DATA MINING AND BUSINESS INTELLIGENCE

DATA MINING AND BUSINESS INTELLIGENCE

VIVEK BHAMBRI
MCA, M.Phil, Ph.D. (Pursuing)
Assistant Professor,
HOD, Department of Computer Science
Desh Bhagat Institute of Management and Computer Sciences, Mandi Gobindgarh

BABITA CHOPRA
MCA, M.Phil, P.HD
Assistant Professor,
Department of Computer Science
Desh Bhagat Institute of Management and Computer Sciences, Mandi Gobindgarh

BALRAM KRISHAN
MCA, M.Phil, Ph.D. (Pursuing)
Assistant Professor,
Department of Computer Science,
Desh Bhagat Institute of Management & Computer Sciences
Mandi Gobindgarh (Punjab)

KHANNA BOOK PUBLISHING CO. (P) LTD.

::: *Publisher of Engineering and Computer Books* :::

Head Office : 4C/4344, Ansari Road, Darya Ganj, New Delhi-110002
Phone: 011-23244447/48 Fax: 011-23244447

Regd. Office : 1694-95, Nai Sarak, Delhi-110006
Phone: 011-23283211 Fax: 011-23256658

E-Mail : contact@khannabooks.com

Website : www.khannabooks.com, www.khannapublishers.com

DATA MINING AND BUSINESS INTELLIGENCE
Balram Krishan, Vivek Bhambri and Babita Chopra

ISBN: 978-93-82609-27-8
First Edition: 2014

Published by:
Khanna Book Publishing Co. (P) Ltd.
4C/4344, Ansari Road, Darya Ganj, New Delhi-110 002
Phone: 011-23244448 Telefax: 011-23244447
E-mail: contact@khannabooks.com
Website: www.khannabooks.com, www.khannapublishers.com

Regd. Off: 1694-95, 1st Floor, Nai Sarak, Delhi-110006 (India)
Phone: 011-23283211 Telefax: 011-23256658

Printed in India by:
S.P.S. Printers & Binders, Delhi

Preface

The IT revolution is the biggest achievement of mankind in last few decades. The technology is changing just at the blink of the eye and the innovation, adoption and implementation of the new technologies is the success mantra for the organizations around the global. The technology has entered into every sphere of our day to day operations, starting from waking up by an alarm, cooking the food, getting ready for the day, shopping, communicating to the friends and relatives. Everywhere we go and perform any job we are generating a huge amount of data everywhere. So we are producing a vast amount of data, but the problem is that we fail to organize it, and hence are not able to get the full benefit from this huge data repositories.

The ever growing size of a data has created the need for automated tools that can assist the decision makers in transforming the data into information and hence to the knowledge. This has led to the birth of techniques of data warehouse and data mining. ***Data mining is the science of extracting useful information from large data sets or databases.***

Data mining emerged during the late 1980s and continues to flourish till date. This book provides the basic knowledge about the techniques and tools of data warehouse and data mining and these tools can be used for making efficient decisions. Nemati & Barko has rightly said that

"Data Mining is capable of answering questions about the past (what has happened), the present (what is happening), and the future (what might happen)"

This book can be used as reference and text book for the Undergraduate and Post Graduate students of Computer Science.

Full care has been taken to explain the concepts in the best way possible; the constructive feedback to make this book better is always welcomed.

Wishing the readers a thoughtful learning experience.

All the best to student community for their future endeavors.

Acknowledgement

A lot of people have helped us in this project and we relish the opportunity to thank them.

Our first gratitude is towards the Almighty for showering His blessings and making us capable of completing this project.

We are indebted to our parents, teachers and colleagues who guided and inspired us to do the work.

We express our heartfelt thanks to ***Dr. Shalini Gupta (Pro-VC, Desh Bhagat University)*** and ***Ms. Nidhi Gupta(Director, USMCS, Desh Bhagat University)*** for their constant encouragement and cooperation in bringing out this book.

We express our deep gratitude to our family members for their constant support.

I, (Vivek Bhambri) thank my father, Sh. Vijay Mohan Bhambri and wife Nisha Bhambri and beloved son Vansh, for their constant support and encouragement and for bearing a lot during my involvement in this project.

I, (Babita Chopra) thank my family, for their constant support and encouragement and for bearing a lot during my involvement in this project.

I, (Balram Krishan) thank my family, for their constant support and encouragement and for bearing a lot during my involvement in this project

The writing of a book of this nature would not have been possible without consulting the writings of many learned writers. We are thankful to all of them. We thank Mr. Mukul Seth, Managing Director, Khanna Book Publishing Co. Pvt. Ltd. for having confidence in us and our work.

We thank the whole team at Khanna Book Publishing Co. Pvt. Ltd. for converting our endeavors into reality.

Brief Table of Contents

Detailed Table of Contents

CHAPTER 1

INTRODUCTION TO DATA WAREHOUSING

In the era of globalization and cut throat competition, the organizations today are striving to gain a competitive edge over each other. The survival mantra in the present day environment of globalization and cut throat competition is to find out the power of invisible force which runs the whole show *i.e. the knowledge*. The technological revolution and the era of IT and IT enabled services has showcased a scenario that in every aspect revolves around the data, its use and the interpretation of data as per the need of the users. Moreover,

- Apart from execution of business processes, the creation of knowledge base and its utilization for the benefit of the organization is becoming a strategy tool to compete.
- The organizations and individuals having *right access to the right information at the right moment of time will be the one to rule the system.*
- The organizations around the globe are collecting a variety of information electronically.
- The computerization of business operations, connectivity through World Wide Web and the support of automated softwares has completely changed the basic concept of generating and managing data.
- The irony of the situation is that in spite of collection of huge amount of data from the various transactions and other sources, the organizations are not able to fully capitalize the benefits which can be reaped from these huge data bases.
- The organizations have realized that their biggest asset *is the knowledge and not the financial resources* and are using the techniques of knowledge management, data warehousing and data mining for customer segmentation and profitability, marketing, risk management and customer relationship management.

The use of information technology is very much prominent in all organizations irrespective of their size.

According to Danziger & Andersen, "Information and Communication Technologies (ICTs) are now widely accepted as key forces in shaping the economic landscape, transforming the way we live, learn, work and play".

According to Sivakumaran- "The adoption of technology has led to the following benefits: greater productivity, profitability, and efficiency, faster service and customer satisfaction, convenience and flexibility, 24*7 operations and space and cost savings".

1.1 THE BASIC CONCEPTS

Today, we consciously or unconsciously diffuse our data somewhere. Whenever we shop, use credit card, rent a movie, withdraw money from ATM, write a check and log on the internet, our data go somewhere. Virtually, every aspect of our life discloses information about us. With the development of computing and communication technology, now data can be captured, recorded, exchanged, and manipulated easier than before.

It is normally said that "***we are living in the information age***" but actually "***we are in the data age***". Because terabytes of data related to business, science, social interactions, operations and almost every aspect of the life move through our computer networks and is stored at various sites. The advent and development of powerful tools for data collection and storage has further intensified the process of data generation. Like a business organization stores data about sales transactions, stock trading records, product descriptions, sales promotions, customer profiles, their purchasing behaviors, company profiles and customer feedback and expectations. But actually, ***we are becoming data rich and information poor***. The meaning is that we are not able to draw the required information from various data items collected and hence are not able to use this information to enhance and enrich our knowledge base.

Before going in to the details of the concepts of data warehousing, it is mandatory to distinguish between data, information and knowledge.

Data: Data is any fact, numbers or text that can be processed by a computer.

- Data is composed of observable and recordable facts that are often found in operational or transactional systems.
- Data is mostly unstructured, factual, and many a times numeric, and reside in database management systems.
- It is entered into the system, whenever a transaction is performed.
- The main examples of data are weights, prices, employee names, addresses, registration numbers etc.
- Data is generated when a transaction is performed like by swapping an ATM card, student or employee marking his attendance, purchasing a commodity in a store, transferring cheque from account A to B and employee payroll databases etc.
- Data can be processed further to form the information and hence can be converted into knowledge.
- *Broadly, the data may be classified into following categories*:
    - Operational or transactional data such as sales, cost, inventory, payroll, and accounting.
    - Meta data - data about the data itself, It contains logical database design or data dictionary definitions required to understand the meaning of the data stored.

Information: The data items collected randomly, when organized and presented in the form which has a value to the end-users, it becomes the information.

- It is an integrated, organized collection of facts which can be used as the basis for decision making.

- Information is factual, but structured and crisp.
- It has some value for the decision maker.
- Information can be processed further to form the knowledge.
- The examples of information are: Time Table, Report Card, Pay Slips, Reports, analysis of retail point of sale transaction data can yield information on which products are selling and when.

Difference between Data and Information

Table 1.1: Difference between Data and Information

Data	Information
Data is raw facts and figures. For Example: 67	Information is a processed form of data. For Example: When 67 is stored as shown below, it becomes information, Weight: 67, shows that 67 is the weight of the entity in question.
Data is not directly significant for decision makers.	Information is significant for decision makers, as depending upon the information obtained the decisions can be taken.
Data is an atomic form.	Information is an integrated form of data.
Data is processed to form the information.	Information is processed to form the knowledge.
Data is mostly unstructured and factual.	Information is factual, but structured and crisp

Another term related to data and information is the *knowledge*.

Knowledge: Knowledge in the most basic sense is defined ***as a derivative of information, which in turn is derived from the data.***

- Knowledge is the information or data which has been organized in a meaningful way.
- Knowledge is inferential, abstract, and is needed to support decision making.
- Information about historical patterns and future trends can be converted into *knowledge*.

For example, summary information on retail supermarket sales can be analyzed in light of promotional efforts to provide knowledge about buying behavior of the customer. Thus, a manufacturer or retailer could determine which items are most susceptible to promotional efforts.

Knowledge and knowledge management are being used interchangeably.

Knowledge Management is being used in our society since time immemorial. Its origin can be related to the time when languages were discovered. Human beings leant how to communicate with each other and this was probably the first medium through which transfer of information took place. The transfer of knowledge took place from parents to children, teacher to the taught and from educated to the uneducated through the verbal or non-verbal mediums of communication. This knowledge transfer was informal and was transferred to generations through customs and folklore. Till the time, the society was not widespread; these means of knowledge dissemination were successful even in the small organizations also. The major problem in this process was faced when the organizations started growing in size and magnitude, the work pressures on employees and ever changing demands of the industry posed by cut throat competitions started increasing. The solution to this problem lies in implementation of techniques of knowledge management and dissemination.

1.2 THE EVOLUTION OF DATA WAREHOUSING (THE HISTORICAL CONTEXT)

- In the competitive customer service sector companies need to have accurate, up-to-date information for making various decisions for operational and strategic levels.
- The organizations around the globe have invested heavily in information technology to help them manage their businesses more effectively and to gain a competitive edge over others.
- Over the last three decades, increasingly large amounts of critical business data have been stored electronically and this volume is expected to grow considerably in the near future.
- The growing size of the data in the organizations and the need of the data for making the future decisions and expansions in an organization have led to the importance of the data.
- Research is going on for finding out the various ways to manage the data optimally and extracting it intelligently and moreover presenting it to fulfill the user's requirements.

The organizations are realizing that data is the most important asset of the organization. It's the data which can make or mar the survival of the organization. The organizations are collecting huge amount of data through various transactions executed every second, but they fail to fully capitalize the benefits from these huge data bases only because they do not have some strong mechanism for knowledge collection, organization, dissemination and hence are not able to use this knowledge for the survival and growth of the organization.

In the nutshell, ***we are drowning in data, but starving for knowledge***!- ***The solution is to design a data warehouse***.

The evolution of data warehousing can be visualized as the outcome of natural evolution and growth of information technology. Since 1960s the database and information technology has progressed hand in hand, systematically from basic file processing systems to sophisticated and powerful database systems for transaction processing and then to analytical processing of data. The database and database management systems were evolved in the development of data warehouses. The evolution process of data base technology can be visualized as:

1. **Before 1960s**: ***Data Collection and Database Creation***. Primitive file processing systems were used and the emphasis was on methods of data storage, retrieval and transaction processing.

2. **1970s to Early 1980s**: ***Birth of Database Management Systems:***
   - Birth and Evolution of Hierarchical, Network and Relational Database Systems.
   - Data Modeling through Entity Relationship Models.
   - Use of Query Languages like SQL.
   - Use of User Interface through Forms and Reports.
   - Query Processing and Optimization.
   - Online Transaction Processing(OLTP)
   - Transaction Management, Concurrency Control and Recovery.

3. **Mid 1980s: *Advanced Database Systems***:
   - Birth of Advanced Data Models like Extended Relational, Object Relational and Deductive Models.
   - Management of Complex Data of various forms: Spatial, Temporal, Multimedia and Moving objects.
   - Use of Web based databases like XML and Semantic web.
   - Integration of data from heterogeneous sources.
   - Integration of text database systems with the various methods of information retrieval.
   - Performance evaluation and maintenance through methods for database tuning and adaptive systems.
   - Attention towards issues related to data privacy and security and methods to maintain security and privacy were evolved.
   - Birth of the concept of cloud computing and parallel data processing.

4. **Late 1980s to Present**: ***Emphasis on Advanced Data Analysis***.
   - Data Warehouse and OLAP.
   - Data Mining and Knowledge discovery and use of various data mining techniques like- ***classification, clustering, association and correlation, trend and deviation analysis, pattern recognition and interpretation***.
   - Application of data mining in business, banking, telecommunication, retail.
   - Mining complex types of data: Streams, Sequence, Text, Spatial, Temporal, Multimedia, Web.
   - Privacy Preserving Data Mining, Mining Social and Information Networks.

Table 1.2 given below shows the evolution of database systems since 1960s till date.

Table 1.2: Evolution of Data Ware House.

Evolutionary Step	Business Question	Enabling Technologies
Data Collection and Data Base Creation (1960s)	"What was my total revenue in the last ten years?"	Computers, tapes, disks, File Processing Systems
Birth of Database Management Systems: Data Access (1980s)	"What were the unit sales in Unit I last March?"	Relational databases (RDBMS), Data Modeling Structured Query Language (SQL), Query Processing and Optimization, ODBC
Advanced Database Systems Data Warehousing & Decision Support (1990s)	"What were unit sales in Unit I last March? Drill down to Unit 10."	On-line analytic Processing (OLAP), multidimensional databases, Integration of heterogeneous data, birth of data warehouses
Advanced Data Analysis Data Mining (Emerging Today)	"What's likely to happen to sales at Unit I next month? And to predict the reasons for the same?"	Advanced algorithms, Multiprocessor computers, Massive data bases, Privacy and Security Concerns.

The evolution of database technology is supported by the progress in hardware technology, where hardware has grown to be more powerful and affordable for one and all. It has provided a boost to the data and information industry, where huge amount of databases are available for transaction management, information retrieval and data analysis.

1.3 OPERATIONAL & INFORMATIONAL DATA STORES:

Operational data stores are created when any transaction is performed;

- It stores the data pertaining to the day-to-day operations of the organization.
- Each department in the organization maintains its own operational data.
- It is of huge size and cannot be used for decision making purposes directly.
- It is transaction or process-oriented.

Whereas, the informational data stores, also known as data warehouse data,

- Store the processed form of operational data, which can be used by decision makers directly.
- It is subject-oriented, geared toward flexible analytical processing of high volumes of business data.

Table 1.3: Comparison of Operational Data and Data Warehouse Data

S.No	Operational data	DW data
1.	The operational data is application oriented i.e each application/ department stores data pertaining to their operations only.	The data warehouse data is subject oriented, i.e stores data on basis of a particular subject like customer, product etc.
2.	It holds current data i.e data related to the day to day transactions.	It holds historical data i.e data is summarized over any time dimension like weekly, monthly or weekly.
3.	Operational data is highly dynamic in nature, as it changes every now and then.	Data warehouse data is static in nature.
4.	It is in detailed and raw form.	It is summarized, otherwise refined.
5.	It is accurate, as of the moment of access.	It represents data over a particular time.
6.	It serves the middle and operational level management.	It serves the management at top level.
7.	It can be updated.	It cannot be updated.
8.	The requirements for processing are understood before initial development.	The requirements for processing are not completely understood before development.
9.	The data stored is transaction driven.	The data stored is analysis driven.
10.	Data is not redundant.	Data is redundant as same data items may be stored over different subject lines more than once.
11.	For processing the operational data, small amount of data is used in a process.	A large amount of data is used in a process.
12.	It offers high level of transaction output.	It offers medium to low level of transaction throughput.
13.	The usage pattern is predictable in nature. So serves as a source for repetitive type of queries.	The usage pattern is unpredictable. So serves as a source for ad-hoc queries.

Operational systems storing operational data were unable to meet to user's expectations due to following reasons:

1. The processing load reduced the response time of operational system.
2. The database design of operational system was not optimized for information analysis and reporting.
3. Most organizations had more than one operational system, so company-wide reporting could not be supported from a single system.
4. Development of reports in operational systems required writing specific computer programs which is a slow and expensive process.
5. Consolidation of data from a wide variety of data sources was a difficult job.

1.4 MEANING AND CHARACTERISTICS OF DATA WAREHOUSE

Meaning of Data Warehouse: A Data warehouse provides mechanism to systematically organize, understand and use the organizational data to make strategic decisions. The organizations around the globe have realized this fact that in order to compete in this era of globalization and cut throat competition, data ware house is a must. The data warehouse is that portion of an overall architected data environment that serves as the single integrated source of data for processing information.

Data warehouse is a process of organizing the storage of large, multivariate data sets in a way that facilitates the retrieval of information for analytical purpose.

A data warehouse is the main repository of the organization's historical data, its corporate memory. It contains the raw material for management's decision support system.

According to William H. Inmon – "A data warehouse is a subject-oriented, integrated, time-variant and non-volatile collection of data in support of management's decision making process".

Characteristics of Data Warehouse: The major characteristics of a data warehouse are:

1. Subject-Oriented: It means that the data in the database is organized so that all the data elements relating to the same real-world event or object are linked together. The information is presented according to specific subjects or areas of interest, not simply as computer files. Data is manipulated to provide information about a particular subject. For example, the data warehouse in a business organization is organized around the major subject areas like customers, suppliers, product and sales. So, data warehouse provides a simple and concise view of data for the decision makers on a particular subject matter by excluding data that is not useful for the decision support process.

2. Integrated: The data warehouse over rules the concept of small islands of data at various places by various departments and tries to consolidate the data at one place and the data becomes a shared resource. In the process of integration, multiple heterogeneous sources of data such as relational databases, flat files and records of online transactions are consolidated into one. The major issue to be taken care in the process of integration is to ensure consistency in naming conventions, encoding structures and attribute measures.

3. Non-Volatile: It means that data in the database is never over-written or deleted, but is retained for future reporting, such historical data helps in studying the past or future trends of market. Data in the data warehouse is permanent asset of the organization and is not to be deleted by one and all. The data can be preserved on any time dimension. This is possible because data in the data warehouse is totally different from the operational data due to which data warehouse does not require transaction processing, recovery and concurrency control mechanisms. Data is initially loaded and is further accessed.

4. Time-Variant: Data is stored to provide information from a historic perspective. The changes to the data in the database are tracked and recorded so that reports can be produced showing changes over time. This feature of data warehouse has fulfilled the need of historical data. Data about a particular month, season or a specific period can be made available.

5. Accessible: The primary purpose of a data warehouse is to provide readily accessible information to end-users.

6. Process-Oriented: It is important to view data warehousing as a process for delivery ofinformation. The maintenance of a data warehouse is ongoing and iterative in nature.

1.5 THE NEED FOR DATA WAREHOUSING

Data warehouses are widely used within the largest and most complex businesses in the world. Since 1970s organizations gained competitive advantage through the use of systems that automate the business processes that offer most cost effective services to the customers. These systems were termed as operational database stores, the major job done by these systems is ***online transaction processing***, which covers most of the day to day operations of an organization like purchasing, manufacturing, banking, accounting etc, whereas the decision making in the present day environment of competition needs much more than the operational data, as decisions now a days involve analytical processing of lot many factors, so organizations tend to turn their archives of data into a source of knowledge, so that a single integrated / consolidated view of the organization's data can be presented to the users. As a result, ***data warehouse systems also known as online analytical processing systems are required***. These data warehouse systems can be visualized as a ***repository of multiple heterogeneous data sources*** organized under a common schema at a common site to help the decision makers in making timely, accurate and reliable decisions. The users often expect that they can perform online analytical processing directly on such databases rather than creating a separate warehouse.

The various reasons for having a separate data warehouse are:

1. First and foremost reason is to ensure high performance for both the systems.
2. An operational database is designed and tuned for the known tasks and can answer customized queries only, whereas there are some complex queries which involve the computation of large data groups at summarized levels and data from diverse sources. If such analytical queries are processed in operational data bases, it will degrade their performance, so separate data warehouse is needed.

3. An operational database supports concurrent processing of multiple transactions, and in such a scenario concurrency control and recovery mechanisms hold special importance, whereas the analytical query processing often needs read only access of data records. If concurrency control and recovery mechanisms are applied for such operations, then it will reduce the efficiency of transaction system also.
4. The content and structure of the data in an operational system is the current data, whereas decision support systems often require the historic data also, so in spite of the huge collection of data in the operational systems, it is not sufficient for decision making.
5. Due to the vast expansion of the horizons of the data and its multivariate uses, the organizations and the individuals are feeling the need for some centralized data management and retrieval system. The centralization of the data is required basically for better processing and in turn facilitating the user access and analysis.
6. The decisions now a days are not based on a single factor only, rather it needs an interdisciplinary approach. For example in a manufacturing concern, if the decision for product is to be made then it is required to analyze it across all products by location, time and channel. The required data is probably there but not integrated and organized in a way required for decision making. Data Warehouse serves not only as a repository for historical data but also as an excellent data integration platform. The data in the data warehouse is integrated, subject oriented, time-variant and non-volatile to enable the user to get a 360° view of his organization.
7. The data warehouse is designed specifically to support querying, reporting and analysis tasks. The data model is flattened (de-normalized) and structured by subject areas to make it easier for users to get even complex summarized information with a relatively simple query and perform multi-dimensional analysis. Multi-level trend analysis provides the ability to analyze key trends at every level across different dimensions, e.g., Organization, Product, Location, Channel and Time, and hierarchies within them. Most reporting, data analysis, and visualization tools take advantage of the underlying data model to provide powerful capabilities such as drilldown, roll-up, drill-across and various ways of slicing and dicing data. The flattened data model makes it much easier for users to understand the data and write queries rather than work with potentially several hundreds of tables and write long queries with complex table joins and clauses.
8. To provide an environment where a relatively small amount of knowledge of the technical aspects of database technology is required to write and maintain queries and reports and/or to provide a means to speed up the writing and maintaining of queries and reports by technical personnel.
9. To make it easier, on a regular basis, to query and report data from multiple transaction processing systems and from external data sources or from data that must be stored for query or report purposes only.

The data warehouses were able to bring in data from a range of different data sources, such as mainframe computers, minicomputers, as well as personal computers and office automation software such as spreadsheet, and integrate this information at a single place. This capability, coupled with user-friendly reporting tools and freedom from operational impacts, has led to a growth of this type of computer system. For organizational learning to take place, data from many sources must be gathered and organized in a consistent and useful way. Data warehouse enhances end-user access to a wide variety of data, where decision makers can obtain various kinds of trend reports e.g. the item with the most sales in a particular area/country for the last two years.

1.6 ROLE AND STRUCTURE OF A DATA WAREHOUSE

Role of a Data Warehouse: In every industry across the world, from retail chain stores to financial institutions, from manufacturing enterprises to government departments, and from airline companies to utility businesses, data warehousing is revolutionizing the way people perform business analysis and make strategic decisions. In the present day challenging times good decision-making is very critical. The best decisions are made when all the relevant data available is taken into consideration. The best possible source for that data is a well-designed data warehouse. Data is extracted periodically from the applications that support business processes and copied onto special dedicated computers. There it can be validated, reformatted, reorganized, summarized, restructured, and supplemented with data from other sources. The resulting data warehouse becomes the main source of information for report generation, analysis, and presentation through ad hoc reports, portals, and dashboards. Executives cannot afford to make decisions based on financial statements that compare last month's results to a budget created up to a year ago. These system information that helps them in answering the basic questions which are not directly based on the quantitative data stored in the data bases, but needs to explore some qualitative aspects like: What still works? What continues to sell? What is the purchasing pattern of customers? What is their taste and preferences? What costs can be cut without causing long-term harm? Business intelligence systems provide the ability to answer these critical questions by turning the massive amount of data from operational systems into a format that is current, actionable, and easy to understand. These system provide information that is decision ready and allow you to analyze current and long-term trends, alert you instantly to opportunities and problems, and give you continuous feedback on the effectiveness of your decisions. The largest and best-managed organizations in the world have been making use of it for more than a decade. It has been truly said that – ***the path to true business intelligence passes through a data warehouse***. The Data Warehousing Institute defines business intelligence as: "***The process, technologies, and tools needed to turn data into information, information into knowledge, and knowledge into plans that drive profitable business action. Business intelligence encompasses data warehousing, business analytic tools, and content/ knowledge management.***"

Unfortunately, the data warehouse is not getting its true value as it is a back end technology and works from behind the scenes. Its job is to provide data to the high-profile front end tools and applications with which users interact.

Data warehousing suggests that data can be restructured and reformatted to facilitate query and analysis by novice users. The goal of a data warehouse is to bring data together from a variety of existing databases to support management and reporting needs. The generally accepted principle is that data should be stored at its most elemental level because this provides the platform for the most useful and flexible basis for use in reporting and information analysis. The data warehouse architecture describes the overall system from various perspectives such ***as data, process, and infrastructure needed to communicate which includes the structure, function and interrelationships of each component.***

In spite of the fact that the operational data is a key asset to the organization, such data is generally not utilized to its full potential. So, to facilitate the user to explore the benefits of operational data to its full extent the technique of data warehousing is being used.

The major goals achieved by using data warehousing are:

1. It enables the users to provide an appropriate access to a homogenized and comprehensive view of the organization data which in turn supports forecasting and decision-making processes at the enterprise level.
2. Data warehouse helps to achieve information consistency. By bringing data from disparate data sources into a centralized repository.
3. The data warehouse provides an unified view of the organization's data. Users from across the organization making use of the data warehouse, all view a single and consistent version of the truth.
4. The metadata layer of the data warehouse enforces information consistency by allowing data within the data warehouse to be defined in business terms as opposed to using general language of databases.
5. As the data in the data warehouse is generally non-volatile, the data warehouse must be designed to adapt to change. In the present time as the business rules and terms of an organization' change over time. The data warehouse environment must be flexible enough to incorporate such changes.
6. Business executives use the data in data warehouses to perform analysis and making strategic decisions. It helps in multidimensional analysis and sophisticated slice and dice operations.
7. The data ware houses clubbed with data mining techniques can further enhance the utility of decisions and can strengthen the knowledge discovery process, in this concern the data warehousing tools can be categorized into access and retrieval tools, database reporting tools, data analysis tools and data mining tools.
8. Data warehouse can be employed for the following applications:
   - **(a)** ***Information Processing***: These applications support querying, basic statistical analysis and reporting using crosstabs, tables, charts or graphs. The low cost web based accessing tools can be integrated with web browsers.
   - **(b)** ***Analytical Processing***: These applications support basic OLAP operations, which includes slice and dice, drill down, roll up and pivoting. It operates on historic data in both the summarized and detailed forms. The major plus point of analytical processing over information processing is multidimensional analysis of data stored in data warehouses.

(c) ***Data Mining***: These applications supports knowledge discovery by finding hidden patterns and associations, constructing analytical models, performing classification and prediction and hence presenting the results obtained using visualization tools.

Structure of Data Warehouse: The structure of data warehouse consists of the following:

1. Physical Data Warehouse: Physical data warehouse is the database in which all the data for the warehouse is stored, along with metadata and processing logic for scrubbing, organizing, packaging and processing the detailed data. The physical store for the data warehouse includes one database that the user can query by using SQL queries. It contains all the data that you have imported from different sources. During the unpacking process, Commercial Servers automatically build the physical store for the data warehouse in both the SQL Server database and the OLAP database.

2. Logical Data Warehouse: It contains metadata, including enterprise rules, processing logic for scrubbing, organizing, packaging and processing data, but does not contain actual data. Instead, it contains the information necessary to access the data wherever it resides. This structure is effective only when there is a single source for the data and when the data in the source is accurate and timely. The logical schema provides an understandable view of the data in the data warehouse, and supports an efficient import process. For example, a site developer uses the logical schema to modify the location of data stored in the underlying physical tables. When a site developer writes code to add, update, or delete data in the data warehouse, the developer interacts with the logical schema. When Commerce Server accesses data in the data warehouse, it accesses the data through the logical schema. Only the site developer needs detailed knowledge of the logical schema. A logical schema includes the following:

- **Class:** A logical collection of data members. For example, the RegisteredUser class contains data members describing a registered users.
- **Data Member:** A structure that stores a piece of data. For example, the E-mail data member of the RegisteredUser class stores the e-mail address for a registered user.
- **Relation:** A connection between two classes is a parent-child relationship. The parent-child relationship defines the number of instances (1 or many) a child can have with a corresponding instance in the parent. For example, RegisteredUser is a parent to the child class Request. There can be many requests for one registered user.
- **Data Mart:** It is a subset of an enterprise - wide data warehouse, which typically supports the enterprise element (department, region, function, etc.). As part of an iterative data warehouse development process, an enterprise build a series of physical (or logical) data marts over time and links them via an enterprise - wide logical data warehouse or feeds them from a single physical warehouse.

The following figure shows the relationship between the physical store and the logical schema.

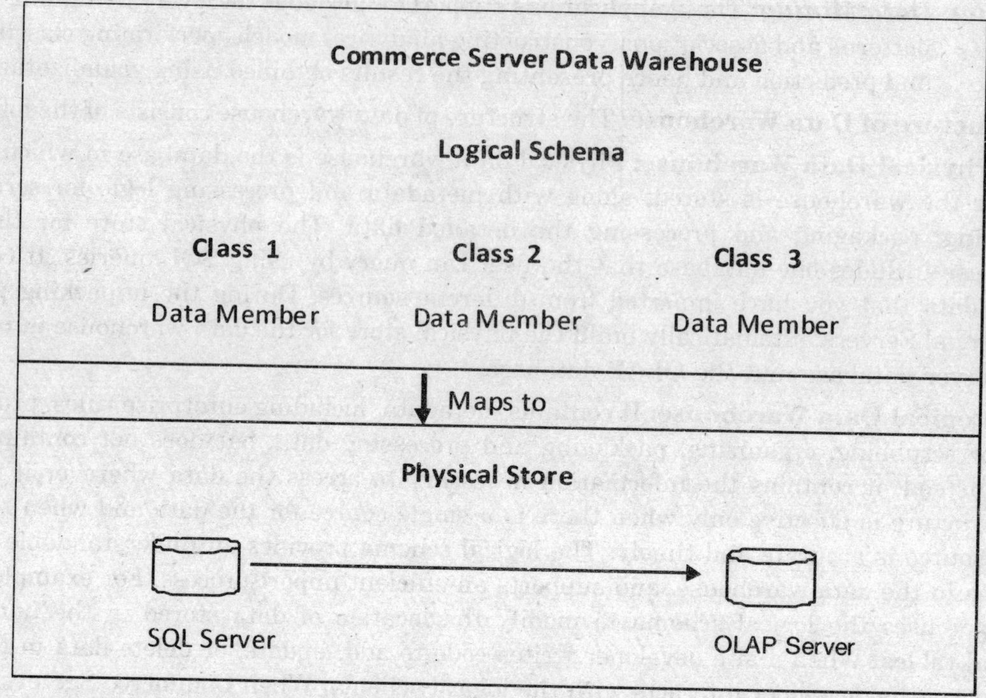

Fig. 1.1. Relationship between Physical Store and Logical Schema

1.7 THE COST OF WAREHOUSING DATA

After studying the basic structure of data warehouse and its various components, it is clear that that data warehouses cost a lot of money. Building and implementing a data warehouse will have a great impact on the corporate budget. The major components of the cost of a data warehouse are:

1. Consultation and Development Costs: Consulting and development costs are those costs that relate to building of the data warehouse. These costs include data modeling, design, mapping, ETL and data population costs. These operations can be done in-house or by having a contract with a consulting firm, or both. A huge investment is required to be done on the design, development, and deployment of the data warehouse. But this cost diminishes over time, as it is one time investment, once the basic data warehouse structure has been developed, the money will be spent only on the few adaptive changes required from time to time. Major investment is required in the initial years of data warehouse construction, after the first little iterations the development work degenerates to maintenance work.

2. Storage and Storage Infrastructure Costs: Storage costs include the cost of storage and the infrastructure required for storing the huge amount of data. The cost of storage in the first few years of the data warehouse is not high because in the first few years there is relatively little historical data, and there are only a few subject areas that are built into the data warehouse. It is over time that large amounts of history appears and that lots of subject areas are entered into the data warehouse.

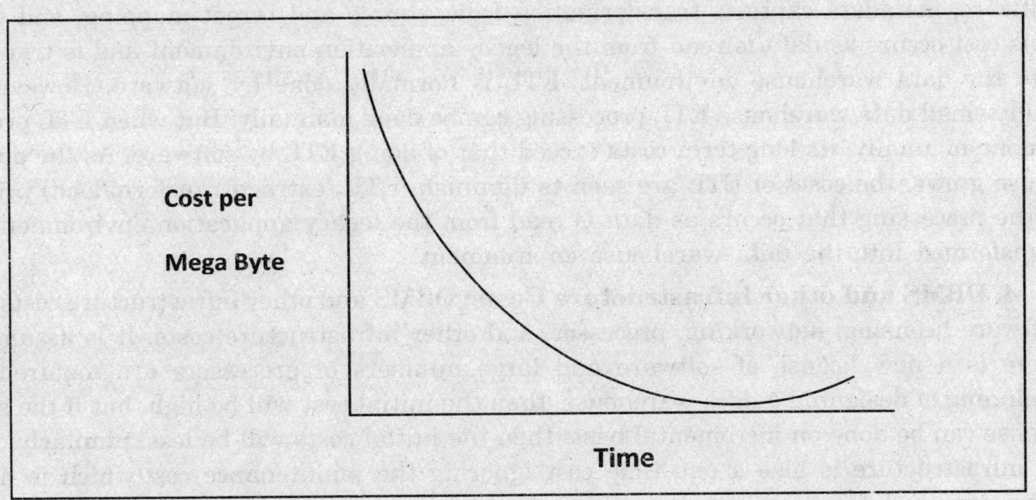

Fig. 1.2: The classical curve of declining cost of storage

Fig 1.2 shows that the unit cost of storage is getting less expensive every year. That means we should not worry about the storage cost. The other side of the picture is that while the unit cost of storage is dropping, the demand for storage is increasing i.e the consumption of storage by the industry is increasing rapidly as shown in Fig. 1.3 given below.

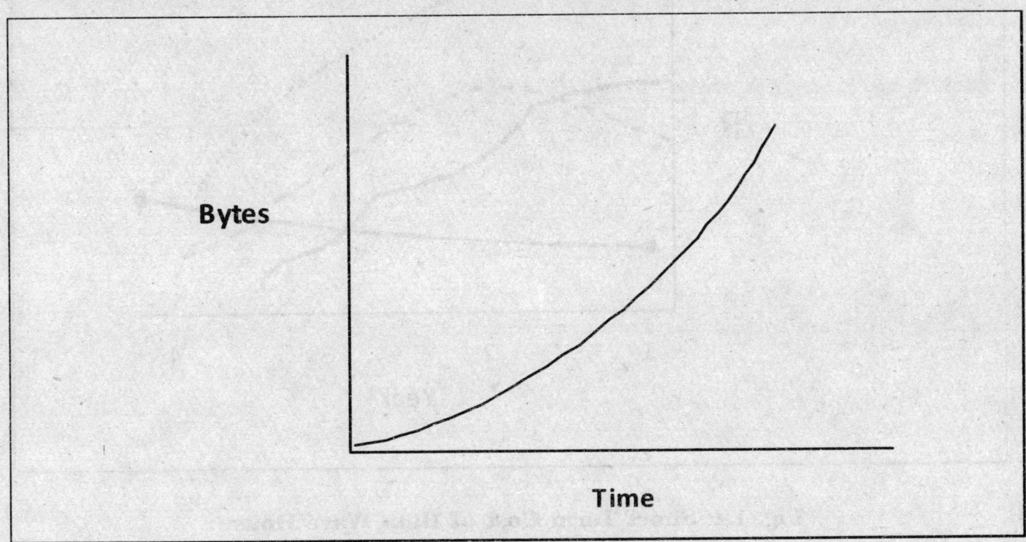

Fig.1.3: The Storage Consumption Curve

The third factor to be taken into consideration is that as volume of data increases, the infrastructure cost for the management of data increases manifold and it is quite high in the companies where huge amount of data is being stored.

3. ETL Costs: This cost is the cost on **extraction/transformation and loading** of the data, that is why it is termed as ETL cost. ETL costs are software costs that include the ETL software, metadata capture, transformation logic, source and target mapping, and so forth. This cost occurs as data is read from the legacy application environment and is transformed into the data warehouse environment, ETL is normally done by software. However, for a really small data warehouse ETL processing can be done manually. But when ETL processing is done manually, its long-term costs exceed that of doing ETL by software. As the data ware house grows, the costs of ETL are seen to diminish. ETL (extract/transform/load) processing is the processing that occurs as data is read from the legacy application environment and is transformed into the data warehouse environment.

4. DBMS and other Infrastructure Costs: DBMS and other infrastructure costs include software licensing, networking, processor, and other infrastructure costs. It is assumed that there is a new license of software and large numbers of processors are required in the beginning of designing a data warehouse, then the initial cost will be high. but if the software license can be done on incremental basis then the initial costs will be less. Similarly, the cost on infrastructure is also a one time cost ignoring the maintenance cost(which is normally very less)

The Fig. 1.4 given below show the short-term (up to 4 year) costs associated with the building and operation of a data warehouse.

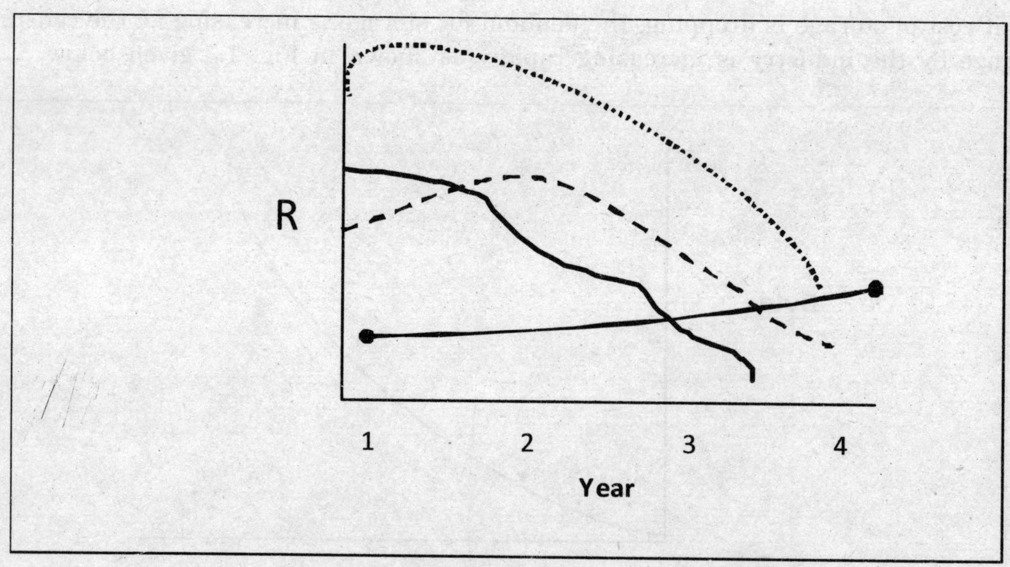

Fig. 1.4: Short Term Cost of Data Ware House

- ***Dotted Curve shows Consulting Cost,***
- ***Dashed Curve shows ETL Cost***
- ***Bold line Curve shows DBMS Cost and***
- ***Curve with Arrows both at the beginning and the end shows the Storage Cost.***

It is clear from the Figure 1.3 that:

1. The Consulting and development cost is the major cost item. A lot of money will be

spent on the design, development, and deployment of the data warehouse. This cost diminishes over time.

2. The cost of storage in the first few years of the data warehouse is not high. In the first few years there is relatively little historical data, and there are only a few subject areas that are built into the data warehouse. It is over time that large amounts of history appear and that lots of subject areas are entered into the data warehouse. The cost of storage is not particularly significant in the life of the building and usage of the data warehouse in the short term.
3. The costs of ETL are seen to diminish as the data warehouse becomes mature.
4. It is seen that as time passes the costs for DBMS and processors diminish after the initial purchase and acquisitions are made.

The Long-Term Costs of a Data Warehouse

The long-term picture for the costs of data warehousing looks considerably different however. Fig. 1.4 shows the long-term picture of the costs of the data warehouse. The picture of costs of a data warehouse seen in Fig. 1.4 is considerably different than the picture of costs seen in Fig. 1.3. Fig. 1.4: depicts the costs of data warehousing over the time frame of ten-years.

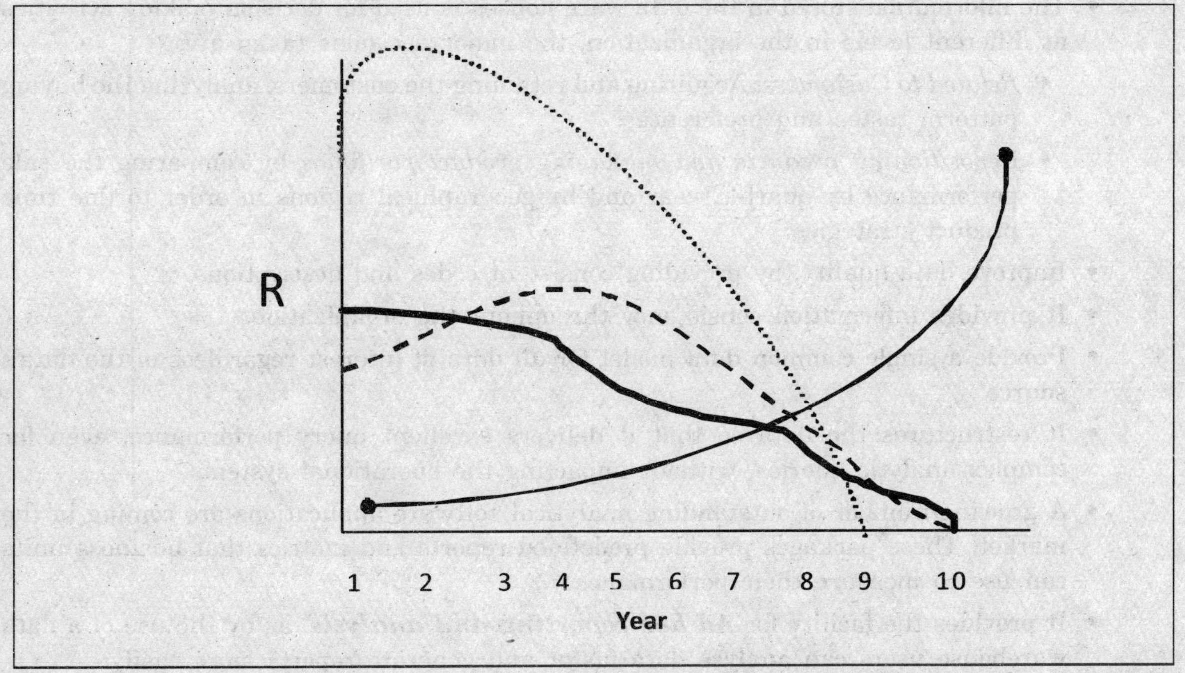

Fig. 1.4: Long Term Cost of Data Ware House

- ***Dotted Curve shows Consulting Cost,***
- ***Dashed Curve shows ETL Cost***

- ***Bold line Curve shows DBMS Cost and***
- ***Curve with Arrows both at the beginning and the end shows the Storage Cost***

In Fig. 1.4 it is seen that at the end of ten years – far and away – the costs of the data warehouse are dedicated to storage. In fact it is because of the large amounts of storage and the infrastructure needed to manage that volume of data that the cost of data warehousing is so large over a lengthy period of time.

1.8 BENEFITS OF DATA WAREHOUSE

Data warehouse stores the information required to make the strategic decisions. It is constructed by integrating data from multiple heterogeneous sources to support structured or unstructured queries, analytical reports and strategic decision making. A data warehouse maintains a copy of information from the transaction systems.

The major benefits of data warehouse are:

- Integrate data from multiple source systems, enabling a central view across the enterprise. It is mandatory because the organizations collect diverse kinds of data and maintain large databases from multiple, heterogeneous, autonomous and distributed information sources.
- The information stored in the data ware houses is used for decision making activities at different levels in the organization, the major decisions taken are:
  - *Related to Customers*: Acquiring and retaining the customers, analyzing the buying pattern, tastes and preferences.
  - *Repositioning products and managing product portfolios* by comparing the sale performance by quarter, year and by geographical regions in order to fine tune product strategies.
- Improve data quality, by providing consistent codes and descriptions.
- It provides information consistency throughout the organization.
- Provide a single common data model for all data of interest regardless of the data's source.
- It restructures the data so that it delivers excellent query performance, even for complex analytic queries, without impacting the operational systems.
- A growing number of outstanding analytical software applications are coming in the market. These packages provide predefined reports and metrics that business units can use to measure their performance.
- It provides the facility for ***Ad hoc reporting and analysis***, as by the use of a data warehouse users can analyze data faster and generate reports more easily.
- A growing number of managers want access to an interactive display of up-to-date critical management data. Sophisticated displays that show real time information in creative, highly graphical form are often called dashboards. The use of data warehouses facilitates ***dynamic presentation through dashboards.***

- The strategic decision making process now a days requires a deep analysis of various aspects to make a viable and appropriate decision, which requires that the data is to be d*rilled down to various dimensions.* The presence of a data warehouse makes it practical to use this capability as per the need of decision makers.
- The data stored in the data warehouses is to be extracted through the use of *data mining techniques and the use of data warehouse builds a ground for the application of data mining techniques.*
- A data warehouse makes it much easier to provide secure access to those that have a legitimate need to specific data and to exclude others.

Data Warehouse Tools/Software

Table 1.4: Data Warehouse Tools/Software

Component	**Product used by Institutional Research**	**Component Description**
Reporting	Crystal Reports	Create presentation style reports with chart and graphs. It can be used to access any type of data source.
Querying	Access 2000	Create complex ad-hoc queries against a variety of data sources using ODBC access to DW databases. It is able to export the data to other types of formats such as text files.
OLAP	Crystal Analysis	Professional Access data cubes for designing views to pivot, filter and aggregate facts on pre-defined dimensions for specific subject areas such as enrollment, degrees conferred, etc.
Data Mining/Statistical Analysis	SAS	Statistical Analysis using ODBC access to IR DW

1.9 CHALLENGES IN IMPLEMENTING DATA WAREHOUSING

According to the Data Warehouse Institute, the top technical challenges facing companies implementing these solutions are:

Data Quality and Security Issues: Data collected from various heterogeneous sources contains a lot of irrelevant data, and some of the values in data may be missing and sometimes noisy data is also inserted in the data collected (all these problems in data may occur intentionally or un-intentionally), but such a data if processed as such will provide wrong results and hence wrong interpretation followed by wrong decision.

Moreover, in the present era of competition and fast changing global scenarios, where a number of transactions are done with a blink of eye, the data changes at a very fast rate and a result of which the results obtained and hence the interpretation done may not be relevant after some time, so data mining techniques should be robust enough to handle the dynamic environments. The unauthorized access to the user's information is a direct attack on the privacy of the individual and hence the concept of invisible data mining is creeping out, where smart softwares like search engines, intelligent database systems incorporate data mining in its functional components, about which the user is not aware of.

***Lack of business case and funding*:** the structure, deployment and execution of a data warehouse needs proper understanding of the user's and business requirements, projection about the possible expectations from the system and ability to handle the forthcoming changes. The design and implementation of data warehouse systems require huge investment, so the process should be handled with proper care.

***Poor data integration infrastructure*:** In data warehouse, as data from various heterogeneous sources is extracted and used, so proper integration of these data items is very important.

Metadata Management Issues: The meta data is the data about data, where this information is to be stored, in what form, and should it be accessible to all or not are the major issues to be taken into account.

***Lack of IT Data Integration Skills*:** The implementation and handling of the whole data warehouse project needs expertise in technical, managerial and operational skills. So, skilled manpower is required to handle this critical and sensitive project.

***Data Transformation and Aggregation*:** The data transformation and aggregation of data should be taken care properly.

1.10 DATA WAREHOUSE: BUILD VERSUS BUY?

Three options are available to obtain a data warehouse:

- Buy readymade system.
- Build it using frameworks.
- Develop a custom warehouse.

Buy a Readymade System: The easiest and most cost effective way to get the data warehouse you need is to buy it. Numerous options are available, especially for the most popular ERP suites including those from SAP and Oracle. The better pre-built solutions make it possible to have a data warehouse up and running quickly, sometimes in just a few weeks. The biggest advantage of buying a readymade system is that the user can see a live demonstration using your own data before committing to its purchase. When a complete pre-built data warehouse solution is not available it is sometimes possible to buy frameworks from which a data warehouse can be created. This approach involves less time, cost, and risk than building your own warehouse.

Build it Using Frameworks: In many cases, the frameworks can be customized to your special needs. However, doing so is not always easy, inexpensive, or foolproof. Success is highly dependent on the skills of those doing the customization. Ongoing maintenance and support can be a major problematic area for those that choose to use frameworks.

Develop a Custom Warehouse: The least attractive option is to create a completely custom data warehouse. Doing so can sound simple – obtain an ETL tool and use it to move data from application databases into a data warehouse. In practice, this option turns out to be far more complicated. A significant percentage of those that have tried to do it themselves have either failed or spent far more money and time than planned. Many companies have spent more than a million over the course of a year or more without being satisfied with the results. The available prebuilt options should always be examined before trying to build it yourself or contracting to have it done for you.

1.11 EVALUATING PRE-BUILT DATA WAREHOUSES

A growing number of fully and partly built data warehouses have become available. When more than one option is available it is necessary to evaluate the pros and cons of each. Obviously the first concern is whether the applications you use are fully supported including every version, module and release in use.

Other criterias to be considered include:

- *Time to value*: How long does it take to get the warehouse operational?
- *Design and Stability of the data model*: The design of the data model should be able to adapt to the changes in the scenario.
- *Quality of metadata*. Well-designed metadata that is enhanced over time can be invaluable.
- *Availability of analytics and reports*: The best options include useful prebuilt reports, dashboards and analytics.
- *Real time updating*: How often is the data warehouse synchronized?
- *Which BI tools are supported*? The system should be able to support the most of BI tools.
- *Track record*. What is the performance track record of the system, when used in other business settings.
- *Quality of maintenance and ongoing support*. Will the user be able to get the required support for regular maintenance or not?
- *Technical environment*. Which servers, operating systems, databases and other tools are supported by the system?

SUMMARY

- Era of globalization and cut throat competition has led to the importance of invisible force which runs the whole show *i.e.* ***the knowledge.***
- *The organizations and individuals having right access to the right information at the right moment of time will be the one to rule the system.*
- The computerization of business operations, connectivity through World Wide Web and the support of automated softwares has completely changed the basic concept of generating and managing data.
- *The organizations are becoming data rich and information poor.*
- ***Data*** is any fact, number or text that can be processed by a computer. Data is mostly unstructured, factual, and many a times numeric, and reside in database management systems.
- The data items collected randomly, when organized and presented in the form which has a value to the end-users, it becomes the ***information***.
- ***Knowledge*** is the information or data which has been organized in a meaningful way. It is inferential, abstract, and is needed to support decision making.
- *We are drowning in data, but starving for knowledge!* The solution is to design a data warehouse.
- The organizations have realized that their biggest asset is the knowledge and not the financial resources and are using the techniques of knowledge management, data warehousing, data mining and business intelligence for customer segmentation and profitability, marketing, risk management and customer relationship management.
- ***Business Intelligence*** is the process, technologies, and tools needed to turn data into information, information into knowledge, and knowledge into plans that drive profitable business action. Business intelligence encompasses data warehousing, business analytic tools, and content/ knowledge management.
- The dataware house data is subject oriented, i.e stores data on basis of a particular subject like customer, product etc.
- ***Data Warehouse*** is a subject-oriented, integrated, time-variant and non-volatile collection of data in support of management's decision making process.
- *Data warehouse* enables the users to provide an appropriate access to a homogenized and comprehensive view of the organization data which in turn supports forecasting and decision-making processes at the enterprise level.
- Data warehouses cost a lot of money.
- ***Consulting and Development Costs*** are those costs that relate to the building of the data warehouse. These costs include data modeling, design, mapping, ETL and data population costs.
- ***Storage Costs*** include the cost of storage and the infrastructure required for storing the huge amount of data.
- ***ETL Cost,*** This cost is the cost on extraction/transformation and loading of the data. ETL costs are software costs that include the ETL software, metadata capture, transformation logic, source and target mapping, and so forth. This cost occurs as data is read from the legacy application environment and is transformed into the data warehouse environment.
- ETL is normally done by software.

- ***DBMS and other Infrastructure Costs*** include software licensing, network, processor, and other infrastructure costs. It is assumed that there is a new license of software and large numbers of processors are required in the beginning of designing a data warehouse, then the initial cost will be high.
- ***The major benefits of data warehouse are***:
  - Integrate data from multiple source systems.
  - Provides information for decision making.
  - Improve data quality, by providing consistent codes and descriptions.
  - Provides information consistency throughout the organization.
  - Provide a single common data model for all data of interest regardless of the data's source.
- Challenges in implementing data warehousing are issues related to data quality and security issues, lack of business case and funding, poor data integration infrastructure, issues related to metadata management, lack of IT data integration skills and difficulty in data transformation and aggregation.
- It is important to decide whether data warehouse should be built or it should be bought, the various options are available to obtain a data warehouse, buy readymade system, build it using frameworks or develop a custom warehouse.

CHAPTER 2

DATA WAREHOUSE MODELING

2.1 ONLINE TRANSACTION PROCESSING & ONLINE ANALYTICAL PROCESSING

The use of databases to manage the businesses is very common now a days. Every day billions of transactions are conducted, stored and transferred from one system to another. Each department in any organization is performing its own transactions and storing them for the future references, day to day and long term strategic decisions to be taken later on.

These systems are characterized into two categories, ***offline transactions processing systems and online transaction processing systems.***

- Both types of these systems cover the day to day operations of organizations like purchasing, inventory management, manufacturing, payroll, accounting etc.
- These systems are updated every now and then and are dynamic in nature, as the records in these databases are updated whenever a transaction occurs.
- The data stored in these systems serves the purpose of short term decisions and cater the needs of middle or operational level managers.

But the today's, highly competitive environment requires that the strategic decisions of an organization should take into account the multiple factors from various prospectives. To make it possible the data collected in the online transaction systems provides the basis. And this data collected over a large duration of time becomes the fixed data repository of the organization, also termed as the data warehouse or ***online analytical processing system***. The data collected in an OLAP serve the users at the top or middle level of management for making strategic decisions. These systems present the data from various prospectives and in various data formats to accommodate the diverse needs of different users. OLTP and OLAP are complementing technologies.

Both OLTP and OLAP are two of the common systems for the management of data. OLTP (***Online Transaction Processing***) is a category of systems that manages transaction processing. OLAP (***Online Analytical Processing***) as the name suggests, is a compilation of ways to query multi-dimensional databases. OLAP is a BI (Business intelligence) tool. BI refers to computer-based methods for identifying and extracting useful information from business data.

OLAP helps the user to synthesize enterprise information through comparative, personalized viewing, as well as through analysis of historical and projected data in various "what-if" data model scenarios. This is achieved through the use of an OLAP Server. An OLAP server is a high-capacity, multi-user data manipulation engine specifically designed to support and operate on multi-dimensional data structures. A multi-dimensional structure is arranged so that every data item is located and accessed based on the intersection of the dimensions which define that item. The OLAP term dates back to 1993, but the ideas, technology and even some of the products have origins long before then.

Databases configured for OLAP employ a multidimensional data model, allowing for complex analytical and ad-hoc queries with a rapid execution time. They borrow aspects of navigational databases and hierarchical databases that are speedier than their relational kin. Nigel Pendse has suggested that an alternative and perhaps more descriptive term to describe the concept of OLAP is **Fast Analysis of Shared Multidimensional Information** (FASMI).The output of an OLAP query is typically displayed in a matrix (or pivot) format.

What is OLTP System?

- It is a category of systems that are dedicated for managing applications that are oriented towards transactions.
- The OLTP system is customer oriented and is used for transaction or query processing by clients, users, staff members at operational level.
- These systems facilitate data entry and retrieval for transaction processing. Here, a transaction may refer to computer or database transaction or business commercial transactions.
- An OLTP system manages the current data that is in very comprehensive form and can not be used for decision making purpose directly.
- An OLTP system consists of short, atomic transactions which are updated very often (many times a day) and by multiple users.
- An OLTP system is characterized by a large number of short online transactions like insert, update & delete etc.
- OLTP systems are typically able to respond to user requests immediately. For example, ATM (Automatic Teller Machines) is an example of commercial transaction processing.
- Recent OLTP systems are able to span more than one company and may work over a network.

What is an OLAP System?

- It is a category of systems, which provide answers to multi-dimensional queries. OLAP is implemented in a multi-user client/server mode and offers consistently rapid response to queries, regardless of database size and complexity.
- Databases used for OLAP are configured for complex and ad-hoc queries with a quick performance in mind.

- An OLAP system is market-oriented, and is used for data analysis by mangers, executives, decision makers at the top level of management, government policy makers etc.
- An OLAP system support read only operations most of the time.
- An OLAP system is characterized by low volume of transactions and queries in these systems are very complex.
- An OLAP system manages large amount of data in summarized and aggregated form, which can be presented from various prospectives as per the requirements of the decision makers.
- Typically OLAP is used for marketing, budgeting, forecasting and similar applications. For example, it can be used to find out the sales of this year as compared to last year? What is the prediction on the sales for the next quarter? What can be said about the trend by looking at the percentage change?
- OLAP functionality is characterized by dynamic multi-dimensional analysis of consolidated enterprise data supporting end user analytical and navigational activities which includes:
  - (A) Trend analysis over sequential time periods.
  - (B) Slicing subsets for on-screen viewing.
  - (C) Drill-down to deeper levels of consolidation.
  - (D) Reaching out to the underlying detail data.
  - (E) Provides rotational view to project data from various different dimensions and prospective.

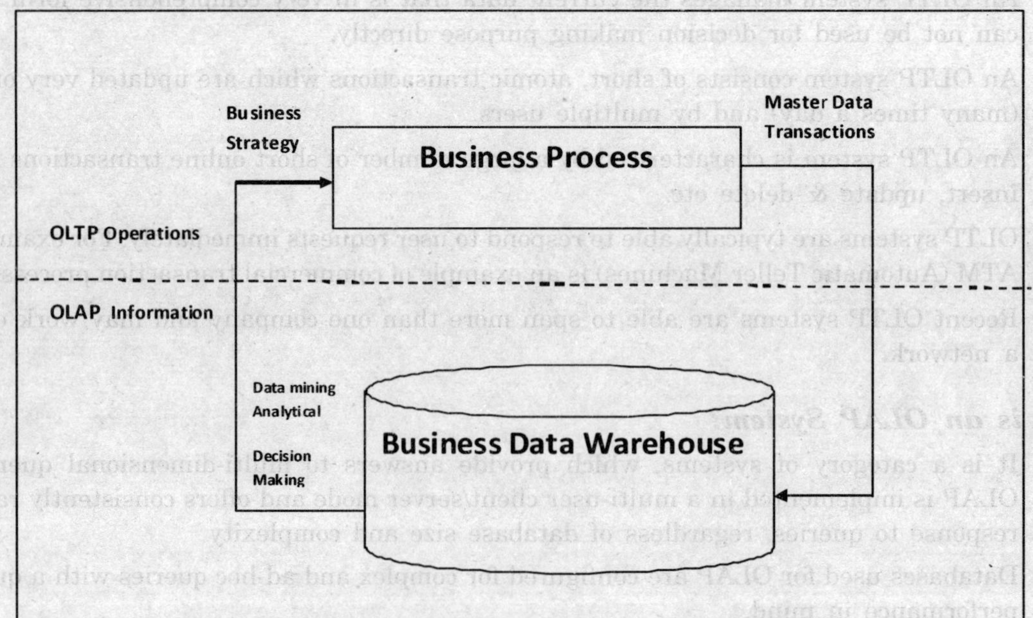

Fig. 2.1: Difference between OLTP & OLAP

An OLTP system provides source data to data warehouses, and OLAP system helps to analyze it. OLAP was conceived for Management Information Systems and Decision Support Systems but is still widely underused. Even today people are making out business intelligence from OLTP data only.

The Fig. 2.1 given above differentiates between an OLTP and OLAP systems, the OLTP systems are concentrated on the business operations, master data transactions and help to design the business strategy to handle the day to day operations, the OLTP systems work as a source of data for the business data warehouse and it becomes the OLAP information which becomes the basis for analytical decision making by using the techniques and tools of data warehouse.

2.2 DIFFERENCE BETWEEN OLTP & OLAP

Many a times it is argued that an operational systems store huge amounts of data, the user can perform on-line analytical processing directly on such databases, instead of having a separate OLAP system. The basic reason for having separate systems is that, these systems have different basis of structure, operations and functionality and the following table shows that these differences are so diverse and prominent, that it is better to have separate systems so that both systems can work efficiently and can deliver the required performance. The following table summarizes the major differences between OLTP and OLAP system design.

Table 2.1: Difference between OLTP and OLAP

S.No	Feature	OLTP Systems	OLAP Systems
1.	Source of Data	The source of this data is the day to day transactions performed at various levels of the organization, by the various in house or outside users. This is the place where data is originated. It has data in detailed and comprehensive form.	The source of OLAP data is OLTP databases; it has consolidated and summarized data.
2.	Purpose of Data	The main purpose of the data is to control and run fundamental business tasks.	The main purpose of OLAP data is to help the decision makers for strategic planning and problem solving.
3.	Type of data	These systems store current data, guaranteed to be up-to-date. The data is highly primitive and is in highly detailed form.	These systems store historic data, where accuracy is maintained over time. The data is summarized and consolidated.
4.	Characteristic	These systems are used for operational processing.	These systems are used for information processing

5.	Orientation	The main orientation of the system is transaction storage and their processing.	The main orientation of these systems is analysis of transactions summarized over a period of time.
6.	Users	The users of these systems are the end users, users at middle and operational level, clerical staff, and data base professionals. The number of users is in thousands.	The users of these systems are managers, executives and members of top level management. The number of users is in hundreds.
7.	View of data	These systems store snapshot of ongoing business processes.	These systems store multi-dimensional views of various kinds of business activities, i.e projects the data from the user's perspective which is required for a particular decision making scenario.
8.	Frequency of Operations	Frequency of operation is high, short and fast updates are done quite often and are initiated by the end users. Operations are done on daily basis.	Frequency of operations is low, periodic long running batch processing is done.
9.	Help for planning	These systems help the short term planning	These systems help the long term planning.
10.	Types of queries handled	These systems run relatively standardized and simple queries. The queries return a few records only.	These systems run complex, ad hoc queries.
11.	Requirement of space	These systems require lesser storage space as only the current data is stored. The storage requirement in giga or tera bytes.	These systems require large storage space, as historic data over a period of time is stored. The storage requirement is more than tera bytes.
12.	Data Base Design	The design of these systems is application oriented and is entity-relationship based.	The design of these systems is subject oriented, multidimensional and is star/snowflake based.
13.	Type of Access	The access is either read or write.	The access is read only.
14.	Focus of Operation	Most of operations in these systems are related to in flow of data.	Most of the operations in these systems are related to outflow of the information.
15.	Database Design	The data base design in these systems is highly normalized with many tables.	The data base design is de-normalized with fewer tables.
16.	Backup and Recovery	Operational data is critical to run the business; data loss may lead to significant financial, legal and reliability problems. Rigorous back up and recovery procedures are required.	These systems store historic data, therefore simple backup and recovery methods will work.

Many vendors of operational relational database management systems have started to optimize such systems for OLAP queries, and the difference between OLTP and OLAP system is diminishing.

2.3 MULTIDIMENSIONAL DATA MODEL

In multidimensional data model the data is viewed as a data cube. Data cubes are used to model n-dimensional data. Where the data can be viewed on the basis of multiple dimensions and hence the better decisions taking into account the multiple facts can be taken.

The following related terminology is in use in data base:

Dimensions: These are the perspectives or entities about which an organization wishes to keep the records. These are the categories of information that organize the warehouse data, such as time, geography, organization, and so on. For example in a sales data warehouse the data can be stored w.r.t various dimensions like: time, item, branch and location. These dimensions allow the user to keep track of the things like monthly sales of items, sales based on the branches, sales based on the locations at which the items were sold etc.

Dimensions may be hierarchical in nature that one member may be a child of another member.

For example, A geography dimension may contain data by country/region, state, and city. A city member is a child to a state member, which is in itself a child to a country member. Thus, the dimension is comprised of three hierarchical levels: all countries, all states, and all cities in the dimension table. To support this, the dimension table should include the relationship of each member to the higher levels in the hierarchy.

Each dimension has a table associated with it and this table is termed as **dimension table**.

2.3.1 Dimension Table

Dimension tables encapsulate the attributes associated with facts and separate these attributes into logically distinct groupings, such as time, geography, products, customers, and so forth. A dimension table may be used at multiple places if the data warehouse contains multiple fact tables or contributes data to data marts. Like the dimension table for item may contain the attributes like item-name, brand and type. The various types of constraints can be applied on the data stored in the dimension tables in order to maintain the data integrity. The data stored can be used to refer the data stored in the fact table, such as product descriptions, customer names and addresses, and suppliers. Dimension tables do not contain as many rows as fact tables, and dimensional data is subject to change, as when a customer's address or telephone number changes. Dimension tables are structured to permit change.

2.3.2 Fact Table

A fact table can contain fact's data on detail or aggregated level. Facts are numeric measures, or the quantities by which the user wishes to analyze relationship between dimensions. Fact tables can contain data aggregations, such as sales per month per region. Because fact tables contain the vast majority of the data stored in a data warehouse, it is important that the table structure should be correct before data is loaded. Expensive table restructuring can be necessary if data required by decision support queries is missing or incorrect.

A fact table typically has two types of columns:

- ***The columns that contain facts and***
- ***The columns that are foreign keys to dimension tables.***

Like facts for a sales data warehouse may be number of units sold, amount spent on the units sold etc. The fact table contains the name of facts or measures as well as the keys to each of related dimension tables. The data cubes in a data warehouse can be n-dimensional. Like it may be 2-D, 3-D or 4-D.

2.3.3 Dimension Table Vs Fact Tables

A product dimension may be used with a sales fact table and an inventory fact table in the data warehouse, and also in one or more departmental data marts. A dimension such as customer, time, or product that is used in multiple schemas is called a conforming dimension if all copies of the dimension are the same.

- In contrast to a fact table, dimension tables are usually small and change relatively slowly. Dimension tables are seldom keyed to date.
- The records in a dimension table establish one-to-many relationships with the fact table. For example, there may be a number of sales to a single customer, or a number of sales of a single product.

Table 2.2: Difference between Dimension Table and Fact Table

S.No	Dimension Table	Fact Table
1.	Numbers of rows are few; normally range from hundreds to thousands.	Numbers of rows are large in number, normally in billions.
2.	The data stored is textual in nature.	The data stored is numeric in nature.
3.	It has multiple columns that are used to manage dimension hierarchies.	It has multiple rows that are used to store data.
4.	The data stored is dynamic in nature and is updated quite often.	The data stored is static in nature.
5.	It has one primary key.	It has multiple foreign keys.

2.3.4 From Tables and Spreadsheets to Data Cubes

An OLAP cube is a data structure that allows fast analysis of data. The arrangement of data into cubes overcomes the limitation of relational databases. Relational databases are not well suited for near instantaneous analysis and display of large amounts of data. Instead, they are better suited for creating records from a series of transactions known as OLTP or On-Line Transaction Processing. Although many report-writing tools exist for relational databases, these are slow when the whole database must be summarized.

The OLAP cube consists of numeric facts called measures which are categorized by dimensions.

The cube metadata is typically created from a star schema or snow flake schema of tables in a relational database. Measures are derived from the records in the fact table and dimensions are derived from the dimension tables. A data cube allows data to be modeled and viewed in multiple dimensions. It is defined by dimensions and facts.

The 2-D data cube is normally used for simple applications and these are used since a long time and these are termed as table or spreadsheets. For example Table 2.3 shows the sales data for items sold per quarter in the city New Delhi.

2-D Data Cubes: A 2-D data cube is basically a table or a spreadsheet. The data presented in such tables or spreadsheets is based on 2-dimensions, like in the Table 2.3 given below; the sales data has been shown on the basis of items sold per quarter in a particular city over a particular time dimension. In the Table 2.3, the items are categorized on the basis of type of items sold and time dimension is the dimension on which time slices are divided(like here we are considering a quarter as the time dimension). The fact or measure is displayed in number of items sold.

Table 2.3: 2-D View of Sales data according to Time and Item for a particular Location.

Type of items for location = 'New Delhi"			
Time	**Computer**	**Cell Phone**	**LCD**
Quarter I	500	876	234
Quarter II	560	777	678
Quarter III	765	888	456

3-D Data Cubes: These types of data cubes allow the data to be viewed on a third dimension also, like the user wish to view the same sales data on the basis of location also. These 3-D data cubes are represented as a series of 2-D tables (as shown in Table 2.4) or can be represented as a 3-D cube (as shown in Fig. 2.2).

Table 2.4: 3-D view of sales data according to Time, Item and Location.

	Items for location = 'Ludhiana'			Items for location = 'Amritsar"			Items for location = 'New Delhi"		
Time	Computer	Cell Phone	LCD	Computer	Cell Phone	LCD	Computer	Cell Phone	LCD
Quarter I	676	234	90	555	789	666	500	876	234
Quarter II	564	245	235	345	456	457	560	777	678
Quarter III	245	777	123	345	123	253	765	888	456

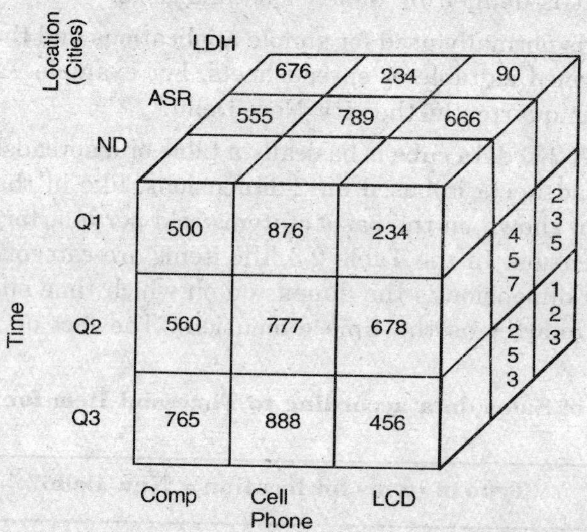

Fig. 2.2: 3-D Data Cube representation of the data, according to Time, Item and Location

4-D Data Cubes: These types of data cubes are used when the user wishes to view the data on the basis on a fourth dimension also, like in our example the user wishes to project the data on the basis of supplier also. Designing and visualizing a 4-D data cube is quite difficult and 4-D data cubes can be visualized as a series of 3-D data cubes as shown in the Fig. 2.4 given below.

Moving on this pattern the user is capable of displaying n-dimensional data as a series of n-1 dimensional cubes.

The cuboid that holds the lowest level of summarization is called a base cuboid. The 4-D cuboid shown in the Figure 2.4 is the ***base cuboid*** for given time, item, location and supplier dimensions.

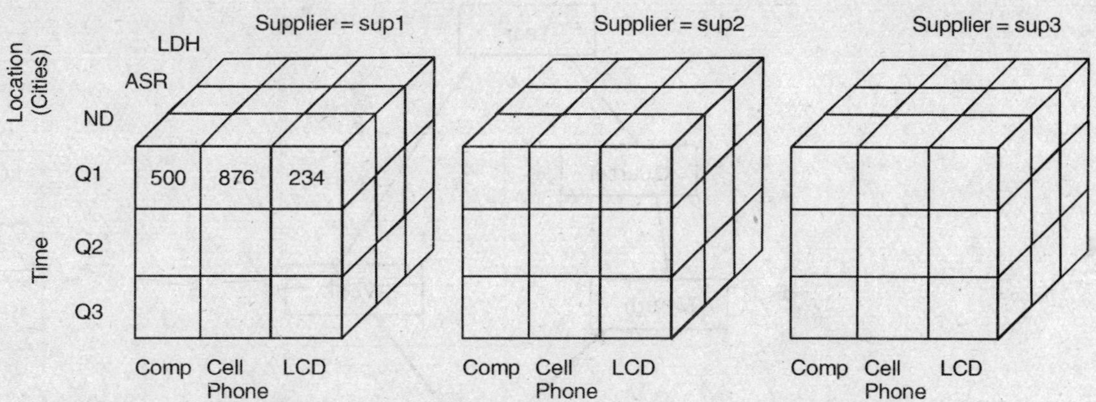

Fig. 2.4: 4-D data cube representation of sales data according to Time, Item, Locatio and Supplier.

2.3.5 The Concept of Hierarchies

A concept hierarchy defines a sequence of mappings from a set of low-level concepts to higher level in a more generalized fashion. Let us consider the concept hierarchy for the dimension location. City values for location include Khanna, Doraha and each city can be mapped to the district it belongs to like Khanna and Doraha belong to district Ludhiana, and then in turn the districts can be mapped further to various states, depending upon the state to which the district belongs to. These mappings form a hierarchy for the dimension location, mapping a low level concept i.e city to higher level more general concept i.e countries. The concept hierarchy is shown in Fig. 2.5.

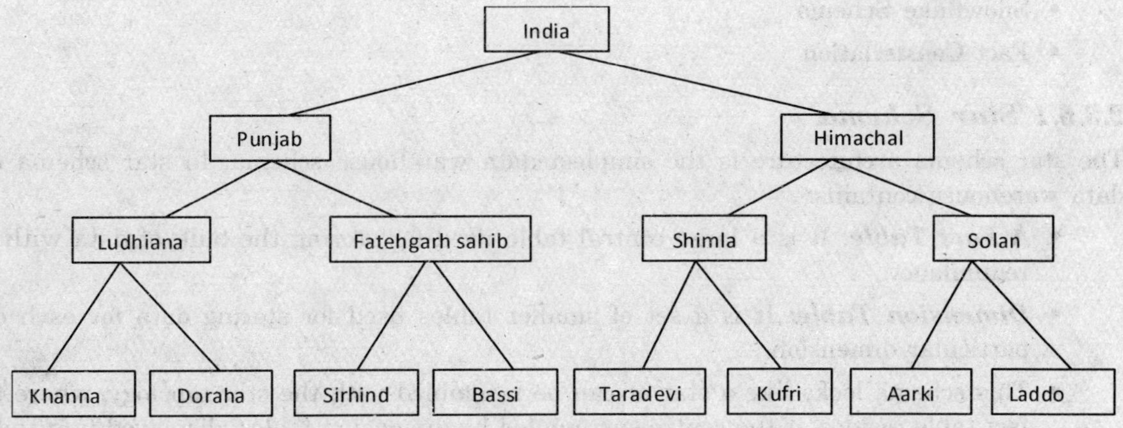

Fig. 2.5: A Concept Hierarchy for Location

The attributes of a dimension may be organized in a partial order forming a lattice, an example of a partial order for the time dimension is shown below in the Fig. 2.6, which shows the attributes, day, week, month, quarter and year.

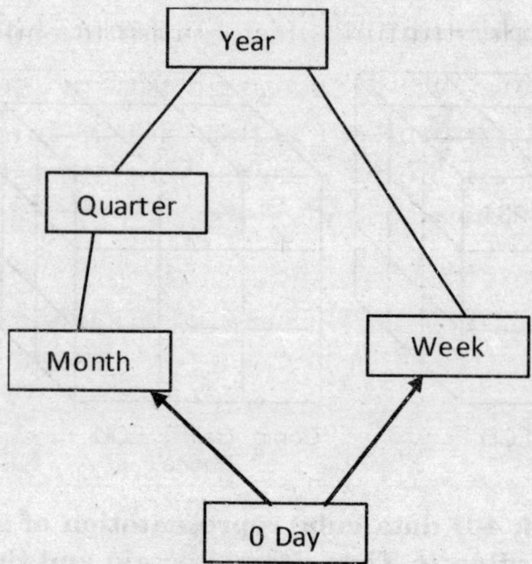

Fig. 2.6: A Lattice for Time.

2.3.6 Schemas for Multidimensional Data (Data Warehouse Schemas)

For representing a relational data base, the entity relationship model is used, where the database schema consists of a set of entities, their attributes and the relationship between the entities. These systems are suitable for Online Transaction Processing Systems. But in data warehouse such a model is not found to be suitable, as in data warehouse we need a concise, subject oriented schema that should facilitate the on line data analysis. For this purpose a multidimensional data model is used and in this case following schemas exists:

- Star Schema
- Snowflake Schema
- Fact Constellation

2.3.6.1 Star Schema

The star schema architecture is the simplest data warehouse schema. In star schema the data warehouse contains:

- ***A Fact Table***: It is a large central table used for storing the bulk of data with no redundancy.
- ***Dimension Table:*** It is a set of smaller tables used for storing data for each one particular dimension.
- This schema looks like a star or can be resembled with the star topology, where the fact table resides at the centre surrounded by dimension tables, displayed in a radial pattern.
- The definition of a Star Schema is one in which all dimension tables are directly related to the fact table through foreign key relationships. It is the simplest form of Data Warehouse design where complex dimension relationships are collapsed into a single layer of dimension tables.

- This schema has simple structure which is easy to understand.
- It has small number of tables to join, so queries can be run effectively.
- The fact tables in a star schema are in third normal form(3NF) whereas dimensional tables are de-normalized. Despite the fact that the star schema is the simplest architecture, it is most commonly used nowadays and is recommended by Oracle.
- It is widely supported by a large number of business intelligence tools.
- Dimensions are represented by one dimension table and each dimension table is related to fact table.

For Example: The following Fig. 2.7 shows the star schema, where the sales have been considered on four dimensions namely, customer, product, location and time. The schema contains:

- ***One Central Fact Table i.e Sales Table and***
- ***Four Dimension Tables: Location, ProductInfo, Time and Customer.***

In star schema each dimension is represented by only one table and each table contains a set of attributes.

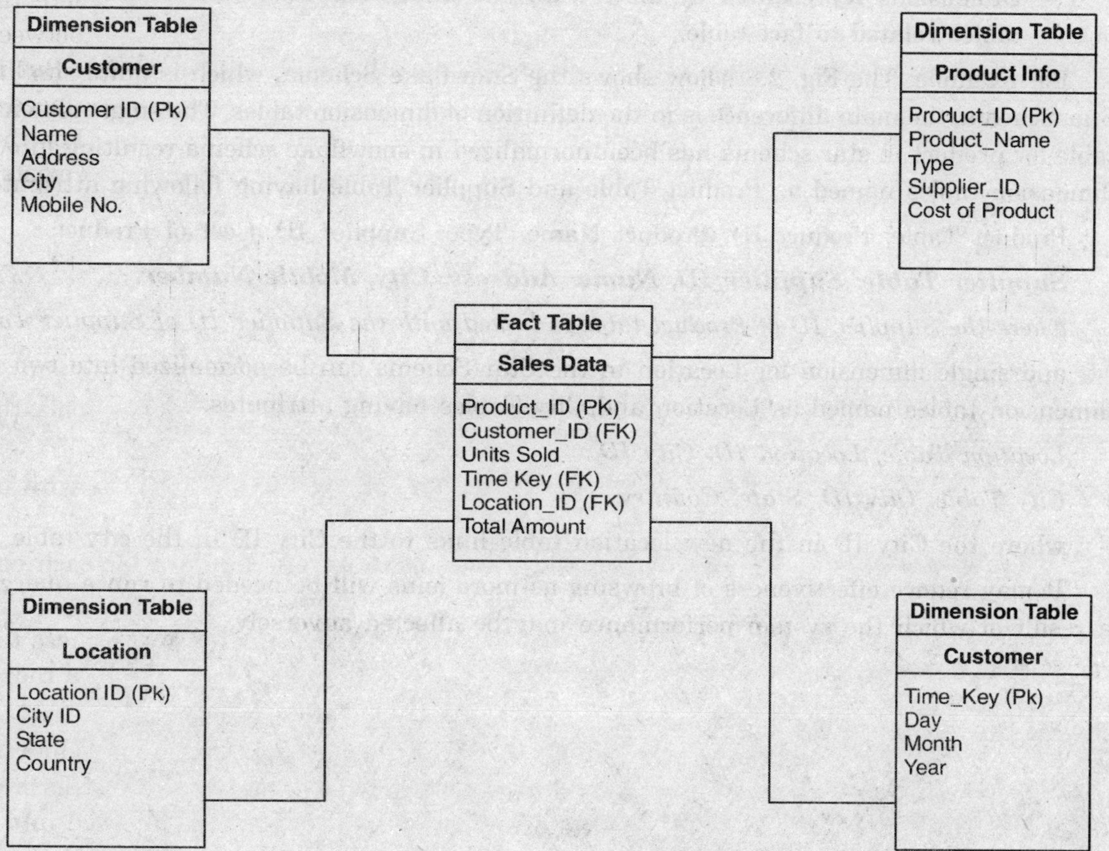

Fig. 2.7: Star Schema

In the Fig. 2.7, the location table contains the attribute set: location id, street, city, state and country. This constraint may result into some redundancy, as Ludhiana and Amritsar are both cities in the state Punjab in the country India. Entries for such cities in location dimension table will create redundancy among the attributes state and country as these will be entered as Ludihana-Punjab- India and Amritsar- Punjab- India.

2.3.6.2 Snowflake Schema

This schema is a variant to Star Schema. The snowflake schema came into existence to reduce the redundancies present in the star schema. In Snowflake Schema:

- Some dimension tables are normalized by splitting the data into additional tables.
- It will result in saving of storage space; however this saving is quite less as comparison to the total magnitude of the fact tables.
- The Snowflake Schema is more normalized and saves space and redundancy.
- Snowflake schemas are generally used when a dimensional table becomes very big and when a star schema can't represent the complexity of a data structure.
- Dimensions represented by more than one dimension table and not all dimension tables related to fact table.

For example, The Fig. 2.8 below shows the Snowflake Schema, which is quite similar to Star Schema, the main difference is in the definition of dimension tables. The single dimension table for product in star schema has been normalized in snowflake schema resulting into two dimension tables named as Product Table and Supplier Table having following attributes:

Product Table: Product_ID, Product_Name, Type, Supplier_ID, Cost of Product.

Supplier Table: Supplier_ID, Name, Address, City, Mobile Number.

where the Supplier_ID of Product table is linked with the Supplier_ID of Supplier Table.

and single dimension for Location in the Star Schema can be normalized into two new dimension tables named as Location and City Tables having attributes:

Location Table: Location ID, City ID.

City Table: City ID, State, Country.

where the City ID in the new location table links to the City ID in the city table.

It may reduce effectiveness of browsing as more joins will be needed to run a query. As a result of which the system performance may be affected adversely.

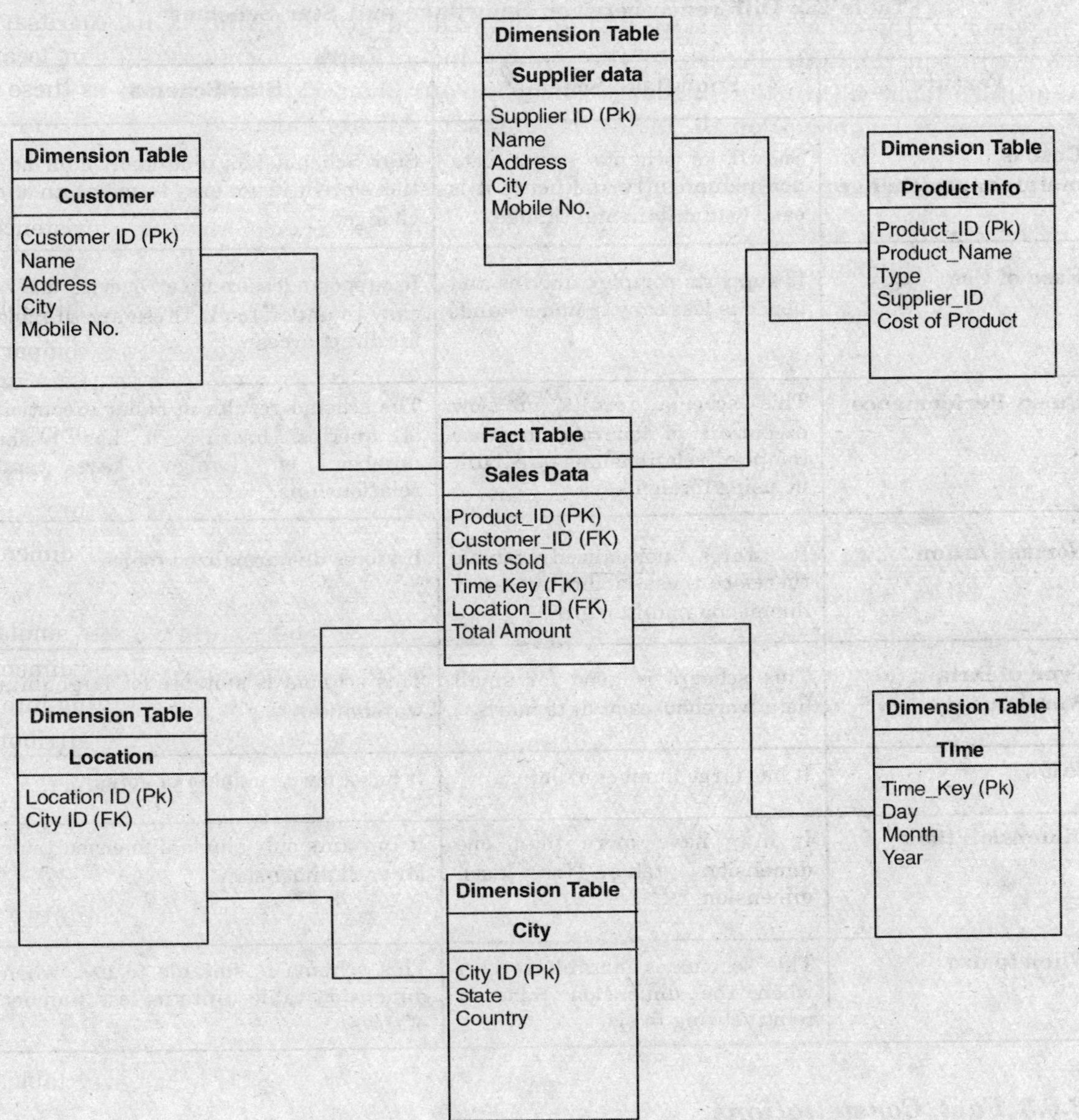

Fig. 2.8: Snow Flake Schema

The table 2.5 shows difference between Snowflake and Star Schemas.

Table 2.5: Difference between Snowflake and Star Schemas

Feature	Snowflake Schema	Star Schema
Ease of maintenance/change	Snowflake schema stores data non-redundantly and hence it is easy to maintain and change.	Star Schema has redundant data and therefore it is not easy to maintain and change.
Ease of Use	It supports complex queries and hence is less easy to understand.	It supports less complex queries and is easy to understand. These are suitable for direct access.
Query Performance	This schema results in slow execution of queries, because complex relationships are built by using foreign keys.	The schema results in faster execution of queries, because it has lesser number of foreign keys and relationships.
Normalization	It stores normalized tables, therefore these facilitates easier dimension maintenance	It stores de-normalized tables.
Type of Data Warehouse	This schema is good for small data warehouses or data marts.	This schema is suitable for large data warehouses.
Joins	It has large number of Joins.	It has a fewer number of Joins.
Dimension table	It may have more than one dimension table for each dimension.	It contains only single dimension table for each dimension.
When to use	This schema is suitable to use, when the dimension table is relatively big in size.	This schema is suitable to use, when dimension table contains less number of rows.

2.3.6.3 *Fact Constellations*

Many applications may allow multiple fact tables to share dimension tables. This kind of schema can be viewed as a collection of stars and is called as ***galaxy schema or a fact constellation***. For each star schema or snowflake schema it is possible to construct a fact constellation schema.

This schema is more complex than star or snowflake architecture, which is because it contains multiple fact tables. This allows dimension tables to be shared amongst many fact tables. That solution is very flexible, however it may be hard to manage and support.

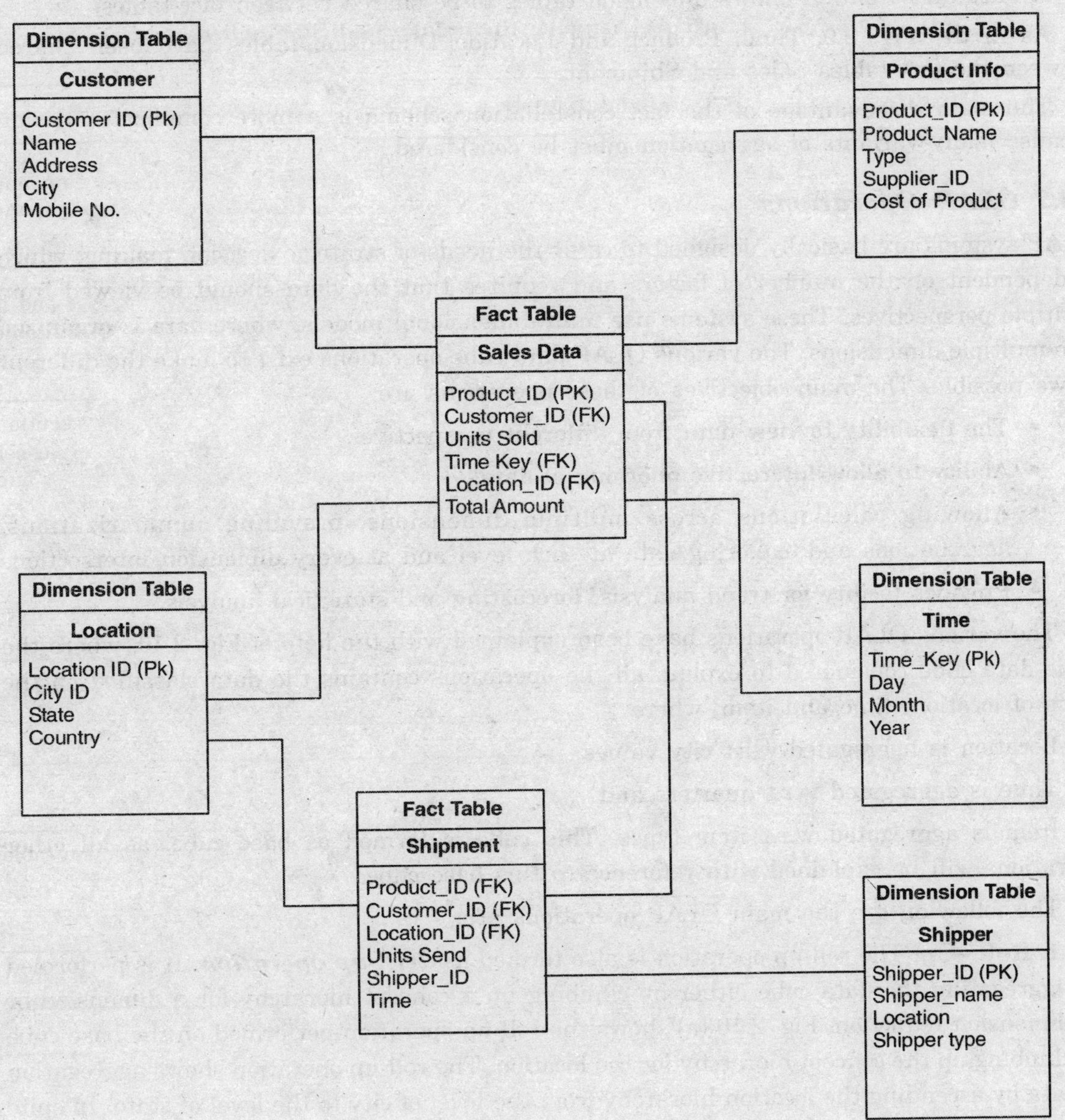

Fig. 2.9: Fact Constellation Schema

The above Fig. 2.9 shows a Fact Constellation, it has 2 Fact Tables - *Sales Table* and *Shipment Table*.

Sales Table has the dimensions: Product ID, Customer ID, Location ID, Units Sold, Time, Total Amount.

Shipment Table has the dimensions: Product ID, Customer ID, Location ID, Units Send, Time, Supplier ID.

A Fact Constellation allows dimension tables to be shared between fact tables.

As in the Fig. 2.9, Time, Product and Location Dimension tables have been shared between the fact tables Sales and Shipment.

The main disadvantage of the fact constellation schema is a more complicated design because many variants of aggregation must be considered.

2.3.7 OLAP Operations

OLAP systems are basically designed to cater the needs of strategic decision making, which is dependent on the number of factors and requires that the data should be viewed from multiple perspectives. These systems use multidimensional models, where data is organized into multiple dimensions. The various OLAP data cube operations exist to make the different views possible. The main objectives of these operations are:

- The flexibility to view data from different perspectives.
- Ability to allow interactive querying of data.
- Allowing calculations across multiple dimensions, providing summarizations, aggregations and exploring data at each level and at every dimension intersection.
- Provides facility for trend analysis, forecasting and statistical analysis.

The various OLAP operations have been explained with the help of Fig. 2.10, where the basic data cube considered to explain all the operations contains the data classified on the basis of location, time and item, where

Location is aggregated w.r.t city values,

Time is aggregated w.r.t quarters and

Item is aggregated w.r.t item types. This cube is termed as base cube, as all other operations will be explained with reference to this base cube.

The following are the main OLAP operations are:

1. Roll –Up: The roll-up operation is also termed as ***drill-up operation***. It is performed by aggregating the data cube either by climbing up a concept hierarchy for a dimension or by dimension reduction. Fig. 2.10 (a) shows the roll-up operation performed on the base cube by climbing up the concept hierarchy for the location. The roll-up operation shows aggregation of data by ascending the location hierarchy from the level of city to the level of state. In spite of grouping the data by city, the resulting cube groups the data by state. In case the roll-up operation is performed by dimension reduction, then one or more dimensions are removed from the given cube. Like if the data cube is structured based on the dimensions location and time, then the roll-up operation may be performed by removing either of the dimension, like the user has removed the location dimension, then the data cube will show the data on the basis of time only.

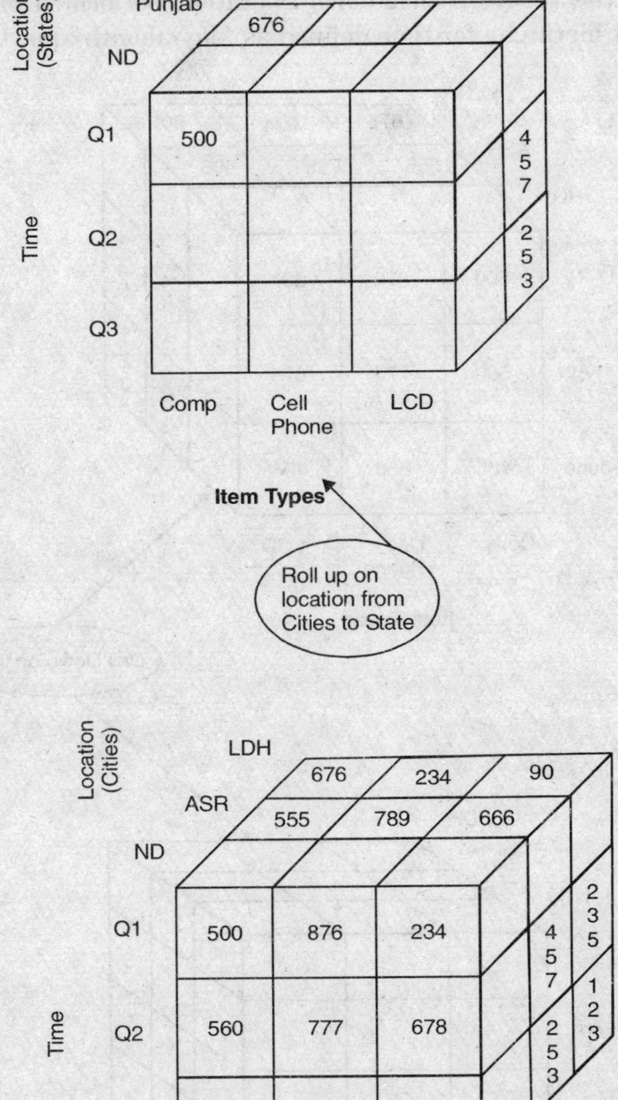

Fig. 2.10(a): Roll Up Operation

2.Drill-Down: This operation is the reverse of roll-up. It moves from less detailed data to more detailed data. There are two methods to perform the drill-down operation:

- ***By stepping down a concept hierarchy for a dimension.***
- ***By introducing an additional dimension.***

Fig. 2.10(b) shows the result of drill-down operation performed on the basic cube by stepping down a concept hierarchy for time defined as "day<month<quarter<year". Drill down

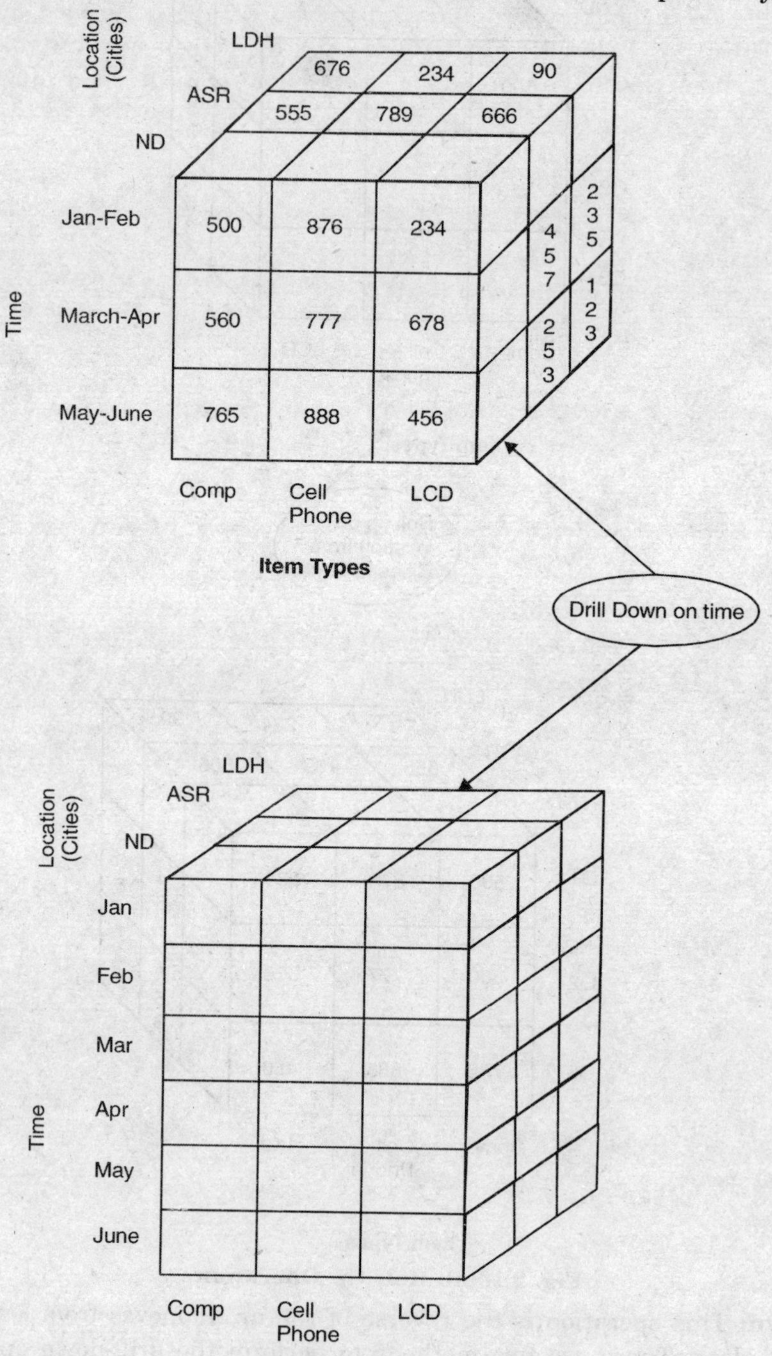

Fig. 2.10(b): Drill down Operation

occurs by descending the time hierarchy from the level of quarter to the more detailed level of month. The resulting data cube shows the details of total sales per month rather than summarizing them by a quarter. Drill-down operation can be performed by adding a new dimension to a cube. For Example: in the base cube defined in Fig. 2.10(b) and additional dimension like customer-group can be added, to provide more detailed information.

2. Slice: The slice operation performs :

- A selection of some specified data based on one dimension of the given cube.
- The result comes out to be a subset of the base cube and can be named as the sub-cube.
- The operation reduces dimensionality of the cubes.
- Sets one or more dimensions to specific values and keeps a subset of dimensions for selected values.

Fig. 2.10 (c)shows a slice operation where the sales data has been selected from the base cube for the dimension time using the criteria time = "Q1"

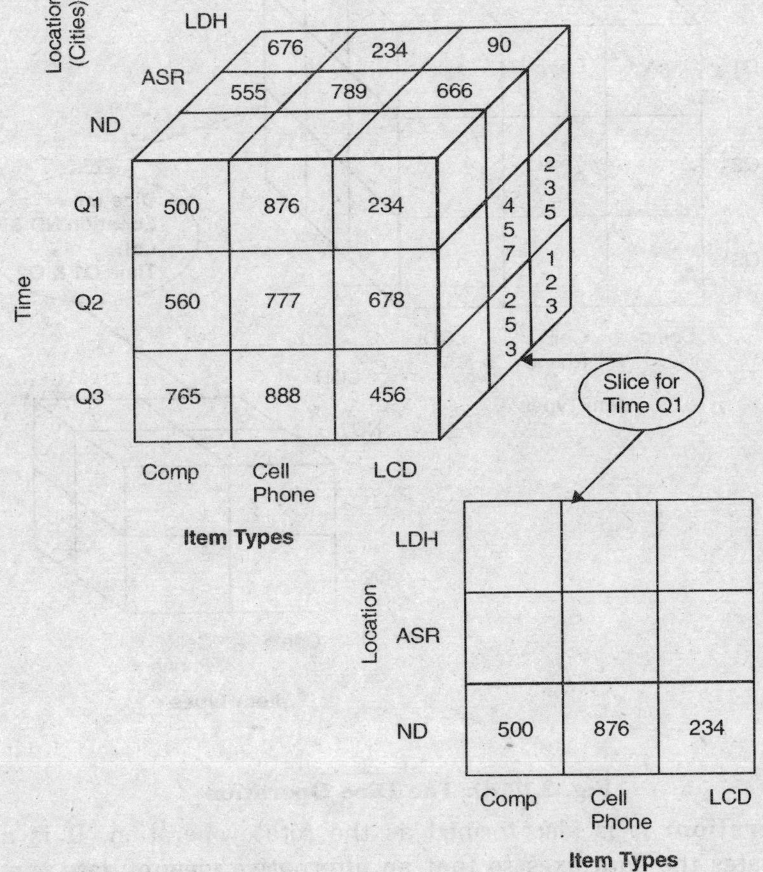

Fig. 2.10(c): Slice Operation

3. Dice Operation: The dice operation performs:

- A selection of some specified data based on two or more dimensions of the given cube.
- The resulting sub cube satisfies the criteria's mentioned in the condition.
- Reduces the number of member values of one or more dimensions.

Fig. 2.10(d) shows a dice operation on central cube based on the criteria that involve three dimensions:

Location = LDH or ND
Time = Q1 or Q2 and
Item = Computer or LCD.

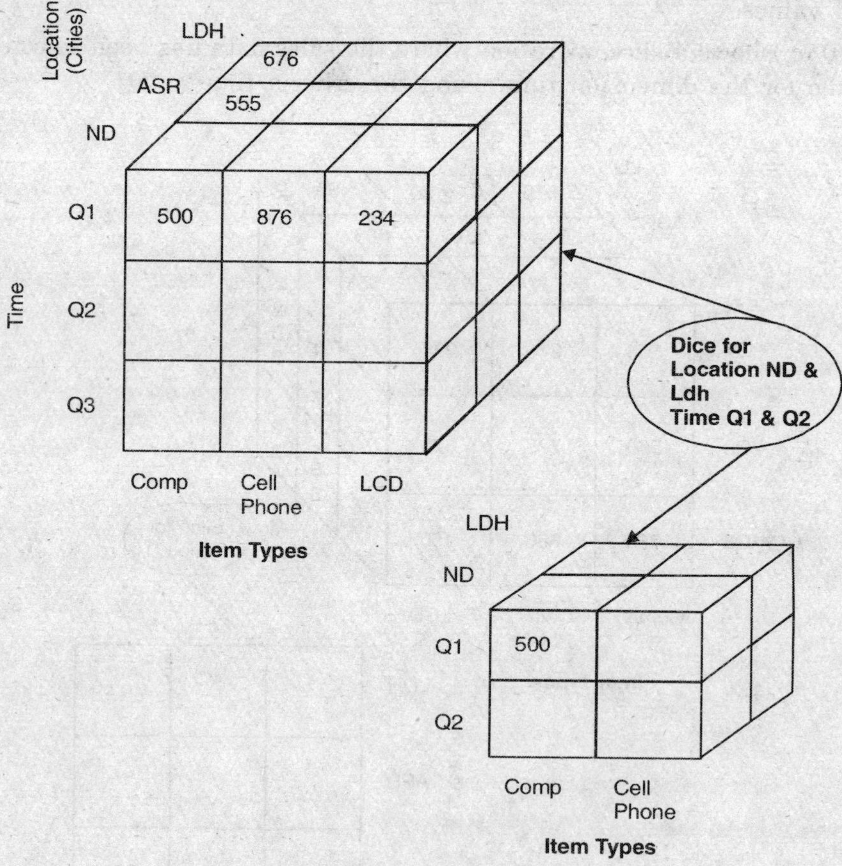

Fig. 2.10(d): The Dice Operation

4. Pivot Operation: It is also termed as the rotate operation. It is a visualization operation that rotates the data axes so that an alternative view of data can be presented. Fig. 2.10(e) shows the pivot operation where the item and location axes in a 2-D slice are rotated.

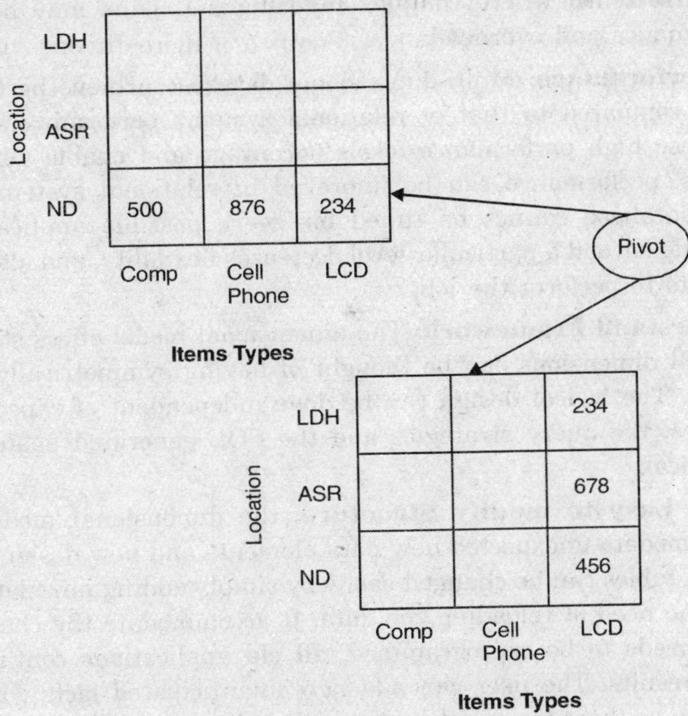

Fig. 2.10(e): The Pivot Operation

5. Drill Across and Drill Through: These two drilling operations perform additional drilling operations. For drill-across, executes queries involving more than one fact table, where as drill through operation uses relational SQL facilities to drill through the bottom level of a data cube down to its back end relational tables.

6. Mathematical Operations: Apart from these basic operations there may be some basic mathematical operations that can be performed on the data cubes, these are:

- Ranking top n or bottom n items.
- Finding Maximum or Minimum in the list.
- Calculating Averages, interests, depreciations.
- Performing Currency conversions.
- Performing various statistical Functions.

The main advantages of Multi-Dimensional Data Model are:

Enhanced Data Presentation and Navigation: The multi-dimensional databases provide intuitive spreadsheet-like views of the data, such views are difficult to generate in relational systems without the use of complex SQL queries, while others cannot be performed by SQL at all, e.g. top ten exam results.

Ease of Maintenance: Multi-dimensional databases are very easy to maintain, because data is stored in the same way as it is viewed, that is according to its fundamental attributes, so no additional computational overhead is required for queries of the database. To compare this to relational systems, where complex indexing and joins may be used that require significant maintenance and overhead.

Increased Performance: Multi-dimensional database achieve performance levels that are far better as compared to that of relational systems performing similar data storage requirements. These high performance levels encourage and enable OLAP applications. In many applications, performance can be improved in relational systems through database tuning, but the database cannot be tuned for every possible applications and business requirement. Tuning beyond a particular level decreases flexibility, and also requires expensive database specialists to perform the job,.

Easy to understand Framework: The dimensional model offers standard type of joins and framework. All dimensions can be thought of having symmetrically equal entry points into the fact table. The logical design can be done independent of expected query patterns. The user interfaces, the query strategies and the SQL generated against the dimensional model is symmetrical.

Flexible and Easy to modify Structure: the dimensional model can be extended smoothly to accommodate unexpected new data elements and new design decisions. Both the fact and dimension tables can be changed easily by simply adding new data rows in the table. It does not have the need of reloading the data. It accommodate the changes the query tool or reporting tool needs to be reprogrammed, all old applications continue to run without yielding different results. The user can add new unanticipated facts , add completely new dimensions, (as long as there is a single value of that dimension defined for each existing fact record) , add new unanticipated dimensional attributes and breaking existing dimension records down to a lower level of granularity from a certain point in time forward, without changing the basic structure.

Difference between ER Diagram and Dimensional Model

	E-R diagram	Dimensional model
1.	An E-R diagram (used in OLTP or transactional system) has highly normalized model (Even at a logical level	Dimensional model aggregates most of the attributes and hierarchies of a dimension into a single entity.
2.	An E-R diagram is a complex maze of hundreds of entities linked with each other	the Dimensional model has logical grouped set of star-schemas
3.	E-R diagram is split as per the entities	A dimension model is split as per the dimensions and facts
4.	In an E-R diagram all attributes for an entity including textual as well as numeric, belong to the entity table	'Dimension' entity in dimension model has mostly the textual attributes, and the 'fact' entity has mostly numeric attributes.
5.	A single ER model serves many purposes and is general in nature.	Multidimensional Model serves a single purpose.

SUMMARY

- **Operational Database Systems** can be characterized into two categories, offline transactions processing systems and online transaction processing systems.
- An OLTP system manages the current data that is in very comprehensive form and cannot be used for decision making purpose directly, whereas, an OLAP system is market-oriented, and is used for data analysis by mangers, executives, decision makers at the top level of management, government policy makers etc.
- OLAP functionality is characterized by dynamic multi-dimensional analysis of consolidated enterprise data supporting end user analytical and navigational activities which includes, trend analysis over sequential time periods, Slicing subsets for on-screen viewing, Drill-down to deeper levels of consolidation, Reaching out to the underlying detail data and provides rotational view to project data from various different dimensions and prospective.
- OLTP systems store current data, guaranteed to be up-to-date. The data is highly primitive and highly detailed, whereas, OLAP systems store historic data, where accuracy is maintained over time. The data is summarized and consolidated.
- In multidimensional data model the data is viewed as a data cube. Data cubes are used to model n-dimensional data.
- Dimension tables encapsulate the attributes associated with facts and separate these attributes into logically distinct groupings, such as time, geography, products, customers, and so forth. A dimension table may be used at multiple places if the data warehouse contains multiple fact tables or contributes data to data marts.
- A fact table can contain fact's data on detail or aggregated level. Facts are numeric measures, or the quantities by which the user wishes to analyze relationship between dimensions. Fact tables can contain data aggregations, such as sales per month per region.
- An OLAP cube is a data structure that allows fast analysis of data. The arrangement of data into cubes overcomes the limitation of relational databases.
- A concept hierarchy defines a sequence of mappings from a set of low-level concepts to higher level, more generalized fashion.
- A datacube consists of a lattice of cuboids each corresponding to a different degree of summarization of the given multidimensional data.
- A multidimensional data model is used to design corporate data warehouses, this model can adopt a ***Star Schema, Snowflake Schema or a Fact Constellation***.
- ***Star Schema*** architecture is the simplest data warehouse schema. It consists of a *fact table and a number of dimension tables.* This schema looks like a star or we can resemble it with the star topology, where the fact table resides at the centre surrounded by dimension tables, displayed in a radial pattern.
- ***Snowflake Schema*** was designed to overcome the limitations of star schema. Some dimension tables are normalized by splitting the data into additional tables. It will result in saving of storage space. The Snowflake Schema is more normalized and saves space and redundancy.
- ***Fact Constellation*** allows multiple fact tables to share dimension tables. This kind of schema can be viewed as a collection of stars and is called as galaxy schema or a fact constellation. For each star schema or snowflake schema it is possible to construct a fact constellation schema.
- ***OLAP operations*** provides the flexibility to view data from different perspectives, ability to allow interactive querying of data, allow calculations across multiple dimensions, providing summarizations, aggregations and exploring data at each level and at every dimension intersection and provides facility for trend analysis, forecasting and statistical analysis.
- The various OLAP operations are ***roll-up, drill-down, drill across, slice and dice, pivot*** and statistical operations like ranking and computing moving averages etc.

CHAPTER 3

BUILDING A DATA WAREHOUSE

In the present day business environment, to cope up with the challenges of global market and to face the strong competition prevailing all around, the organizations need to store more and more data about their business operations as well as the data about the competitors. This data has an essential role in the decision making process. Data in the operational systems which covers a short period of time, cannot provide the required basis for the strategic decisions. The industry decision makers are frustrated as the reports produced by the company's system are inflexible and business conditions change all the time and the right data to solve the business problem is not available. The decision makers require the data from different sources integrated together to make a decision viable and acceptable for all departments of an organization. So analytical systems are required in which information is integrated from internal as well as external sources, and is organized over the major subjects of the organization over a long period of time. So the data ware houses have been developed to answer the increasing demands of quality information required by the top managers and economic analysts of organizations.

Data warehouses offer support for decision-making process, allowing complex analyses which cannot be properly achieved from operational systems.

The data warehouse environment is built in an entirely different way than the classical operational environment has been built. The classical operational environment has been built on the system development life cycle - the SDLC - that requires that requirements be identified, then analysis proceed, followed by design and programming. Next testing occurs, and is completed by implementation. The SDLC is fine where requirements can be known in advance. But the DSS analyst - who is the ultimate beneficiary of the data warehouse - does not and cannot know his/her requirements in advance. The requirements of DSS analysts' are discovered in a hit and trial manner. So, there is an entirely different mode of development that is required for data warehouse development.

3.1 DESIGNING A DATA WAREHOUSE

Data warehouse development is a continuous process, evolving with the organization. A data warehouse is not a concept; it is a business application that must provide a return on the company's investment just like any other project. The data warehouse project must be driven by user needs. The organizations are usually familiar with structure and implementation of information systems, but issues related to data warehouse are quite different, in this case the organization has to make arrangements for information flow from various internal information systems and from internal sources of information. To make it possible the user should be fully involved in identifying the information requirements and identifying the data from internal and external data sources.

Why to Design a Data Warehouse?

- Data warehouse provide a competitive advantage by presenting relevant information to the users at the various levels in the organization.
- Data warehouse helps in increasing business productivity, as it is able to gather information describing the organization quickly and efficiently.
- Data warehouse facilitates customer relationship management as it provides a holistic view of data from different perspectives as required by the customers and items across all lines of business, all departments and all markets.
- Data warehouse implementation leads to cost reduction as through it is easier o track trends, patterns and expectations over a long period of time in a consistent anc reliable manner.
- Data warehouse provides the understanding of the significance of data it contains, and ability to understand and translate the business requirements into queries.
- It must deliver a great user experience—*user acceptance is the measure of success.*
- It should function without interfering with OLTP systems.
- It should be flexible enough to cope up with the changing business and user requirements.

A data warehouse implementation represents a complex activity including two major stages:

- In the first stage, of *system configuration*, the data warehouse conceptual model is established, in accordance with the users' demands (data warehouse design).
- Then data sources are established, as well as the way of extracting and loading data (data acquisition).
- Finally, the storage technology is chosen and it is decided on the way the data will be accessed.

Before embarking on the design of a data warehouse, it is imperative that the architectural, organizational and design goals of the data warehouse should be clear and well understood. Because the purpose of a data warehouse is to serve users, it is also critical to understand the various types of users, their needs, and the characteristics of their interactions with the data warehouse.

Data Warehouse Design Issues

The major design issues are:

1. The design of data warehouse should be exhaustive and it should consider a holistic view of data requirements from various sources, the aim is to cover all data sources for designing a data warehouse which will meet the requirements of users at various levels in the organization.
2. As the data is to be collected from heterogeneous sources, the other major design issue is to harmonize the data (which covers data conversion and merging etc) while maintaining the integrity, reliability and authenticity of data.
3. Although the data warehouse is meant for storing the historical data, but while designing the data warehouse it must be ensured that the old data is relevant and is useful for data warehouse. Data too old to be relevant should not be entered in the data warehouse.
4. The data ware houses grow with the passage of time, the designers should decide to limit the size of data ware house by dropping old data and selecting suitable data to be included into the warehouse.
5. Data warehouse design should be business driven and should be based on specific business goals to be achieved by OLAP system.
6. The data warehouse design should be flexible enough to cope up with the changing user and business requirements.

3.2 ARCHITECTURAL ISSUES IN DESIGNING A DATA WAREHOUSE

A data warehouse exists to serve its users—analysts and decision makers. A data ware house can be built either on a ***top-down*** or on a ***bottom-up*** approach.

There are two approaches for this:

Bottom up Approach

Building a data warehouse with the bottom-up approach is often simpler and less ambitious. It is done by implementing **data marts**.

1. The bottom-up approach describes the process of building individual and independent data marts for departments, or specific business areas, and then joining them to providethe data for the entire organization.
2. It is a flexible method that allows the organization to go further with lower costs, as separate data marts are created at low cost and then these are integrated together.
3. The main sources of input in this approach are:
   - The content of the enterprise's transaction processing systems like: order entry, invoicing, accounting, personnel, shipping etc.
   - All the existing reporting systems.
   - All desired and projected reporting requirements and finally what external data users may need. Then, we build an all-encompassing data model.

4. The bottom-up approach is a fast one and is based on experiments and prototypes.
5. This approach to design, development and deployment of independent data marts provides flexibility, low cost and rapid return on investment.
6. This approach is useful in the early stages of business modeling and technology development. It allows the organization to move forward gradually at less expense and to make technological benefits before making significant commitments.

The problems with this approach are:

- Integration of individual data marts into a consistent enterprise data warehouse is quite difficult.
- Most of the times, in the beginning of developing data warehouse the data definitions are created by consulting only a few business lines, and the solution could be rejected by the next business line involved.

Top-down Approach

The top-down approach suits the vision of Bill Inmon, who considers that the data warehouse must respond to the requirements of all the users in the organization, and not of only a certain group.

- One can built a global data warehouse for entire organization and split it into individual data marts or sub data warehouses dedicated for individual departments.
- The top-down approach is a mature one and it is used when the technology and the economic problems are well known.
- This approach achieves the synergy between the business subjects and provides a single version of the truth.
- Top-down approach describes the process of building a data warehouse for the entire organization, containing data from multiple, heterogeneous, operational sources.
- It is a systemic method which minimizes the integration problems, but is expensive.
- The smaller scale is easier to deliver as an end result quickly.
- This approach is used in the environments where the business problems to be solved are clear and well understood.
- It is an expensive method and takes a long time to develop.
- It lacks flexibility due to difficulty in achieving consistency and consensus for a common data model for the entire organization.

The two approaches may be combined to get the advantages provided by each of them, by using the combined approach, the user can exploit the planned and strategic nature of top-down approach while retaining the rapid implementation and opportunistic approach of bottom-up approach.

From software engineering point of view, one of the following ***methods*** *can be used:*

Waterfall approach, which requires a structured and systematic analysis at each step, before going forward;

Spiral Approach, which allows fast generation of more and more developed functional systems, with short intervals between successive releases.

The most adequate method for developing a data warehouse is the iterative one. In this approach, more iterations are made, and a new version emerges at every iteration. The business subjects are approached one after the other. The method provides a scalable architecture and answers the informational demands of the whole organization. It also allows an efficient management of the users' requirements and reduces the possible risks.

Which Approach is best? - Top Down or Bottom Up?

- Top Down approach is a systemic method which minimizes the integration problems, but is expensive, takes a long time to develop and has a low flexibility. It is difficult to achieve consistency and consensus for a common data model for the entire organization.
- Bottom Up approach to design, development and deployment of independent data marts provides flexibility, low cost and rapid return on investment. But it can lead to problems while integrating various disparate data marts into a consistent data warehouse.

Keeping the pros and cons of both the methods, it is always better to develop a data warehouse in an incremental and evolutionary manner as shown in the Fig. 3.1(a) given below: and the step by step procedure can be enumerated as:

1. ***In the Step I***, a high level corporate model is defined which provides a corporate-wide, consistent, integrated view of data among different subjects and its potential usages, keeping the varied requirements of potential users at the various levels of the organization in mind.
2. ***In the step II***, independent data marts can be implemented in parallel, which should be in line with the corporate model defined in step I.
3. ***In step III***, distributed data marts can be constructed to integrate different data marts.
4. Finally, a multitier data warehouse is constructed where the enterprise warehouse is the sole owner of all warehouse data, which is then distributed to the various dependent data marts.

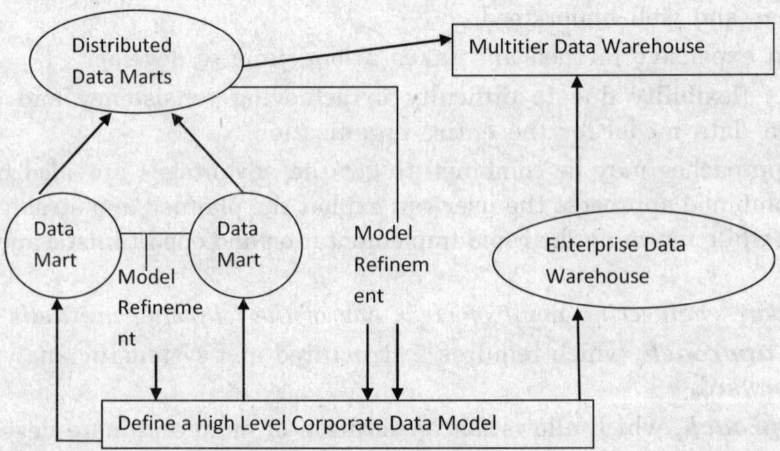

Fig. 3.1(a): A Recommended approach for data warehouse development.

3.3 ORGANIZATIONAL ISSUES IN DESIGNING A DATA WAREHOUSE

The first and foremost issue is why the organization should go for the development and deployment of the data warehouse. What are the prospective benefits which the organization can reap from this project implementation, some of the common benefits include:

- The data warehouse provides relevant information to make critical strategic decisions well in time which is required to win over the competitors and will provide a competitive advantage to the organization.
- Data warehouse facilitates the quick and efficient collection, interpretation and use of information by the various users at the various levels in an organization and hence enhances the overall productivity of the organization.
- Data warehouse helps in tracking trends, patterns and expectations over a long period of time and hence lead to overall cost reduction.

3.4 DATA WAREHOUSE PERFORMANCE ISSUES IN DESIGNING A DATA WAREHOUSE

The actual performance requirements may vary from application to application and business to business. The usage patterns of data warehouse vary and are unpredictable, so the traditional database design and tuning techniques may not work in data warehouse environment, so for maintaining the good performance the user's requirements should be well understood in the design phase itself, but the common performance issues which should be kept in mind while designing a data warehouse are:

1. The interaction with the user should be on-line, interactive and rapid. (Although very strict real time responses may not be required, this is required in OLTP Systems).
2. The response time requirements vary from business to business and application to application, good and acceptable response time criteria's should be maintained.
3. Good query optimization mechanism should be made operational, specialized de-normalized views containing specific, summarized, derived and aggregated data should be used to improve the query response time.
4. Deliver a great user experience — user acceptance is the measure of success.
5. Data warehouse should function without interfering with the OLTP systems.
6. It should provide a central repository of consistent data.
7. It should answer complex queries quickly.
8. It should provide a variety of powerful analytical tools, such as OLAP and data mining.

3.5 SKILLS REQUIRED TO BUILD A DATA WAREHOUSE

Building and using a data warehouse is a complex task and data warehouse development team should have multidisciplinary skills to understand, analyze and hence implement the user's requirements and to convert their data requirements into reality. The basic skills required are:

Business Skills, these skills include:

- The ability to understand the business environment and its operations.
- The ability to understand the data requirements of the users.
- The ability to understand how systems store and manage their data.
- The ability to think how to build extractors that transfer data from operational system to data warehouse.
- The ability to design/implement warehouse refresh software that helps the users to keep the data warehouse up-to-date with the data in the operational systems.

Technical Skills, these skills include:

- The ability to understand and implement the required technology suitable for data warehousing.
- The ability to choose suitable hardware and software platforms required.
- The ability to discover trends and patterns and to guide the decision makers.
- The ability to make assessments from quantitative information and to derive facts based on conclusions drawn from historic information stored in the data warehouse.
- The ability to extrapolate trends based on history.
- The ability to keep a check on anomalies and outliers.

Program Management Skills, these skills include:

- The ability to handle multiple technologies, vendors and end users.
- The ability to deliver the desired product well in time keeping all constraints in mind.
- The ability to choose work as a member or to lead the team as a leader.

3.6 STEPS IN DEVELOPING A DATA WAREHOUSE

The process of designing and implementing a data warehouse is very challenging and difficult task. The top management asks the data warehouse designer "Take all enterprise data and build a data warehouse such that the management can get answers to all their queries".

The stages of building a data warehouse are not too much different of those of a database project. Specific to data warehouse is the fact that they are built through an iterative process, which consists of an identification of business requirements, development of a solution in accordance with these requirements and implementation of data warehouse architecture. The phases or steps of a data warehouse project development listed below are similar to those of most database projects, starting with identifying requirements and ending with deploying the system:

1. Development of a Feasibility Study.
2. Design the dimensional model.
3. Selection of the technological Solution.

4. Develop the data ware house architecture, including the Operational Data Store (ODS)
5. Design the relational database and OLAP cubes- Extracting and loading data into the data warehouse.
6. Develop the data maintenance applications and project iterations.
7. Data ware-house testing and implementation- Develop analysis applications
8. Test and deploy the system and roll out.

1. Development of a Feasibility Study: The feasibility study defines the activities, costs, benefits and critical factors for the success of proposed system. The data warehouse will be built in a number of designing, developing and refining iterations according to the tactical and strategic business requirements. In this stage, both short term and long term strategies are pursued, the immediate and future costs are identified, so that a proper budget plan could be prepared. The feasibility study is presented to some important managers within the organization to determine the future demands. The following goals must be achieved in this stage are:

- Achieve a global view on organization's activity and users' requirements.
- Establish the scope of data ware house.
- Identifying the business directions and purposes.
- Establishment of the priorities of users' requirements.
- Establishment of the necessary data for solving the requirements.
- Defining the process for data warehouse iterative population and for data validation according to the business requirements.
- The mission and functions of the group or department, the key performance indicators used and the critical factors for success.
- An idea about the products manufactured, the providers and customers of the organization.
- The information systems and applications used; the manual transformations necessary to get the data that is not available.

The major steps carried out in the feasibility study are:

(a) Business Lines Analysis (Building a business case): It is an important stage in the data warehouse development cycle. Its main purpose is to have an understanding of the business and identification of business requirements. The users of a data warehouse form a heterogeneous group and they will formulate varied requirements, which only partly can be foreseen in data warehouse development stage. Building the business case is common at the beginning of any project. It involves determining the business needs of the project, the costs of the project, and the return on the investment. First of all the corporate model is built which highlights the major functional entities in the company, the data elements used by them and the relationship between them. The objective of this phase is to understand the business before entering into discussion with the users. The objectives of the users, their challenges and how they go about making business decisions is defined and understood.

(b) ***Determining business, users and their requirements:*** After having an idea about the business and the various business operations, the next step is to have an idea about the user requirements, where the interview and work with the users, not the data is important. The objective is to put yourself in their shoe and to get an idea about the information the users will need for being successful at their jobs and then work on the data that should be in the data warehouse which can easily be converted into the information required by the users. Business users should be closely tied to the design team during the logical design process; they are the people who understand the meaning of existing data. It is important that business users feel ownership for the resulting system. Find out from the experts what data exists and where it resides, but only after you understand the basic business needs of the end users.

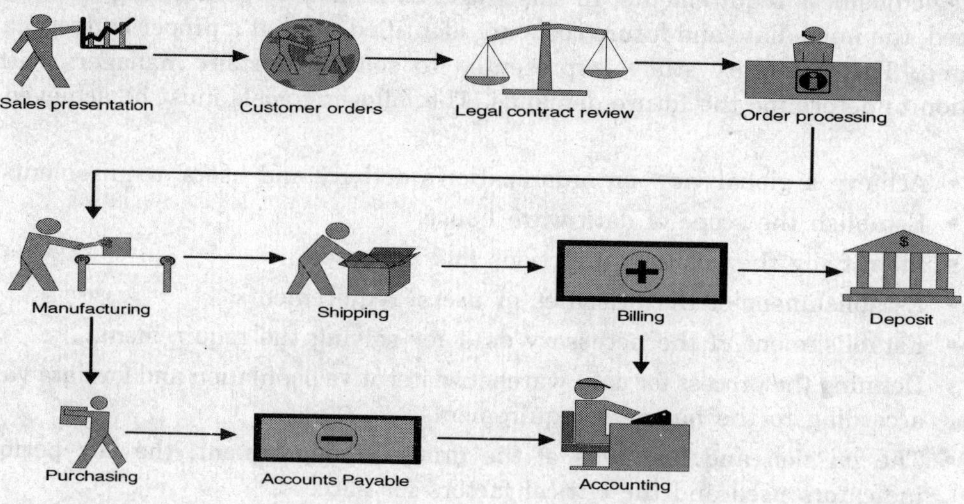

(c) **Determining the technical requirements.** The technical requirements may involve determining:

- Hardware platforms for data warehouse.
- DBMS for supporting data warehouse.
- Backup and Recovery mechanisms.
- Communication and Network Infrastructure for a data warehouse.
- System Management and Operating System Platforms required.
- The Software Tools for building, operating and using data warehouse.
- Security Mechanisms.
- Methods of Loading and Transforming data from Operational Systems to the Data Warehouse.

(d) **Defining standard reports required by users:** The ultimate success of a data ware house depends on the factor that how much it satisfies the user requirements. For the system to be more viable, standard reports required by users should be analyzed to determine the tables, columns, and selection criteria necessary to create the reports, and the frequency in which they are generated. Provisions should also be made for expanding or modifying the scope of reports as required. Client application tools should be analyzed to determine if they can provide enhanced processing capabilities that will help in processing data, performing queries, or generating reports.

When the organization has decided to build the data warehouse and has defined the business requirements and has agreed upon the scope of the application, then the conceptual design is created. Then the need is to translate the system requirements into a system deliverable. To do so, the logical and physical design for the data warehouse is created. To do so:

- The specific data content is defined.
- The relationships within and between groups of data is identified and enumerated.
- The system environment required to support and manage the data warehouse is identified and arranged accordingly i.e either purchased or built.
- The data transformations required are identified and carried out.
- The frequency with which data is refreshed is calculated.

The logical design is more conceptual and abstract than the physical design.

In the logical design, the logical relationship among the objects is identified. In the physical design, the most effective way of storing and retrieving the objects as well as handling is decided and carried out.

The ultimate aim is to design the data warehouse toward the needs of the end users. The aim of the users is to perform analysis and look at aggregated data, rather than at individual transactions. However, end users may not know what they need until they see it and visualize it. So the design should be in line with the user's expectations and requirements.

The logical design should result in:

- A set of entities and attributes corresponding to fact tables and dimension tables.
- A model of operational data from the source into subject-oriented information in the target data warehouse schema.

The logical design is an activity that is done without considering any technical requirements and is usually done by using a pen and paper, but now a days various automated design tools such as **Oracle Warehouse Builder** (specifically designed to support modeling the ETL process) or **Oracle Designer** (a general purpose modeling tool) are available that support and facilitates the design process and make it easy.

2. Design the Dimensional Model: After gathering and analyzing the user requirements, the main functional entities are identified from the basic corporate model of the company, and the relationship between them is identified so that the data model and dimensional model covering all the functional entities of the system can be created. Designing and building the database is a critical part of building a successful data warehouse. This step is often performed by experienced database designers because it can involve taking data from multiple (most of the time heterogeneous) sources and combining it into a single, logical model. The model designed must satisfy the following requirements:

- It must suit the requirements of the users.
- It should support ease of use for direct access.
- It should be easy to maintain and should be flexible enough to adapt to future changes.
- The model designed must be in line with the relational database that supports OLAP cubes.
- It must provide the facility of "instantaneous" query results for analysts.

The basic components of schema design are dimensions, keys, fact and dimension tables (These topics have already been discussed in Chapter 2)

Data warehouses use either the relational or dimensional models. Each model has benefits and drawbacks.

The data warehouse architecture must be de-signed so that it can allow further development with a minimal impact on the existing model. It must present the relational and multidimensional databases used for the data warehouse and the data marts, their localization and interconnection, as well as the access tools.

The various steps carried out in preparation of design are:

1. The data warehouse *logical architecture* is defined. This is the configuration of the required data collections: a central repository storing the data of the entire organization, an optional operational data store, one or more data marts and one or more metadata repositories.
2. As the overall aim of data warehouse design is to fulfill the user requirements: The following four architectures are designed:

The data architecture: The purpose is to organize the data sources and collections and to define the quality and management standards, both for data and metadata. This general model presents the business areas and their relations.

The application architecture: *It* presents the software components that provide the implementation of the business functionality within the data warehouse, as well as the data transfer from its source to users, that is data extracting, cleaning, transforming, loading, refreshing and accessing.

The technical architecture *It* provides the proper infrastructure for data and application architectures. It includes the server, network, hardware and software components for connecting and communication, and the users' workstations. The technical architecture must respond to the requirements of scalability, performance, availability, stability and security. It must be robust, reliable, flexible, extensible and parallel.

The support architecture includes tools for backup/recovery, archiving, performance monitoring, as well as the organizational functions necessary for proper functioning of the organization.

Dimensional Model: It stores data in a data cube or multi-dimensional matrix. A data cube is shown in the Fig. 3.1(b) given below, it is a three-dimensional matrix with market locations along one side, products and time dimension along the other two, and the cells containing the data facts for each market/product/period intersection

This matrix structure allows access to any market location/product/time dimension cell directly. It can extract a slice or a block of data quickly by rotating its axes and re-ordering data easily. This is useful for statistical analysis (cross tabulating and correlation) and for output formatting.

Due to these features of dimensional models, almost all Business Intelligence (BI) products employ a cube or matrix structure for their internal working data storage.

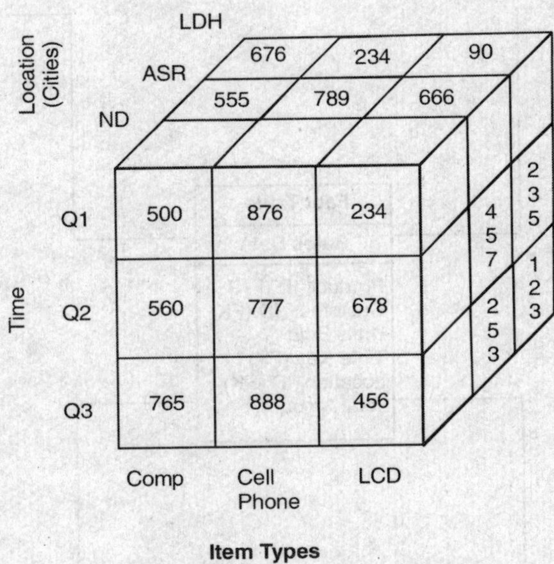

Fig. 3.1(b): A Data Cube

Relational Model: The relational model uses a straightforward database table to store fact information. With the relational model the non-existing data intersections simply do not exist in the data table. This minimizes data storage and permits much larger databases. New intersections are appended to the end of the table.

Query retrieval times for small databases are comparable between relational and dimensional products, but are, far superior with the relational model for large databases.

Generally, the relational model is preferred for data warehousing because:

· It is easy to update

· It can support very large databases

· Almost all companies already own a relational DBMS product with the corresponding skilled engineers.

· The dimensional model products are proprietary.

Dimensional Model Schemas: The principal characteristic of a dimensional model is a set of detailed business facts surrounded by multiple dimensions that describe those facts. When realized in a database, the schema for a dimensional model contains a central fact table and multiple dimension tables. A dimensional model may produce a star schema or a snowflake schema.

Star Schemas:

- A schema is called a star schema if all dimension tables can be joined directly to the fact table. The Fig. 3.2 shows a classic star schema.

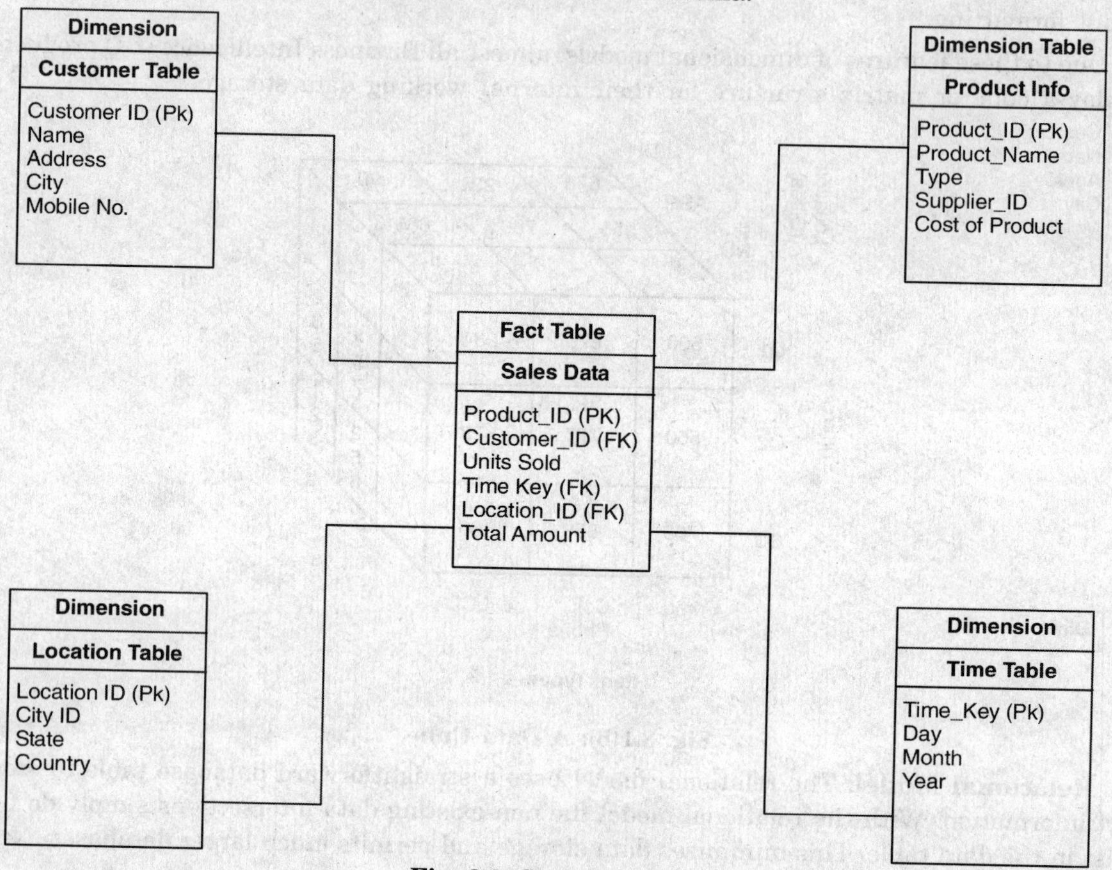

Fig. 3.2: Star Schema

Snowflake Schemas

- A schema is called a snowflake schema if one or more dimension tables do not join directly to the fact table but must join through other dimension tables. For example, a dimension that describes products may be separated into three tables (snow flaked) as illustrated in the following Fig. 3.3.
- Both Star and Snowflake schemas are dimensional models; the difference is in their physical implementations. Snowflake schemas support ease of dimension maintenance because they are more normalized. Star schemas are easier for direct user access and often support simpler and more efficient queries. The decision to model a dimension as a star or snowflake depends on the nature of the dimension itself, such as how frequently it changes and which of its elements change, and often involves evaluating tradeoffs between ease of use and ease of maintenance. It is often easiest to maintain a complex dimension by snowflaking the dimension. Snow flake schema allows the data to be stored in separate tables by doing so the referential integrity between the levels of the hierarchy is guaranteed.

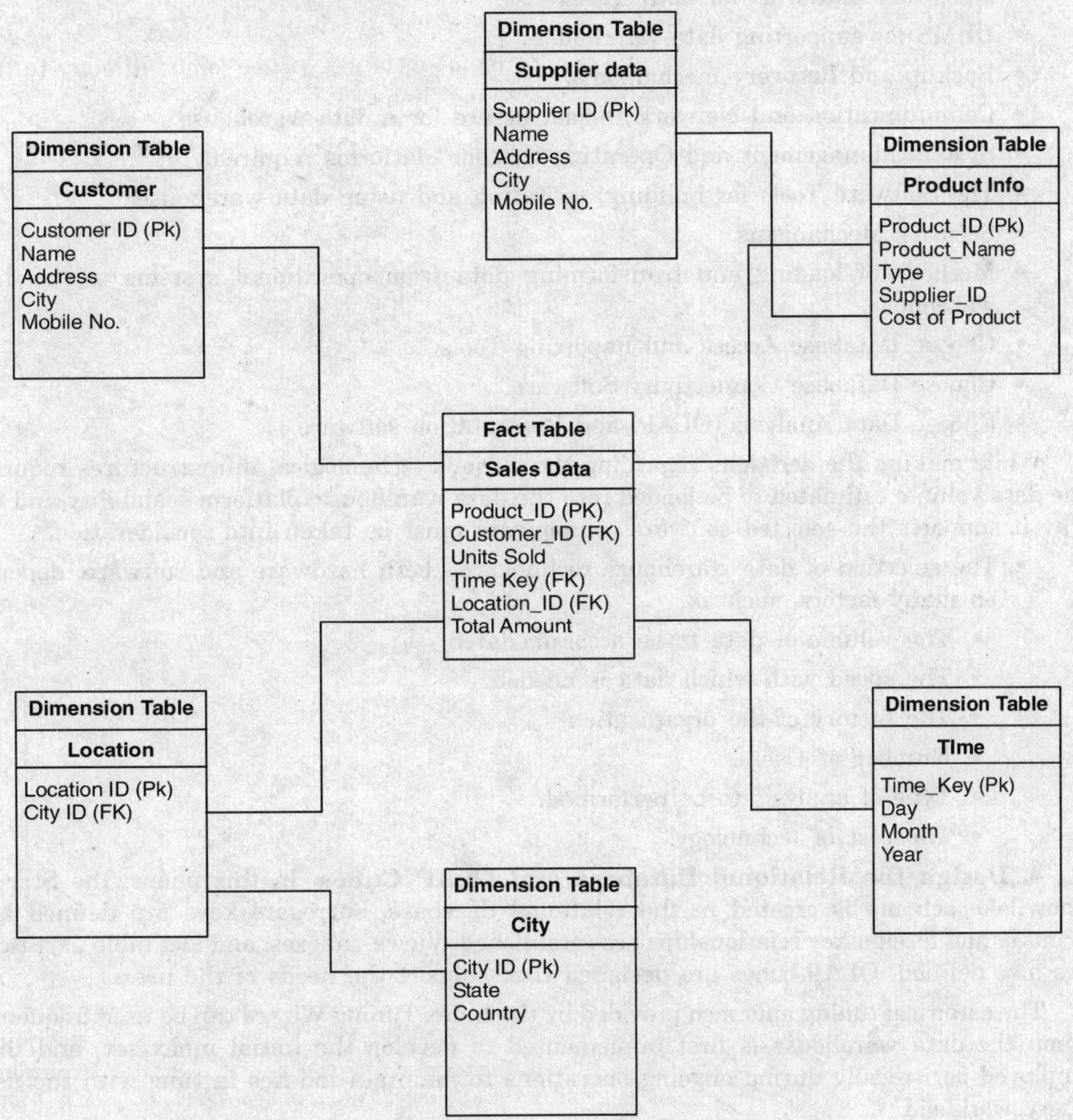

Fig. 3.3: Snowflake Schema

[*Note: Difference between Star and Snowflake Schemas is given in Chapter 2*]

3. Selection of the Technological Solution: The purpose of this stage is to identify the possible tools for implementing data and application architecture and for providing technical support functions. These must be selected and acquired to fulfill the business and technical requirements that have been defined by the data warehouse architecture. This selection must take into consideration the existing technical infrastructure of the organization. The major technological infrastructure required is:

- Hardware platforms for data warehouse.
- DBMS for supporting data warehouse.
- Backup and Recovery mechanisms.
- Communication and Network Infrastructure for a data warehouse.
- System Management and Operating System Platforms required.
- The Software Tools for building, operating and using data warehouse.
- Security Mechanisms.
- Methods of loading and transforming data from operational systems to the data warehouse.
- Choose Database Access and Reporting Tools.
- Choose Database Connectivity Software.
- Choose Data Analysis (OLAP) and Presentation software.

While making the decisions regarding the various technological infrastructures required the data volume estimated to be loaded into the data warehouse, platform scalability and the way it supports the selected software components must be taken into consideration.

- The selection of data warehouse technology - both hardware and software, depends on many factors, such as:
  - The volume of data to be accommodated.
  - The speed with which data is needed.
  - The history of the organization.
  - Number of Users.
  - Type of analysis to be performed.
  - The cost of technology.

4. Design the Relational Database and OLAP Cubes: In this phase, the Star or Snowflake schema is created in the relational database, surrogate keys are defined and primary and foreign key relationships are established. Views, indexes, and fact table partitions are also defined. OLAP cubes are designed that support the needs of the users.

The empirical tuning approach provided by the Index Tuning Wizard can be used frequently when the data warehouse is first implemented to develop the initial index set, and then employed periodically during ongoing operations to maintain indexes in tune with the user query workload.

Views should be created for users who need direct access to data in the data warehouse relational database. Users can be granted access to views without having access to the underlying data. Indexed views can be used to improve performance of user queries that access data through views.

5. Loading the Data in the Data Warehouse: The primary source of data for a data warehouse is the company's own transaction processing systems. Even if the company has re-engineered its systems with an ERP system (Enterprise Resource Planning) where all company functions are built into a consistent data structure, there will still be other sources to bring into the warehouse. The data from the external sources like external users, business rules and policies are also a source of data for the data warehouse. Extract the data from operational data sources, transfer it, clean-up and load into the data warehouse model or data mart. The Operational Data Store (ODS) is an operational construct that has elements of both data warehouse and a transaction system. This store contains data consolidated from multiple systems and grouped by subject area. Like a transaction system, it may be updated by business users, and contains relatively little historical data. Implementations of the operational data source vary widely depending on business requirements. The disparate data elements identified for the data warehouse have a surprising degree of inconsistency. The usual approach to solve this problem is to transform the data before loading it to the warehouse. There is a better way is not to transform but to harmonize the data at a later stage.

6. Develop the Data Maintenance Applications: It has been rightly said that the *data ware houses are not built; rather these are evolved with the passage of time.* The data warehouse implemented grows as the user keep on revising his business and technical requirements. It may also be possible that the initial study has concentrated on a few subject areas only, and later on new dimensions to the business operations may require adding the new subject areas. This iterative process keeps on and data warehouse life cycle keeps on rolling till the data warehouse is in use. In the initial iterations the scope of data warehouse is reviewed, all constraints imposed by the source system are identified and documented and these documentations are shown to the users and the management to make sure that the management expectations and the established goals will be achieved. The data maintenance applications, including extraction, transformation, and loading processes, must be automated, often by specialized custom applications, the common automated tools are:

- Data Transformation Services (DTS) in SQL Server 2000
- Transact-SQL
- Applications developed using scripting such as Microsoft Visual Basic

7. Data Warehouse Testing and Implementation: Once the planning and design stages are completed, the current iteration for data warehouse implementation may start. In this stage, the development and testing environments are established, the hardware and software components are installed and the configuration management process is implemented. Referring to the *specified aspects* of the installed database management system, the data warehouse logical and physical design are finalized:

- The physical design of the fact and dimension tables are finalized;
- The most proper indexes are established, taking into consideration the estimated size of thedata warehouse and the queries supposed to be performed;
- A decision about table partitioning is taken, knowing that it's easier to manage a partitioned data warehouse, but its performances are lower.

At the same time, programs are developed or configured for data extracting, cleaning, transforming, loading and periodically refreshing. The initial data is loaded along with the technical and business metadata. User interfaces and production reports are developed, sample ad-hoc queries are run against the test database, and the results are validated. The data access is established and the user training is done. Support procedures are implemented for database security, backup and recovery, disaster recovery and data archiving.

After the initial test is made by the development team, the final users are involved. They have to use the system as they will do after data warehouse transition to production. This manner makes possible to find out and correct the errors, to identify the requirements for performance enhancement, and to allow the users to become familiar with the new system. It's possible that other changes will need to be done after the transition to production, but starting this activity with a proper performance represents one of the project success keys.

8. Deployment and Roll-Out: In this stage the production database is created and the programs for extracting, cleaning, transforming and loading data are run against the source systems. The users' training is compl ed, the team for change management is created, and the control procedures for future development cycles are established. It is important to involve users in the testing phase. After initial testing by development and test groups, users should load the system with queries and use it the way they intend to, before the system is brought on line. Substantial user involvement in testing will provide a significant number of benefits. The main benefits are:

- Discrepancies can be found and corrected.
- Users become familiar with the system.
- Index tuning can be performed.

It is important that users exercise the system during the test phase with the kinds of queries they will be using in reality. This can enable a considerable amount of empirical index tuning to take place before the system becomes online. Additional tuning needs to take place after deployment, but starting with satisfactory performance is a key to success. Users who have participated in the testing and have seen performance, will be able to improve the system in future also. continually improve as the system is exercised will be inclined to be supportive during the initial deployment phase as early issues are discovered and addressed

In the operation stage, besides the data ware-house employment by the final users, its maintenance and development are provided too. The IT specialists have to do several specific activities for achieving this purpose, some of these activities are:

- *Periodical refreshing of the data warehouse-* From time to time, the new changes made in the operational systems have to be loaded into the data warehouse, so that its users could have the most recent information at their disposal.
- *Computing certain statistical indicators-* To pursue the data warehouse evolution, performance and maintenance. Some of these indicators are: number of queries performed in a certain day, average response time, number of users per day, frequency of using data warehouse subjects, average duration of a work session.
- Evaluation *of the database size- The* size of data warehouse increases at every loading operation and can cause serious troubles. There are several techniques that can be used for reducing the negative consequences the increase of the data warehouse volume over certain limits, aggregating the detailed data, and then archiving and deleting it from the data warehouse, limiting the storing interval at a certain period of time, deleting the unused data, which can be identified on the basis of statistical indicators regarding the data warehouse.
- *Database disaster recovery.* The information within the data warehouse have a strategic importance for the managers of the organization. That is why a special attention has to be given to disaster recovery procedures.

SUMMARY

- Data Warehouse is not a concept; it is a business application that must provide a return on the company's investment just like any other project.
- Data warehouse development is a continuous process, evolving with the organization.
- Data warehouses offer support for decision-making process, allowing complex analyses which cannot be properly achieved from operational systems.
- A data warehouse must be designed to satisfy the user's requirements, should function without interfering with OLTP systems and should be flexible enough to cope up with the changing business and user requirements.
- A data warehouse can be built either on a ***top-down*** *or on* ***a bottom-up approach***.
- The ***bottom-up approach*** describes the process of building individual and independent data marts for departments, or specific business areas, and then joining them to provide the data for the entire organization.
- The ***bottom-up approach*** is flexible, less costly and provides rapid return on investment, but integration of individual data marts into a consistent enterprise data warehouse is quite difficult.
- The ***top-down approach*** the user can build a global data ware house for entire organization and split it into individual data marts or sub data warehouses dedicated for individual departments.
- The ***top-down approach*** is a mature one and it is used when the technology and the economic problems are well known, it is a systemic method, minimizes the integration problems, but is expensive, of long standing and has a low flexibility and takes a long time to develop.
- The most adequate method for developing a data warehouse is the ***iterative one***. In this approach, more iterations are made, and a new version resulting at every iteration.
- Data warehouse design is surrounded by ***organizational, technical and design issues***.
- Data warehouse ***organizational issues*** involve the relevance of the design for the organization and to investigate whether the data warehouse will help in tracking trends, patterns and expectations over a long period of time and hence can lead to overall cost reduction or not.
- Data warehouse ***design issues*** emphasize that the design should be exhaustive and should provide a holistic view of data, ability to harmonize the data while maintaining the integrity, reliability and authenticity of data.
- Data warehouse ***performance issues*** suggests that the actual performance requirements may vary from application to application and business to business, but the common performance issues require that the interaction with the user should be on-line, interactive and rapid, and good response time of queries, query optimization mechanism and overall good user experience are the prerequisite performance factors.
- The skills required for building a data warehouse are ***Business Skills, Technical Skills*** and ***Program Management Skills***.
- ***Business Skills*** include, the ability to understand the business environment and its operations, to understand how systems store and manage their data, how to build extractors that transfer data from operational system to data warehouse and the ability to design/implement warehouse refresh software that helps the users to keep the data warehouse up-to-date with the data in the operational systems.
- ***Technical Skills,*** include the ability to understand and implement the required technology

(hardware and software) suitable for data warehousing, to discover trends and patterns and to guide the decision makers and the mechanism to check on anomalies and outliers.

- ***Program Management Skills,*** include the ability to handle multiple technologies, vendors and end users, to deliver the desired product well in time keeping all constraints in mind and ability to work as a leader or a member.
- **Steps in Developing a Data Warehouse are d**evelopment of a feasibility study, design the of dimensional model, selection of the technological solution, develop the data ware house architecture, design the relational database and OLAP cubes- Extracting and loading data into the data warehouse, develop the data maintenance applications and project iterations, data ware-house testing and implementation and finally test and deploy the system and roll out.

CHAPTER 4

DATA WAREHOUSE ARCHITECTURE

A data warehouse provides:

- Competitive advantage by presenting relevant information using which the decision makers can make critical judgments in order to win in the competitive market space.
- Enhanced productivity since it can quickly gather information about the activities of the organization.
- Enhanced customer relationship management since it provides consistent view of the customers and items along all lines of the business, all departments and all markets.
- The benefit of cost reduction by tracking trends, patterns and exceptions over long periods of time in a reliable and a consistent manner. The business analysis framework must be understood in order to create an efficient data warehouse.

4.1 PRINCIPLES OF DATA WAREHOUSING

1. ***Data is an enterprise asset*** and is viewed as belonging to a particular individual or as a part of an application. It is important to note that while data is a shared asset, the IT department should have organizational responsibility for managing the technology infrastructure that supports this asset. It means that the enterprise data model should be shared among the various users and effective integration of various data warehouse components should be achieved. It emphasizes on greater use of metadata, careful schema version management and support for an enterprise data warehouse.
2. ***The business is the guardian for data:*** Data assets should have owners in the business. These owners are known as data guardians and data stewards, these guardians should be involved in the definition of business operations and entities and attributes required to represent the business model. Data stewards should have an active role in defining data quality specifications such as valid values, required relationships, etc. All of this metadata should be stored in a centrally managed "metadata repository" – an on line data dictionary, that describes the corporate data asset and the rules that protect it. *Data stewards* should also have a role in determining the appropriate security levels for the data assets.

3. ***Data should be secured based on risk analysis:*** The appropriate level of security should be implemented for each data element within the enterprise. A risk-based cost analysis should drive all security decisions. Stakeholders should balance the *cost of strict security measures* and the potential for blocking legitimate accesses against the potential risks presented by having less stringent policies in place. This implies that the IT department place sufficient security infrastructure around data assets, and that data guardians make well reasoned choices regarding legitimate access needs versus the cost of inadequately secured data.
4. ***Data should be stored in fewer databases:*** As it is better to maintain a few large multi-subject-area databases, rather than many application-specific databases;
5. ***Limit dependence on physical data structures:*** It must be ensured that business logic is insulated from the details of database structures. The end user should not bother about the internal hardware level details.
6. ***Single point for data manipulation:*** There should be a single application, function library, or component that manages all manipulation of data that is stored in systems of record (SOR's). This principle recognizes that data quality should begin at the source system where data is created, updated and deleted.

4.2 DATA WAREHOUSING COMPONENTS

A data warehouse always consists of a number of components, including:

1. Operational data sources.
2. Design/development tools.
3. Data extraction and transformation tools.
4. Data warehouse management system and data.
5. Data access and analysis tools.
6. System Management tools.

1. Operational Data Sources: The first component of a data warehouse is the data obtained from various sources, which may be internal or external. A significant portion of implementation effort is spent extracting data from operational systems and putting it in a format suitable for informational applications that run off the data warehouse.

2. Design and Development Tools: It includes the components required to design and develop the basic data warehouse structure. It includes various designing tools.

3. Data Extraction and Transformation Tools: The data sourcing, cleanup, transformation and migration tools perform all of the conversions, summarizations, key changes, structural changes and condensations needed to transform disparate data into information that can be used by the decision support tool. Thc functionality includes:

- Removing unwanted data from operational databases.
- Converting heterogeneous data items to common data names and definitions.
- Establishing defaults for missing data.
- Accommodating source data definition changes.

The data sourcing, cleanup, extract, transformation and migration tools have to deal with some significant issues including: database heterogeneity, DBMSs are very different in data models, data access language, data navigation, operations, concurrency, integrity, recovery etc.

4. Data Warehouse Management System and Data: The central data warehouse database is the basis of the data warehousing environment. Most of the time, this database is implemented on the relational database management system (RDBMS) technology. The traditional RDBMS products are optimized for transactional database processing but keeping in mind the basic data warehouse attributes, such as very large database size, ad hoc query processing and the need for flexible user view creation including aggregates, multi-table joins and drill-downs, have forced the developers to design data warehouse management system on the following approaches:

- Parallel relational database designs for scalability that include shared-memory, shared disk, or shared-nothing models implemented on various multiprocessor configurations (symmetric multiprocessors or SMP, massively parallel processors or MPP, and/or clusters of uni- or multiprocessors).
- To speed up a traditional RDBMS by using new index structures to bypass relational table scans.
- Multidimensional databases (MDDBs) that are based on proprietary database technology; conversely, a dimensional data model can be implemented using a familiar RDBMS. Multi-dimensional databases are designed to overcome any limitations placed on the warehouse by the nature of the relational data model. MDDBs enable on-line analytical processing (OLAP) tools that architecturally belong to a group of data warehousing components jointly categorized as the data query, reporting, analysis and mining tools. It includes Meta data and Data Marts (These topics have been covered later on in this chapter)

5. Data Access and Analysis Tools: The main purpose of data warehousing is to provide information to business users for strategic decision-making. These users interact with the data warehouse using front-end tools. Many of these tools require an information specialist, although many end users develop expertise in the tools. The tools required for this purpose fall into four main categories: ***Query and reporting tools, application development tools, online analytical processing tools, and data mining tools***.

Query and reporting Tools: These reporting tools let companies generate regular operational reports or support high-volume batch jobs such as calculating and printing paychecks. Managed query tools shield end users from the complexities of SQL and database structures by inserting a meta layer between users and the database. These tools are designed for easy-to-use, point-and-click operations that either accept SQL or generate SQL database queries.

***OLAP Tools*:** These tools are based on the concept of dimensional data models and corresponding databases, and allow users to analyze the data using elaborate, multidimensional views. Typical business applications include product performance and profitability, effectiveness of a sales program or marketing campaign, sales forecasting and capacity planning. These tools assume that the data is organized in a multidimensional model.

***Application Development Tools*:** these tools are required to built the proposed application.

Data Mining Tools: These tools allow the discovery of meaningful new correlations, patterns and trends by digging into large amounts of data stored in the warehouse using artificial intelligence, statistical and mathematical techniques.

6. System Management Tools: Data Warehouse Administration and Management Data warehouses tend to be as much larger as related operational databases, reaching terabytes in size depending on how much history needs to be saved. They are not synchronized in real time to the associated operational data but are updated as often as once in a day if the application requires it. In addition, almost all data warehouse products include gateways to transparently access multiple enterprise data sources without having to rewrite applications to interpret and utilize the data. Furthermore, in a heterogeneous data warehouse environment, the various databases reside on disparate systems, thus requiring inter-networking tools. The need to manage this environment is obvious. Managing data warehouses include security and priority management; monitoring updates from the multiple sources; data quality checks; managing and updating meta data; auditing and reporting data warehouse usage and status; purging data; replicating, sub-setting and distributing data; backup and recovery and data warehouse storage management.

Microsoft recognized the need for a set of technologies that would integrate these components. To cater to this need of large scale enterprise, Microsoft created the **Microsoft Data Warehousing Framework**. It provides the basic guidelines for the development of Microsoft products such as SQL Server 7.0, and provides a basis for the integration of products from other vendors. The goal of the Microsoft Data Warehousing Framework is to simplify the design, implementation, and management of data warehousing solutions. The Data Warehousing Framework has been designed keeping the requirements of the end users in mind; it provides an open architecture that can be extended easily by Microsoft customers and third-party businesses using industry-standard technology. This allows organizations to choose best-of-breed components and still be assured of integration.

The main features of this are:

1. It provides an Open architecture that can be integrated easily and allows that the existing architecture can be extended by third-party vendors.
2. It provides the facility to import data from heterogeneous sources.
3. It provides the facility to export data to multiple, heterogeneous and physically separated data sources.
4. It provides the facility for data validation at various levels as and when required.
5. It facilitates the construction and use of integrated metadata for data warehouse design.
6. It provides facility for data extraction and transformation as per the requirement of the end users.
7. It facilitates optimal server management.
8. It provides a large number of analysis tools which can be used by the end users for analyzing the data and for providing the customized reports.

9. It provides a platform for optimal usage of various resources and provides a basis for scheduling, storage management, performance monitoring, alerts/events, and notification.

The data warehouse architecture must support the following four *different views of the data warehouse, these are:*

- **The Top-Down View:** It allows the selection of relevant information necessary for the data warehouse. The information matches the current and the forthcoming needs of the business.
- **The Data Source View:** It exposes the way in which the data is captured, stored and managed by a data warehouse system. Each user designs the individual source tables which are integrated as per the requirements. These source tables may be detailed at various levels of accuracy. Normally CASE tools or entity relationship models hold the traditional data sources.
- **The Data Warehouse View:** It includes the fact tables and dimension tables. It represents the information that is stored within the data warehouse as well as information regarding the data, time of origin of the source data to provide the historical context.
- **Business Query View:** It is the perspective view of data in the data warehouse from the point of view of the end user.

4.3 ESSENTIAL PROPERTIES FOR A DATA WAREHOUSE

The following are the essential properties for designing a data warehouse system:

1. **Separation:** Analytical and transactional processing should be kept apart as much as possible.
2. **Scalability:** The data warehouse should be scalable so as to cater to the changing requirements of the user, to accommodate the increased number of users, to cope up with the changing business scenarios. i.e if number of users or the requirements of the user changes, then the system should be able to implement it without changing the basic structure.
3. **Extensibility:** The architecture should be able to host new applications and technologies without redesigning the whole system. As the business scenarios changes rapidly and new technologies are invented and implemented every now and then, the data warehouse design should be able to be extended to incorporate the changes.
4. **Flexibility:** The architecture should be flexible enough to accommodate the changes done while performing the scalability and extensibility operations.
5. **Security:** As data is the most important asset of the organization. Maintaining the security and privacy of data is of paramount importance. The architecture should ensure the security and privacy of data stored in the data warehouse to ensure that the right person should get the right access to the right data and to monitor the unauthorized access and to take remedial actions as per the need and policy of the organization.

6. **Administerability:** Data warehouse management should not be overly difficult to manage. The various components should be correlated to each other in such a way that these can be supervised, organized and managed easily and conveniently.
7. **Ease of Use:** The data warehouse should be designed in such a way that it should be easy to understand and use by the various users having varying degree of technical, operational and analytical skills.

4.4 DATA WAREHOUSE ARCHITECTURE

Building a data warehouse is a daunting task and requires efforts from all levels of the organization. As discussed earlier, data warehouses are not built; rather these are evolved with the passage of time. Many methodologies have been proposed to simplify the information technology efforts required to support the data warehousing process. The data warehouse architecture is based on a relational database management system which server the function of central repository for informational data. Operational data and processing is completely separated from data warehouse processing. The main objective of this central information repository, surrounded by a number of key components, is to make the entire environment functional, manageable and accessible by both the operational systems that feed data into the warehouse and by end-user query and analysis tools.

A Data Warehouse Architecture (DWA) is a way of representing the **overall structure of data, communication, processing and presentation** that exists for end-user computing within the enterprise. The data warehouse is an enterprise wide framework for managing informational data with in the organization. the basic terms related to this are:

Enterprise Data Warehouse: It contains enterprise-wide information obtained from multiple operational data sources and from external information providers, which is then integrated and consolidated at one place, which can be used for data analysis. It is built by composing the data from various subject areas like customers, products, and sales, and is used for both tactical and strategic decision making. The enterprise data warehouse contains both detailed point-in-time data and summarized information, and its size ranges from gigabytes (GB) to more than 1 terabyte. Enterprise data warehouses can be very expensive and time-consuming to build and manage. It is designed in a top down approach.

Data Mart: It contains a subset of enterprise-wide data that is built for use by an individual department or division in an organization. The data mart is usually built from the bottom approach up by departmental resources for a specific decision-support application or group of users. Data marts contain summarized and often detailed data about a subject area. The scope is confined to a particular specific area. The information in the data mart can be a subset of an enterprise data warehouse (dependent data mart) or can come directly from the operational data sources (independent data mart).

Virtual Warehouse: A virtual warehouse is a set of views over operational databases created for some specific purpose by a particular user. For efficient query processing, only some of the possible summary views may be materialized. A virtual warehouse is easy to build and it requires excess capacity on the operational database servers.

Three basic types of data warehouse architecture exist and these are:

4.4.1 Single-Layer Architecture

Single-layer architecture is not frequently used in practice. Its goal is to minimize the amount of data stored and to reach at this goal, it removes data redundancies. Fig. 4.1 given below shows that the only layer physically available is the source layer. In this case, data warehouses are virtual. This means that a data warehouse is implemented as a multidimensional view of operational data created by specific middleware, or an intermediate processing layer.

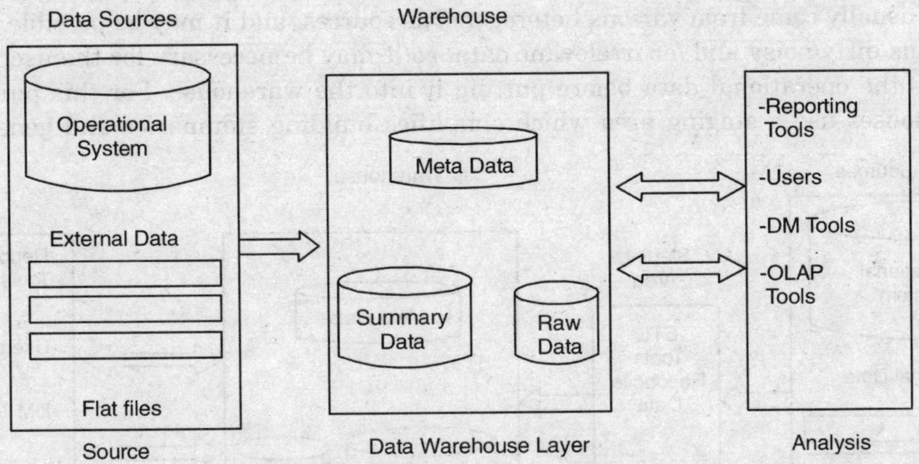

Fig. 4.1: Single Layer Architecture

The basic architecture has been divided into three parts:

Data Sources: It represents the various sources of information for the data warehouse, the sources many be internal like corporate relational databases or legacy operational Systems and flat files available within the organization at various levels or may come from information systems outside the organization.

Warehouse: It is the common data repository which stores the data on the permanent basis, it includes, metadata, summary data, and raw data. Raw data and metadata is also present in the traditional OLTP systems, the data warehouses include a special kind of data termed as summary data, which stores the results of various standard queries run by the users. These are also termed as materialized views.

Analysis: The third component is the users who access the data warehouse for getting the required information as per their requirements. At this layer the integrated data is efficiently and flexibly accessed to issue reports, dynamically analyze information and simulate business scenarios. The users use various tools for analysis, reporting, and mining the data. These users create various customized views required for various types of decisions required. Aggregate data navigators, complex query optimizers and user-friendly GUIs are used to make the analysis possible.

The problem with this approach is that it fails to meet the requirement for separation between analytical and transactional processing. Analyzed queries are submitted to operational data after the middleware interprets them. In this way, the queries affect regular transactional workloads. Although this architecture can meet the requirement for integration and correctness of data, it cannot log more data than sources do. For these reasons, a virtual approach to data warehouses can be successful only if analysis needs are particularly restricted and the data volume to analyze is huge.

4.4.2 Two-Layer Architecture

Two-layer architecture highlights a separation between physically available sources and data warehouses; it actually consists of four subsequent data flow stages. The data fed into data warehouse usually come from various heterogeneous sources, and it may be possible that this data contains dirty/noisy and /or irrelevant data, so it may be necessary for the user to clean and process the operational data before putting it into the warehouse. For this purpose the data warehouses use a staging area which simplifies building summaries and general.

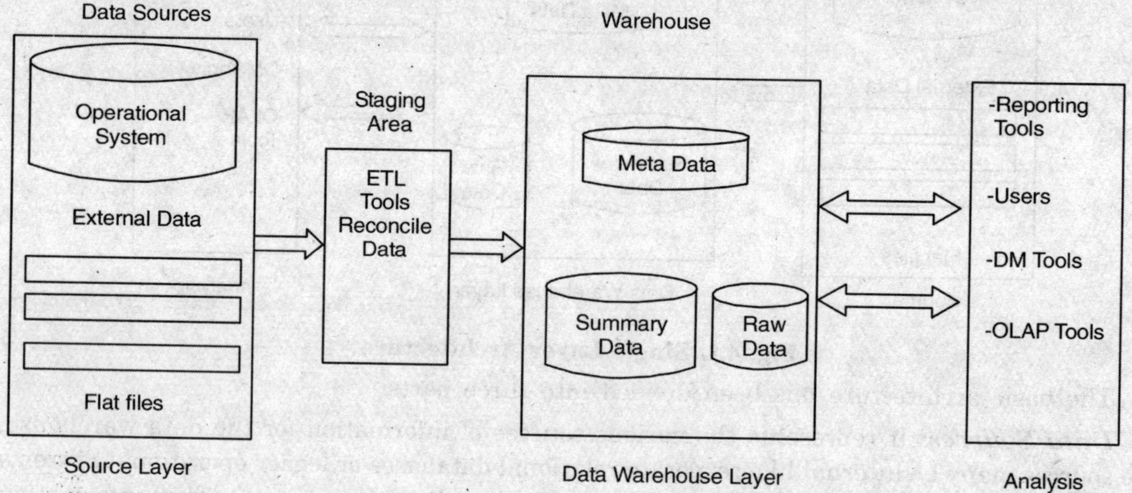

Fig. 4.2: Two Layer Architecture

Warehouse management. Fig. 4.2 given above shows the architecture of data warehouse with staging area, the data warehouse architecture in this case has been divided into four parts:

- Data Sources
- Staging Area (where data sources go before the warehouse)
- Warehouse
- Analysis

The components: data sources, warehouse and analysis are same as in the case of single layer architecture, but the new component staging area has been added, this is the component where data goes before entering into the data warehouse.

Staging Area: In this phase, *cleaning, preprocessing and filtering* of data is done. In this area:

- The data stored at various sources is extracted, cleansed to remove inconsistencies and fill gaps, and is integrated to merge heterogeneous sources into one common schema.

- It decouples extraction process from cleaning process.
- It performs the transformation of data received in various formats from disparate systems to a single target data warehousing technology platform.
- Extraction, Transformation, and Loading tools (ETL) can merge heterogeneous schemas.
- ETL process actually feed the reconciled data layer—a single, detailed, comprehensive, and top-quality data source— that in its turn feeds the data warehouse. For this reason, the ETL process operations as a whole can be termed as reconciliation.
- Data staging operations are the most complex and technically challenging among all the data warehouse process phases.
- ETL takes place once when a data warehouse is populated for the first time, then it occurs every time the data warehouse is regularly updated.

Fig. 4.3 given below shows that ETL consists of four separate phases: extraction capture, cleansing, transformation, and loading.

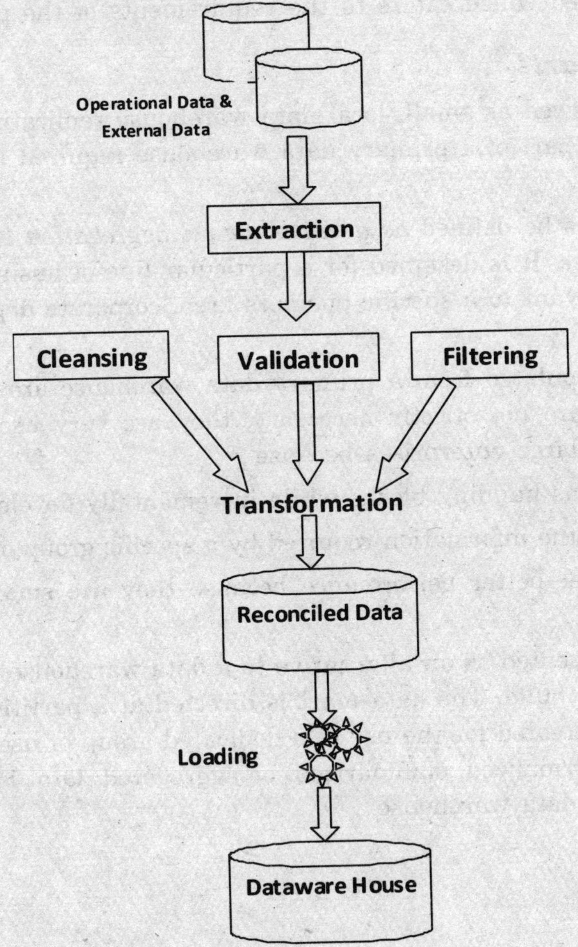

Fig. 4.3: Phases of ETL

4.4.3 Three-Layer Architecture

As discussed earlier, the ultimate aim of data warehouse is to present the data to the users at the various levels as per their requirements so that they can take the decisions well in time. The different users require customized view of the data which can cater to their specific requirements, to make it possible the data warehouse architecture is customized for different groups within your organization, by adding data marts. The main components of this architecture are:

- Data Sources
- Staging Area
- Warehouse
- Data Marts (purchasing, sales, and inventory)
- Analysis

The components, data sources, staging area, warehouse and users are same as in the case of previous version of architecture (Two Layer Architecture), but the new component **data mart** has been included which caters to the requirements of the particular department.

What is a Data Mart?

Data Marts can be viewed as small, local data warehouse replicating (and summing up as much as possible) the part of a primary data warehouse required for a specific application domain.

Data Mart can also be defined *as a subset or an aggregation of the data stored in the primary data warehouse*. It is designed for a particular line of business. It includes a set of information pieces relevant to a specific business area, corporate department, or category of users.

The data marts populated from a primary data warehouse are often called dependent. Although data marts are not strictly necessary, they are very useful for data warehouse systems in midsize to large enterprises because

- They are used as building blocks while incrementally developing data warehouses;
- They mark out the information required by a specific group of users to solve queries;
- They can deliver better performance because they are smaller than primary data warehouses.

Data marts are presented as an alternative to a data warehouse that takes significantly less time and money to build. The data mart is directed at a partition of data (often called a subject area) that is created for the use of a dedicated group of users. A data mart might, in fact, be a set of denormalized, summarized, or aggregated data. Fig. 4.4 shows the three layered architecture of data warehouse.

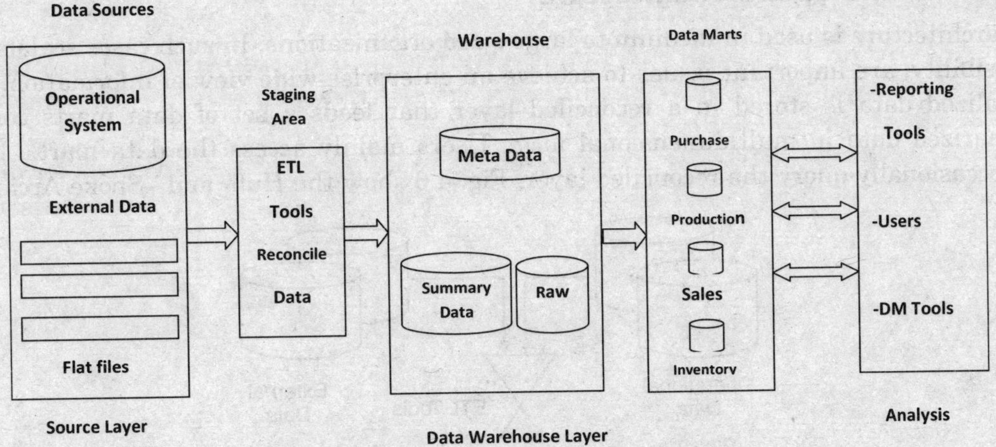

Fig. 4.4: Three Layered Architecture

Apart from these basic structures, the following important architecture schemas are also used:

Independent Data Marts Architecture: In this approach different data marts are separately designed and built in a nonintegrated fashion. This architecture can be used at the initial stages when a strong sponsorship toward an enterprise-wide warehousing project is not available or when the different departments of the organization are loosely coupled. This architecture is not very popular as it fails to achieve data integration and cross-reporting. Fig. 4.5 given below show the independent data mart architecture.

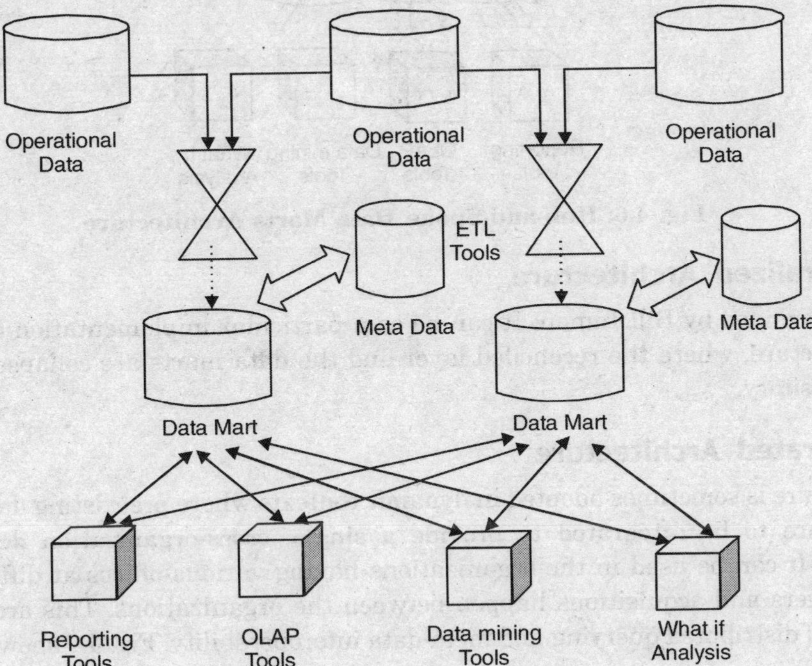

Fig. 4.5: Independent Data Marts Architecture

4.4.5 Hub-and-Spoke Architecture

This architecture is used in medium to large sized organizations. In such cases scalability and extensibility, are important issues to achieve an enterprise-wide view of information. Atomic, normalized data is stored in a reconciled layer that feeds a set of data marts containing summarized data in multidimensional form. Users mainly access the data marts, but they may occasionally query the reconciled layer. Fig. 4.6 show the Hub- and –Spoke Architecture.

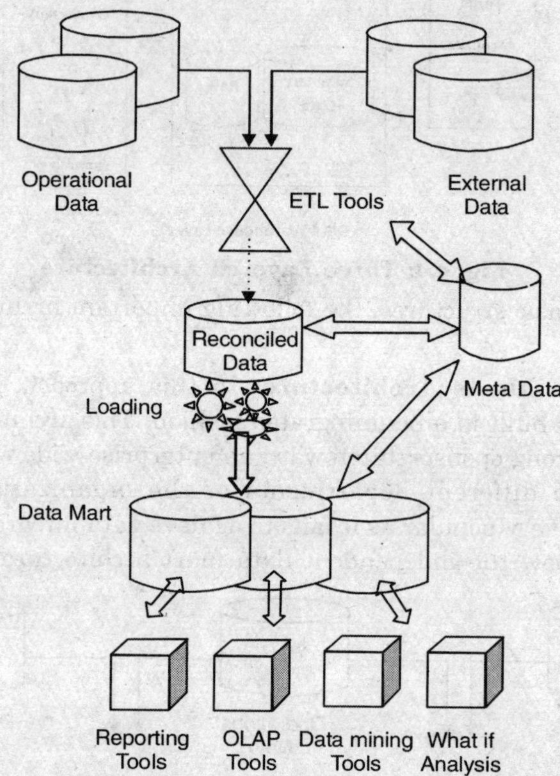

Fig. 4.6: Hub-and-Spoke Data Marts Architecture

4.4.6 Centralized Architecture

It was recommended by Bill Inmon. It can be as a particular implementation of the hub-and-spoke architecture, where the reconciled layer and the data marts are collapsed into a single physical repository.

4.4.7 Federated Architecture

This architecture is sometimes adopted in dynamic contexts where preexisting data warehouses/ data marts are to be integrated to provide a single, cross-organization decision support environment. It can be used in the organizations having various offices at different locations or when mergers and acquisitions happen between the organizations. This architecture uses the concepts of distributed querying and meta-data interoperability. Fig. 4.7 shows the federated architecture.

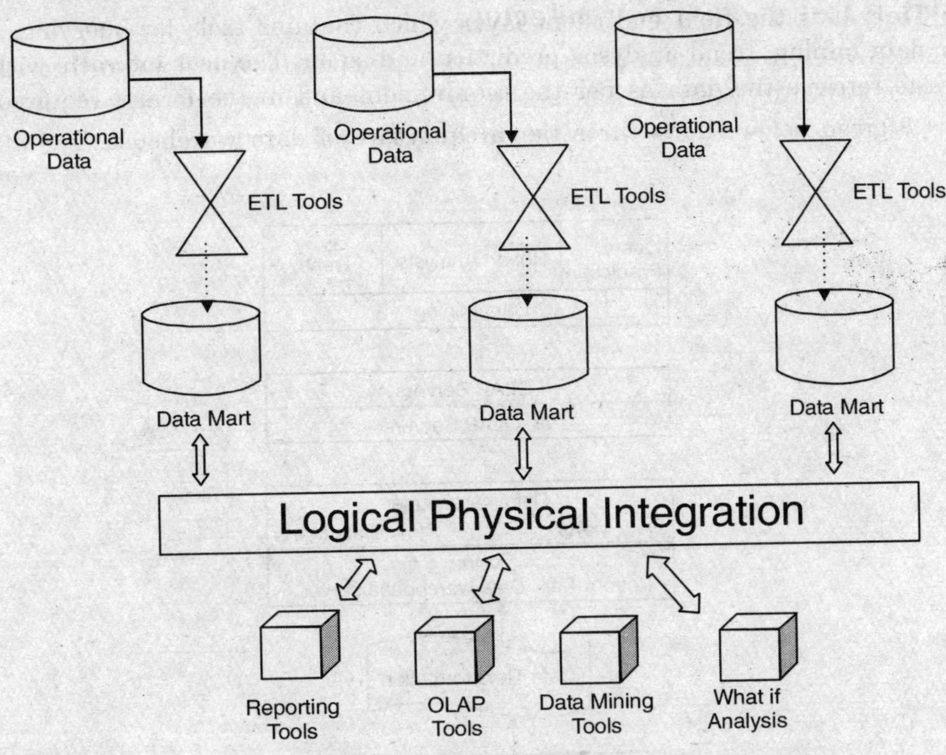

Fig. 4.7: Federated Architecture

4.5 THREE TIER ARCHITECTURE FOR DATA WAREHOUSING

Bottom Tier: It is a warehouse database server, which is almost always a relational database system. The main source of data in this stage may be internal or external, where the internal sources include back end tools and utilities from operational databases and the data from external sources like customer profile information, information about the competitors provided by any external agency. Data obtained from the various heterogeneous sources are transformed by using various back end tools and utilities, These tools and utilities perform data extraction, cleaning and transformation e,g to merge similar data from different sources into a unified format, as well as to load and refresh functions to update the data warehouse. The data is extracted using application program interfaces known as gateways. A gateway is supported by the underlying DBMS and allows client programs to generate SQL code to be extracted at a server. Examples of gateway include Open Database Connection and Object linking and Embedding Database by Microsoft and Java Database connection. This tier also contains a metadata repository which stores information about the data warehouse and its contents.

Middle Tier: It is an OLAP server that is implemented by:

- Using a relational OLAP model, this is an extended relational DBMS that maps operations on multidimensional data to standard relational operations.
- A multidimensional OLAP is a special purpose server that directly implements multidimensional data and operations.

Top Tier: It is the front end client layer which contains tools for querying, reporting, analysis, data mining, trend analysis, prediction and so on. The user interacts with this tier and tries to retrieve the data as per the requirement and in the format required.

Fig. 4.8 given below shows three tier architecture of data warehouse.

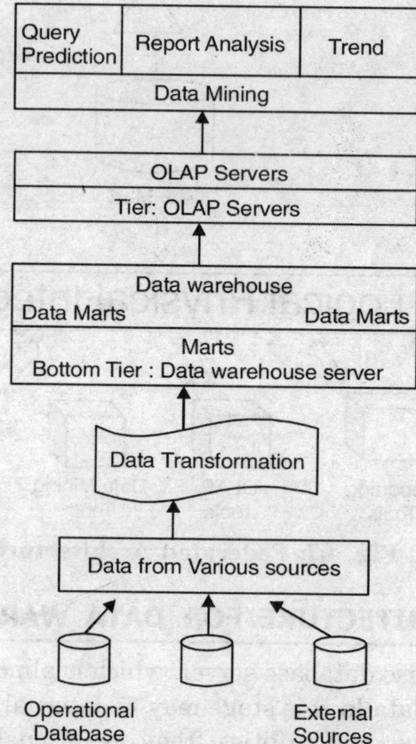

Fig. 4.8: Three Tier Architecture

The organization can choose any of the above mentioned architectures depending on the organizational structure, its business operations and user requirements. The working of all these layers, can be explored further as shown in the Fig. 4.9 given below:

- Information Access Layer
- Data Access Layer
- Data Warehouse Layer
- Data Staging Layer
- Operational Database/External Database Layer
- Data Directory (Metadata) Layer
- Process Management Layer

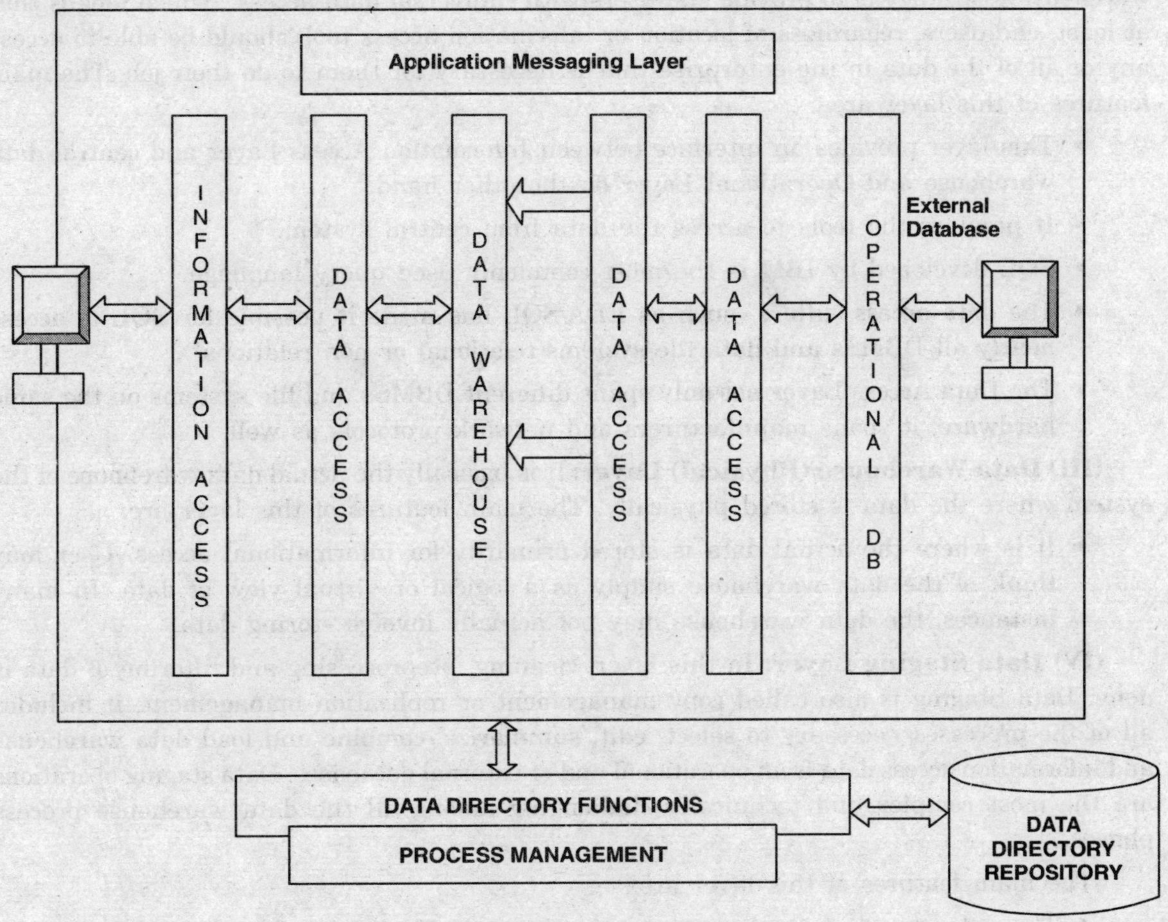

Fig. 4.9: Data Warehouse Architecture

(I) Information Access Layer: This is the outer most layer of architecture which interfaceswith the end user. The main features of this layer are:

- This layer is used as an interface with the end users.
- This layer includes the hardware and software involved in displaying and printing reports, spreadsheets, graphs and charts for analysis and presentation.
- The user uses various sophisticated tools on desktop for manipulating, analyzing and presenting data.
- The various automated presentation tools used are Excel, Lotus 1-2-3, Focus, Access, SAS, etc.
- The major problems faced in handling this layer are: handling the data obtained from heterogonous sources and to use a common data language that can be used throughout the enterprise.

(II) Data Access Layer: As discussed earlier, one of the key issue for the success of data warehousing strategy is to provide end-users with "universal data access", which means that at least, end-users, regardless of location or information access tool, should be able to access any or all of the data in the enterprise that is necessary for them to do their job. The main features of this layer are:

- This layer provides an interface between Information Access Layer and central data warehouse and Operational Layer on the other hand.
- It provides the tools to access the data from central system.
- SQL developed by IBM is the most commonly used query language.
- The data access "filters" such as EDA/SQL has made it possible for SQL to access nearly all DBMSs and data file systems(relational or non relational).
- The Data Access Layer not only spans different DBMSs and file systems on the same hardware, it spans manufacturers and network protocols as well.

(III) Data Warehouse (Physical) Layer: It is basically the actual data warehouse of the system where the data is stored physically. The main features of this layer are:

- It is where the actual data is stored primarily for informational access. User may think of the data warehouse simply as a logical or virtual view of data. In many instances, the data warehouse may not actually involve storing data.

(IV) Data Staging Layer: In this layer, cleaning, preprocessing and filtering of data is done. Data Staging is also called copy management or replication management, it includes all of the processes necessary to select, edit, summarize, combine and load data warehouse and information access data from operational and/or external databases. Data staging operations are the most complex and technically challenging among all the data warehouse process phases.

The main features of this layer are:

- The data stored at various sources is extracted, cleansed to remove inconsistencies and fill gaps, and is integrated to merge heterogeneous sources into one common schema.
- Extraction, Transformation, and Loading tools (ETL) can merge heterogeneous schemas.
- ETL process actually feed the reconciled data layer—a single, detailed, comprehensive, top-quality data source—that in turn feeds the data warehouse. For this reason, the ETL process operations as a whole can be termed as reconciliation.
- ETL takes place once when a data warehouse is populated for the first time, then it occurs every time the data warehouse is regularly updated.
- Data Staging may also involve data quality analysis programs and filters that identify patterns and data structures within existing operational data.

Fig. 4.10 given below shows that ETL consists of four separate phases: ***extraction capture, cleansing, transformation, and loading.***

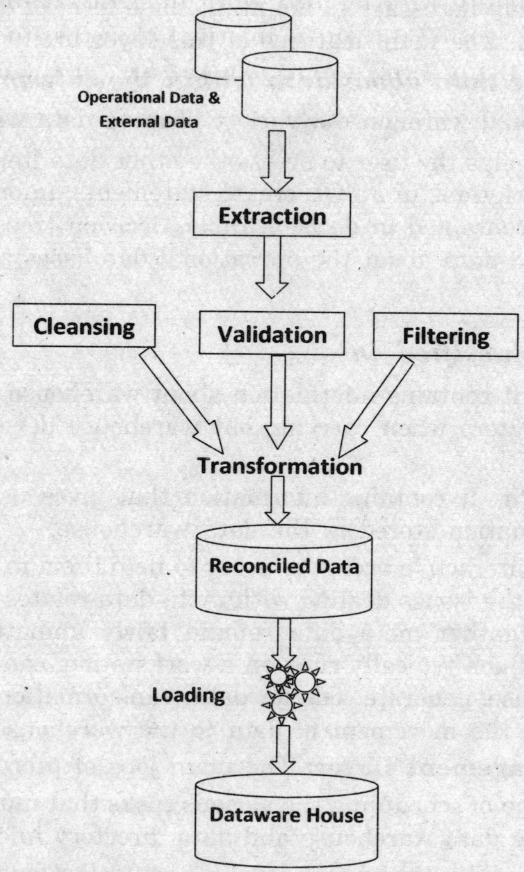

Fig. 4.10: Phases of ETL

(V) Operational Database/External Database Layer: This layer provides the data relevant to each user in the customized form. The main features of this layer are:

- This layer processes data to support critical operational needs.
- These databases are created to provide an efficient processing structure for a relatively small number of well-defined business transactions.
- Clearly, the goal of data warehousing is to free the information that is locked up in the operational databases and to mix it with information from other, often external, sources of data.
- As the operational systems have limited focus, the databases designed to support operational systems have difficulty in accessing the data for other management or informational purposes. This difficulty in accessing operational data is amplified by the fact that many operational systems are often 10 to 15 years old. The age of some of these systems means that the data access technology available to obtain operational data is itself outdated.

(VI) Data Directory (Metadata) Layer: In order to provide the facility of universal data access, it is absolutely necessary to maintain some form of data directory or repository of meta-data information. The main features of this layer are:

- ***Meta-data is the data about data within the enterprise.***
- In a fully functional warehouse a variety of meta data will be available.
- Any data which helps the user to access the other data items is termed as meta data. Like Record descriptions in a SQL create statements, information in an ER diagram, the information contained in decision table, decision trees, data about the end-user views of data and data about the operational databases are all considered as meta-data.

Meta data can be classified into:

Technical Meta Data: It contains information about warehouse data for use by warehouse designers and administrators when carrying out warehouse development and management tasks.

Business Meta Data: It contains information that gives users an easy-to-understand perspective of the information stored in the data warehouse.

Meta data provides interactive access to users to help them in understanding the content and to find data. One of the issues dealing with meta data relates to the fact that many data extraction tool used to gather meta data remain fairly immature. Meta data repository management software, which typically runs on a workstation, can be used to map the source data to the target database; generate code for data transformations; integrate and transform the data; and to control the movement of data to the warehouse.

(VII) Process Management Layer: The main jobs of process management layer are:

- It performs the job of scheduling the various tasks that must be accomplished to build and maintain the data warehouse and data directory information.
- It works as a scheduler or the high-level job controller for the processes or procedures to ensure that data warehouse should be kept up-to-dated.

(VIII) Application Messaging Layer: It is the transport system underlying the data warehouse. It is also termed as **middleware.** The main features of this layer are:

- It deals with transporting information around the enterprise computing network.
- It works much more than the networking protocols. It can be used to isolate applications, operational or informational, from the exact data format on either end.
- Application Messaging can also be used to collect transactions or messages and deliver them to a certain location at a certain time.

4.6 DATA WAREHOUSE IMPLEMENTATION

Data warehouses store huge amount of data and the decision makers require that these huge volumes of data should be processed in fractions of seconds. So the proper implementation of data warehouse is of utmost importance, for this purpose the emphasis should be on:

- Efficient cube computation Techniques.
- Efficient Data Access Methods.
- Efficient Query Processing Techniques.

4.6.1 Efficient Data Cube Computation techniques

The data warehouses storing huge volumes of data require multidimensional analysis and efficient computation of aggregations across many set of dimensions. In normal SQL terminology, these aggregations are refered as *group-by*, where each group-by is represented as a cubiod and a set of group-by's forms a lattice of cuboids, which define a data cube. For this purpose ***compute cube*** operator is used,

This operator computes aggregates over all subsets of dimensions specified in the operation. It requires large storage space, particularly when the number of dimensions is large in number. Lets consider the same example which we discussed in Chapter 3, for an inventory system, where the data base contains the data on city, product and year. For these three dimension a total of $2^3 = 8$ cuboids or group-by's can be computed for this data. The possible combinations are:

{(city, product, year), (city, product), (city, year), (product, year), (city),(product),(year),( )}, where ( ) means that the group-by is empty(i.e the dimensions are not grouped). These group-by's form a lattice of cuboids for the data cube as shown in the Fig. 4.11 given below,

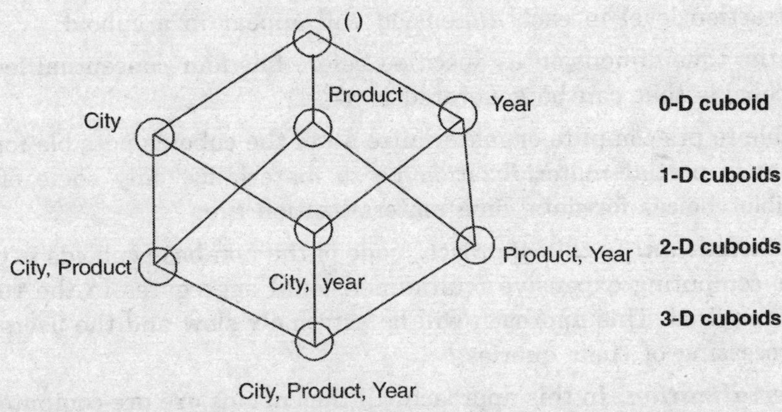

Fig. 4.11: Lattice of Cuboids, making a 3-D data cube.

Base Cuboids: The base cuboid contains all three dimensions i.e city, product and year. It can return the total sales for any combination of three dimensions. It is least generalized, most specific of all the cuboids.

Apex Cuboids: It is also termed as 0-D cuboid, refers to the case where the group-by is empty. It is most generalized or least specific of all the cuboids.

If the user starts at the apex cuboid and explore downward in the lattice, it is also termed as ***drilling down*** within a data cube.

And if the user starts at the base cuboid and explore upward, it is termed as ***rolling up.***

For a cube with n dimensions, there are a total of 2n cuboids, the following statement

compute cube sale_cube,

It would instruct the system to compute sales aggregate cuboids for all eight subsets of the set {city, product, year}, including the empty subset. The cube computation operator was first proposed by Gray et al.

OLAP may need to access different cuboids for different queries, it is better to compute in advance all or at least some of the cuboids in a data cube. It leads to fast response time and avoids some redundant computation. All OLAP products support pre-computations of multidimensional aggregates. The biggest problem in this pre-computation is that if all the cuboids are pre-computed then the storage space will be used in excess and if the cubes have many dimensions then this problem will increase many fold. If there are no hierarchies associated with each dimension then total number of cuboids for an n-dimensional data cube will be 2^n. And if the dimensions have associated concept hierarchies with multiple levels then this problem will be more intensive, For example: the dimension time has many hierarchies associated with it, it is not exploded at just one conceptual level i.e year but it is explored at multiple conceptual levels such as in the hierarchy" day-> month -> quarter -> year" . For n-dimensional data cube, the total number of cuboids that can be obtained are:

Total Number of Cuboids = π (i = 1 to n) (Li + 1)

Where Li is the number of levels associated with the dimension *i*. Here it is assumed that at most, one abstraction level in each dimension will appear in a cuboid.

For example, the time dimension as specified before has four conceptual levels, then the total number of cuboids that can be generated is 4^{10}.

It is not possible to pre-compute or materialize all of the cuboids possible for a data cube, the possible option is partial materialization i.e to materialize only some of the possible cuboids, the possible choices for data cube materialization are:

- ***No Materialization:*** In this approach, none of the non-base cuboids is pre-computed. It leads to computing expensive multidimensional aggregates in the run time i.e as and when required. This approach will be extremely slow and the users have to wait for the processing of their queries.
- ***Full Materialization:*** In this approach, all the cuboids are pre-computed in advance. The resulting lattice of computed cuboids is referred to as the full cube. It requires large amount of memory space in order to store all the pre-computed cuboids, but it results in fast execution of the user's queries and hence the response time reduces drastically.
- ***Partial Materialization:*** In this approach, only a few selected cuboids are pre-computed. This selection is usually done keeping the user's requirements in mind. That means the cuboids which are required quite often by a user or by a set of users are computed in advance, while the others are computed as per the demand by the user. Partial materialization represents a trade-off between storage space and response time. This method should consider the following factors:

  (a) Identify the subset of cuboids or sub-cubes to materialize.

  (b) Exploit the materialized cuboids or sub-cubes during query processing,

  (c) Efficiently update the materialized cuboids or sub-cubes during load and refresh.

The selection of the subset of cuboids to materialize should take into account:

- *The workload of the queries.*
- *The frequency of occurrence of queries.*
- *The cost of execution of queries.*
- *The cost of accessing the data.*
- *The cost for incremental updates.*
- *Total storage requirements.*
- *Physical database design.*
- *Method for generation and selection of indices.*

4.6.2 Efficient Data Access Methods

The fast access to data is the first and foremost requirement of the users. To facilitate efficient data accessing, data warehouses support index structure and materialized views using cuboids. The most common methods used to index the OLAP data are:

(a) Bitmap Indexing

(b) Join Indexing.

(a) Bit Map Indexing: It is the most popular method in OLAP products as it allows quick searching in data cubes. In the bitmap index for a given attribute, there is a distinct bit vector Bv, for each value v in the domain of attribute. If the given attribute's domain consists of n values, then n bits are needed for each entry in the bitmap index (i.e there are n bit vectors). If the attribute has the value v for a given row in the data table, then the bit representing that value is set to 1 in the corresponding row of bitmap index. All other bits for that row are set to 0. It can be considered as an alternative method for representation of record_id list.

Example: Consider the example of college database, consider the following data has been stored about the entity student:

registration number, name, father's name, course, city, phone number.

Suppose the dimension course at the top level has four values (showing the type of courses), like: MCA, BCA, B.Tech, M.Sc. each value is represented by a bit vector in the course bitmap index table. Suppose that the cube is stored as a relation table with 1000 rows. As the domain of course consists of four values, the bitmap index table requires four bit vectors, each with 1000 bits. The Fig. 4.12 (a) to (c) given below shows:

- A base table, containing the data about the dimensions course and city.
- Course bitmap index table and city bitmap index table, which shows the mapping of the data from the base tables to these two tables.

Base Table		
Record Id	**Course**	**City**
101	MCA	New Delhi
102	BCA	Chandigarh
103	B. Tech	New Delhi
104	BCA	New Delhi
105	MCA	Chandigarh
106	B. Tech	Chandigarh
107	M. Sc	New Delhi
108	MCA	New Delhi
109	B. Tech	Chandigarh
110	MCA	New Delhi

Fig. 4.12(a)

Course Bitmap Index Table				
Record Id	**MCA**	**BCA**	**B. Tech**	**M. Sc**
101	1	0	0	0
102	0	1	0	0
103	0	0	1	0
104	0	1	0	0
105	1	0	0	0
106	0	0	1	0
107	0	0	0	1
108	1	0	0	0
109	0	0	1	0
110	1	0	0	0

Fig. 4.12(b)

City Bitmap Index Table		
Record Id	**New Delhi**	**Chandigarh**
101	1	0
102	0	1
103	1	0
104	1	0
105	0	1
106	0	1
107	1	0
108	1	0
109	0	1
110	1	0

Fig. 4.12(c)

Fig. 4.12(a) to (c): Indexing OLAP data using bitmap indices.

Advantages:

1. This method is advantageous as compared to hash and tree indices. It is particularly useful for low cardinality domains as comparison, join and aggregation operations are reduced to bit arithmetic, which reduces the processing time to a greater extent.
2. This method leads to significant reductions in space and input/output as a string of characters can be represented by a single bit. For higher cardinality domains, this method can be adapted using compression techniques.

(b) Join Indexing: This method was used in relational data base query processing also. Traditional indexing maps the value in a given column to a list of rows having that value. In contrast, join indexing registers the joinable rows of two relations from a relational database. For example, if two relations R (RID, A) and S (B, SID) join on the attributes A and

B, then the join index record contains the pair (RID, SID), where RID and SID are record identifiers from the relations R and S. So the join index record can identify joinable tuples without performing costly join operations.

This scheme is useful for maintaining the relationship between a foreign key and its matching primary keys from a joinable relation.

The star schema model of a data warehouse makes join indexing attractive for cross table search, as the linkage between a fact table and its corresponding dimension table comprises the fact table's foreign key and the dimension table's primary key.

Join indexing maintains relationships between attribute values of a dimension (e.g within a dimension table) and the corresponding rows in the fact table. Join indices may span multiple dimensions to form composite join indices.

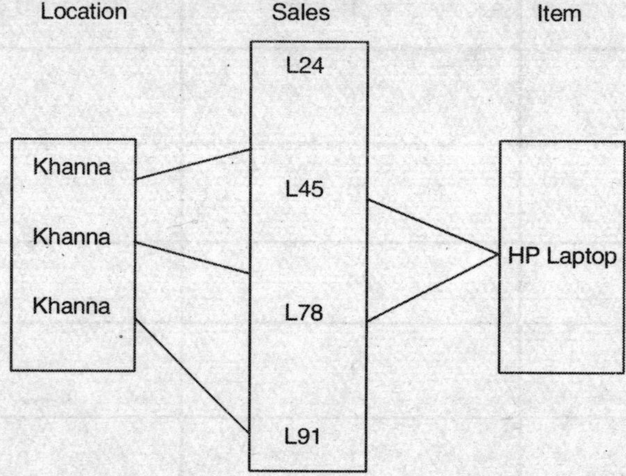

Fig. 4.13: Linkages between a sales fact table and location and item dimension tables.

Join Index for Location/Sales Key

Location	Sales Key
Khanna	L24
Khanna	L45
Khanna	L78

Join Index Table for Item/Sales key

Item	Sales Key
HP Laptop	L24
HP Laptop	L45
HP Laptop	L78

Join index table linking location and item to sales key

Location	Item	Sales Key
Khanna	HP Laptop	L24

Fig. 4.14: Join index tables based on the linkages between the sales fact table and location and item dimension tables.

To further speed up the query processing, the join indexing and the bitmap indexing methods can be integrated to form bitmapped join indices.

4.6.3 Efficient Processing of OLAP Queries

The ultimate aim of the data warehousing and data mining technology is to provide fast access to the data and it is necessary that the queries must be executed efficiently, i.e these should consume limited resources and must provide results as early as possible. The purpose of materializing cuboids and constructing OLAP index structure is to speed up query processing in data cubes. For a materialized view, query processing should follow the steps given below:

- ***Find out which operations should be performed on the available cuboids:*** It deals with transforming any selection, projection, roll-up and drill down operations specified in the query into corresponding SQL and/or OLAP operations. For Example, slicing and dicing a data cube may correspond to selection and/or projection operations on a materialized cuboid.
- ***Find out to which materialized cuboid the relevant operations should be applied:*** It deals with identifying all of the materialized cuboids that may potentially be used to answer the query, pertaining the set using knowledge of dominance relationships among cuboids, estimating the costs of using the remaining materialized cuboids.

Example OLAP Query Processing: Let us suppose that the data cube for student data base has an enrolment_cube{time, item, location}. The dimension hierarchies used are:

<day, month, year> for time,

<course-name, department, type of course(professional/non-professional)> for course, and

<street, city, district, state, country> for location.

Let the query is to be executed on {department, state} with the selection year = 2009. And the following materialized cubes are available:

- Cuboid I: {year, course-name, city}
- Cuboid II: {year, department, country}
- Cuboid III:{year, department, state}
- Cuboid IV: {course-name, state} where year = 2009.

Which of these four cuboids should be used to process the query?

Cuboid II can not be used because country is more general concept than country.

Cuboids I, III or IV can be used because: these contain the same set or a superset of the dimensions in the query and selection clause in the query can imply the selection in the cuboid

4.7 ONLINE ANALYTICAL MINING (OLAM)

Online Analytical Processing (OLAP) technology helps the decision makers to visualize huge operational data in one go for quick, consistent, interactive and timely analysis of the data, hence it can be considered as an essential element of the decision support system. It can be visualized as a powerful data analysis method for multi-dimensional analysis of data warehouses. But now a days, data mining techniques are also used with OLAP to analyze large data sets which makes OLAP more useful and easier to apply in decision support systems. The OLAP technology is integrated with data mining as a result of which a new promising direction of Online Analytical Mining (OLAM) has emerged.

In simple words, OLAM can be defined as

OLAM = OLAP + Data Mining

OLAM can be viewed as an integration of Data Mining and Data Warehousing and OLAP Technologies. It came into existence due to the necessity of mining knowledge and patterns at different levels of abstraction by drilling/rolling, pivoting, slicing/dicing, etc. Various data mining techniques used are: Interactive Characterization, Comparison, Association, Classification, Clustering, and Prediction.

In the last few years, OLAP systems are the predominant front-end tools used in data warehousing environments for multi-dimensional analysis, the reasons for this rapid development are as follows:

- These systems are used by decision makers to get quick answers of complex queries on their huge operational data.
- These systems allow users to perform quick, efficient and interactive analysis on organizational historical data.
- These systems support the retrieval of higher level summary information from detailed data.

But with the fast spread globalization and cut throat competition among companies and the increasing size of data bases has forced the users to take the help of latest technologies to improve the performance of these systems. Data mining is such a technology that can help in knowledge discovery in databases (KDD) and data mining techniques like Association, Classification, Clustering and Trend Analysis can make OLAP more useful and easier to apply in decision support systems.

4.7.1 Need of OLAM

1. Most data mining tools need to work on integrated, consistent, and cleaned data, which requires costly data cleaning, data transformation and data integration as preprocessing steps. A data warehouse constructed by such preprocessing serves as a valuable source of cleaned and integrated data for OLAP as well as for data mining.
2. Effective data mining needs exploratory data analysis. A user often likes to traverse flexibly through a database, select any portion of relevant data, analyze data at

different granularities, and present results in different forms. On-line analytical mining provides facilities for data mining on different subsets of data and at different levels of abstraction, by drilling, pivoting, filtering, dicing and slicing on a data cube and on some intermediate data mining results.

3. Most of the times, the users are not able to predict what kind of knowledge is to be mined from the huge databases. The integration of OLAP with multiple data mining functions provides flexibility for users to select desired data mining functions and swap data mining tasks dynamically.
4. OLAM facilitates OLAP-based, interactive, exploratory analysis. It helps the user to traverse database, select relevant data, present constraints and expected mining results, and analyze data at different levels of granularities, so that the varying demands of the users can be fulfilled.
5. OLAM allows on-line flexible selection of data mining functions, flexible selection of desired mining functions and dynamic change of data mining tasks.
6. It provides the ability to mine anywhere. Any portion of data base can be carved by drilling, dicing, filtering, etc.
7. It allows discovery-driven exploration of multi-feature cubes. Spatial and multimedia dimensions/measures.

4.7.2 Architecture for On-line Analytical Mining

An OLAM engine may perform multiple data mining tasks, such as concept description, association, classification, prediction, clustering, time-series analysis, etc. So, an OLAM engine is more sophisticated than an OLAP engine as it usually consists of multiple mining modules which may interact with each other for effective mining. There is no fundamental difference between the data cube required for OLAP and that for OLAM, although OLAM analysis may often involve the analysis of a larger number of dimensions with finer granularities, and thus require more powerful data cube construction and accessing tools than OLAP analyses. Since OLAM engines are constructed either on customized data cubes which often work with relational database systems, or on top of the data cubes provided by the OLAP products, it is suggested to build on-line analytical mining systems on top of the existing OLAP and relational database systems, rather than from the ground up.

- OLAM and OLAP have an integrated architecture because an OLAM engine performs analytical mining in data cubes in a similar manner as an OLAP engine performs on-line analytical processing.
- Both the OLAM and OLAP engines accept user's on-line queries (instructions) and work with the data cube in the analysis.
- Since some requirements in OLAM, such as the construction of numerical dimensions, may not be readily available in the commercial OLAP products, we have chosen to construct our own data cube and build the mining modules on such data cubes.

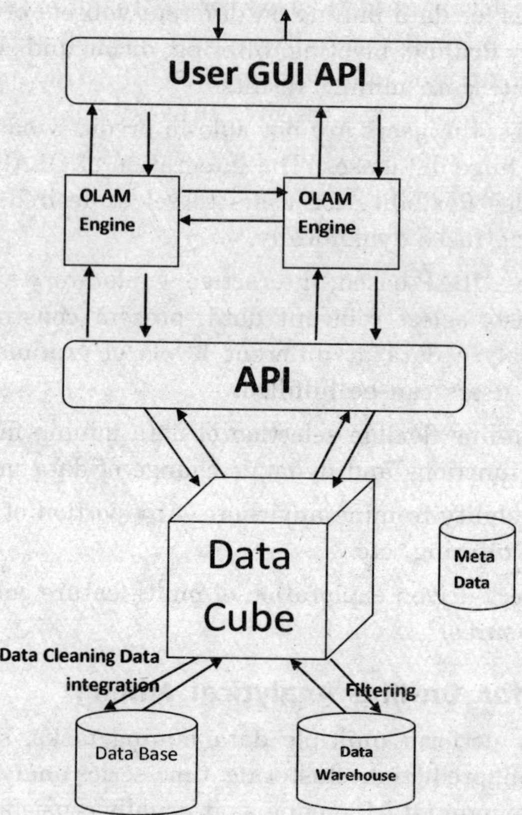

Fig. 4.15: An Integrated OLAM and OLAP Architecture

4.8 DISCOVERY DRIVEN EXPLORATION OF DATA CUBES

A data cube as discussed may have a large number of cuboids, where each cuboid may contain a large number of cells. In such a scenario, it is not possible to go through a cube thoroughly. So the need is felt to develop the tools which will help the user in exploring the huge aggregated space of a data cube, one such technique fulfilling this requirement is discovery-driven approach. In this technique, pre-computed measures showing the data exceptions are used to guide the user in the data analysis process, at all aggregation levels. These measures are also termed as exception indicators, where an exception is a data cell value that is significantly different from the value anticipated, based on a statistical model. The model considers variations and patterns in the measure value across all the dimensions to which a cell belongs to. For example; In student data base, if the attendance of a particular student is considered, it shows that the number of days for which the student was absent is more in a particular month, then it can be treated as an exception. However, it is not an exception if the student dimension is considered, as there are some other students who were absent in that month for same number of days.

The model considers exceptions hidden at all aggregated group-by's of a data cube. Visual cues, like, background color, is used to show the degree of exception at each cell, based on the pre-computed exception indicators. There are a variety of methods available for cube construction and the computation of exception can be clubbed with cube construction, so that overall construction of data cubes for discover driven exploration is sufficient.

Exception Indicators to find Data Anomalies: There are various measures which can be used as exception indicators which will help in identifying the data anomalies. These measures show the variation in the actual and expected value for the quantity in a cell. The measures are computed and associated with every cell for all aggregation levels. These are:

- ***SelfExp:*** It shows the degree of surprise of the cell value as comparison to other cells at the same aggregation level.
- ***InExp:*** It shows the degree of surprise somewhere below the cell, if we drill down from it.
- ***PathExp:*** It shows the degree of surprise for each drill-down path from the cell.

Example: Let us consider the example of college attendance records, where we want to analyze the monthly attendance as a percentage difference from the previous month. The Fig. 4.16 given below show the data aggregated over all students for each month.

To find out the exception indicators, the option ***highlight exception*** is used. It converts the SelfExp and InExp values into visual cues, which is shown with each cell. The background color of the cell is based on its SelfExp value, and a box is drawn around each cell, where the thickness and color of the box are related to its InExp value. Thick boxes show high InExp Value, and in both the cases, darker the color the greater is the degree of exception. Like, dark, thick boxes for attendance in a particular month shows that the user should explore the lower-level aggregations of these cells by drilling down.

Drill downs can be run along the aggregated student dimensions. To find out that which path has more exceptions, the user selects a cell of interest and run a path exception module that colors each dimension based on PathExp value of the cell. It shows the degree of surprise for that path.

A drill down along item results in a cube slice, like the Fig. 4.17 below shows attendance over month for each student. Then the user will have many different attendance values to analyze and the option highlight exception shows the exceptional values in the data.

	Attendance					
	Jan	**Feb**	**Mar**	**Apr**	**May**	**June**
Total	78%	80%	80%	83 %	86%	**38 %**

Fig. 4.16: Attendance Record for one Semester

Attendance			Month			
Name of Student	Jan	Feb	Mar	Apr	May	June
Ajay	78%	79%	88%	81%	36%	88%
Sameer	65%	66%	23%	89%	56%	44%
Rajat	86%	79%	78%	88%	77%	89%

Fig. 4.17: Student Wise Attendance Record

Consider the difference in attendance for student Ajay in May, this cell has dark background which shows that it has high SelfExp value, meaning that the cell is an exception.

The InExp values can be used to show the exceptions at lower levels that are not visible at the current level. Consider the cells for the student Sameer in March, it has been encircled indicating high InExp value. The user may wish to explore the details by drilling down along the various subjects. The result has been shown in the Fig. 4.18 given below, where exception has been highlighted and it is clearly visible that exceptional attendance is in subject DBMS.

Attendance			Month			
Subject Name	Jan	Feb	Mar	Apr	May	June
IT	67%	66%	50%	78%	66%	89%
DBMS	56%	67%	11%	63%	61%	78%
Lab	77%	78%	45%	90%	67%	88%

Fig. 4.18: Attendance record for the Student - 'Sameer'.

These exception values SelfExp, InExp and PathExp measures are based on a statistical method for table analysis. They take into account all the group-by's in which a given cell value participates. A cell value is considered as an exception based on how much it differs from its excepted value. The difference between a given cell value and its expected value is called as residual. Where, larger the residual, the more the given cell is an exception.

The data cube can be constructed for discovery driven exploration using following steps:

1. Compute the aggregate values defining the cube such as sum or count, over which the exceptions will be found.
2. Model fitting is done, in which coefficients mentioned before are determined and used to compute the standardized residuals.
3. In the last step, SelfExp, InExp and PathExp values are computed based on standardized residuals.

4.9 ATTRIBUTED-ORIENTED INDUCTION

As large amount of data is stored in databases, it is advisable to describe concepts in concise and generalized forms. It helps the user in examining the general behavior of data. For Example, in a customer database, the decision makers may not be interested in examining the transactions of individual customers, they will be interested to view the data generalized to higher levels like customer groups according to sex, geographic region and customer income group. Data generalization summarizes data by replacing relatively low level values(e.g. numeric values for an attribute age) with higher-level concepts(e.g. young, middle-aged and senior)or by reducing the number of dimensions to summarize data in concept space involving fewer dimensions. The most common form of data generalization is concept description. A concept typically refers to a data collection like common buyers, graduate student and so on. Concept description generates descriptions for data characterization and comparison.

Characterization provides a concise and distinct summarization of given data, where as comparison provides descriptions comparing two or more data collections.

Attribute Oriented Induction for Data Characterization: This approach was proposed in 1989, a few year before the introduction of data cube technology. In the data cube technology, the views were pre-computed in the data warehouse before the users actually ask for it, these views are termed as materialized views and perform offline aggregations. On the other hand, in case of attribute oriented induction approach, the queries are computed online as and when required. Actually this distinction between these two approaches is not very prominent, because some aggregations in the data cube can be computed online, whereas some offline pre-computations can be used in the case of attribute oriented induction. The general method of attribute oriented induction is:

- Collect the task relevant data using a database query.
- Perform generalization based on the examination of number of each attribute's different values in the relevant data set. The generalization can be performed by
  (*a*) Attribute Removal Method.
  (*b*) Attribute Generalization Method.

The following example illustrates the process of attribute induction. First of all characterization process is carried out followed by class comparisons.

Example; Lets consider an example of College database named as CDB, given the attributes: Registration Number, Name, Gender, Birth place, DOB, Residence, Phone Number, Father's name, Qualification and Rank.

A data mining query for this characterization can be expressed in data mining query language as:

use CDB

mine characteristics as *"Computer Students"*

in relevance to registration number, name, gender, DOB, Birth Place, Phone Number, Qualification, rank

from student

where status in "graduate"

Before applying attribute oriented induction, following jobs are to be done,

Data Focusing: As the name specifies in this step specification of task relevant data is provided. The relevant data based on the query submitted by the user is fetched, by fetching only the relevant data the data mining process becomes more efficient and better results can be obtained as compared to the situation when the entire data base is mined. Many a times, specifying the relevant attributes may be difficult for the user. A user may select a few attributes but may leave a few attributes which might be useful for the analysis. For example, let the dimension time is defined by the attributes, year-month-date-time, if the user has included only the date in the query , in order to provide generalization on time, the other attributes defining the dimension may also be included, i.e the system automatically includes year and month. On the other hand the user may include all the attributes by using the clause relevance to *, in this case, all the attributes in the relation will be available for the analysis, but many of these attributes do not contribute to reach at some useful result, that means too many attributes are available. In order to find out the relevant attributes, a relevance analysis can be performed, by which statistically irrelevant attributes are removed from the descriptive mining process.

Data Generalization: The second step to perform attribute oriented induction is to perform data generalization; there are two methods to perform data generalization:

- ***Attribute Removal:*** It is based on the following rule:

  If there is a large set of distinct values for an attribute of the initial working relation, but either there is no generalization operator on the attribute(i.e there is no concept hierarchy defined for the attribute) or its higher-level concepts are expressed in terms of other attributes, then the attribute should be removed from the working relation.

- ***Attribute Generalization:*** It is based on the following rule:

  If there is a large set of distinct values for an attribute in the initial working relation and there exists a set of generalization operators on the attribute, then a generalization operator should be selected and applied to the attribute.

Both these methods for data generalization claim that if there is a large set of distinct values for an attribute, then further generalization should be applied. Then how; large a set of distinct values for an attribute should be considered. User may prefer some attributes to remain at a low level abstraction while others may be generalized to higher levels. If the attribute is generalized too high, it may lead to over-generalization and on the other hand, if the attribute is not generalized to a sufficiently high level then under-generalization may result. Therefore a balance should be maintained in attribute-oriented generalization, for this purpose various attribute generalization control strategies can be used, the most common strategies in this category are: attribute generalization threshold control and generalization relation threshold control.

Table 4.1: Initial working relation: A Collection of Task Relevant Data

Registration Number	Name	Sex	Stream	Father's Name	Date of Birth	Birth Place	Residence	Phone Number	gpa
11101101	Amit	M	CS	Vinod	11-2-89	New Delhi	Ekta Enclave	98101-89123	8.84
11101102	Ajay	M	CS	Munish	12-3-90	New Delhi	Ekta Enclave	97123-45678	8.70
11101103	Sushma	F	Mgt	Amar	14-9-90	Mumbai	Sabzi Mandi	98444-12345	7.13
11101104	Rajni	F	FT	Munish	25-09-91	Karachi, Pakistan	Aamir Apartments	98544-19990	4.56

How Attribute-Oriented Induction is performed on the initial working relation of the table above:

For each attribute of the relation, the generalization proceeds as follows:

1. **Registration Number, Name, Father's name:** As a large number of distinct values are available for these three attributes, so no generalization operation is defined on it, hence these attributes are removed.
2. **Sex:** As there are only two distinct values for this attribute i.e either Male or Female, this attribute is retained and no generalization is performed on it.
3. **Stream:** Let us suppose that a concept hierarchy has been defined that allows the attribute steam to be generalized to values {computer science, management, engineering, fashion technology}. Let the attribute threshold is set to 4 and there are more than 10 different values exist in the initial working relation. So by attribute generalization and attribute generalization control, stream is generalized by climbing the given concept hierarchy.
4. **Date of birth:** For this attribute there exists a hierarchy that can generalize date of birth to age and then age to age-range and the number of age-ranges is small w.r.t attribute generalization threshold, so the generalization of date of birth should take place.
5. **Birth Place:** This attribute has a large number of different values, let a concept hierarchy exists for birth place, defined as "city-state-country". We may wish to generalize it.

   If the number of different values for country > Attribute Generalization Threshold, then birth-place should be removed.

   Number of different values for country < Attribute Generalization Threshold, the birth-place should be generalized to birth-country.

6. **Phone Number:** As in the case of attributes in category I, this attribute also has too many distinct values and therefore should be removed in generalization.
7. **gpa:** Let there is a concept hierarchy for gpa that groups the values for grade point average into numeric values like{0-5, 5-7.5, 7.5-10} which again can be grouped into descriptive values like{average, very good, excellent}, the attribute therefore cane be generalized.

Table 4.2: Generalized Relation obtained by Attribute Oriented Induction on the data of Table 4.1

Sex	Major	Birth-country	Age-range	Residence-city	gpa
M	Science	India	24-30	New Delhi	excellent
F	Mgt.	India	24-31	Mumbai	very good
F	FT	Pakistan	22-30	Karachi	average

Algorithm: Attribute-Oriented Induction: Suppose a user has submitted a data mining request, and the following procedure generalizes mining characteristics in a relational database:

Input:

Dbase a relational database,

Dquery, a data mining query,

list, a list of attributes containing the attributes ai

gen(ai), a set of concept hierarchies or generalization operators on attributes ai;

a-generalization-threshold,represents attribute generalization threshold for each attribute ai.

Output: O, a Prime_generalized_relation.

Procedure:

1. W <- get-task-relevant-data(Dquery,Dbase),W, the work relation holds the task relevant data.
2. Preparation-for-generalization(W):
   (a) Scan W and collect the distinct values for each attribute ai
   (b) For each attribute ai, find whether ai should be removed, if not, compute its minimum desired level Li, based on its given or default attribute threshold, find out the mapping pairs(v,v'), where v is a distinct value of ai in W and v' is its corresponding generalized value at level Li.
3. O <- generalization(W)

The prime-generalized-relation, O is derived by replacing each value v in W by its corresponding v' in the mapping while calculating count and computing any other aggregate values. This step can be implemented efficiently using either of the two following variations:

(a) For each generalized tuple, insert the tuple into a sorted prime relation P by a binary search, if the tuple is already in O, increase its count and other aggregate values accordingly, else insert it into O.

(b) As in most of the cases the number of distinct values at the prime relation level is small, the prime relation can be coded as an m-dimensional array, where m is the number of attributes in O, and each dimension contains the corresponding generalized attribute values. Each array element holds the corresponding count and other aggregation values. The insertion of a generalized tuple is performed by measure aggregation in the corresponding array element.

The efficiency of the algorithm can be analyzed as follows:

Step I: In the first step the task relevant data is collected into working relation W. its efficiency depends on: *size of the data base, the query processing method used.*

Step II:

(a) Statistics on the working relation is collected, for this purpose the working relation is scanned.

(b) Minimum Desired level and Mapping pairs for each attribute are determined- it depends on the number of distinct values available for each attribute.

Step III: In this step the prime relation, O is derived. It is performed by scanning each tuple in the working relation and inserting generalized tuples into O. there are a total of W tuples in W and o tuples in O.

For each tuple t in W, its attribute values is substituted based on the derived mapping pairs., which results in a generalized tuple t'.

If 3(a) is used, each t' takes O(log p) to find the location for the count increment., so the total complexity comes out to be:

O(|W| * log p) for all generalized tuples.

If 3(b) is used, each t' takes O(1) to find the tuple for the count increment. So the total complexity comes out to be:

O(N) for all generalized tuples.

SUMMARY

- Data warehouse architecture support four different views of the data warehouse, top-down view, data source view, data warehouse view and Business Query View.
- A Data Warehouse Architecture (DWA) is a way of representing the overall structure of data, communication, processing and presentation that exists for end-user computing within the enterprise.
- Essential Properties for a Data Warehouse are Separation, Scalability Extensibility Flexibility Security Administerability and Ease of Use.
- Single-layer architecture is not frequently used in practice. Its goal is to minimize the amount of data stored and to reach at this goal, it removes data redundancies. It has three components: *Data Sources, Warehouse and Analysis.*
- The problem with single layer architecture is that it fails to meet the requirement for separation between analytical and transactional processing.
- Two-Layer Architecture has four components, Data Sources, Staging Area (where data sources go before the warehouse) and Warehouse and Analysis.
- In the Staging Area cleaning, preprocessing and filtering of data is done.
- ETL consists of four separate phases: extraction capture, cleansing, transformation, and loading.
- The components of three-layer architecture are: Staging Area, Warehouse, Data Marts (purchasing, sales, and inventory) and Analysis.
- Data mart is defined *as a subset or an aggregation of the data stored in the primary data warehouse.* It is designed for a particular line of business. It includes a set of information pieces relevant to a specific business area, corporate department, or category of users.
- Other common architecture schemes are, centralized architecture, federated architecture, hub and spoke and independent architecture.
- The various layers of data ware house architecture can be enumerated as- Information Access Layer, Data Access Layer, Data Warehouse Layer, Data Staging Layer , Operational Database/ External Database Layer, Data Directory (Metadata) Layer , Process Management Layer and Application Messaging Layer
- Meta-data is the data about data within the enterprise.
- Various types of meta data are Technical Meta Data and Business Meta Data:
- Data cube computation and exploration play an essential role in data warehousing and is important for flexible data mining in multidimensional space.
- A data cube consists of a lattice of cuboids. Each cuboid corresponds to a different degree of summarization of a given multidimensional data.
- Full materialization refers to the computation of all the cuboids in a data cube lattice. Partial materialization refers to the selective computation of a subset of the cuboid cells in the lattice.
- The Bitmap Indexing and Join Indexing are most common methods for efficient data access.
- OLAM (Online Analytical Mining) integrates the OLAP technology with data mining.
- OLAM facilitates OLAP-based, interactive, exploratory analysis. It helps the user to traverse database, select relevant data, present constraints and expected mining results, and analyze data at different levels of granularities, so that the varying demands of the users can be fulfilled.

- OLAM allows on-line selection of data mining functions, flexible selection of desired mining functions and dynamic change of data mining tasks.
- OLAM and OLAP have an integrated architecture because an OLAM engine performs analytical mining in data cubes in a similar manner as an OLAP engine performs on-line analytical processing.
- Both the OLAM and OLAP engines accept user's on-line queries (instructions) and work with the data cube in the analysis.
- The general method of attribute oriented induction performs, collection of task relevant data using a database query and performing generalization based on the examination of number of each attribute's different values in the relevant data set.
- The generalization can be performed by Attribute Removal Method and Attribute Generalization Method.

CHAPTER 5

DATA MINING

The huge amount of data collected through various internal and external sources has resulted in a situation where the decision makers have no time to go through these huge data repositories for making profitable, widely accepted long sighted decisions. The organizations are becoming *data rich and information poor.* The data collected in large repositories become data archives that are visited rarely. It is almost impossible to analyze this huge amount of data without the help of powerful analysis tools. So the decision makers are making strategic decisions depending on their intuition and experience rather than on the basis of *information-rich data* stored in the repositories. The advancement has been done to design the expert system and knowledge based technologies which rely on users or domain experts to manually input knowledge into knowledge bases. This method of manual knowledge input is prone to biases and errors and is time consuming also. So the need is to develop some data mining tools that can turn data tombs into shrine of knowledge, which can be used by decision makers directly.

5.1 MEANING OF DATA MINING

Data Mining is the process of extracting knowledge hidden from large volumes of raw data. The knowledge must be new, not obvious, and one must be able to use it.

Data mining has been defined as ***"the nontrivial extraction of implicit, previously unknown, and potentially useful information from data"***.

It is basically "***the science of extracting useful information from large data sets or databases***". It involves sorting through large amounts of data and picking out relevant information. Data Mining is an analytic process designed to explore data (usually large amounts of data - typically business or market related) in search of consistent patterns and/ or systematic relationships between variables, and then to validate the findings by applying the detected patterns to new subsets of data.

Data Mining is developed with the goal of providing tools for automatically and intelligently transforming large amount of data in to knowledge relevant to the users. The extracted knowledge is often expressed in the form of association rules, decision tress or clusters that allows one to find interesting patterns buried deeply in the data which facilitate decision making process.

5.2 DEFINITIONS OF DATA MINING

Table 5.1: Data Mining defined throughout the Literature

Author	**Definition**
Cabena et al.	Data mining is defined as the process of extracting previously unknown, valid, and actionable information from large databases and then using the information to make crucial business decisions.
Fabris	Data mining is described as the automated analysis of large amounts of data to find patterns and trends that may have otherwise gone undiscovered.
Chung and Grey	The objective of data mining is to identify valid, novel, potentially useful, and understandable correlations and patterns in existing data.
Insightful Miner 3.0User Guide	Data mining is the application of statistics in the form of exploratory data analysis and predictive models to reveal patterns and trends in very large data sets.
Gartner Group	Data mining is the process of discovering meaningful new correlations, patterns and trends by sifting through large amounts of data stored in repositories, using pattern recognition technologies as well as statistical and mathematical techniques.
Fayyad et al., (1996)	Data mining is a step in the knowledge discovery in databases (KDD) process and refers to algorithms that are applied to extract patterns from the data. The extracted information can then be used to form a prediction or classification model, identify trends and associations, refine an existing model, or to provide a summary of the database being mined.
Two Crows Corporation (1999)	Data mining is a process that uses a variety of data analysis tools to discover patterns and relationships in data that may be used to make valid predictions.
Hand (1998)	Data mining is the process of secondary analysis of large databases aimed at finding unsuspected relationsbips which are of interest or value to the database owners.
Newing (1996)	Data mining is the process of extracting valid, previously unknown and ultimately comprehensible information from large databases and using it to make critical business decisions.
Brabazon (1997)	Data mining is the discovery of new, non-obvious, valuable information from a large collection of raw data.

Berry and Linoff (1997)	Data mining is 'the process of exploration and analysis, by automatic or Semiautomatic means, of large quantities of data in order to discover meaningful patterns and rules.
Nemati & Barko (2002)	Data mining is a process that uses statistics, artificial intelligence and machine learning techniques to extract and identify useful information, and subsequent knowledge, from large databases.
Liao (2003)	Data Mining (DM) is an interdisciplinary field that combines artificial intelligence, computer science, machine learning, database management, data visualization, mathematic algorithms and statistics. DM is a technology for knowledge discovery in databases (KDD). This technology provides different methodologies for decision making, problem solving, analysis, planning, diagnosis, detection, integration, prevention, learning and innovation.
Wen (2004)	Data mining is the process of discovering patterns in data. The process must be automatic or semi-automatic. The patterns discovered must be meaningful in that they lead to an increase in the quality of decision making.
Dan et al., 2001	Data mining is a variety of techniques such as neural networks, decision trees or standard statistical techniques to identify nugget of information or decision-making knowledge in bodies of data, and extracting these in such a way that they can be put to use in areas such as decision support, prediction, forecasting, and estimation.
Greengard (1999)	Data mining is a group of analytical applications that search for hidden patterns in a database.
Smith (2002)	Data mining is a process that uses a variety of data analysis tools to discover patterns and relationships in data and using them to make valid predictions.

Data mining is a process of analyzing the data from various perspectives and summarizing it into valuable information. Data mining assists the users to look for hidden patterns in a group of data to discover new relationships in the data.

Data mining consists of five major elements:

- Extract, transform, and load transactional data onto the data warehouse system.
- Store and manage the data in a multidimensional database system.
- Provide data access to business analysts and information technology professionals.
- Analyze the data by application software.
- Interpretation of data on multiple criterias.
- Present the data in a useful format, such as a graph or table.

5.3 IMPORTANCE OF DATA MINING

Several areas of science, business, and other environments deal with immense amount of data, which requires to be turned into something meaningful known as *knowledge*. Data mining is repeatedly unnoticed but it can offer very interesting information that statistical methods are unable to make or produce properly.

Major Data Requirements of the Industry are:

1. What is the profile, tastes, preferences and purchasing behavior of the customers?
2. What is the transaction behavior of the various customers?
3. Which products are often purchased together by the customers of which particular profile?
4. What services and benefits would the current customers likely desire?
5. Identifying the customers who are getting all types of services from the company.
6. Which set of customers are Loyal and which one are disloyal?
7. What set of transactions lead to a fraud?
8. Will the customer be able to repay the loans or not?
9. To predict the future trends and hence to design the future road map.

Major Goals the organization needs to achieve are:

1. Cross Selling the products.
2. Differentiating between Loyal and Disloyal Customers.
3. Target Marketing to focus on prospective customers.
4. Prevention of defaults, bad loans.
5. To increase customer retention.
6. To increase customer satisfaction.

Data Mining Services can be used for the following functions:

- **Research and Surveys.** Data mining can be used for product research, surveys, market research and analysis. Information can be gathered that is quite useful in driving new marketing campaigns and promotions.
- **Information Collection.** During the web scraping process it is possible to collect information regarding investors, investments and funds by scraping through related websites and databases.
- **Customer Opinions.** Customer views and suggestions play an important role in the way a company operates. The information can be readily found on forums, blogs and other resources where customers freely provide their views.
- **Data Scanning.** Data collected and stored will not be important unless scanned. Scanning is important to identify patterns and similarities contained in the data.
- **Extraction of Information.** This is the process of identifying the useful patterns in data that can be used in decision making process. This is so because decision making must be based on sound information and facts.

- **Pre-processing of data.** Usually the data collected is stored in the data warehouse. This data needs to be pre-processed. Where pre-processing means that some data items which are insignificant may therefore removed manually by data mining experts.
- **Web data.** Web data usually caused many challenges in mining. This is so because of its nature. For instance, web data can be believed as dynamic as it keeps on changing from time to time. As a result, the process of data mining should be repeated in regular intervals.
- **Competitor Analysis.** There is a need to understand how our competitors are working in the business market. We need to know both their weaknesses and strengths. Their methods of marketing and distribution can be mined.
- **Online Research.** The internet is highly regarded for its vast information. It is obvious that it is the largest source of information. It is possible to gather a large number of information regarding different companies, customers and our business clients. It is possible to detect frauds through online means.
- **News:** Nowadays with almost all major newspapers and news sources posting their news online it is possible to gather information regarding trends and other critical areas. In this way, it is possible to be in the better position of competing in the market.
- **Updating Data**: Data collected will be a waste of time unless it is updated. This is to ensure that the information is appropriate so that right decision can be made at the right time.

The areas in which the data mining techniques can be implemented are:

1. Marketing: The data mining techniques can be used to know the customers well and to plan that how the organization can market their products in a better way.

- Data Mining is used to determine that how customers will react to new products and offers, which customers will be likely to accept the new product offers, the risk profile of a customer segments for defaulting on loans etc.
- Data mining technique can be used to profile the like minded customers in to one group and hence they can be dealt accordingly, As we know that, the customers of a given geographic location and of a particular job profile demand a particular set of services, like in banking sector the customers from the service class always demand for the policy which ensures more security as they are not intending to take risks, likewise the same set of service class people in rural areas have the preferences for some particular brands which may differ from their counterparts in the urban areas.

Instead of mass pitching a certain "hot" product, the customer service representatives of the company can be equipped with data pertaining to customer profiles enriched by data mining that will help them to identify which products and services are more relevant to the callers.

- Retaining the existing customers and selling the new products to the existing customers is a very important factor for the success of the organization. Instead of approaching to the new customers for selling the new products, reaching out to the existing customers is termed as cross-selling. The data collected about the taste and preferences of the existing customers can be mined and they can be informed about the latest products and policies launched.

This technique will help the management in finding the solution of 80/20 principle of marketing, which says: Twenty per cent of our customers will provide the 80 per cent of our profits, then problem is to identify those 20 % and the techniques of clustering will help in achieving the same.

- The reaction of the customers for the existing and new products can be recorded, according to which the future strategies can be designed.

2. Risk Management: The customer and the companies while dealing with each other will always try to cover the risk factor. The company will not be interested in dealing with the customers who are not honest in their dealings. It is more important in financial organizations like banks, insurance sector, telecom sector and now a days it has been used in medical diagnosis and treatment also. Like in financial sector, data mining techniques help to distinguish borrowers who repay loans promptly from those who don't. It also helps to predict when the borrower is at default, whether providing loan to a particular customer will result in bad loans or not. Bank executives by using data mining technique can also analyze the behavior and reliability of the customers. It also helps to predict when the borrower is at fault, whether providing loan to a particular customer will result in bad loans or not.

3. Customer Relationship Management: In the era of cut throat competition the customer is considered as the king and it is the customer only who is ruling the whole show. The huge data bases of various organizations are storing billions of data items about the customers.

- Data mining technique can be used to create customer profile to group the like minded people and hence they can be dealt accordingly. Like in a student data base, the students who are interested in programming languages can be grouped together and they can be offered the courses of their interest, while the group of students interested in networking can be provided the customized courses in their area of interest.[here the technique of clustering is used]
- Data mining can be useful in all the three phases of a customer relationship cycle: Customer Acquisition, Increasing value of the customer and Customer retention. The information collected can be used for different purposes like making new marketing initiatives, market segmentation, risk analysis and revising company customer policies according to the need of the customers.
- The profiling can be done on the basis of demographic characteristics, life style and previous transactional behavior of a particular customer. Customer profiling is to characterize features of special customer groups. Which customers in particular the organization will wish to keep? Which customers will drive most of the profits? Which customers might switch to our competitors and why? Which customers are dissatisfied with our services and products? If the organization has the answers to these questions then they will be able to design customized services and offers, which will enhance customer satisfaction.

4. Predicting the Future Trends: Data mining will help in predicting the future trends and organizations can offer the products accordingly, like if a customer has availed a home loan, then after some time he/she can be contacted again for buying furniture or refrigerator or TV etc. As these are the obvious requirements after the purchase of a home. By predicting customer needs in advance, businesses can then market their products in a better way. Customer satisfaction can also be improved through more effective marketing.

5. Attrition Analysis: In the present day environment of cut throat competition, the customers are in a fix and are shifting from one company to other quite often. The studies show that customers switch from one company to other, when they observe that the other companies are providing better customized facilities. The company then need to classify the customers to identify that which set of customers might switch to the competitors and why? Which set of customers are dissatisfied with our services and products? The analysis will help the bank to identify such customers and hence the organization can plan strategies to prevent the attrition.

6. Fraud Detection: While dealing with the companies, the customers and the companies have the chances of falling an easy prey to the frauds. So both the parties wish to be secure while dealing with each other. The data mining techniques can help them to detect and hence prevent frauds. The study presented here will focus on the ways and means of analyzing the customer data in order to identify the patterns that can lead to frauds.

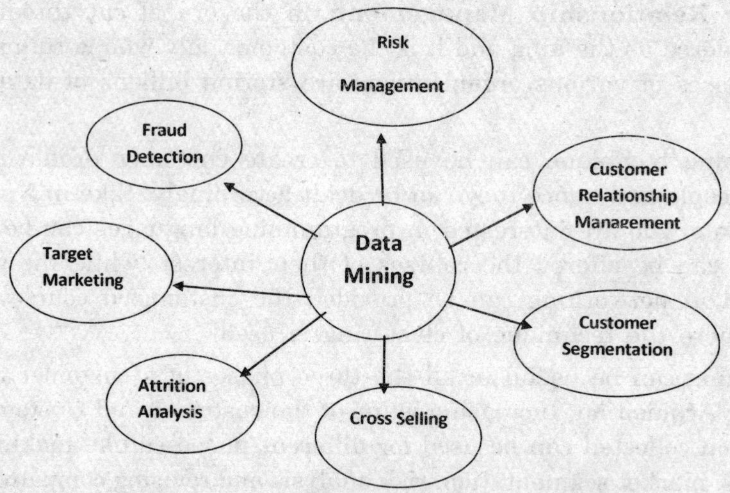

Fig. 5.1: Application Areas of Data Mining

The other benefits include:

1. The reaction of the customers for the existing and new products can also be known based on which organization will try to promote the product, improve on the quality of products and services and can gain competitive advantage over the other organizations.
2. Analysts can also analyze the past trends to determine the present demand and forecast the customer behaviour of various products and services in order to grab more business opportunities and anticipate behavior patterns in the future.

3. Data mining techniques also help to distinguish between profitable and non-profitable customers.
4. Data mining techniques help to distinguish between the borrowers who repay loans promptly from those who do not.
5. Organization's executives by using data mining technique can also analyze the behavior and reliability of the customers while selling cards related products. It also helps to analyze whether the customer will make prompt or delay payment if the credit cards are sold to them.

Thus organizations using the tools and techniques of data mining can be able to answer the following questions:

- ***Which segment of population is most likely to respond to a particular service?***
- ***Whether two market segments have similar characteristics?***
- ***Identifying the level (satisfaction) of a particular product/service***
- ***Ideal conditions for launching a new product/service.***

Data Mining helps to increase sales by targeting the right customers and to make the right offers to customers. Organizations, who have their ears to the ground regarding their customer's tastes and preferences, gather a lot of data. What data mining does is that it filters through all the huge data and chalk out a pattern, which enable the organization to personalize its communication towards the customer as much as possible. With data mining, organizations can get a better understanding of what drives the customer relationship

5.4 DATA MINING LIFE CYCLE

The life cycle of a data mining project consists of six phases. The sequence of the phases is not rigid. Moving back and forth between different phases may be required. It depends on the outcome of each phase. The main phases are:

1. **Business Understanding:** This phase focuses on understanding the project objectives and requirements from a business perspective, then converting this knowledge into a data mining problem definition and a preliminary plan is designed to achieve the objectives.
2. **Data Understanding:** It starts with an initial data collection, to get familiar with the data, to identify data quality problems, to discover first insights into the data or to detect interesting subsets to form hypotheses for hidden information.
3. **Data Preparation:** It covers all activities to construct the final dataset from the initial raw data. In this step the data received from various distributed, heterogeneous and varied sources is collected and after removing the dirty data, the data from various sources is combined into a particular form as per the requirements of the user and business.
4. **Modeling:** In this phase, various modeling techniques are selected and applied and their parameters are calibrated to optimal values.

5. **Evaluation:** In this stage the model is thoroughly evaluated and reviewed. The steps executed to construct the model should make it sure that it properly achieves the business objectives. At the end of this phase, a decision on the use of the data mining results should be reached.
6. **Deployment:** The purpose of the model is to increase knowledge of the data, the knowledge gained is to be organized and presented in a way that the customer can use it. The deployment phase can be as simple as generating a report or as complex as implementing a repeatable data mining process across the enterprise.

5.5 TYPES OF DATA USED IN A DATA WAREHOUSE

Technically data mining is not specific to any one type of media or data. Data mining can be applied to any kind of data. The most common forms of data for data mining are ***database data, data warehouse data and transactional data***. But the techniques of data mining can be applied to other types of data also, like:

- ***Data Streams***
- ***Ordered/Sequence Data***
- ***Graph or Networked Data***
- ***Spatial Data***
- ***Multimedia Data***
- ***Different types of databases, including relational databases, object-relational databases and object-oriented databases,***
- ***Data Warehouse***
- ***Unstructured and Semi-structured repositories such as the World Wide Web***
- ***Time-Series Databases***
- ***Textual Databases and***
- ***Flat Files.***

However, algorithms and approaches may differ when applied to different types of data. The various types of data used in data mining is:

Flat Files: Flat files are actually the most common data source for data mining algorithms, especially at the research level. Flat files are simple data files in text or binary format with a structure known by the data mining algorithm to be applied. The data in these files can be transactions, time-series data, scientific measurements, etc.

Database Data or Relational Databases: A database system is also known as database management system consists of a collection of interrelated data, known as database, and a set of programs to manage and access the data. The software programs provide the facility for defining and implementing database and data storage structures, for defining methods for concurrent, shared or distributed access and for ensuring consistency and security of information.

A relational database consists of a set of tables, consisting of set of *attributes* (depicted as table columns) and *tuples* (depicted as table rows). An entity relationship model is constructed for relational data bases; such a model shows entities, their attributes and the relationship between the entities. Table 5.2 (a) to (c) present some relations in a Student Data Base, namely Student, Teacher, Projects showing the activity of a project allocation system. These entities have following attributes:

Student (Registration-Number, Name, Course, Contact-Number, Email-id)

Teacher (TID, Teacher-Name, Designation, Contact-number, Department, Email-id)

Project (Project-ID, Project-name, Number of students, Technology used, Project Leader, Project Guide)

Table 5.2(a) Student Data Base, *Relation: Student*

Registration-Number	Name	Course	Contact-Number	Email-id
101010	Ajay	MCA	9867779000	ajay@gmail.com
101110	Sanjana	MCA	981234589	sanjana@gmail.com

Table 5.2(b) Student Data Base, *Relation: Teacher*

TID	Teacher-Name	Designation	Contact-Number	Department	Email-id
1010	Gurpal	AP	919191919	CS	gurpal@gmail.com

Table 5.2(c) Student Data Base, *Relation: Project*

Project-ID	Project-name	Number of students	Technology used	Project Leader	Project Guide
12	Hotel Mgt.	3	.net	Sameer	Gurpal

The data in relational scheme can be extracted by using database queries and the most commonly used query language for relational database is SQL, which allows retrieval and manipulation of the data stored in the tables, as well as the calculation of aggregate functions such as average, sum, min, max and count. For instance, an SQL query to select the number of projects in .net technology can be obtained as:

Select count(*) from Projects Where technology = .net GROUP BY technologyused.

Data mining algorithms using relational databases can be more versatile than data mining algorithms specifically written for flat files, since they can take advantage of the structure inherent to relational databases. While data mining can benefit from SQL for data selection, transformation and consolidation, it goes beyond what SQL could provide, such as predicting, comparing, detecting deviations, etc.

Data Warehouses: A data warehouse as a storehouse is a repository of data collected from multiple data sources (*often heterogeneous*) and is intended to be used as a whole under the same unified schema. A data warehouse gives the option to analyze data from different sources under the same roof. Data warehouse is build via a process of data cleaning, data integration, data transformation, data loading and periodic refreshing of data. The data in data warehouse is organized over a number of subject areas, and provides information from historical prospective. Let us suppose that franchises belonging to same company may have different databases and different structures. If the executive of the company wants to access the data from all stores for strategic decision-making, future direction, marketing, etc., it would be more appropriate to store all the data in one site with a homogeneous structure that allows interactive analysis. In other words, data from the different stores would be loaded, cleaned, transformed and integrated together.

To facilitate decision-making and multi-dimensional views, data warehouses are usually modeled by a *multi-dimensional data structure*. Data in a data warehouse is modeled by multidimensional data structure known as a *data cube* in which each dimension corresponds to an attribute or a set of attributes in the schema. A data cube provides multidimensional view of data and allows fast access of summarized data.

Example: 3-D Data Cube: This types of data cubes allow the data to be viewed on a third dimension also, like the user wish to view the same sales data on the basis of location also. These 3-D data cubes are represented as a series of 2-D tables (as shown in Table 5.3) or can be represented as a 3-D cube (as shown in Fig. 5.2).

Items for location = 'Ludhiana' **Items for location = 'Amritsar"** **Items for location = 'New Delhi"**

Table 5.3: 3-D view of sales data according to Time, Item and Location.

	Items for location = 'Ludhiana'			Items for location = 'Amritsar"			Items for location = 'New Delhi"		
Time	Computer	Cell Phone	LCD	Computer	Cell Phone	LCD	Computer	Cell Phone	LCD
Quarter I	676	234	90	555	789	666	500	876	234
Quarter II	564	245	235	345	456	457	560	777	678
Quarter III	245	777	123	345	123	253	765	888	456

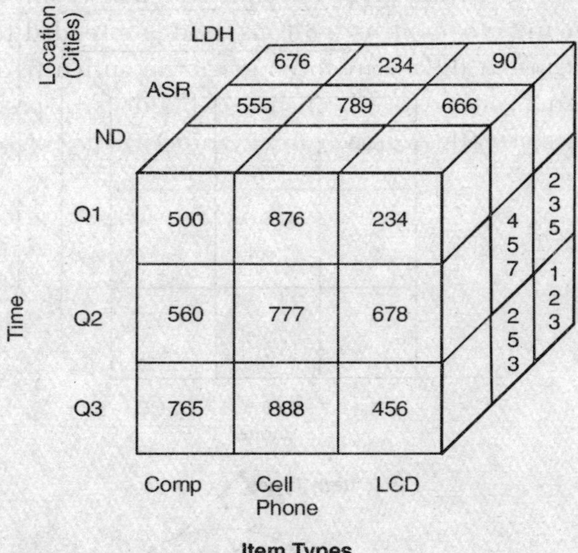

Fig. 5.2: 3-D Data Cube representation of the data, according to Time, Item & Location

As data warehouse helps in providing multidimensional views of data and hence can be used successfully for online analytical processing. And various OLAP operations can be performed on the data cube, some of these operations are drill-down and roll-up, slice which provides the user with the customized views of the data.

Roll –Up: The roll-up operation is also termed as ***drill-up operation***. It is performed by aggregating the data cube either by climbing up a concept hierarchy for a dimension or by dimension reduction. Fig. 5.3 shows the roll-up operation performed on the base cube by climbing up the concept hierarchy for the location. The roll-up operation shows aggregation of data by ascending the location hierarchy from the level of city to the level of state. In spite of grouping the data by city, the resulting cube groups the data by state. In case the roll-up operation is performed by dimension reduction, then one or more dimensions are removed from the given cube. Like if the data cube is structured based on the dimensions location and time, then the roll-up operation may be performed by removing either of the dimension, like the user has removed the location dimension, then the data cube will show the data on the basis of time only.

**Other OLAP operations, drill-down, slice, dice and pivot have already been explained in Chapter 2.*

Transactional Databases: A transaction database is a set of records representing transactions, each with a time stamp, an identifier and a set of items. Associated with the transaction files could also be descriptive data for the items. The data about customer's purchase, issue of books from library, amount withdrawn from a bank account or a click on a web page. A transaction is identified by a transaction id. Transactions can be stored in a table with one record per transaction. A snap shot of transactional data base is shown below in the Table 5.4, the library department stores the list of books issued in a transactional database as:

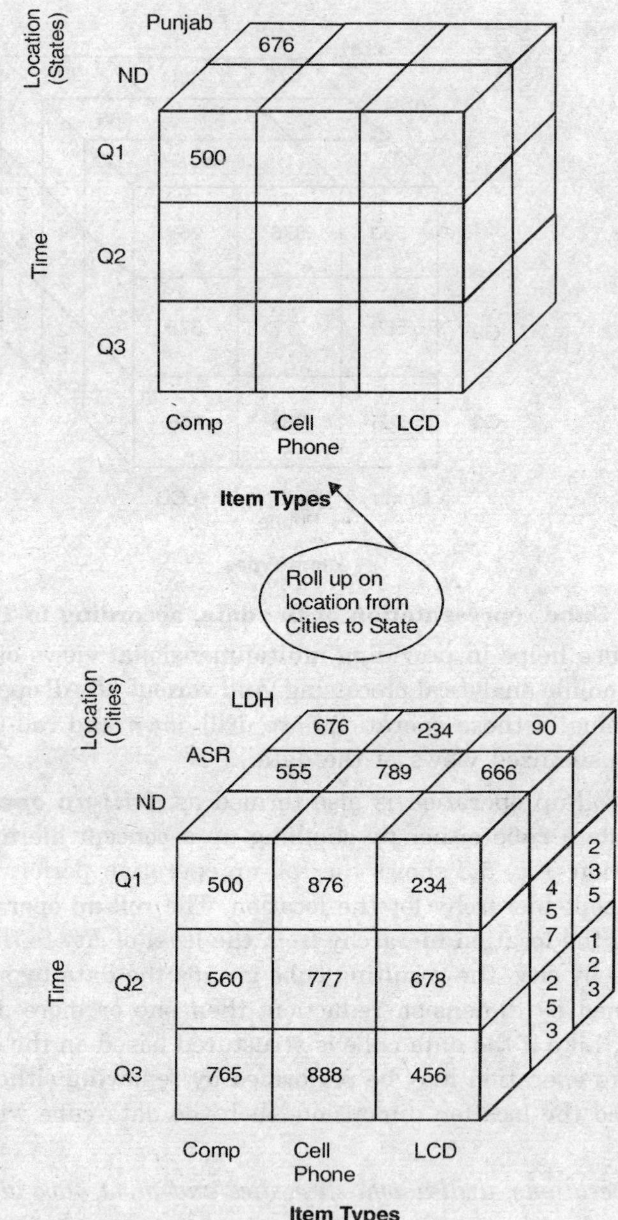

Fig. 5.3: Roll Up Operation

Table 5.4: A Snapshot of Transactional Database

Transaction ID	Rollno	NOB Issued	Date of Issue
101010	12378	2	23-04-13
101011	56234	1	24-04-13

Multimedia Databases: Multimedia databases include videos, images, audio and text media. They can be stored on extended object-relational or object-oriented databases, or simply on a file system. Multimedia is characterized by its high dimensionality, which makes data mining even more challenging. Data mining from multimedia repositories may require *computer vision, computer graphics, image interpretation, and natural language processing methodologies*.

Spatial Databases: Spatial databases are databases that, in addition to usual data, store geographical information like maps, and global or regional positioning. Such spatial databases present new challenges to data mining algorithms.

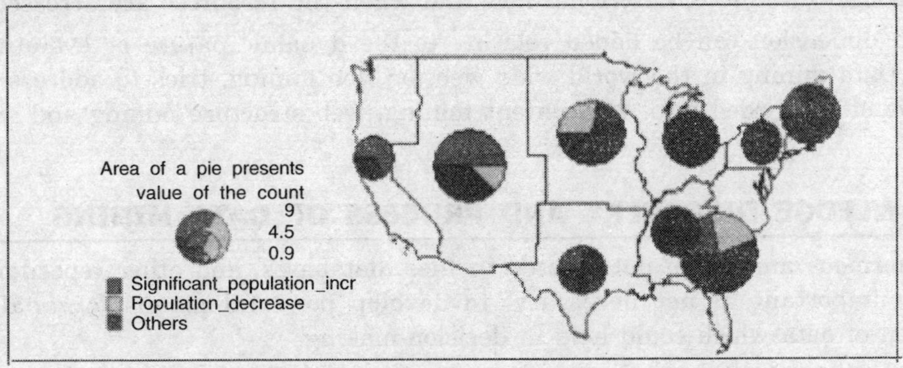

Fig. 5.4: A Snapshot of Spatial Database

Time-Series Databases: Time-series databases contain time related data such as stock market data or logged activities. These databases usually have a continuous flow of new data coming in, which sometimes causes the need for a challenging real time analysis. Data mining in such databases commonly includes the study of trends and correlations between evolutions of different variables, as well as the prediction of trends and movements of the variables in time. Fig. 5.5 shows some examples of time-series data.

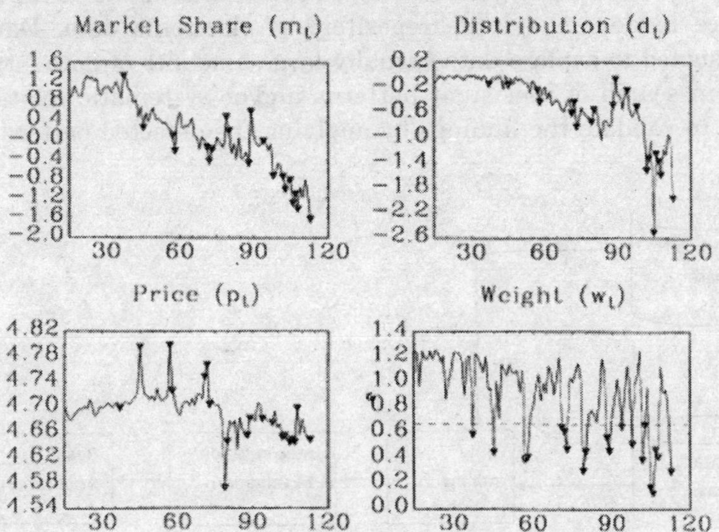

Fig. 5.5: A Snapshot of Time-Series Database

World Wide Web: The World Wide Web is the most heterogeneous and dynamic repository available. A very large number of authors and publishers are continuously contributing to its growth and a massive number of users are accessing its resources daily. Data in the World Wide Web is organized in inter-connected documents. These documents can be text, audio, video, raw data, and even applications. Conceptually, the World Wide Web is comprised of three major components:

- *the content of the web*, which encompasses documents available;
- *the structure of the web*, which covers the hyperlinks and the relationships between documents; and
- *the usage of the web*, describing how and when the resources are accessed.

A fourth dimension can be added relating to the dynamic nature or evolution of the documents. Data mining in the world wide web, or web mining, tries to address all these issues and is often divided into web content mining, web structure mining and web usage mining.

5.6 KNOWLEDGE DISCOVERY AND PROCESS OF DATA MINING

With the enormous amount of data stored in files, databases, and other repositories, it is increasingly important, if not necessary, to develop powerful means for analysis and interpretation of data which could help in decision-making.

Data Mining, is also known as *Knowledge Discovery in Databases* (KDD), refers to the nontrivial extraction of implicit, previously unknown and potentially useful information from data in databases. While data mining and knowledge discovery in databases (or KDD) are frequently treated as synonyms, data mining is actually part of the knowledge discovery process.

Data Mining Process

Data mining is a process of analyzing data using powerful analysis tools capable of extracting business intelligence hidden in a large repository of electronic data. Data Mining is an analytic process designed to explore data (usually large amounts of data - typically business or market related) in search of consistent patterns and/or systematic relationships between variables, and then to validate the findings by applying the detected patterns to new subsets of data.

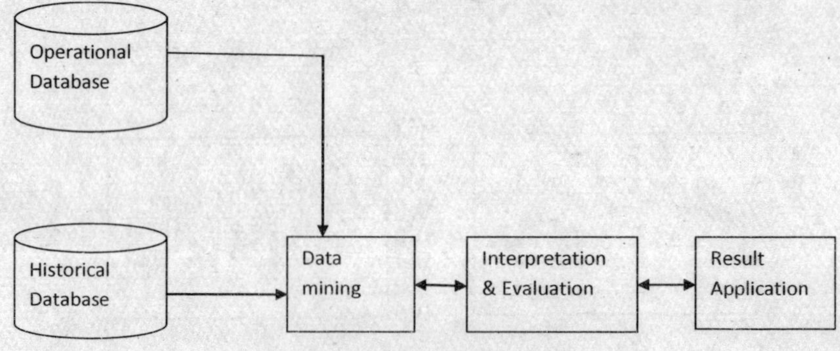

Fig. 5.6: Process of Data Mining

Data mining is developed with the goal of providing tools for automatically and intelligently transforming large amount of data in knowledge relevant to users. The extracted knowledge is often expressed in the form of association rules decision tress or clusters that allows one to find interesting patterns buried deeply in the data which facilitate decision making process.

Data Mining is operated on a data warehouse model of gathering all the data into central site, then running an algorithm against that data.

The following Fig. 5.7 shows data mining as a step in an iterative knowledge discovery process. The Knowledge Discovery in Databases comprises of a few steps leading from raw data collections to some form of new knowledge. During this whole process the original raw data passes through various stages and finally it comes out as knowledge and this transistion is shown in the Fig. 5.8. The iterative process consists of the following steps:

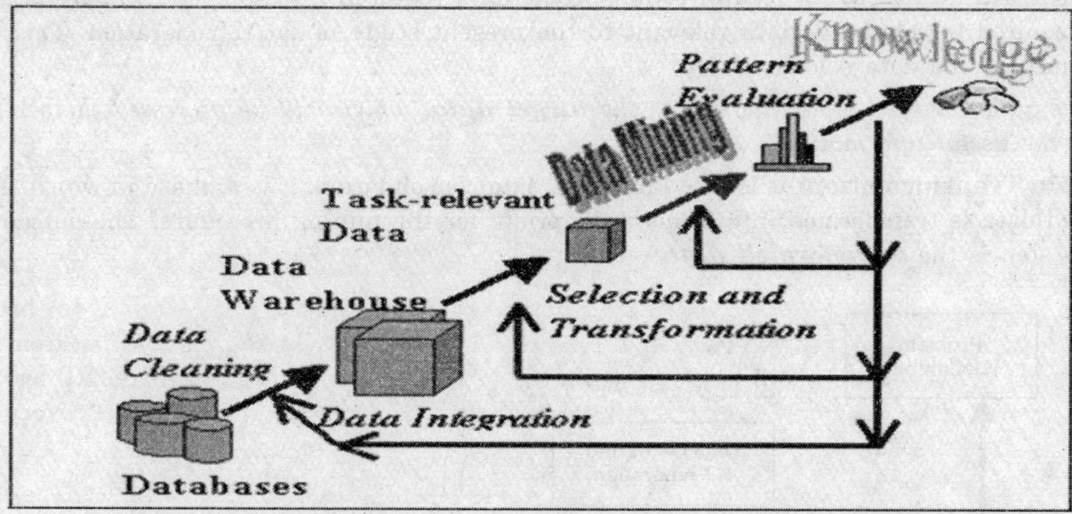

Fig. 5.7: Data Mining as a Part of Knowledge Discovery Process

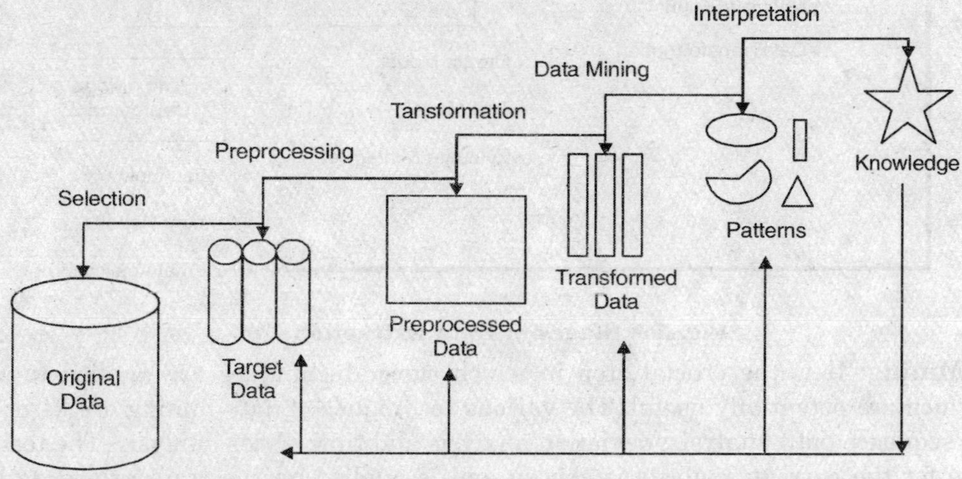

Fig. 5.8: Stages of Data during Knowledge Discovery Process

Data Cleaning: This step is also known as *data cleansing*, it is a phase in which noise data and irrelevant data is removed from the data collected. Most of the times, the real-world data tend to be incomplete, noisy and inconsistent. Data cleaning routines attempt to ûll in the missing values, smooth out noise while identifying outliers, and correct inconsistencies in the data. Data cleaning is usually performed as an iterative two-step process consisting of *discrepancy detection and data transformation.*

Data Integration: At this stage, the data collected from multiple heterogeneous sources is combined in a common source.

After these two steps, the original raw data is converted into the form which can be used for further processing and the data now can be treated as ***clean data****.*

Data Selection: All the data stored in the data repositories is not required all the time. The user will always be in need of some specific data required for the current analysis, so it is required to select the data relevant to the present study under consideration. This is performed at the data selection step.

The data obtained after this step is the ***target data****, which will be processed further to derive the useful information.*

Data Transformation: It is also known as data consolidation, it is a phase in which the selected data is transformed into forms appropriate for the mining procedure. The outcome of this step is the ***transformed data***.

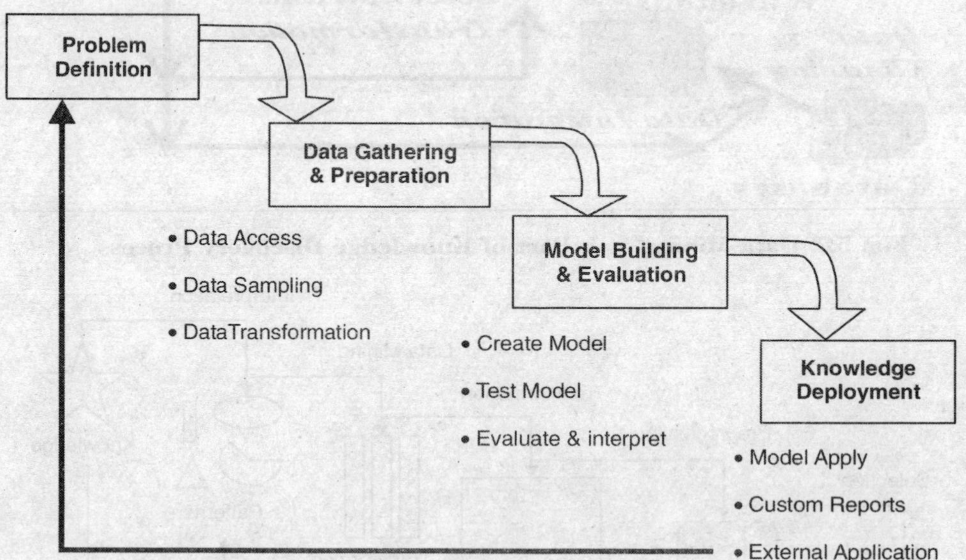

Fig. 5.9: Stages of Data Extraction

Data Mining: It is the crucial step in which clever techniques are applied to extract patterns which are potentially useful. The various techniques of data mining are association, clustering, sequence path analysis, deviation analysis and time series analysis. The technique appropriate for the current analysis is chosen and is applied on the transformed data.

Pattern evaluation: In this step, strictly interesting patterns representing knowledge are identified based on given measures.

Knowledge Representation: It is the final phase in which the discovered knowledge is visually represented to the user. This essential step uses visualization techniques to help users understand and interpret the data mining results.

The final outcome is the ***knowledge*** extracted through this knowledge discovery process.

Some of the steps in this whole process can be combined together. For instance, *Data Cleaning* and *Data Integration* can be performed together as a pre-processing phase to generate a data warehouse. *Data Selection and Data Transformation* can also be combined where the consolidation of the data is the result of the selection, or, as for the case of data warehouses, the selection is done on transformed data.

The KDD is an iterative process. Once the discovered knowledge is presented to the user, the evaluation measures can be enhanced, the mining can be further refined, new data can be selected or further transformed, or new data sources can be integrated, in order to get different, more appropriate results.

5.7 THE KNOWLEDGE DISCOVERY PROCESS

Knowledge Discovery in Databases KDD is defined as: the non-trivial process of identifying valid, novel, potentially useful, and ultimately understandable patterns in the data. Data mining is one of the tasks in the process of knowledge discovery from the databases. It combines techniques from many fields, including databases, artificial intelligence, statistics and visualization. The process itself has many stages and is highly iterative. It concerns the entire knowledge extraction process, including how data is stored and accessed, how to use efficient and scalable algorithms to analyze massive datasets, how to interpret and visualize the results and how to model and support the interactions between human and machine. The knowledge discovery process developed by Cios et al (source: http://www.crisp-dm.org/) consists of following steps:

1. Understanding of the Problem Domain: The first and the foremost step in knowledge discovery is developing and understanding of the application domain and the goals from business and user's perspective. The large numbers of users in the organization normally have conflicting requirements, and then the need is to construct a common set of requirements acceptable to all users. At this stage the organizational requirements always get higher priority over the individual requirements. This step converts the requirements collected into data mining problem definition and designs the preliminary project plan to achieve the objectives. This step requires high degree of analytical and logical interpersonal and intrapersonal skills.

2. Understanding of the Data: This step begins with initial data collection and familiarization with the data. The data set relevant for the analysis is selected from the large and huge database. It begins with an initial insight into the data and detection of interesting data subsets. Data collected is checked for completeness, redundancy, missing values and plausibility of attribute values. It can be visualized as a combination of following activities:

- Collection of initial data.
- Description of data.
- Exploration of data.
- Verification of data quality.

3. Preparation of the Data: This step covers all activities needed to construct the final datasets, which will be fed into data mining tools in the subsequent steps. It begins with selection of data relevant to the application under consideration, cleaning of data to remove noisy, dirty and irrelevant data from the collection, using transformation methods to reduce the search space and deriving new attributes, combining heterogeneous data items from multiple data sources into one source and then formatting it according to the requirements. The cleaned data may further be processed by feature selection and extraction algorithms (to reduce dimensionality) by derivation of new attributes and summarization of data.

4. Data Mining: It is a crucial step in which clever techniques are applied to extract potentially useful patterns. This decision depends upon the goal of the KDD process, the type of data and techniques available. Data mining tasks include discovering association rules, sequential patterns, and time sequences, predicting a classification, discovering clusters and predicting values. Further the selection also depends on the goal of the process, i.e. whether it is predictive, descriptive, etc.

5. Evaluation of the discovered Knowledge: It includes understanding the results, checking whether the discovered knowledge is novel and interesting or not. The knowledge discovered is interpreted by domain experts and then the impact of discovered knowledge is checked. In this step, interesting patterns representing knowledge are identified based on given measures. The identification and analysis of the patterns relevant to the individual and organization is quite cumbersome task and it requires high degree of expertise.

6. Use of the discovered knowledge: It is the final phase in which the discovered knowledge is visually presented to the user. This essential step uses visualization techniques to help users to understand and interpret the data mining results.

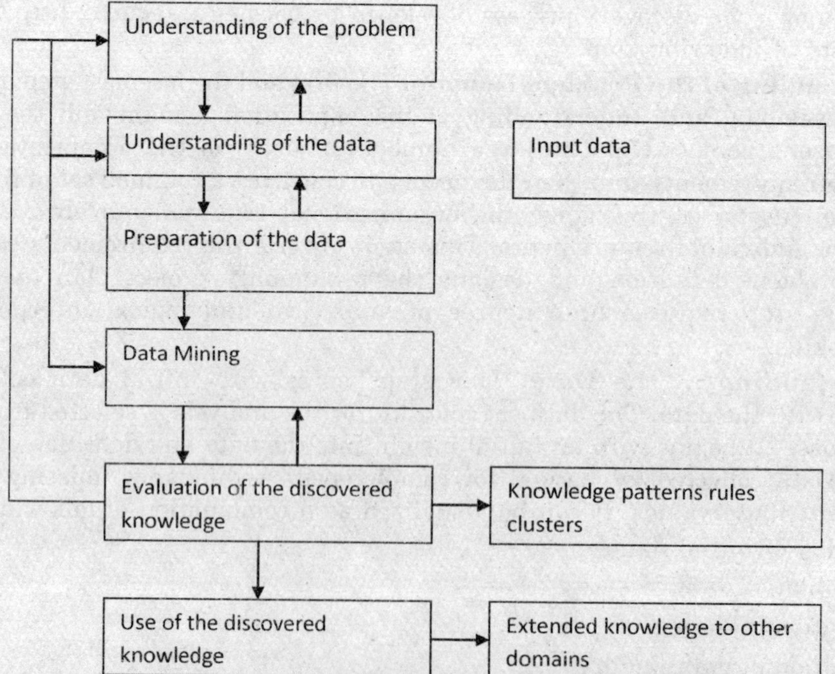

Fig. 5.10: The Knowledge Discovery Process Model

KDD is an iterative process: the results of one step may mean that a previous step needs to be revisited. Although the computation of data mining step is usually the most expensive one, the choices made in these steps depend on the domain knowledge of the user and can have a great influence on the quality of the outcome of the KDD process.

5.8 DATA MINING VS QUERY TOOLS

Query Tools are tools that help analyze the data in a database. They provide query building, query editing, searching, reporting and summarizing functionalities. On the other hand, data mining is a field in computer science, which deals with the extraction of previously unknown and interesting information from raw data. Data stored in databases is used as the input for the data mining process. Users who are inclined towards statistics use Data Mining. They utilize statistical models to look for hidden patterns in data. Data miners are interested in finding useful relationships between different data elements, which is ultimately profitable for businesses.

Data Mining

Data mining is also known as Knowledge Discovery in Data (KDD). As mentioned above, it is a field of computer science, which deals with the extraction of previously unknown and interesting information from raw data. Due to the exponential growth of data, especially in areas such as business, data mining has become very important tool to convert this large wealth of data in to business intelligence, as manual extraction of patterns has become seemingly impossible in the past few decades. For example, it is currently been used for various applications such as social network analysis, fraud detection and marketing. Data mining usually deals with following four tasks: clustering, classification, regression, and association. Clustering is identifying similar groups from unstructured data. Classification is learning rules that can be applied to new data and will typically include following steps: preprocessing of data, designing modeling, learning/feature selection and Evaluation/validation. Regression is finding functions with minimal error to model data. And association is looking for relationships between variables. Data mining is usually used to answer questions like what are the main products that might help to obtain high profit next year.

Query Tools

Query Tools are tools that help to analyze the data in a database. Usually these query tools have a GUI front end with convenient ways to input queries as a set of attributes. Once these inputs are provided the tool generates actual queries made up of the underlying query language used by the database. SQL, T-SQL and PL/SQL are examples of query languages used in many popular databases today. Then, these generated queries are executed against the databases and the results of the queries are presented or reported to the user in an organized and clear manner. Typically, the user does not need to know a database-specific query language to use a query tool. Key features of query tools are integrated query builder and editor, summary reports and figures, import and export features and advanced find/ search capabilities.

What is the difference between Data Mining and Query Tools?

Query tools can be used to easily build and input queries to databases. Query tools make it very easy to build queries without even having to learn a database-specific query language. On the other hand, Data Mining is a technique or a concept in computer science, which deals with extracting useful and previously unknown information from raw data. Most of the times, these raw data are stored in very large databases. Therefore data miners can use the existing functionalities of query Tools to preprocess raw data before the data mining process. However, the main difference between data mining techniques and using query tools is that, ***in order to use query tools the users need to know exactly what they are looking for, while data mining is used mostly when the user has a vague idea about what they are looking for.***

5.9 CLASSIFICATION OF DATA MINING SYSTEMS

There are many data mining systems available or are being developed. Some are specialized systems dedicated to a given data source or are confined to limited data mining functionalities, other are more versatile and comprehensive. Data mining systems can be categorized according to various criterias and classifications as follows:

1. **Classification of data mining systems according to the type of data source mined:** This classification is according to the type of data handled such as spatial data, multimedia data, time-series data, text data, World Wide Web, etc.
2. **Classification of data mining systems according to the data model:** This classification is based on the data model involved such as relational database, object-oriented database, data warehouse, transactional database, etc.
3. **Classification of data mining systems according to the kind of knowledge discovered:** This classification is based on the kind of knowledge discovered or data mining functionalities, such as characterization, discrimination, association, classification, clustering, etc. Some systems tend to be comprehensive systems offering several data mining functionalities together.
4. **Classification of data mining systems according to mining techniques used:** This classification is according to the data analysis approach used such as machine learning, neural networks, genetic algorithms, statistics and visualization techniques.

5.10 ARCHITECTURES OF DATA MINING SYSTEM

With popular and diverse applications of data mining, it is expected that a good variety of data mining systems will be designed and developed in future years. For designing a successful data mining systems, the architecture and design of a data mining system is critically important. A good system architecture and design will facilitate the system to make best use of the software environment, accomplish data mining tasks in an efficient and timely manner and will facilitate the exchange of information with other information systems, and will adapt to user's diverse requirements hanging with the passage of time. A huge amount of data and information have been stored and integrated in data warehouse systems. Moreover, comprehensive information processing and data analysis infrastructure have been or will be continuously and semantically constructed surrounding database systems and data warehouses. These include accessing, integrating, consolidation, and transformation of multiple, heterogeneous databases, ODBC/OLE DB connections web-accessing and service facilities and reporting and OLAP analysis tools.

Under this situation, a critical question in the design of a data mining system becomes whether we should couple or integrate a data mining (DM) system with a data base system and/or a data

warehouse (DW)system , and if we should, how to do it correctly? To answer these questions, we need to examine the possible ways of coupling or integrating a DM system and a DB/DW system. Based on different architecture designs, a DM system can be integrated with a DB/DW system using the following coupling schemes-

- *No Coupling.*
- *Loose Coupling.*
- *Semi-tight Coupling and*
- *Tight coupling.*

No Coupling: No coupling means that a data mining system will not utilize any function of a data base or data warehouse system. It may fetch data from a particular source (such as a file system), process data using some data mining algorithm, and then store the mining results in another file. Such a system, though simple, suffers from several drawbacks.

- A database system provides a great deal of flexibility and efficiency at storing, organizing, accessing, and processing data. Without using a data base or warehouse system, a data mining system may spend a substantial amount of time finding, collecting, cleaning, and transforming data.
- In database or warehouse systems, data tend to be well organized, indexed, cleaned, integrated, or consolidated, so that finding the task-relevant, high-quality data becomes an easy task.
- There are many tested, scalable algorithms and data structures implemented in data base and warehouse systems. It is feasible to realize efficient, scalable implementations using such systems.
- Most of the data have been or will be stored in data base or warehouse systems. Without any coupling of such systems, a data mining system will need to use other tools to extract data, making it difficult to integrate such a system into an information processing environment.

In the nutshell, no coupling represents a poor design.

Loose Coupling: Loose coupling means that a data mining system will use some facilities of a database or data warehouse system, fetching data from a data repository managed by these systems, performing data mining, and then storing the mining results either in a file or at a specified place in a database or data warehouse.

- Loose coupling is better than no coupling since it can fetch any portion of data stored in databases or data warehouses by using query processing.

- It provide advantages of the flexibility, efficiency, and other features provided by such systems. However, many loosely coupled mining systems are mainly memory-based. Since mining itself does not explore data structures and query optimization methods provided by database or data warehouse systems.
- The major problem with loose coupling is that it is difficult to achieve high scalability and good performance with large data sets.

Semi tight Coupling: Semi tight coupling means that besides linking a data mining system to a data base and data warehouse system, efficient implementations of a few identical data mining functions can be provided in the data base or data warehouse system. These primitives can include sorting, indexing, aggregation, histogram analysis, multilayer join, and precipitation of some essential statistical measures, such as sum, count, max, min, standard deviation and so on. Moreover, some frequently used intermediate mining results can be pre-computed and stored in the data base and data warehouse system. Since these intermediate mining results are either pre-computed or can be computed efficiently, this design will enhance the performance of a data mining system.

Tight Coupling: Tight coupling means that a data mining system is smoothly integrated into the data base or data warehouse system. The data mining subsystem is treated as one functional component of an information system. Data mining queries and functions are optimized based on mining query analyses, data structures, indexing schemes, and query processing methods of a database and data warehouse system. With further technology advances, data mining, database, and data warehouse systems will evolve and integrate together as one information system with multiple functionalities. This will provide a uniform information processing environment. This approach is highly desirable since it facilitates efficient implementations of data mining functions, high system performance, and an integrated information processing environment. With this analysis, one can see that mining system should be coupled with database/data warehouse system.

Loose coupling, though not efficient, is better than no coupling since it makes use of both data and system facilities of a database system. Tight coupling is highly desirable, but its implementation is nontrivial and more research is needed in the area. Semi tight coupling is a compromise between loose and tight coupling. It is important to identify commonly used data mining primitives and provide efficient implementations of such primitives in DB or DW systems.

5.11 DATA MINING LANGUAGES

Data mining query language is designed to support the features that make the data mining an interactive process. The importance of the design of a good data mining query language can also be obtained by observing the history of relational data base systems. Relational data base systems have dominated the database market for decades. The standardization of relational query languages, which occurred at the early stages of relational database development, is widely credited for the success of the relational database field. The standardization of relational query languages provided a foundation on which relational systems were developed and evolved. It facilitated information exchange and technology transfer, and promoted commercialization and wide acceptance of relational database technology. The recent standardization activities in database systems, such as work relating to SQL-3, and so on, further illustrate the importance of having a standard database language for success of development and commercialization of database systems. Hence, having a good query language for data mining may help in standardizing the development of platforms for data mining systems.

Designing a comprehensive data mining language is challenging because data mining covers a wide spectrum of tasks, from data characterization to mining association rules, data classification, and evolution analysis. Each task has different requirements and the design of an effective data mining query language requires a deep understanding of the power, limitation, and underlying mechanisms of the various kinds of data mining tasks. How would we design a data mining query language? It depends on:

- The set of task-relevant data to be mined.
- The kind of knowledge to be mined.
- The background knowledge to be used in the discovery process.
- The interestingness measures and thresholds for pattern evolution.
- The expected representation for visualizing the discovered patterns.

Based on these primitives, we design a query language for data mining called DMQL (data mining query language), DMQL allows the ad hoc mining of several kinds of knowledge from relational databases and data warehouses at multiple levels of abstraction. The language adopts an SQL-like syntax, so that it can easily be integrated with the relational query language SQL.

Various ways of using DM Query Language are

Syntax for Task-Relevant Data Specifications: The first step in defining a data-mining task is the specification of the task-relevant data, that is the data on which mining is to be performed. This involves specifying the database and tables or data warehouse containing the relevant data, conditions for selecting the relevant data, the relevant attributes or dimensions for exploration, and instructions regarding the order or grouping of the data retried.

DMQL provides clauses for the specification of such information, as follows:

- *use database (database_name) or use the data warehouse (data_warehouse_name): the use clause directs the mining task to the database or data warehouse specified.*
- *from (relation (s)/cubes(s)) [ware (condition)]: the from and where clauses respectively specify the database tables or data cubes involved, and the conditions defining the data to be retrieved*
- *In relevance to (attribute_or_dimensionlist): This clause lists the attributes or dimensions for exploration.*
- *Order by (order list): The order by clause specifies the sorting order of the task-relevant data.*
- *group by (grouping_list): The group by clause specifies criteria for grouping the data. Having (condition):*
- *having clause specifies the condition by which groups of Data are considered relevant.These clauses form an SQL query to collect the task-relevant data.*

Syntax for Specifying the Kind of Knowledge to be mined: The (Mine_Knowledge_Specification) statement is used to specify the kind of knowledge to be mined. In other words, it indicates the data mining functionality to be performed. Its syntax is defined below for characterization, discrimination, association, and classification. Characterization:

(Mine_Knowledge_Specification) ::

=mine characteristics [as (pattern_name)]

For [target_classn where atarget_condition]

{versus[contrast_class_i] where[constrast_condition_i]}

Analyze (measure(s))

This specifies that characteristic descriptions are to be mined. The analyze clause, when used for characterization, specifies aggregate measure, such as count, sum, or count%(percentage count, i.e., the percentage of tuples in the relevant data set with the specified (characteristics).

Syntax for Concept Hierarchy: Specification Concept hierarchies allow the mining of knowledge at multiple levels of abstraction. In order to accommodate the different viewpoints of users with regard to the data, there may be more than one concept hierarchy per attribute or dimension. For instance, some users may prefer to organize branch locations by provinces and states, while others may prefer to organize them according to languages used. In such cases, a user can indicate which concept hierarchy is to be used with statement.

use hierarchy (hierarchy_name) for {attribute _or_dimension)

Otherwise, a default hierarchy per attribute or dimension is used.

Syntax for Interestingness Measure Specification: The user can help control the number of uninteresting patterns returned by the data mining system by specifying measures of pattern interestingness and their corresponding thresholds. Interestingness measures and thresholds can be specified be the user with the statement

with [(interest_measure_name)] threshold-(threshold_value)

Syntax for Pattern Presentation and Visualization Specification: "How can users specify the forms of presentation and visualization to be used in displaying the discovered patterns?" Our data mining query language needs syntax that allows users to specify the display of discovered patterns in one or more forms, including rules, tables, cross tabs, pie or bar charts, decision trees ,cubes ,curves or surfaces-We define the DMQL display statement for this purpose;

display a (Result _form) Where the (result_form) could be any of the knowledge presentation or visualization forms listed above.

Interactive mining should allow the discovered patterns to be viewed at different concept levels or from different angles. This can be accomplished with roll-up and drill-down operations. Patterns can be rolled up, or viewed at a more general level, by climbing up the concept hierarchy of an attribute or dimension (replacing lower-level concept values by higher-level values). Dropping attributes or dimensions can also perform generalization. For example, a pattern contains the attribute city given the location hierarchy city < state<country <continent, then dropping the attribute, state, the patterns can be drilled down on, or viewed at a less

general level, by stepping down the concept hierarchy of an attribute or dimension patterns can also be made less general by adding attributes or dimensions to their description. The attribute added must be one of the attributes listed in the in relevance to clause for task-relevant specification. The user can alternately view the patterns at different levels of abstractions with the use of following DMQL syntax:

(Multilevel_Manapulation)::= roll up on

(attribute_or_dimension)

|drill down on (attribute_or_dimension)

|add (attribute_or_dimension)

|drop(attribute_or_dimension)

Designing Graphical User Interfaces Based on a Data Mining Query Language: A data mining query language provides necessary primitives that allow users to communicate with data mining systems. However, inexperienced users may find data mining query languages difficult to use and remember. Instead, users may prefer to communicate with data mining systems through a graphical user interface (GUI). In relational data base technology, SQL serves as a standard "core" language for relational systems, on top of which GUI's can easily be designed. Similarly, a data mining query language may serve as a "core language" for data mining system implementation providing a basis for the development of GUI's for effective data mining. A data mining GUI may consist of the following functional components:

- *Data collection and data mining query compositions*: This component allows the user to specify task-relevant data sets and to compose data mining queries. It is similar to GUI's used for the specification of relational queries.
- *Presentations of discovered patterns*: This component allows the display of the discovered patterns in various forms, including tables, graphs, charts, curves and other visualization techniques.
- *Hierarchy specification and manipulation*: This component allows for concept hierarchy specification, either manually by the user or automatically (based on analysis of the data at hand). In addition, this component should allow concept hierarchies to be modified by the user or adjusted automatically based on the given data set distribution.
- *Manipulation of data mining primitives*: This component may allow the dynamic adjustment of the data mining thresholds, as well as the selection, display and modification of concept hierarchies. It may also allow the modification of previous data mining queries or conditions.
- *Interactive multilevel mining*: This component should allow roll-up or drill-down operations on discovered patterns.
- *Other miscellaneous information*: This component may include on-line help manuals indexed search, debugging, and other interactive graphical facilities. The design of a graphical user interface should also take into consideration different classes of users of a data mining system. In general, Users of data mining systems can be classified into two categories: *Business analysts and Business executives*: Business analysts would like to have flexibility and convenience in selecting different portions of the

data manipulating dimensions and levels, setting mining parameters, and tuning data mining processes. On the other hand, a business executive needs clear presentation and interpretation of data mining results, flexibility in viewing and comparing different data mining results and easy integration of data mining results. A well-designed data mining systems should provide friendly user interfaces for both kinds of users.

Standardization of Data Mining Language Primitives: Apart from DMQL the research is going on to design other data mining languages which can be used for multiple platforms. The standardization will help to strengthen the development of data mining platforms and will facilitate the sharing of data mining results.

MSQL is a data mining query language proposed by Imielinski and Virmani. The language uses SQL like syntax and SQL primitives including sorting and group-by. As a number of rules can be generated in data mining, MSQL provides the options like GetRules and SelectRules for both the rule generation and rule selection.

Other research efforts on data mining language design include the **MINERULE** operator, proposed by Meo, Psaila and Ceri. It follows SQL like syntax and serves as rule generation queries for mining association rules.

Microsoft proposed a data mining language called **OLE DB** for data mining. This is considered as a notable step towards standardization.

CRISP (Cross Industry Standard Process for Data Mining) is another standardization effort related to data mining.

5.12 DATA MINING TECHNIQUES

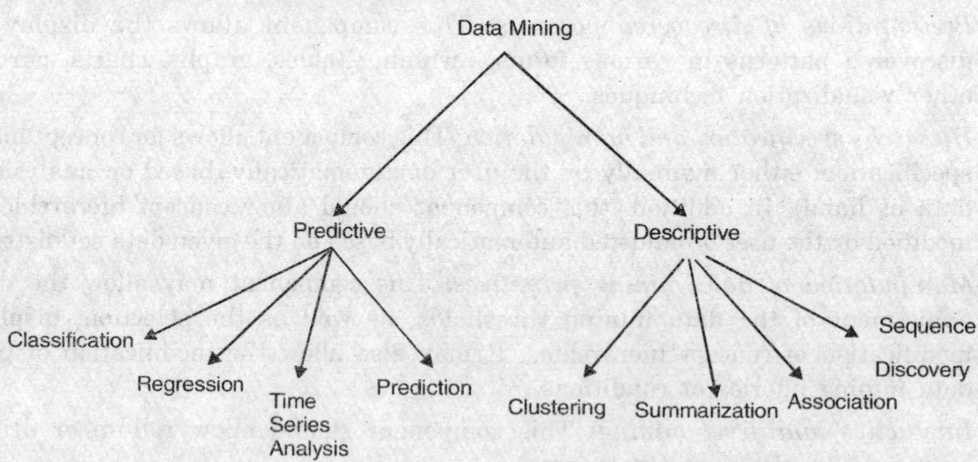

Fig. 5.11: Techniques of Data Mining

The data mining techniques can be broadly categorized into two categories:

1. Predictive: Classification, Regression, Deviation Detection.

2. Descriptive: Association, Clustering, Sequential Pattern discovery,

The various techniques of data mining are:

A. Association: Association and correlation is usually to find frequently used data items in the large data sets. It is the technique of finding patterns where one event is connected to another event. It tries to explore the dependency rules which will predict occurrences of an item based on occurrences of other items. This technique uses the frequency counts of a certain item or event and measures how items are related to each other. The objective is to find out the items/events which occur together most of the times. This type of findings help businesses to make certain decisions regarding pricing, selling and to design the strategies for marketing, such as catalogue design, cross marketing and customer shopping behavior analysis. However, the number of possible association rules for a given dataset is generally very large and a high proportion of the rules are usually of little value. For example: In a supermarket the association rule on the inventory data base to find out that every time a customer buys garlic he usually buys onions also. It will help in designing price policy, promotional schemes, store layout and designing strategies for providing customized services. The various types of associations include: Multilevel association rule, Multidimensional association rule, Quantitative association rule, Direct and Indirect association rules.

B. Clustering: Clustering can be defined as identification of similar classes of objects. This is the technique of combining the transactions with similar behavior into one group, or the customers with same set of queries or transactions into one group. Classification approach can also be used as an effective way of distinguishing groups from each other. So, clustering can be used as preprocessing approach for attribute subset selection and classification. The technique collects different attributes of customers based on their geographical and lifestyle related information, cluster them together and then customize the services according to the general requirements of the cluster. Like if we consider the customers of the banking sector, the customers from different job sectors or the customers from fixed salary background or from business class, have different set of choices for the type of accounts they open and the requirements of services from the banks. If the customers have been clustered into categories then the bank can offer the services as per the requirement of the cluster members and hence the effort from the bank side will reduce and on the other hand the satisfaction level of the customers will increase many fold.

C. Regression: Regression technique can be adapted for prediction. Regression analysis can be used to model the relationship between one or more independent and dependent variables. In data mining independent variables are attributes already known and dependent variables are what we want to predict. Unfortunately, many real-world problems are not simply prediction. For instance, sale volumes, stock prices, and product failure rates are all very difficult to predict because they may depend on complex interactions of multiple predictor variables. Therefore, more complex techniques (e.g., logistic regression, decision trees, or neural nets) may be necessary to forecast future values. This technique of data mining will help in discovering patterns from which one can make the reasonable predictions.

D. Classification: Classification is the most commonly applied data mining technique, which employs a set of pre-classified examples to develop a model that can classify the population of records at large. The criteria for classification vary from organization to organization and it will depend on the objectives for which the classification is to be done. The classification will help the organization to do the focused marketing. Fraud detection and credit risk applications are particularly well suited to this type of analysis. This approach frequently employs decision tree or neural network-based classification algorithms. The data classification process involves learning and classification. In Learning the training data is analyzed by the classification algorithm. In classification test data is used to estimate the accuracy of the classification rules. If the accuracy is acceptable, the rules can be applied to the new data tuples. For a fraud detection application, this would include complete records of both fraudulent and valid activities determined on record-by-record basis.

E. Sequential Pattern Discovery: This technique is basically used to predict the future actions of the customers relating to the sequence in which they will be executing the various events. For Example in the banking sector, if a customer has taken loan for the construction of the house in year 2010 then in 2011 he/she can be contacted to take loan for the purchase of the furniture or any electric appliance, as these are the products which are purchased after construction of a house. If a student has purchased a book on C then after some time the sequence of purchase of books can be predicted as: Book on C++, Test our programming skills and then programming in Java.

F. Deviation Detection: This technique tries to observe any detection in the normal execution of the events. Knowledge of deviations from normal is extremely important for any organization. A deviation can be an anomaly or a fraud or a change. As it normally leads to fraud or attrition of the customers from one organization to another. In the past, such deviations were difficult to detect in time to take corrective action. Data mining tools provide powerful means such as neural networks for detecting and classifying such deviations. For example, a higher than normal credit purchase on a credit card can be a fraud anomaly. Once a deviation has been discovered as a fraud, the organization takes steps to prevent such frauds and initiates corrective action. If the deviation has been discovered as a change, further information collection is necessary. For example, a change can be that a customer got a new job and moved to a new house. In this case, organization has to update the knowledge about the customer.

5.13 MAJOR ISSUES IN DATA MINING

While data mining is still in its infancy, it is becoming a trend and ubiquitous. Before data mining develops into a conventional, mature and trusted discipline, many still pending issues have to be addressed. Some of these issues are addressed below.

Security and Social Issues: Security is an important issue with any data collection that is shared and/or is intended to be used for strategic decision-making. In addition, when data is collected for customer profiling, user behavior understanding, correlating personal data with other information, etc., large amounts of sensitive and private information about individuals or companies is gathered and stored. This becomes controversial given the confidential nature of some of this data and the potential illegal access to the information. Moreover, data mining could disclose new implicit knowledge about individuals or groups that could be against privacy policies, especially if there is potential dissemination of discovered information. Another issue that arises from this concern is the appropriate use of data mining. Due to the value of data, databases of all sorts of content are regularly sold, and because of the competitive advantage that can be attained from implicit knowledge discovered, some important information could be withheld, while other information could be widely distributed and used without control.

It is important to study the impact of data mining on society and the individuals in particular, the improper disclosure or use of data and potential violation of individual privacy and data protection rights are the areas of concern.

User interface issues: The knowledge discovered by data mining tools is useful as long as it is interesting, and above all understandable by the user. Good data visualization eases the interpretation of data mining results. Many data exploratory analysis tasks are significantly facilitated by the ability to see data in an appropriate visual presentation. There are many visualization ideas and proposals for effective data graphical presentation. However, there is still much research to accomplish in order to obtain good visualization tools for large datasets that could be used to display and manipulate mined knowledge.The major issues related to user interfaces and visualization are "screen real-estate", information rendering, and interaction. Interactivity with the data and data mining results is crucial since it provides means for the user to focus and refine the mining tasks, as well as to picture the discovered knowledge from different angles and at different conceptual levels.

Mining Methodology Issues: These issues pertain to the data mining approaches applied and their limitations. Topics such as versatility of the mining approaches, the diversity of data available, the dimensionality of the domain, the broad analysis needs (when known), the assessment of the knowledge discovered, the exploitation of background knowledge and metadata, the control and handling of noise in data, etc. are all examples that can dictate mining methodology choices. Many new data mining methodologies have been developed in the recent past. For instance, it is often desirable to have different data mining methods available since different approaches may perform differently depending upon the data at hand. Moreover, different approaches may suit and solve user's needs differently. The need is to investigate new kinds of knowledge, mining in multidimensional space, integrating methods from various fields and creating semantic ties among data objects.

Most algorithms assume the data to be noise-free. This is of course a strong assumption. Most datasets contain noise, exceptions, invalid or incomplete information, etc., which may complicate, if not obscure, the analysis process and in many cases compromise the accuracy of the results. As a consequence, data preprocessing (data cleaning and transformation) becomes vital.

The knowledge requirements of every individual or the organization vary, so the data mining system should provide a wide range of knowledge discovery capabilities. The data mining tasks vary from data characterization and discrimination to association and correlation analysis, classification, regression, clustering, outlier analysis and trend analysis. These tasks may use the same database in different ways and require development of various data mining techniques.

Mining knowledge in multidimensional space is important because it is important to search for the interesting patterns among combination of dimensions at varying levels of abstraction. Data can be aggregated as a multidimensional data cube which will enhance the power and flexibility of data mining.

More than the size of data, the size of the search space is even more decisive for data mining techniques. The size of the search space is often depending upon the number of dimensions in the domain space. The search space usually grows exponentially when the number of dimensions increases. This is known as the *curse of dimensionality*. This "curse" affects so badly the performance of some data mining approaches that it is becoming one of the most urgent issues to solve.

The power of data mining can be enhanced by integrating new methods from multiple disciplines, like to mine data with natural language text, it is desirable to use the methods of information reterival and natural language processing.

Most of the data reside in linked environment whether it is web, database relations, files or documents. Semantic links across multiple data objects can be used to take full advantage of data mining.

Performance Issues: Many artificial intelligence and statistical methods exist for data analysis and interpretation. However, these methods were often not designed for the very large data sets data mining is dealing with today. Terabyte sizes are common. This raises the issues of scalability and efficiency of the data mining methods when processing considerably large data. Algorithms with exponential and even medium-order polynomial complexity cannot be of practical use for data mining. Linear algorithms are usually the norm. In same theme, sampling can be used for mining instead of the whole dataset. However, concerns such as completeness and choice of samples may arise. Other topics in the issue of performance are *incremental updating*, and parallel programming. There is no doubt that parallelism can help solve the size problem if the dataset can be subdivided and the results can be merged later. Incremental updating is important for merging results from parallel mining, or updating data mining results when new data becomes available without having to re-analyze the complete dataset.

Data Source Issues: There are many issues related to the data sources, some are practical such as the diversity of data types, while others are philosophical like the data glut problem. We certainly have an excess of data since we already have more data than we can handle and we are still collecting data at an even higher rate. If the spread of database management systems has helped increase the gathering of information, the advent of data mining is certainly encouraging more data harvesting. The current practice is to collect as much data as possible now and process it, or try to process it, later. The concern is whether we are collecting the right data at the appropriate amount, whether we know what we want to do with it, and whether we distinguish between what data is important and what data is insignificant. Regarding the practical issues related to data sources, there is the subject of heterogeneous databases and the focus on diverse complex data types. We are storing different types of data in a variety of repositories. It is difficult to expect a data mining system to effectively and efficiently achieve good mining results on all kinds of data and sources. Different kinds of data and sources may require distinct algorithms and methodologies. Currently, there is a focus on relational databases and data warehouses, but other approaches need to be pioneered for other specific complex data types. A versatile data mining tool, for all sorts of data, may not be realistic. Moreover, the proliferation of heterogeneous data sources, at structural and semantic levels, poses important challenges not only to the database community but also to the data mining community.

User Interaction Issues: the user is a very important component of the data mining process. It is important to learn how to interact with a data mining system, the kinds of knowledge mined by the user, the ability to mine knowledge at multiple granularities, the use of domain knowledge, how to handle unplanned mining, and knowledge visualization and interpretation of mined results.

- Mining different kinds of knowledge databases: Data mining should cover a wide variety of data analysis and knowledge discovery tasks and should be able to cater the diverse requirements of users at the various levels.
- Interactive mining of knowledge at multiple levels of abstraction: The data mining process should be interactive. Interactive mining allows users to focus the search for patterns, providing and refining data mining requests based on returned results. Designing flexible interfaces is very important to make the system interactive and user friendly.
- Incorporation of background knowledge: Background knowledge may be used to guide the discovery process and allow discovered patterns to be expressed in concise terms and at different levels of abstraction. If the user's knowledge about the constraints, rules and other information about the domain under study can be incorporated into knowledge discovery process, then interesting results can be obtained easily.
- Data mining query languages and ad hoc mining: Relational query languages (such as SQL) allow users to pose ad hoc queries for data retrieval. It will enable the user to design and run ad hoc queries.
- Presentation and visualization of Data Mining results: Discovered knowledge should be expressed in high-level languages, visual representations, or other expressive forms so that knowledge can be easily understood and directly usable by humans.

Performance issues: These include efficiency, scalability, and parallelization of data mining algorithms.

- Efficiency and scalability of data mining algorithms: To effectively extract information from a huge amount of data in databases, data mining algorithms must be efficient and scalable. The running time of a data mining algorithm must be predictable, short and acceptable by applications.
- Parallel, distributed, and incremental mining algorithms: The huge size of many databases, the wide distribution of data, and the computational complexity of some data mining methods are factors motivating the development of algorithms that divide data into partitions that can be processed in parallel.

Issues relating to the diversity of database types:

- **Handling of relational and complex types of data:** The data which is being stored in the organization's data base contains various data types, it vary from strauctred data like relational and data warehouse data to unstructured data, from stable data repositories to dynamic data streams, from simple data objects to temporal data, biological sequences, sensor data, spatial data, hyper text data, multimedia data, software program code, web data. It is not possible to have one data mining system which can mine all types of data. So, specific data mining systems should be constructed for mining specific kinds of data.

- **Mining information from heterogeneous databases and global information systems:** Local- and wide-area computer networks (such as the Internet) connect many sources of data, forming huge, distributed, and heterogeneous databases. Mining such huge interconnected information networks will explore new interesting previously unknow patterns.

The above issues are considered major requirements and challenges for the further evolution of data mining technology. Some of the challenges have been addressed in recent data mining research and development, to a certain extent, and are now considered requirements, while others are still in the research stage.

5.14 CHALLENGES IN DATA MINING

Outliers: The outliers are the values which deviate from the rest of the data, the presence of these outliers may lead to wrong observations and calculations. Such values should be checked before providing the data for applying the data mining techniques. The filtering and pre-processing of data is important to handle the outliers properly.

Interpretation of results: The results obtained from data mining if not interpreted properly, can prove to be fatal for the organization, so the interpretation of results as per the requirements of the users is very important and needs careful handling.

Large datasets: the size of data bases is growing at an alarming rate, which makes the analysis of data a difficult job. So the data mining methods should be scalable enough to handle the ever growing databases.

Interactive Data Mining Methods: The user need a friendly interface to deal with any system being used, same is the case of data mining, an interactive, friendly, customizable interface is required.

High dimensionality: The analysis done on the user data, requires that the data should be analyzed on multiple dimensions to make the results more viable and acceptable, so user data should be stored based on multiple dimensions. Such data is difficult to store, handle and interpret.

Handling Irrelevant/Noisy data and data with Missing values: Data collected from various heterogeneous sources contains a lot of irrelevant data, and some of the values in data may be missing and sometimes noisy data is also inserted in the data collected (all these problems in data may occur intentionally or un-intentionally), but such a data if processed as such will provide wrong results and hence wrong interpretation followed by wrong decision.

Changing data: In the present era of competition and fast changing global scenarios, where a number of transactions are done with a blink of eye, the data changes at a very fast and a result of which the results obtained and hence the interpretation done may not be relevant after some time, so data mining techniques should be robust enough to handle the dynamic environments.

Integration: Search engines, database systems, data warehouse systems and cloud computing systems are main information processing and computing systems. It is important to ensure that data mining serves as an essential data analysis component that can be integrated into already existing information processing systems.

Data Warehouse and Data Preprocessing: Data Warehouse and data preprocessing are critical for the success of data mining. The major issue while creating a data warehouse is to handle inconsistent or heterogeneous data collected from various sources at different dimensions of time. These disparities must be tackled properly so that optimal utilization of data mining techniques can be obtained.

Mining Complex Data Types: As discussed earlier, now a days, we deal with the data of various different types, which range from text, multimedia, web data, spatial data which may be in structured or unstructured form. Handling the data of various types and hence applying the data mining techniques is a daunting task which needs proper care and deep understanding of inns and outs of various data mining techniques.

Ability to handle distributed data mining: Traditional data mining methods, were designed to work well in centralized locations, do not work well in many distributed computing environments present today. So the data mining techniques should be advanced to ensure distributed data mining

Need of Visualization Tools: the user now a days demand the graphical representation of results and hence visualization tools are required for scientific data mining systems. And moreover, these tools should be integrated with existing data mining techniques.

Need for Domain Specific Knowledge: the data collected for various application domain varies in various forms and needs to be handled keeping the usage of the data in mind, so domain specific systems are required, which cab cater to the needs of the particular domain and can provide results worth acceptable by the users of that domain.

Unauthorized use of personal data could result in disclosure of confidential information: the unauthorized access to the user's information is a direct attack on the privacy of the individual and hence the concept of invisible data mining is creeping out, where smart softwares like search engines, intelligent database systems incorporate data mining in its functional components, about which the user is not aware of.

Results of Data Mining techniques are not always correct: The results obtained from the data mining algorithms may be wrong, due to error in any stage of the data mining process(starting from input to the final results, it may be due error in input, pre-processing, application of algorithm and evaluation). Moreover, if the results obtained are not interpreted properly, will make the whole process wasteful.

Cost: The data mining systems are costly both in terms of hardware and software cost and huge investment is required at the initial stage and the as the system progresses, the size of database increases and the maintenance cost increases manifold.

SUMMARY

- Decision makers are making strategic decisions depending on their intuition and experience rather than on the basis of *information-rich data* stored in the repositories.
- The need is to develop some data mining tools that can turn data tombs into shrine of knowledge, which can be used by decision makers directly.
- Data Mining is the process of extracting knowledge hidden from large volumes of raw data. The knowledge must be new, not obvious, and one must be able to use it.
- Data mining has been defined as *"the nontrivial extraction of implicit, previously unknown, and potentially useful information from data"*.
- Data mining is defined as the process of extracting previously unknown, valid, and actionable information from large databases and then using the information to make crucial business decisions.
- The techniques of data mining can be used for customer relationship management, fraud detection, marketing, attrition analysis, risk management, Customer Segmentation, predicting the future trends, target marketing and Cross Selling.
- Data Mining Life Cycle consists of six phases, these phases are, Business Understanding, Data Understanding, Data Preparation, Modeling, Evaluation and Deployment. The sequence of the phases is not rigid. Moving back and forth between different phases may be required.
- The most common forms of data for data mining are *database data, data warehouse data and transactional data.*
- The other types of data used in data mining are data streams, ordered/sequence data, graph or networked data, spatial data, multimedia data and studied for databases, including relational databases, object-relational databases and object-oriented databases, data warehouses, transactional databases, unstructured and semi-structured repositories such as the World Wide Web, time-series databases and textual databases, and even flat files.
- Data mining and knowledge discovery in databases (or KDD) are frequently treated as synonyms, *data mining is actually part of the knowledge discovery process.*
- During the knowledge discovery process, the data moves through the various stages, original raw data, target data, transformed data, pattern evaluation and finally the knowledge.
- The Knowledge Discovery Process involves the understanding of the problem domain, Understanding of the Data, Preparation of the Data, Data Mining, Evaluation of the discovered Knowledge and use of the discovered knowledge
- *Query Tools are tools that help analyze the data in a database.* They provide query building, query editing, searching, reporting and summarizing functionalities.
- Data mining systems can be classified according to the type of data source mined, data model used, mining techniques used and according to the kind of knowledge discovered.
- Data Mining softwares are Knowledge STUDIO, Knowledge SEEKER, SPSS, Clementine, Intelligent Miner, Oracle Data Miner and Weka 3.
- Data mining query language is designed to support the features that make the data mining an interactive process.

- Various data mining query languages used are MSQL, MINERULE, CRISP and OLE DB.
- Data Mining system can be integrated with a data base and data warehouse system using the following coupling schemes - *No Coupling. Loose Coupling. Semi-tight Coupling and Tight coupling.*
- Data Mining Techniques: The data mining techniques can be broadly categorized into two categories, Predictive and Descriptive, predictive techniques include Classification, Regression, Deviation Detection and descriptive techniques are Association, Clustering, Sequential Pattern discovery,
- Major Issues in Data Mining include, Security and Social Issues, User interface issues, Mining Methodology Issues, Performance Issues, Data Source Issues, Mining Methodology and User Interaction Issues, Performance issues and Issues relating to the diversity of database types.

CHAPTER 6

ASSOCIATION RULE MINING

Association rule mining finds frequent patterns, interesting associations, causal structures or correlation among a large set of data items or objects in a transactional data base, relational data base or other information repositories. As the size of data bases is growing at an alarming rate, the decision makers are finding it difficult to handle and manage it and hence finding it more difficult to find associations occurring between different data items stored in these huge data repositories. If such associations are made available then it will help the decision makers in making more viable decisions in catalog design, cross-marketing, show room layout and carrying out the analysis of customer shopping *behavior* etc.

The first and the foremost task to find associations among the data items is to find the frequent patterns i.e the patterns which are repeating in the database again and again.

Frequent Patterns are the patterns that appear frequently in a data set.

For example, a set of items, like bread and butter, that appear frequently together in a transaction data set is a frequent item set.

In the same way, buying a book on C is followed by a purchase of book on C++ and then on Java, is the quite obvious purchase pattern for a student of Programming Languages.

If such a pattern appears frequently in the history of data base, then it can be termed as frequent sequential pattern.

Frequent Pattern Mining searches for recurring relationships in a given data set. Such a mining of data leads to the discovery of associations and correlations among items in a large transactional or relational data sets.

Finding Frequent Patterns helps in mining associations, correlations, data classification, clustering and many other data mining tasks.

The most suitable example of frequent item set mining is ***Market Basket Analysis***.

6.1 MARKET BASKET ANALYSIS

This process analyzes the buying habits of the customers by finding associations between different items that customer place in the shopping basket. The knowledge about such associations and correlations will help the decision makers to get knowledge about the purchasing behavior of the customers, i.e which items they buy together most of the times.

It will help them to plan marketing and advertisement strategies, design of store layout etc.

For Example, if customer is buying bread, what is the probability that the customer will buy butter or jam or milk on the same trip to the shopping mall, and again which brand of butter/jam or milk is purchased quite often. Such information will help:

- The store manager to decide which items are to put together with close proximity so that it may encourage the sale of these items together in a single visit to the store.
- The company manager to decide that discounts can be given on which set of items.
- The company manager to contact the customers who are likely to buy the same product.
- The manager will get an idea about the purchasing behavior of the customers and hence will plan the marketing strategies accordingly.

Example: As a manager of a shopping mall, will be interested in finding out the purchasing behavior of the customers, and will be interested in finding out which set of items are purchased together most of the times, in a single trip to the mall. To answer these questions, market basket analysis is performed on the data of customer transactions. The knowledge about such a piece of information will help the decision makers to design store layouts. The different strategies that can be used are:

1. Items that are purchased together are placed close to each other in order to encourage the combined sale of such items. If the customer is buying bread, then placing butter/jam/milk close to it will increase the sale of all these items. Like if a customer is buying computer, also tend to buy mouse pad or antivirus software at the same time, then placing the hardware display close to software display will help in the increased sale of both the items.
2. In an alternative strategy, placing the bread counter at one end of the store and butter/jam/milk counter at the other end of the store, then customer after placing bread in his basket will roam in the store to search for other items (butter/jam/milk) and on the way, he may tend to buy the other items placed in between. Then the customer will move out of the store by not buying just bread and butter/jam/milk but will buy lot many other items also, it will increase the sales of the store.
3. The market basket analysis will also help the store manager to decide which items can be put on sale at the reduced prices, for this purpose following two approaches can be used:
   - ***Directly Associated Products:*** The manager will provide the discount on the purchase of items related to each other directly. As we see if the customer buys bread most of the time he buys butter also, so the manager will put these two items as combo offer, like butter is free with the bread, it will increase the sale of bread. If the customer tends to buy computer and printers together, then having a sale on printers may increase the sale of printers and computers.

- ***Indirectly Associated Products:*** The manager will provide the discount on the purchase of items that are not related to each other directly. It happens because of the reason that if customer buys bread then he buy butter/jam or milk by his own, as it is the necessity (when he eats bread, most of the time he needs either of these items), and will buy of his own, so there is no need to give discount on the related items. So the better option is to give discount on items not related to each other. This normally happens to clear the stock or to motivate the use of the products not purchased quite often or to introduce some new product in the market. Like the company has launched a new brand of biscuits, then offer can be buy bread and get a packet of biscuit.

6.2 ASSOCIATION RULE MINING

Each item in the store has a boolean variable representing the presence or absence of that item. Each basket can be represented by a boolean vector of values assigned to these variables. The boolean vectors are analyzed for buying patterns that reflect items that are frequently associated or purchased together. These patterns can be represented in the form of association rules.

Let I = {I1, I2, I3, I4 ....In} be the item set.

DB is the task relevant data, it is a set of transactions where each transaction T is a non empty itemset such that T is the subset of I.

TID is the unique id associated with each transaction.

A be a set of items, then a transaction T contains A iff A is subset of T.

An Association rule is an implication of the form A=> B, where A is subset of I, B is subset of I and A != Ø and B != Ø and A ∩ B != Ø. Where Ø means that the set is empty.

The association rules are normally measured with the help of following two measures: the rule A => B, holds in the transaction set DB with:

- ***support:*** it is denoted by s, support of a rule indicates how frequently its items appear in the data base. It is the percentage of transactions in DB that contains A U B (i.e both A and B), it is taken to be the P(A U B)

  support (A => B) = P(A U B)

- ***confidence:*** it is denoted by c, confidence of a rule indicates the probability that if the left hand side appears in T, the right hand side will also appear. It is the percentage of transaction in DB containing A that also contain B. It is taken to the conditional probability, P(B | A).

  confidence (A => B) = P(B \ A)

The values of support and confidence occur between 0 % to 100% rather than 0 to 1.

Example of market Basket Transactions: The following example shows 8 baskets picked by different customers and items in the baskets show the items picked up by them,

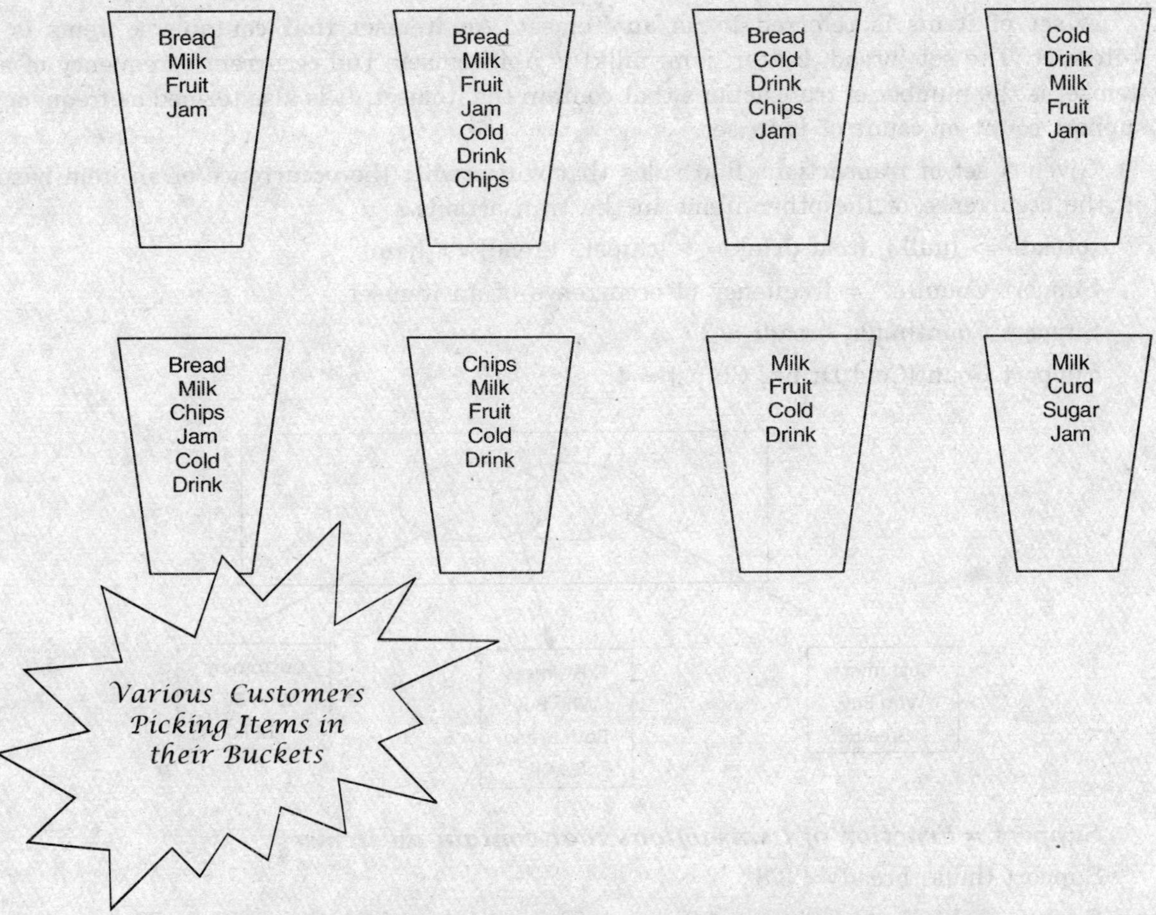

Fig. 6.1: 8 baskets containing different items picked by customers

Table 6.1: An Example of 4-itemset

TID	Items
T101	Bread, Milk, Fruit, Jam, Cold Drink
T102	Bread, Jam, Cold Drink, Chips Milk, Fruit.
T103	Jam, Cold Drink, Chips, Soda, bread
T104	Jam, Cold Drink, Milk, Fruit
T105	Jam, Cold Drink, Chips, Milk, Bread
T106	Fruit, Cold Drink, Chips, Milk
T107	Fruit, Cold Drink, Milk
T108	Fruit, Cheese, Chocolate, Yogurt

A set of items is referred to as an itemset. An itemset that contains k items is a k-itemset. The set {bread, butter, jam, milk} is a 4-itemset. The occurrence frequency of an itemset is the number of transactions that contain the itemset. It is also termed as frequency, support count or count of item set.

Given a set of transactions find rules that will predict the occurrence of an item based on the occurrence of the other items in the transactions.

{bread} => {milk}, {cold drink}= > {chips}, {bread} => {jam}

Support Count(sc) = frequency of occurrence of an itemset.

Support Count{milk, bread} = 3

Support Count{Cold Drink, Chips} = 4.

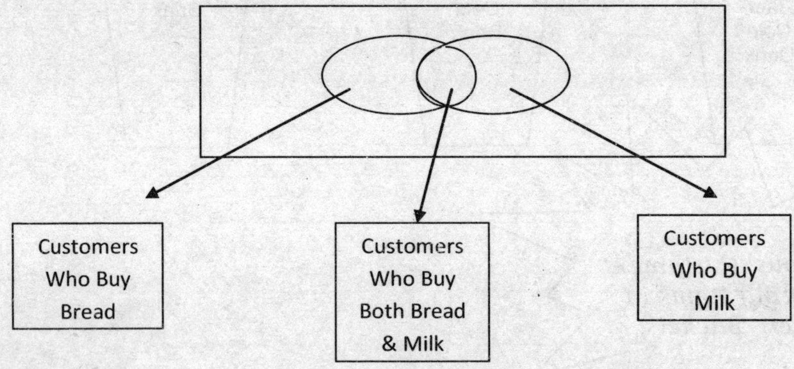

Support = Fraction of transactions that contain an itemset

Support (milk, bread) = 3/8.

Support (cold drink, Chips) = 4/8.

Frequent Itemsets: An itemset whose support is greater than a minsup threshold.

Support(s) = Fraction of Transactions that contain both X and Y.

= sc(Bread, Milk)/ Total Number of transactions = 3/8.

Confidence(c) = measures how often items in Y appear in transaction that contain X.

= sc(bread, milk)/ sd(bread) = 3/4 = 0.75

Given a set of transaction T, the goal of association rule mining is to find all rules having:

Support >= minsup threshold

Confidence >= minconf threshold

{Bread, Jam} => {Milk} s = 0.4, c = 0.75

{Milk, Jam} => {Bread}s = 0.4, c = 0.75

{Bread} => {Milk, Jam}s = 0.4, c = 0.75

{Jam} => {Bread, Milk}s = 0.4, c = 0.75

{Milk} => {Bread, Jam} s = 0.4, c = 0.75

Example I: Find the support and confidence values for the following set of transactions.

TID	Items Bought
10101	{F, A, D, B}
10110	{D, A, C, E, B}
11000	{C, A, B, E}
10100	{B, A, D}

What is the Support and Confidence of {B, D} => {A}?

Solution: Support : Percentage of tuples that contain {A, B, D} = 75 %

Confidence : Number of tuples that contain {A, B, D}/ number of tuples that contain {B,D} = 100%

Example II: Consider the following set of transactions with Minimum Support = 50% and Minimum Confidence = 50%, find the values for A => C.

TID	Items Bought
10101	{A, B, C}
10110	{A, C}
11000	{A, D}
10100	{B, E, F}

Solution:

Frequent Item Sets	Support
{A}	75 %
{B}	50 %
{C}	50%
{A, C}	50%

For Rule A => C

Support = Support (A U C) = 50%

Confidence = Support(A U C) / Support(A) = 66.6 %

Apriori Principle- any subset of a frequent item set must be frequent.

Rules that satisfy both a minimum support threshold(min_sup) and a minimum confidence threshold(min_conf) are called strong.

An item set satisfies minimum support if the occurrence frequency of the itemset >= min_sup * total number of transactions in DB.

The number of transactions required for the itemset to satisfy minimum support is referred to as the minimum support count.

If an itemset satisfies minimum support then it is a frequent itemset, the set of frequent k-itemsets is denoted by Lk.

6.3 PROCESS OF ASSOCIATION RULE MINING

The process of association rule mining is a two-step process:

1. ***Find all Frequent Itemsets:*** The first step is to find out the itemsets that are appearing frequently in the data base. Each of these itemsets will occur at least as frequently as a pre-determined minimum support count, min_sup. The biggest problem in mining frequent itemsets from a large data set is that such mining generates a huge number of itemsets which satisfy minimum support threshold., particularly when min_sup is quite low. It occurs due to the reason that if an itemset is frequent, each of its subset will also be frequent. Find all itemset whose support>= minsup
2. ***Generate Strong Association Rules from the Frequent Item sets:*** The next step is to find out or generate strong association rules from the frequent item sets. These rules must satisfy minimum support and minimum confidence.

Market basket analysis is just one form of association rule mining. In fact, there are many kinds of association rules. These association rules can be classified in various ways, based on the following criteria:

- ***Based on the type of values handled in the rule*:** If the rule concerns association between the presence or absence of the items, it is a Boolean Association Rule. If a rule describes associations between quantitative itemset or attributes, then it is a quantitative association rule. In these rules, quantitative values for items or attributes are partitioned into intervals. The following rule is an example of a quantitative association rule, Where A is a variable representing a customer:

  Age(A, "20-40") ^ income(A, "30000-45000) => buys(A, Laptop)

The quantitative attributes age and income have been discretized.

- ***Based on the dimensions of data involved in the rule:*** If the items or attributes in an association rule refer to only one dimension, then it is a single dimensional association rule. The rule can be written as:

  Buys (A, "Laptop") => Buys (A, cell-phone)

If a rule references two or more dimensions, such as the dimension buys, time-of-transactions and customer-category, then it is a multi-dimensional association rule.

- ***Based on the levels of abstractions involved in the rule set:*** Some method for association rule can find rules at different levels of abstraction. For Example, Let a set of association rules mined include the following rule:

  Age(A, "20-40") => buys(A, "laptop")

  Age(A, "20-40") => buys(A, "Computer)

The items bought are referenced at different levels of abstraction. Like computer is a higher level abstraction of laptop. We refer to the rule set mined as consisting of multilevel association rules. If, instead, the rules within a given set donot reference items or attributes at different levels of abstraction, then the set contains single-level association rules.

-***Based on various extensions to association mining***: Association mining can be extended to correlation analysis, where the absence or presence of correlated items can be identified. It can also be extended to mining maxpatterns i.e maximal frequent patterns and frequent closed itemset where an itemset c is closed if there exists a proper subset of c, c' such that every transaction containing c also contains c'.

6.4 FREQUENT ITEMSET MINING METHODS

The best methods for finding frequent itemsets is the AprioriAlgorithm as discussed below.

6.4.1 Apriori Algorithm

Apriori is an influential algorithm for mining frequent itemsets for boolean association rules. This algorithm was proposed by R. Agarwal and R.Srikant in 1994 for mining frequent itemsets for Boolean association rules.

The name of algorithm is based on the fact that the algorithm uses prior knowledge of frequent itemset properties.

This algorithm implements an iterative approach known as level-wise search, where k-itemsets are used to explore k+1 itemsets.

First of all, the set of frequent 1-itemsets is found, it is denoted by L1,

Then L1 is used to find L2, which is the set of frequent 2-itemsets,

Then L2 is used to find L3 and so on.

To improve the efficiency of the level-wise generation of frequent itemsets, an Apriori Property is used to reduce the search space.

Apriori property states that all non empty subsets of a frequent itemset must also be frequent.

To understand the application of this property in the algorithm, we look at how Lk-1 is used to find Lk for k >= 2, for this purpose a two step procedure is followed:

(i) **Join Step:** To find Lk, a set of candidate k-itemsets is generated by joining Lk-1with itself. This set of candidates is denoted by Ck.

(ii) **Prune Step:** Any (k-1)-itemset that is not frequent cannot be a subset of a frequent k-itemset.

Hence if any k-1 subset of a candidate k-itemset is not in Lk-1, then the candidate cannot be frequent either and so can be removed from Ck. This subset testing can be executed quickly by maintaining a hash tree of all frequent itemsets.

Apirori Algorithm: This algorithm is applied to find frequent itemsets using an iterative level-wise approximation on candidate generation.

Inputs to the Algorithm: (i) A database of Transactions.

(ii) min_sup, the minimum support count threshold.

Outputs of the Algorithm: L, Frequent itemsets in database.

Pseudo-Code:

C_k: Candidate itemset of size k

L_k : frequent itemset of size k

L_1 = {frequent itemsets from database};

for (k = 2; L_{k-1} !=∅; k++) **do begin**

C_{k+1} = candidates generated from L_k;

for each transaction t in database do

increment the count of all candidates in C_{k+1} that are contained in t

L_{k+1} = candidates in C_{k+1} with min_support

end

return $\cup_k L_k$;

How to Generate Candidates?

Suppose the items in L_{k-1} are listed in an order

Step 1: Self-joining L_{k-1}

insert into $\mathbf{C_k}$

select $\mathbf{p.item_1, p.item_2, ..., p.item_{k-1}, q.item_{k-1}}$

from $\mathbf{L_{k-1}\ p, L_{k-1}\ q}$

where $\mathbf{p.item_1=q.item_1, ..., p.item_{k-2} = q.item_{k-2}, p.item_{k-1} < q.item_{k-1}}$

Step 2: Pruning

For all ***itemsets c in*** $\mathbf{C_k}$ do

For all ***(k-1)-subsets s of c*** do

if (s *is not in* L_{k-1}) **then delete** c **from** C_k

Function candidate-gen(F_{k-1})

$C_k \leftarrow \varnothing$

forall $f_1, f_2 \in F_{k-1}$

with $f_1 = \{i_1, \ldots, i_{k-2}, i_{k-1}\}$

and $f_2 = \{i_1, \ldots, i_{k-2}, i'_{k-1}\}$

```
                and i_{k-1} < i'_{k-1} do
    c ← {i_1, ..., i_{k-1}, i'_{k-1}};                    // join f_1 and f_2
    C_k ← C_k È {c};
    for each (k-1)-subset s of c do
        if (s Ï F_{k-1}) then
            delete c from C_k;                           // prune
    end
  end
  return C_k;
```

Example III: This example shows the execution of Apriori Algorithm: The database d is given in the Table 6.2(a). There are 4 transactions in the database, so |D| = 4. The subsequent steps I to VIII and the corresponding tables explains the Apriori algorithm for finding frequent itemsets in D.

Table 6.2(a)

Transaction ID	List of Items
Trans100	1,3,4
Trans101	2,3,5
Trans102	1,2,3,5
Trans103	2,5

Step I: It is observed that each item is a member of the set of candidate 1-itemset, C1. The algorithm scans all the transactions to count the number of occurrences of each item.

Table: C1

Itemset	Support Count
{1}	2
{2}	3
{3}	3
{4}	1
{5}	3

Step II: Let the minimum support count required is 2, i.e min_sup = 2. Using this value the set of frequent 1-itemsets, L1, can be obtained, that consists the list of candidates 1-itemsets satisfying minimum support. Clearly, in the table given below the itemset{4} does not satisfy the given criteria, hence has been removed from the table.

Table: L1	
Itemset	**Support Count**
{1}	2
{2}	3
{3}	3
{5}	3

Step III: The set of 2-itemsets is generated and is named as C2,

Table: C2
Itemset
{1 2}
{1 3}
{1 5}
{2 3}
{2 5}
{3 5}

Step IV: The transactions in D are scanned and the support count of each candidate itemset in C2 is calculated,

Table: C2	
Itemset	**Support**
{1 2}	1
{1 3}	2
{1 5}	1
{2 3}	2
{2 5}	3
{3 5}	2

Step V: The set of frequent 2-itemsets, L2, can be obtained, that consists the list of candidates from 2-itemsets which satisfies minimum support value criteria. Clearly, in the table given below the itemsets {1 2}, {1 5}, does not satisfy the given criteria, hence have been removed from the table.

Table: L2	
Itemset	**Support**
{1 3}	2
{2 3}	2
{2 5}	3
{3 5}	2

Step VI: The set of 3-itemsets is generated and is named as C3,

Table: C3
Itemset
{2 3 5}

Step VII: The transactions in D are scanned and the support count of each candidate itemset in C3 is calculated,

Table: C3	
Itemset	**Support**
{2 3 5}	2

Step VIII: The set of frequent 3-itemsets, L3, can be obtained, that consists the list of candidates from 3-itemsets which satisfies minimum support value criteria. Clearly, all itemsets in the table given satisfy the given criteria, hence nothing has been removed from the table.

Table: L3	
Itemset	**Support**
{2 3 5}	2

6.4.2 Methods to Improve Efficiency of Apriori's Algorithm

Many variations of the Apriori algorithm have been proposed that focus on improving the efficiency of the basic algorithm given in the previous section, some of these variations are:

(a) Hash-based Itemset Counting: In this technique the itemsets are hashed into corresponding buckets. This technique is used to reduce the size of candidate k-itemset, Ck for $k > 1$. A k-itemset whose corresponding hashing bucket count is below the threshold cannot be frequent. Like while scanning each transaction in the database to generate 1-itemsets, L1, the user can generate all the 2-itemsets for each transaction, hash them into different buckets of the hash table structure and increase the bucket count of the corresponding bucket. A 2-itemset with a corresponding bucket count in the hash table that is below the support threshold cannot be frequent and thus should be removed from the candidate set.

(b) **Transaction Reduction:** In this technique number of transactions scanned are reduced in the future iterations. A transaction that does not contain any frequent k-itemset cannot contain any frequent $k + 1$ itemsets. Therefore, such a transaction can be marked or removed from further consideration because subsequent database scans for j-itemsets where $j > k$ will not be required to be considered for the transaction.

(c) **Partitioning:** In this technique the data is portioned to find candidate itemsets. It requires just two scans to mine the frequent itemsets. Fig. 6.2 shows the step by step procedure. The steps have been described as:

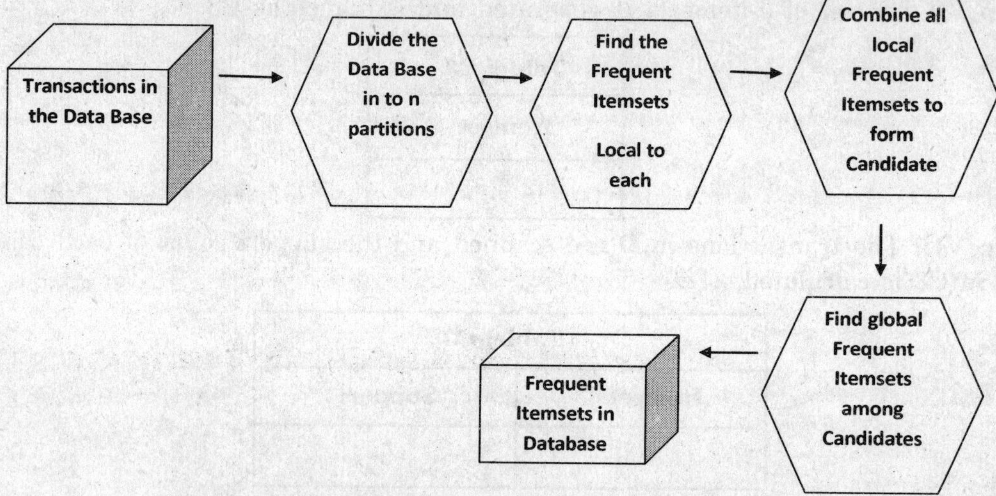

Fig. 6.2: Mining data by Partitioning

Step I: The algorithm divides the transactions of D into n non-overlapping partitions. If the minimum relative support threshold for the transaction in the data base is min_sup, then the minimum support count for a partition is min_sup * number of transactions in that partition. In this case, first of all, all the local frequent itemsets are found, i.e the itemsets which are frequent in partition are found. A local frequent itemset may or may not be frequent w.r.t the entire database, so any itemset that is potentially frequent w.r.t to database must occur as a frequent itemset in at least one of the partitions, so all local frequent itemsets are candidate w.r.t database.

Step II: The second scan of data base D is conducted in which the actual support of each candidate is assessed to determine the global frequent itemsets. The size of each partition and the total number of partitions are set in such a way that each partition can fit into main memory and therefore be read only once in each phase.

(d) **Sampling:** In this technique the frequent itemset is determined on a sample of the database, rather than searching it on the entire database. A random sample s of the given data is picked and then a search for frequent itemsets is made on s rather than on the complete data. This is normally difficult to find out that what should be the size of the sample, the simplest approach is to have the size of sample in such a way that it can be accommodated in the main memory only and hence the searching can be done in minimum time possible. The biggest problem of searching the frequent itemsets in a sample is that while searching the frequent sets in a sample s rather than in the database, the user may miss some of the global frequent itemsets.

(e) Dynamic Itemset Counting: In this technique the new candidate itemsets can be added at any start point, whereas in Apriori algorithm, the new candidate itemsets are determined only before each complete database scan. This technique uses the count-so-far as the lower bound of the actual count, if the count-so-far passes minimum support, then the itemset is added into the frequent itemset collection and can be used to generate longer candidates. It leads to fewer database scans than with Apriori for finding all the frequent itemsets.

6.5 TYPES OF ASSOCIATION RULES

Association rules can be applied in various domains and these rules vary depending on the following criterias:

1. Types of values handled: The association rules in this category are handled by considering the types of values being handled. It can be divided into two broad categories:

Boolean Rules: Rules that concern associations between the presence or absence of items, e.g. *"buys A" or "does not buy A".*

buys(x, "SQLServer") ^ buys(x, "DMBook") => buys(x, "DBMiner") [0.2%, 60%]

Quantitative Rules: Rules that concern associations between quantitative items or attributes.

age(x, "30..39") ^ income(x, "42..48K) => buys(x, "PC") [1%, 75%]

Categorical attributes, like a color of a car, have a finite number of values with no ordering.

Quantitative attributes have numeric values with an implicit ordering: e.g., age, income, height, weight. But the problem with quantitative attributes is that these can have too many values.

The solution is to transform quantitative attributes into categories via discretization _ static discretization, dynamic discretization

An example data set:

From this data set we can get, for example, a rule:

Age(x,"30..39") ^ Married(x,"Yes") => NumCars(x,"2")

when sc = 40% and ã = 50%.

Customer ID	Age	Married	NumCars
101	24	No	1
102	26	Yes	1
103	28	No	0
104	32	Yes	2
105	37	Yes	2

2. Types of dimensions of data involved:

Single-dimensional rules: Items in the rule refer to only one dimension or predicate, e.g., to "buys".

buys(X, "milk") Þ buys(X, "bread")

Single-dimensional rules:

buys(x, "Beer") ^ buys(x, "Chips") => buys(x, "Bread") [0.4%, 52%]

in this case transactional data is used. Items in a rule are assumed to belong to the same transaction.

Multi-Dimensional Rules: If a rule references two or more dimensions, such as the dimensions buys, time_of_transaction and customer_category, then it is a multidimensional association rule. Multidimensional association rules with no repeated predicates are called interdimension association rules. Sometimes the user may be interested in mining multidimensional association rules with repeated predicates. These rules are called hybrid dimension association rules. Items in the rule refer to two or more dimensions or predicates, For Example, the following is an example of such a rule, where the predicate buys is repeated:

age(X, "20...29") ^ buys(X, "laptop") Þ buys(X, "Printer")

Inter-dimension association rules (*no repeated predicates*)

age(X,"19-25") Ù occupation(X,"student") Þ buys(X,"coke")

Hybrid-dimension association rules (*repeated predicates*)

age(X,"19-25") Ù buys(X, "popcorn") Þ buys(X, "coke")

The various attributes in the database can be: categorical or quantitative. Categorical attributes have a finite number of possible values, and these values have no ordering among the values (e.g occupation, brand, color). These attributes are also termed as nominal attributes. On the other hand, quantitative attributes are numeric and have implicit ordering among values like age, income and price.

Techniques for mining multidimensional association rules can be categorized according to the following approaches regarding handling of the quantitative attributes:

- ***Discretizing the attributes using predefined concept hierarchies*:** Most of the times some attributes may have numerous possible values, which becomes difficult to manage, so the process of discretizing is done prior to mining. In this process the possible values for a given attributes are arranged according to concept hierarchies, like for an attribute income, the original numeric values may be replaced by range of values, like 0-10000, 10001-20000, and so on. This discretization is static and predetermined.
- ***Discretizing the quantitative attributes into bins*:** In an approach the quantitative attributes are discretized into bins based on the distribution of the data. These bins can then be further combined during the mining process. This process is dynamic and is done to satisfy some mining criteria. This strategy treats the numeric values as quantities rather than as predefined ranges or categories, so the association rules mined from this approach are also referred to as quantitative association rules.

- ***Discretizing to capture semantic meaning of data*:** In the third approach quantitative attributes are discretized so as to capture the semantic meaning of every data in the interval. This process is dynamic in nature and considers the distance between data points, these quantitative association rules are also named as distance-based association rules.

6.6 MINING MULTI-LEVEL ASSOCIATION RULES IN LARGE DATABASES

Mining of association rules from large data sets has been a focused topic in recent data mining research. Many applications at mining associations require that mining be performed at multiple levels of abstraction. For example, besides finding 80 percent of customers that purchase milk may also purchase bread, it is interesting to allow users to ªdrill-downº and show that 75 percent of people buy wheat bread if they buy 2 percent milk. The association relationship in the latter statement is expressed at a lower level of abstraction but carries more specific and concrete information than that in the former. Therefore, a data mining system should provide efficient methods for mining multiple-level association rules. To explore multiple-level association rule mining, one needs to provide:

1. Data at multiple levels of abstraction, and
2. Efficient methods for multiple-level rule mining.

Multiple-Level Association Rules: However, mining association rules at high concept levels may often lead to the rules corresponding to prior knowledge and expectations, such as "milk => bread", (which could be common sense), or lead to some uninteresting attribute combinations if the minimum support is allowed to be rather small, such as "toy => milk", (which may just happen together by chance). These observations lead us to examine the second choice: applying different minimum support thresholds and possibly different minimum confidence thresholds as well, at mining associations at different levels of abstraction. Especially, we explore the most typical case: progressively reducing the minimum support thresholds at lower levels of abstraction. This leads to mining interesting association rules at multiple concept levels, which may not only discover rules at different levels, but may also have high potential to find nontrivial, informative association rules because of its flexibility for focusing the attention to different sets of data and applying different thresholds at different levels.

6.7 MOVING FROM ASSOCIATION RULES TO CORRELATION ANALYSIS

Most of the association rule mining algorithms employ a support-confidence framework to filter out the uninteresting association rules. But these algorithms are not sufficient enough to provide the desired results, as many rules that are not interesting may still be produced by these methods. It has been observed that all of the strong association rules discovered (i.e the rules satisfying the minimum support and confidence thresholds) may not be important to the users. The biggest problem here is to identify that whether the user will be interested in the given rule or not. This matter can be handled either subjectively or objectively. Most of the times this decision is subjective and is dependent on user's judgement and may differ from one user to another. But in order to measure it objectively, the statistics behind the data can be used as a tool to filter out the uninteresting rules from the data. In this method a correlation measure is used with support-confidence framework for the association rules. This leads to the correlation rules of the form

A => B [support, confidence, correlation]

It states that the correlation rule is measured not only by its support and confidence but also by the correlation between itemsets A and B. there is a variety of correlation measures which can be applied on the data sets, the user need to chose the one depending on the size of data base, the size of data sets under considerations and the requirements of the user.

Lift is a simple correlation measure that states that: ***the occurrence of itemset A is independent of occurrence of itemset B if P(A U B) = P(A) P(B), else the itemsets A and B are dependent and correlated as events.***

It can be measured as

Lift(A, B) = P(A U B)/ P(A). P(B)

The value of Lift indicates the degree of correlation, i.e whether it is positively correlated, negatively coorelated or there exist no coorelation between the itemsets.

Value of Lift(A, B)	Degree of Correlation
< 1	***A and B are negatively correlated.*** The occurrence of A is negatively correlated with the occurrence of B,that means if one of them occurs then it rules out the occurrence of the other one
> 1	***A and B are positively correlated.*** The occurrence of one implies the occurrence of the other.
= 1	***A and B are independent and there is no correlation between them.***

6.8 CONSTRAINT BASED ASSOCIATION MINING

When the process of data mining is applied on a given set of data, then it may uncover thousands of rules, which may not be useful to the user. It results in providing the data which is not required by the user, to overcome this problem, constraint based association mining is used in which ***the mining is performed by applying various kinds of constraints.*** These constraints limit the data which is retrieved during the execution of a particular query. The various types of constraints which can be applied are:

1. ***Knowledge Type Constraints:*** These constraints specify the type of knowledge to be mined.
2. ***Data Constraints:*** These constraints specify the set of task relevant data, like the constraint is applied on the attribute income of the customer, where the query requires the list of customers with income >= 20000.
3. ***Dimension Level Constraint*:** These constraints specify of dimension of data or the levels of the concept hierarchies to be used. Like in the customer data base having the attributes: customerid, name, age, address, mobileno, hobby. The user may not

be interested in all the attributes, so the constraint is applied and the user wish to retrieve only customerid, name and their mobileno only.

These three types of constraints have been discussed earlier in the previous chapters. The new form of constraints that can be applied is the rule constraints.

4. ***Rule Constraints***: these constraints specify the form of rules to be mined. These constraints can be expressed as metarules, as the minimum or maximum number of predicates that can occur in the rule antecedent or consequent or as relationship among attributes, attribute values and /or aggregates.

These constraints allow the user to specify the rules to be mined according to their intention, which will make data mining process more effective and result oriented. Apart from this a sophisticated data mining query optimizer can be used to exploit the constraints provided by the user. This type of mining encourages interactive exploratory mining and analysis.

These metarules allow users to specify the syntactic form of rules that they are interested in mining. Metarules may be based on the experience of analyst, expectations or intuition regarding the data, or may be generated based on the database schema.

Let us suppose, being a librarian in the college library, the data about the students and faculty has been stored with attributes StudentID, name, Course for student and FacultyId, Name, Department and Specialization Area. Apart from this the list of customer transactions is also available. The librarian is interested in finding association between the student/ faculty attributes and the books ordered by them. Inspite of finding all the association rule showing these relationships, the librarian is interested in finding which pairs of student/faculty attributes require the books on Data Mining. A metarule can be used to specify this relationship, the metarule can be defined as:

P1(X, Y) ^ P2(X, W) => demands(X, "Data Mining")

Where P1 and P2 are predicate variables that are instantiated to attributes from the given database during the mining process.

X is a variable representing a Student or Faculty.

Y and W take on values of the attributes assigned to P1 and P2 respectively.

The user will specify a list of attributes that can be considered for P1 and P2, or a default set can be used.

The metarule forms a hypothesis regarding the relationships that the user is interested in searching. The data mining system then searches for rules that match the given meta rule.

SUMMARY

- The discovery of frequent patterns, associations and coorelation relationships in the data items can be used as a tool for making strategic decisions.
- ***Market Basket Analysis*** tries to investigate the buying habits oif the customers by finding out the itemsets that are purchased together or in a sequence.
- ***Association Rule Mining*** finds frequent patterns, interesting associations, causal structures or correlation relationship among a large set of data items or objects in transactional data base, relational data base or other information repositories.
- ***Frequent Patterns*** are the patterns that appear frequently in a data set. Like, a set of items, bread and butter, that appear frequently together in a transaction data set is a frequent item set.
- The association rules are normally measured with the help of following two measures: ***Support and Confidence.***
- ***Support*** of a rule indicates how frequently its items appear in the data base. It is the percentage of transactions in database that contains both A and B, support (A => B) = P(A U B).
- ***Confidence*** of a rule indicates the percentage of transaction in database containing A that also contain B. It is taken to the conditional probability, P(B| A). confidence (A => B) = P(B\A).
- The process of association rule mining is a two-step process: firstly all frequent itemset are found and then strong association rules from the frequent item sets are generated.
- The association rules can be classified on the basis of the *type of values handled in the rule, the dimensions of data involved in the rule, various extensions to association mining and based on the levels of abstractions involved in the rule set.*
- **Apriori** is an influential algorithm for mining frequent itemsets for boolean association rules.
- ***Apriori property*** used in this algorithm is that all non empty subsets of a frequent itemset must also be frequent.
- Various methods to improve efficiency of Apriori's Algorithm are *Hash-based Itemset, Counting, Transaction Reduction, Partitioning Sampling and Dynamic Itemset Counting.*
- ***Coorelation*** may also be calculated along with the support and confidence value.
- ***Lift*** is a simple correlation measure that states that: the occurrence of itemset A is independent of occurrence of itemset B if P(A U B) = P(A) P(B), else the itemsets A and B are dependent and correlated as events.
- In the concept of ***constrained mining***, the mining is performed by applying various kinds of constraints like knowledge type constraints, data constraints, dimension and rule level constraints.
- ***Rule Constraints*** specify the form of rules to be mined. These constraints can be expressed as metarules, as the minimum or maximum number of predicates that can occur in the rule antecedent or consequent or as relationship among attributes, attribute values and /or aggregates.
- ***Constrained Mining*** allow the user to specify the rules to be mined according to their intention, which will make data mining process more effective and result oriented.

CHAPTER 7

CLASSIFICATION

7.1 MEANING OF CLASSIFICATION

A huge amount of information is hidden in the data bases that can be used for making better decisions. The biggest problem is that the huge amount of data stored in the databases is not organized and classified. The data if classified into various classes or categories can be used for making better decisions at a fast rate, which will help the decision makers to predict the future trends.

Classification is the concept which we use in our day to day operations many a times.

A kid is given the task to classify the various objects depending upon some noticeable characteristics. The child may be asked to put all red colored balls into one bucket and blue colored balls into another one.

We classify our friends as loyal or disloyal, our servants as honest or cheaters, our eatables as vegetables or fruits, our computer components as hardware or software, the students of our class as intelligent or duffers.

This classification helps us to categorize the large data objects into different classes and hence these classes can be operated upon as and when required. The different classes can be used for different purposes.

Like after classifying our customers as loyal or disloyal, the company can chalk out a plan to deal with them accordingly. The set of students classified as toppers or average can be given assignments depending on their caliber. Classifying the Post Graduate students of computer science depending on their area of specialization like databases, programming, networking or testing, will help the institute to organize classes depending upon their area of interest and can be given training accordingly.

Classification is the most commonly applied data mining technique, which employs a set of pre-classified examples to develop a model that can classify the population of records at large. The criteria for classification vary from organization to organization and it will depend on the objectives for which the classification is to be done. The classification will help the organization to do the focused marketing and fraud detection. The data classification process involves learning and classification. In Learning the training data is analyzed by the classification algorithm. In classification test data is used to estimate the accuracy of the classification rules. If the accuracy is acceptable, the rules can be applied to the new data tuples. For a fraud detection application, this would include complete records of both fraudulent and valid activities determined on record-by-record basis.

Examples of Classification Task:

- Predicting tumor cells as benign or malignant.
- Classifying credit card transactions as legitimate or fraudulent.
- Classifying secondary structures of protein as alpha-helix, beta-sheet, or random coil.
- Classifying customers as loyal or disloyal.
- Categorizing news stories as finance, weather, entertainment, sports, etc.

7.2 APPLICATIONS OF CLASSIFICATION

- ***Fraud Detection:*** Any financial organization mostly wishes to identify the transactions leading to fraud. Like in banking sector the loan officer wish to analyze its data to find out the loan applications that are safe or risky for the bank. By scanning the transaction data and customer details, the loan applications can be classified into the categories of safe and risky.
- ***Target Marketing:*** The marketing manager wish to analyze the customer data to know whether a customer with a given profile will buy the new product or not. If two new products have been launched by the company and they wish to make their existing and the prospective customers aware about these products, both of these products have different characteristics and the target customers are different. The first option is let the call centre representative inform all the customers about both the products. And the second option is classify the customers into two categories, first one with the group of customers who will be interested in the product type A and the ones interested in product type B and let the representative call the respective group for the product they will be interested in, it will enhance the response rate and the better results can be obtained in the minimum time.
- ***Performance Prediction:*** The decision maker is interested to find out the performance of various machines, men and products used in the production process. The classification technique will help them to classify the machines in to the categories of machines providing high output, average and /or low output and hence can be utilized accordingly. The men can be classified as excellent workers, average workers and below average and hence can be assigned tasks depending on their caliber. Like in a software development company the programmers can be classified according to language they use as development tool and hence can be assigned projects accordingly.
- ***Medical Diagnosis*:** A medical researcher wants to analyze cancer data to predict which one of various treatment patterns available should be given to the patient. Depending on the symptoms of the particular patient the patients can be classified into different categories and accordingly the particular treatment can be given to the patients.

In all these cases, the task of data analysis is termed as classification, where a model or classifier is constructed to predict class or categorical labels such as 'safe' or 'risky' for loan application data, 'yes' or 'no' for the marketing data. These categories can be represented by discrete values where ordering among values have no specific meaning.

General Approach to Classification: The general approach to classification is a two-step process:

Step I: ***Learning Step:*** Build a classification model based on previous data. It is built describing a predetermined set of data classes or concepts. For this purpose the data base tuples described by the attributes are analyzed. Each tuple is assumed to belong to a predefined class.

Step II: ***Classification Step:*** Determine if model is acceptable, then use the model to classify the new data. Before applying the model, the predictive accuracy of the model is estimated. The hold out method is simple technique that uses a test set of class labeled samples. These samples are randomly selected and are independent of training samples. The accuracy of the model on a given test set is the percentage of test set samples that are correctly classified by the model.

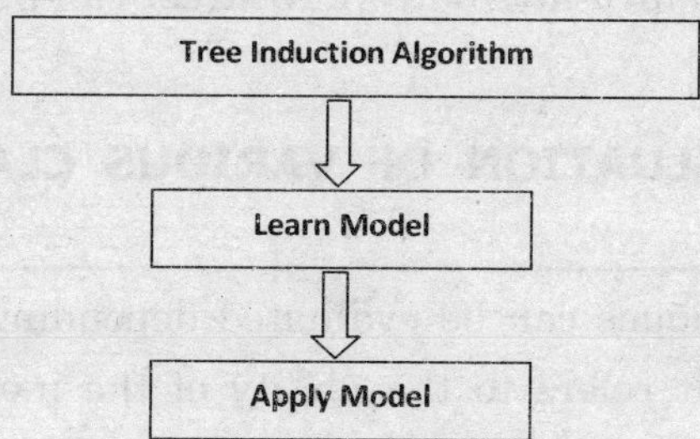

Fig. 7.1: Decision Tree Classification Task

The technique collects different attributes of customers based on their geographical and lifestyle related information, group them together and then customize the services according to the general requirements of the group. Like if we consider the customers of the banking sector, the customers from different job sectors or the customers from fixed salary background or from business class, have different set of choices for the type of accounts they open and the requirements of services from the banks. If the customers have been clustered into categories then the bank can offer the services as per the requirement of the cluster members and hence the effort from the bank side will reduce and on the other hand the satisfaction level of the customers will increase many fold.

7.3 DATA PREPARATION FOR CLASSIFICATION

The following pre-processing steps may be applied to the data in order to improve the accuracy, efficiency and scalability of classification models.

1. **Data Cleaning:** This refers to the preprocessing of data in order to remove or reduce noise, treatment of missing values(like by replacing a missing value with the most commonly occurring value for that attribute or with the most probable value based on statistics).

2. **Relevance Analysis:** Most of the times it has been observed that many attributes in the data may be irrelevant to the classification task. For example, data recording the day of the week on which a bank loan application was filed is unlikely to be relevant for the success of the application. Many a times a number of attributes are recorded which may not be relevant for the current analysis. More over on some occasions redundant attributes are also recorded, which may make the classification process tiresome, or may mislead or slow down the learning step. In order to remove the irrelevant data or the redundant attributes the process of ***relevance analysis*** is carried out. The time spent on relevance analysis when added to the time spent on learning from the resulting reduced feature subset, should ideally be less than the time that would have been spent on learning from the original set of features. The analysis carried out can help in improving the efficiency of classification process.
3. **Data Transformation:** The discrete or continuous values of data items can be transformed into a form which will be helpful in making the analysis process easier and more result oriented. For this purpose data can be generalized to higher level concepts and concept hierarchies can be used for this purpose. Like the numeric values of income may be generalized to discrete ranges like low, medium and high. Similarly, the nominal-valued attributes like street can be generalized to higher level concepts like city.

7.4 CRITERIAS FOR EVALUATION OF VARIOUS CLASSIFICATION TECHNIQUES

The various classification techniques can be evaluated depending on the following criterias:

1. ***Predictive Accuracy*:** It refers to the ability of the model to correctly predict the class label of new or previously unseen data.
2. ***Speed:*** It refers to the computation costs involved in generating and using the model.
3. ***Robustness:*** This is the ability of the model to make correct predictions given noisy data or data with missing values.
4. ***Scalability*:** It refers to the ability to construct the model efficiently given large amounts of data.
5. ***Interpretability:*** It refers to the level of understanding and insight that is provided by the model.

7.5 VARIOUS CLASSIFICATION TECHNIQUES

The common classification techniques are:

1. Decision Tree based Methods
2. Rule-based Methods
3. Memory based reasoning
4. Neural Networks
5. Naïve Bayes and Bayesian Belief Networks
6. Support Vector Machines.

7.5.1 Decision Tree Based Classification

A decision tree is a flow chart like tree structure where each internal node denotes a test on an attribute, each branch represents an outcome of the test and leaf nodes represent classes or class distributions. The top most node in the tree is called the root node. In order to classify a given sample, the attribute values of the sample are tested against the decision tree. The path is traced from the root of the tree to the leaf node till the data matching the sample is not reached. An example of decision tree is shown in the Fig. 7.2 given below, it checks whether the allocation of loan to a particular customer is safe or not. The Table 7.1 given below shows the corresponding data. In the decision tree, the internal nodes are denoted by rectangles and leaf nodes are denoted by ovals. The decision tress prepared may produce binary or non-binary trees, where binary tree is tree in which each internal node branches to exactly two other nodes.

Table 7.1: The Sample Data

Transaction ID	Refund	Martial Status	Income	Cheat
101	Yes	Single	25000	No
102	No	Married	50000	No
103	No	Divorced	40000	Yes
104	Yes	Married	15000	No
105	Yes	Married	35000	No
106	Yes	Single	25000	No
107	No	Single	10000	Yes

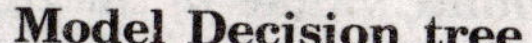

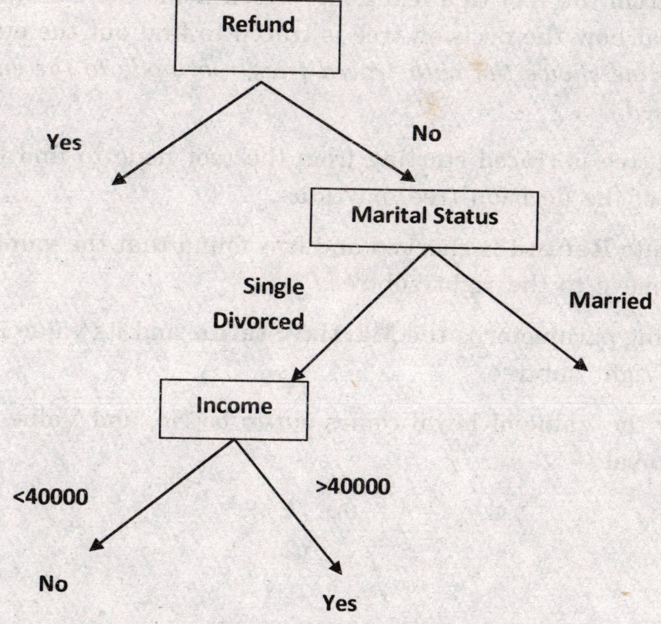

Fig. 7.2: Decision Tree I for Sample Data in Table 7.1

There can be more than one tree that fits the same data. Fig. 7.3 shows the second decision tree for sample data in Table 7.1.

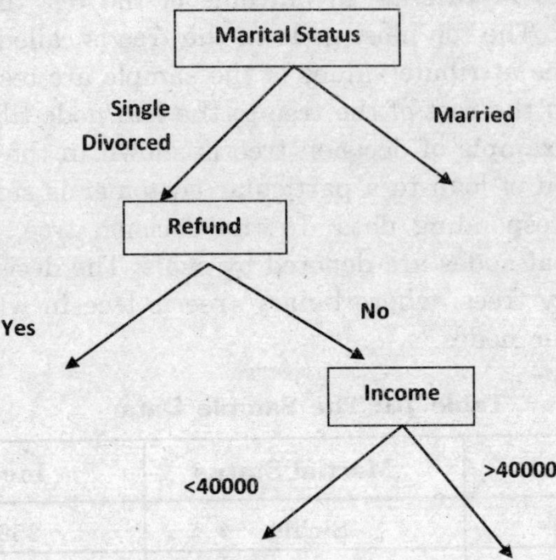

Fig. 7.3: Decision Tree II for Sample Data in Table 7.1

This covers the learning step, and then the second step ***classification Step*** is performed, in which it is evaluated that whether the model is acceptable or not, if yes, then use the model to classify the new data. It is checked that how the decision trees can be used for classification. Given a tuple X, the attribute values of the tuple are tested against the decision tree. A path is traced from the root to a leaf node, which holds the class prediction for that tuple. Fig. 7.4 show that how the decision tree is traced to find out the outcome of the test data given, *the dotted line shows the path traced from root node to the end of the tree, till the result is not obtained.*

The given decision tree is traced starting from the root node to find the test data, the step by step scanning of the decision tree moves as:

1. The first attribute **Refund** is checked and it is found that the value of this attribute is **No** and we move to the right subtree.
2. The next deciding parameter is the **Martial Status**, and its value is **Married,** so we again move to right subtree.
3. And ultimately the Value of Loyal comes out to be No, and Value No is assigned to the attribute Loyal.

Test Data

Refund	Martial Status	Income	Loyal
No	Married	50000	?

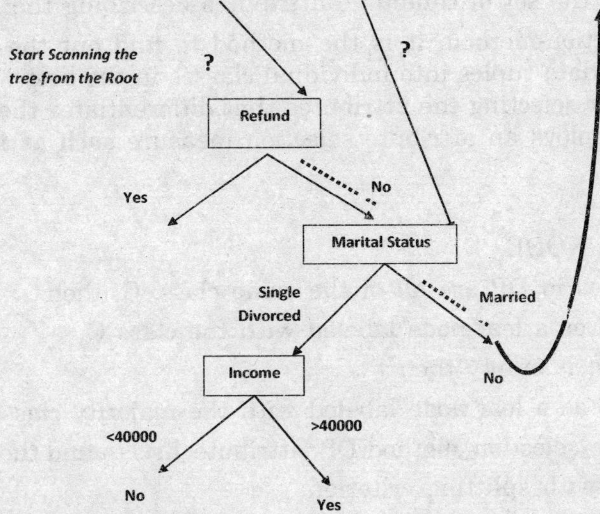

Fig. 7.4: Tracing the Decision Tree to find the Value of Given Attribute

7.5.2 Decision Tree Induction

Decision trees are trees that classify instances by sorting them based on feature values. Each node in a decision tree represents a feature in an instance to be classified, and each branch represents a value that the node can assume. Instances are classified starting at the root node and sorted based on their feature values.

To describe a basic algorithm for leaning decision trees. Following steps are carried out:

- ***Tree Construction***, during this phase attribute selection measures are used to select the attributes that partitions the tuples into distinct classes in the best way possible.
- ***Tree Pruning***: It attempts to identify and remove the branches of tree which may reflect noise or outliers in the training data. It will enhance the classification accuracy on unseen data.

The various Decision Tree Algorithms are:

- ***Hunt's Algorithm (one of the earliest)***
- ***ID3(Iterative Dichotomiser) developed by J. Ross Quinlan***
- ***C4.5 developed by Quinlan***
- ***CART(Classification and Regression Trees) developed by L.Breiman, J. Friedman, R. Olshen and C.Stone.***
- ***SLIQ,SPRINT***

Most of these algorithms adopt ***Greedy Strategy***, in which decision trees are constructed in top-down recursive divide-and-conquer manner. In this approach, the records are split based on an attribute test that optimizes certain criterion, but the major issue in this concern is to determine how to split the records, to what extent these should be splitted and to determine when to stop splitting. The algorithm given below is a version of ID3, a well known decision tree induction algorithm.

Algorithm: Generate_Decision_Tree:

This algorithm will generate a decision tree from the training tuples of data partition, DP.

Inputs to the Algorithm:

1. Data Partition, DP, which is a set of training tuples and their associated class labels.
2. Attribute_list, the set of candidate attributes describing the tuples.
3. Attribute-selection-method, it is the method to find out the splitting criterion that partitions the data tuples into individual classes in the best way possible. It specifies a procedure for selecting the attributes that differentiates the given tuples according to class. It employs an attribute selection measure such as information gain or the Gini index.

Procedure:

1. Create a node NODE,
2. If all the tuples in DP are all of the same class, C, then
3. Return NODE as a leaf node labeled with the class C.
4. If attribute_list is empty then
5. Return NODE as a leaf node labeled with the majority class in data partition, DP
6. Apply attribute_selection_method(DP, attribute_list) to find the best splitting criterion.
7. Label node N with splitting criterion.
8. If splitting_attribute is of discrete value and multiway splits are allowed then remove splitting attribute.
9. For each outcome j of splitting criterion, let Dj be the set of data tuples in DP satisfying outcome j= ai
10. If Dj is empty then, attach a leaf labled with the majority class in DP to node NODE.
11. else attach the node returned by Generate_decision tree(Dj, attribute_list) to node NODE.
12. Return NODE.

The tree starts as a single node representing the training samples in step 1, if all samples belong to the same class, then the node becomes a leaf and is labled with that class (steps 2 and 3), otherwise the algorithm uses an entropy based measure known as *information gain* as a heuristic for selecting the attribute that will best separate the samples into individual classes(step 6). This attribute becomes the test or decision attribute at the node (step 7). A branch is created for each known value of the test attribute and the samples are partitioned accordingly. The algorithm uses the same process recursively to form a decision tree for the samples at each partition. Once an attribute has occurred at a node, it need not be considered in any of the node's descendents (step 11).

The recursive partitioning stops only when anyone of the following conditions is true:

1. All samples for a given node belong to the same class(steps 2 and 3) or
2. There are no remaining attributes on which the samples may be further partitioned (step 4). In this case, majority voting is employed (step 5). This involves converting the given node into a leaf and labeling it with the class in majority among samples. Otherwise the class distribution of the node samples may be stored.

3. There are no samples for the branch test attribute = ai(step 10). In this case, a leaf is created with the majority class in samples.(step 11)

Advantages:

1. The decision trees are inexpensive to construct and the construction of decision tree classifiers does not need any domain knowledge or parameter setting; hence these are best suited for exploratory knowledge discovery.
2. Decision trees can handle multi-dimensional data.
3. These are extremely fast at classifying unknown records.
4. It is easy to interpret if tree is of small-size.
5. Accuracy is comparable to other classification techniques for many simple data sets.

Decision tree induction algorithms have been used for classification in many application areas, like medicine, manufacturing, production, financial analysis, molecular biology, astronomy, marketing etc. The computational complexity of the algorithm given training set D is O(n * |D| * log (|D|)), where n is the number of attributes describing the tuples in D and |D| is the number of training tuples in D. This means that the computational cost of growing a tree grows at most n * |D| * log (|D|) with |D| tuples.

7.6 ATTRIBUTE SELECTION MEASURE

An attribute selection measure is a heuristic for selecting the splitting criteria that separates a given data partition D into individual classes. If we split D into smaller partitions according to the outcomes of the splitting criterion. Then for each partition all the tuples that fall into a given partition would belong to the same class. These measures are also termed as splitting rules, as these determine how the tuples at a given node are to be split. This method provides a ranking for each attribute and the attribute having the best score for the measure is chosen as the splitting attribute for the given tuples. The most common attribute selection measures are:

1. Information gain.
2. Gain ratio.
3. Gini Index.

The following terminology has been used to explain these concepts:

Let D, is the data partition, which contains the training set of class labeled tuples.

The class label attribute has m distinct values defing m distinct classes, Ci(i = 1, 2, ... m). Let Ci, D be the set of tuples of class Ci in D.

Let |D| and |Ci,D| denote the number of tuples in D and Ci, D respectively.

1. Information Gain: This measure is used to select the test attribute at each node in the tree. This measure is known as attribute selection measure or a measure of the goodness of split. This measure is used in ID3 method of classification and is based on the work proposed by Claude Shannon on information theory. ***The attribute with the highest information gain is chosen as the test attribute for the current node.*** This attribute minimizes the information needed to classify the samples in the resulting partitions and reflects the least randomness or impurity in these partitions. This is a theoretical approach which minimizes the expected number of tests needed to classify an object and guarantees that a simple tree is found.

Let node N represent or hold the tuples of partition D. The attribute with the highest information gain is chosen as the splitting attribute for node N. This attribute minimizes the information needed to classify the tuples in the resulting partitions.

The expected information needed to classify a tuple in D is given by:

$$\text{Info (D)} = -\,\Sigma(i = 1 \text{ to } m)\ pi \log_2(pi)$$

Where pi is the non-zero probability that an arbitrary tuple in D belongs to class Ci and it is estimated by |Ci, D|/D|. *A log function to the base 2 is used as the information is encoded into binary form.*

Info(D) is just the average amount of information needed to identify the class label of a tuple in D. Info(D) is also known as the entropy of D.

More information would be required to arrive at an exact classification, this amount is measured by:

$$\text{Info'(D)} = \Sigma\ (j = 1 \text{ to } v)\ |Dj|/|D| * \text{Info(Dj)}$$

Where |Dj|/|D| acts as the weight of the jth partition. It is the expected information required to classify a tuple from D based on the partitioning by A, the smaller the expected information required the greater is the purity of partitions.

Information Gain *is defined as the difference between the original information requirement and the new requirement. The original information requirement is based on the proportion of classes and the new requirement is obtained after partitioning on A.*

$$\text{Therefore, Gain(A)} = \text{Info(D)} - \text{Info'(D)}$$

The attribute A with the highest information gain, Gain(A) is chosen as the splitting attribute at node N.

Example: Table 7.2 given below presents the training data, of class labeled tuples selected randomly from the University Data Base. The class label attribute joins elite club has two distinct values {yes, no}, therefore there are two distinct classes (i.e m = 2).

Table 7.2: Sample Data Base(Training Data)

Sno	Age	Income	Urbanite	Class:Joins_elite_club
1	Youth	High	No	No
2	Youth	High	No	No
3	Youth	Medium	No	No
4	Youth	Low	Yes	Yes
5	Youth	Medium	Yes	Yes
6	Middle_aged	High	No	Yes
7	Middle_aged	Low	Yes	Yes
8	Middle_aged	Medium	No	Yes
9	Middle_aged	High	Yes	Yes
10	Senior	Medium	No	Yes
11	Senior	Low	Yes	Yes
12	Senior	Low	Yes	No
13	Senior	Medium	Yes	Yes
14	Senior	Medium	No	No

Let C1 is the class which corresponds to the response **Yes** and

C2 is the class which corresponds to the response **No**.

There are 9 tuples of class **Yes** and 5 tuples of class **No**.

To find the splitting criterion for these tuples, we must compute the information gain of each attribute. The expected information needed to classify a tuple in D:

$$\text{Info(D)} = -\ 9/14 \log_2(9/14) - 5/14 \log_2(5/14) = 0.940 \text{ bits}$$

If we need to compute the expected information requirement for each attribute. Let the attribute selected is age.

There are three age categories and the number of tuples for each category is shown below in the Table 7.3:

Table 7.3: Information Grouped by the Attribute 'Age'

Category	Number of Tuples with Response - Yes	Number of Tuples with Response - No
Youth	2	3
Middle-aged	4	00
Senior	3	2

The expected information needed to classify a tuple in D, if the tuples are partitioned according to age is

$$\begin{aligned}\text{Info(age)(D)} &= 5/14 * (-2/5 \log_2 2/5 - 3/5 \log_2 3/5) + 4/14*(-4/14 \log_2 4/4) + \\ &\quad 5/14 * (-3/5 \log_2 3/5 - 2/5 \log_2 2/5) \\ &= 0.694\end{aligned}$$

Therefore, the gain in information from such a partitioning would be:

$$\text{Gain(age)} = \text{Info(D)} - \text{Info(age)(D)} = 0.940 - 0.694 = 0.246.$$

Similarly, the user can calculate Gain(Income)

Calculations for Gain (Income)

There are three income categories, namely, high, medium and low and the number of tuples for each category are:

Category	Number of Tuples with Response Yes	Number of Tuples with Response No
High	2	2
Medium	4	2
Low	3	1

The expected information needed to classify a tuple in D if the tuples are partitioned according to income is

Info(income)(D) = 4/14 * (–2/4 $\log_2$ 2/4 – 2/5 $\log_2$ 2/5) + 6/14 * (–4/6 $\log_2$ 4/6 – 2/6 $\log_2$ 2/6) + 4/14 * (–3/4 $\log_2$ 3/4 – 1/4 $\log_2$ 1/4)

= ?

Gain(income) = 0.029 bits

Proceeding in the same way, next the Gain(Locality) is calculated and it comes out to be 0.151.

Upon inspecting the different values of Gain, it is found that ***highest information gain* is for *age* and hence age is selected as the *splitting attribute.*** A node is created and labeled with age and branches are grown for each of the attribute's values. The resultant decision tree is shown below in Fig. 7.5.

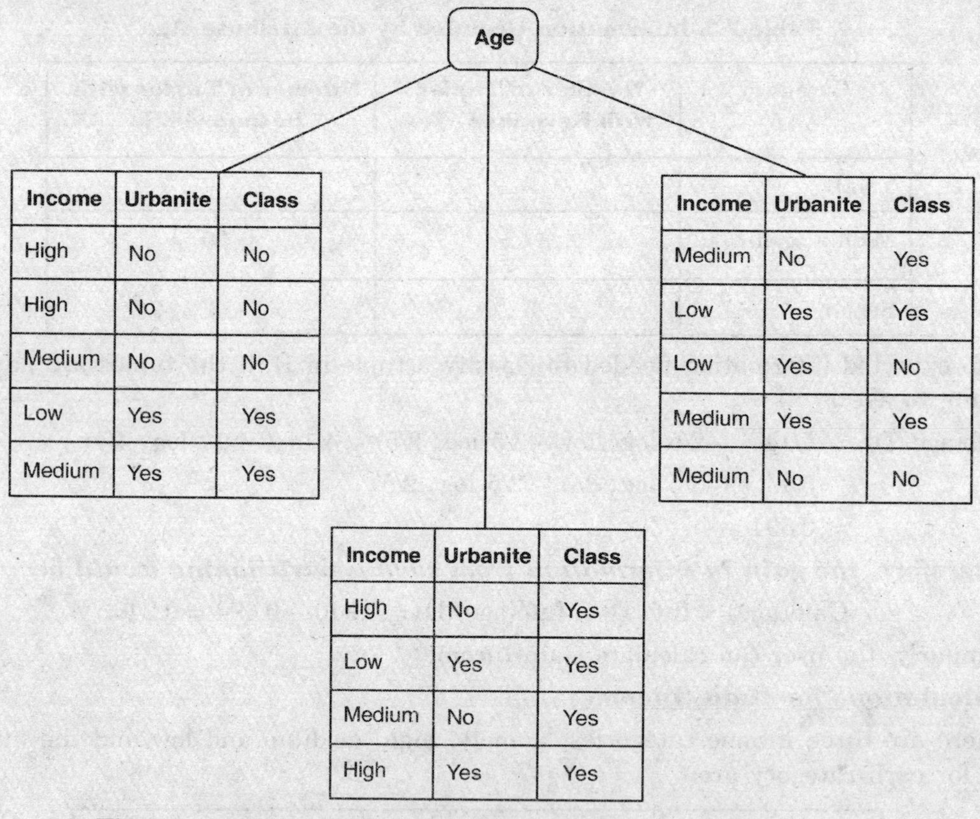

Income	Urbanite	Class
High	No	No
High	No	No
Medium	No	No
Low	Yes	Yes
Medium	Yes	Yes

Income	Urbanite	Class
Medium	No	Yes
Low	Yes	Yes
Low	Yes	No
Medium	Yes	Yes
Medium	No	No

Income	Urbanite	Class
High	No	Yes
Low	Yes	Yes
Medium	No	Yes
High	Yes	Yes

Fig. 7.5: Content of Table 7.2 Splitted Over the Attribute- Age [As Age has Maximum Information Gain]

Limitations: This method is biased towards tests with many outcomes. It selects attributes having a large number of values. Like, for an attribute that acts as a unique identifier like student_id. A split on student_id will result in a large number of partitions,(equal to the number of values for student_id), each one having just one tuple. In this case, each partition is pure and the information required to classify data set D based on this partitioning would be Info(student_id)(D) = 0. So, the information gained by partitioning on this attribute is maximal. It is quite evident that such a partitioning is useless for classification.

2. Gain Ratio: To overcome the limitations of information gain method mentioned above, an extension to this method is used, this new measure is named as *gain ratio*. It is used by the C4.5 algorithm. It tries to apply normalization to information gain using a split information value which is quite similar to Info(D) as:

$$\text{SplitInfoA(D)} = -\ \Sigma(\ j = 1 \text{ to } n)\ |Dj|/|D| * \log_2\ (|Dj|/|Di|)$$

It represents the information generated by splitting training data set D into n partitions. For each outcome, it considers the number of tuples having that outcome w.r.t the total number of tuples in D. The gain ratio is defined as:

$$\text{GainRatio(A)} = \text{Gain(A)} / \text{SplitInfoA(D)}$$

The attribute with maximum gain ratio is selected as the splitting attribute. As the split information approaches to 0, the ratio becomes unstable.

Example: A test on income splits the data into three partitions, low, medium and high, containing 4, 6 and 4 tuples repectively. So the gain ratio is calculated as:

$$\text{SplitInfoincome(D)} = -4/14 \log_2(4/14) - 6/14 \log_2(6/14) - 4/14 \log_2(4/14) = 1.557.$$

As calculated earlier, Gain(income) = 0.029, therefore,

GainRatio(Income) = 0.029/1.557 = 0.019

3. Gini Index: This measure is used in CART. It measures the impurity of D, a data partition or set of training tuples as:

$$\text{Gini(D)} = 1 - \Sigma(i = 1 \text{ to } m)\ pi^2$$

Where pi is the probability that a tuple in D belongs to class Ci and is estimated by |Ci, D|/|D|. This sum is computed over m classes.

Example: Let D be the training data show in Table 7.2, where there are 9 tuples which belong to class joins_elite_class = Yes, and remaining 5 tuples belong to class class joins_elite_class = No. A root node N is created for the tuples in D and the Gini Index to compute the impurity od D:

$$\text{Gini(D)} = 1 - (9/14)^2 - (5/14)^2 = 0.459$$

To find the splitting criterion for the tuples in D, we need to compute the Gini Index for each attribute. Let us consider the attribute income and the possible splitting subsets, let the subset {low, medium}, There are 10 tuples in partition A1 satisfying {low, medium} and the remaining four tuples of D would be assigned to partition A2. The Gini Index value is computed as:

$$\begin{aligned}\text{Gini income}<\{\text{low,medium}\}(D) &= 10/14\ \text{Gini(A1)} + 4/14\ \text{Gini(A2)}\\ &= 10/14\ (1 - (7/10)^2 - (3/10)^2) + 4/14(1 - (2/4)^2 - (2/4)^2)\\ &= 0.443\end{aligned}$$

Gini Index Values for splits on the remaining subsets,

{low, high} and {medium} = 0.458

{medium, high} and {low} = 0.450

The best binary split for attribute income is on {low, medium} and {high}, as it minimizes the Gini Index.

SUMMARY

- This classification helps us to categorize the large data objects into different classes and hence these classes can be operated upon as and when required.
- The various applications areas of Classification are fraud detection, target marketing, performance prediction and medical diagnosis.
- General Approach to Classification is a two-step process, comprising of learning step and Classification Step:
- The process of classification involves data cleaning, relevance analysis and data transformation.
- Criterias for evaluation of various classification techniques are predictive accuracy, speed: robustness, scalability, interpretability.
- The common classification techniques are: decision tree based Methods, rule-based Methods, memory based reasoning method, neural networks, Naïve Bayes and Bayesian Belief Networks and Support Vector Machines.
- Decision tree induction is a top-down recursive tree induction algorithm, which uses the attributes selection measure to select attribute tested for each non-leaf node in the tree.
- The various Decision Tree Algorithms are, Hunt's Algorithm, ID3(Iterative Dichotomiser), C4.5, CART(Classification and Regression Trees), SLIQ and SPRINT.
- The decision trees algorithms are inexpensive to construct, can handle multi-dimensional data, are extremely fast at classifying unknown records and provide accurate results.
- An attribute selection measure is a heuristic for selecting the splitting criteria that separates a given data partition D into individual classes.
- The most common attribute selection measures are: Information gain, Gain ratio and Gini Index.
- Information Gain is defined as the difference between the original information requirement and the new requirement. The original information requirement is based on the proportion of classes and the new requirement is obtained after partitioning on A.
- The attribute with the highest information gain is chosen as the splitting attribute at node N.
- Gain ration is used by the C4.5 algorithm. It tries to apply normalization to information gain using a split information value. The gain ratio is defined as:
- GainRatio(A) = Gain(A)/SplitInfoA(D).
- The attribute with maximum gain ratio is selected as the splitting attribute.
- Gini Index is used in CART. It measures the impurity of D, a data partition or set of training tuples as: Gini(D) = 1 – Σ(i = 1 to m) pi^2.
- The attribute with minimum gini index is selected as splitting attribute.

CHAPTER 8

PREDICTION TECHNIQUES

8.1 MEANING OF PREDICTION

Prediction about the future is a very interesting area. Every body of us is curious to know what will happen in future. The organizations, big or small are always interested in predicting the future trends in the market and the possible outcomes of a particular course of action. They are investing a huge amount of money on men, material and machines, so it is quite obvious that they are more worried about the probable outcomes and wish to secure their return on investment. If any individual or organization is able to predict the future before hand, then they will be able to decide their actions accordingly. For Example, if we have predicted that a particular machinery will fail this year, then we can take remedial actions before hand, if the organizations can predict the frauds and can predict the future course of action of the customers, they can design the strategies accordingly.

Prediction is a combination of various data mining techniques. It involves analyzing trends, classification, pattern matching, and relation. By analyzing past events or instances, the user can make prediction about an event.

Predictive data mining (PDM) works the same way as does a human handle data analysis for a small data set; however, PDM can be used for a large data set without the constraints that a human analyst has. According to Fayyad, data mining can be divided into two tasks: predictive tasks and descriptive tasks. The ultimate aim of data mining is prediction; therefore, predictive data mining is the most common type of data mining and is the one that has the most application to businesses or life concerns. PDM "learns" from past experience and applies this knowledge to present or future situations. Applications suitable for data mining are vast and have not been explored in many areas of business and life concerns.

According to Betts," data mining yields unexpected nuggets of information that can open a company's eyes to new markets, new ways of reaching customers and new ways of doing business."

Predictive data mining has three stages:

1. **Data Preprocessing,** which includes data preparation and data reduction.
2. **Data Mining,** which involves the extraction of data from data warehouses using various data-mining techniques.

3. **Data Post-Processing**, which involves the interpretation of results and demonstrating?

These stages are elaborated upon in Fig. 8.1, which shows a more complete picture of all the aspects of data mining.

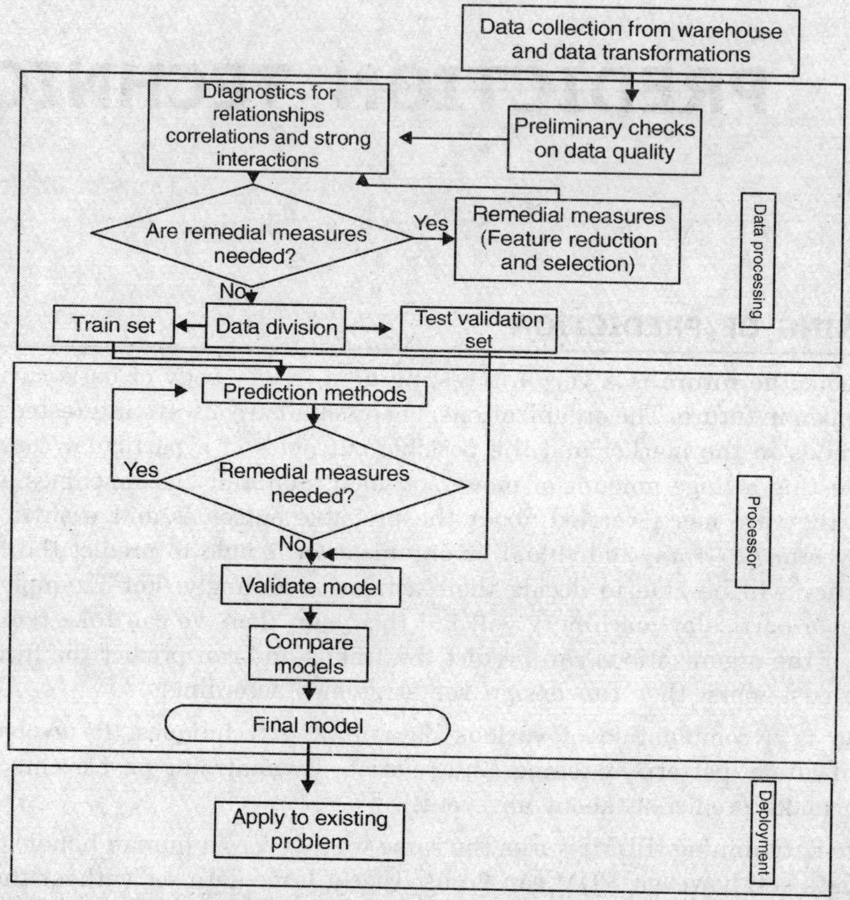

Fig. 8.1: The stages of predictive data mining.

8.2 METRICS FOR EVALUATING THE ACCURACY OF A CLASSIFIER

For a classification model, let the input from the previous years is used to build a classifier to predict the future trends. Then is quite important to estimate how accurately the classifier can predict the purchasing behavior of future customers. Many a times the user prepares more than one classifier and then try to compare their level of accuracy and hence the efficiency. But the important point here is How to measure the accuracy? What methods can be used to measure the accuracy and which method is accurate and why?

It is important to judge that how good or how accurate the classifier is at predicting the class label of tuples. There are two possibilities: the first one considers that class tuples are more or less evenly distributed and in the other case classes are unbalanced. The various measures for classifier evaluation are listed in the Table 8.1 given below:

Table 8.1: Evaluation Measures

Evaluation Measures	
Measure	**Formula**
accuracy, recognition rate	TP + TN/P + N
error rate	FP + FN/P + N
sensitivity, true positive rate, recall	TP/P
specificity, true negative rate	TN/N
precision	TP/TP + FP
F, F1, F-score	2 * precision * recall/precision + recall
Fβ	$(1 + \beta^2)$ * precision * recall/β^2 * precision + recall

Using training data to derive a classifier and then estimate the accuracy of the resulting learned model can result in misleading overoptimistic estimates due to over-specialization of learning algorithm to the data. Instead, it is better to measure the accuracy of the classifier on a test set containing class-labeled tuples that were not used to train the model.

Let us consider the students data base containing the students records, the various tuples in the database can be categorized as:

Positive Tuples: These are the tuples which are of interest for present study, like hostel-facility = yes is a positive tuple,

Negative tuples: These are all other tuples not included in the first category, hostel-facility = no is a negative tuple.

Let P = Number of positive tuples

N = Number of negative tuples.

For each tuple, we compare the classifier's class label prediction with the tuple's known class label. The basic terminology used in measurement of accuracy is:

True Positives (TP): These are positive tuples that were correctly labeled by the classifier.

True Negatives (TN): These are negative tuples that were correctly labeled by the classifier.

False Positives (FP): These are the negative tuples that were incorrectly labeled as positive like tuples of class hostel-facility = no for which the classifier predicted hostel-facility = yes.

False Negatives (FN): These are the positive tuples that were mislabeled as negative. like tuples of class hostel-facility = yes for which the classifier predicted hostel-facility = no

These terms have been explained in the ***Confusion Matrix*** given below in Fig. 8.2.

Confusion Matrix is a powerful tool for analyzing how well the classifier can recognize tuples of different classes. TP and TN tells us when the classifier is getting things right and FP and FN tell us when the classifier is getting things wrong.

Confusion Matrix				
		Predicted Class		**Total**
		yes	no	
Actual Class	yes	TP	FN	P
	No	FP	TN	N
Total		P'	N'	P + N

Fig. 8.2: Confusion Matrix

Given m classes (m > = 2), a confusion matrix is a table of atleast size m * m. An entry i, j in the matrix show the number of tuples of class i that are labeled by the classifier as class j. A classifier will have good accuracy if most of the tuples have been represented along the diagonal of the matrix, and the result of the entries being zero or close to zero. i.e FP and FN are around zero, ideally. From the Fig. 8.2, following observations can be made:

$$P' = TP + FP.$$

$$N' = FN + TN.$$

$$TP + FN + FP + TN = P + N = P' + N'.$$

The various measure to evaluate accuracy of a classifier are:

Accuracy: It is defined as percentage of test set tuples that are correctly classified by the classifier. i.e.

$$\text{Accuracy} = TP + TN/P + N.$$

Error Rate: It is also termed as misclassification rate of a classifier M,

Error rate = 1 – accuracy (M), where accuracy (M) is the accuracy of M.

Error rate = FP + FN/P + N.

Sensitivity: It is defined as true positive rate or recognition rate, it is the proportion of positive tuples that are correctly identified.

$$\text{sensitivity} = TP/P$$

Specificity: It is termed as true negative rate, it is the proposition of negative tuples that are correctly identified.

$$\text{specificity} = TN/N.$$

Moreover, accuracy = sensitivity * P/P+N + specificity * N/P + N.

Precision: It can be considered as a measure of exactness, i.e what percentage of tuples labeled as positive are actually so.

$$\text{Precision} = TP/TP + FP$$

If precision is 1 for a class C, it means that every tuple that the classifier labeled as belonging to class C does indeed belong to class C.

Recall: It can be considered as a measure of completeness, i.e what percentage of positive tuples is labeled as such.

$$\text{Recall} = \text{TP/TP} + \text{FN} = \text{TP/P}.$$

If recall is 1 for a class C, that means that every item from class C was labeled as such, but it does not tell how many other tuples were incorrectly labeled as belonging to class C.

F-measure: It is also known as F1 score or F-Score and Fβ. It is a way to combine precision and recall into a single measure.

$$F = 2 * \text{precision} * \text{recall/precision} + \text{recall}.$$

$$F\beta = (1 + \beta^2) * \text{precision} * \text{recall}/\beta^2 * \text{precision} + \text{recall}.$$

where β is a non-negative real number.

F measure is the harmonic mean of precision and recall, it gives equal weight age to precision and recall.

Fβ is a weighted measure and assigns â times as much weights to recall as to precision. Commonly used Fβ measures are:

F2 it weights recall twice as much as precision.

F0.5 weighs precision twice as much as recall.

Apart from measuring a classifier on basis of accuracy based measures, the classifier can be compared on the following aspects:

- **Speed:** It is the time taken to generate and use the given classifier and hence the cost incurred on this process.
- **Robustness:** It is ability of the classifier to work well even if the input is not proper. Like classifier should be able to make the correct predictions although data with missing values or noisy data has been given as input.
- **Scalability:** It refers to the ability to construct the classifier efficiently given large amounts of data. It is checked with a series of data sets of increasing size.
- **Interpretability:** It is a measure of level of understanding and insight that is provided by the classifier or predictor. It varies from context to context and hence is difficult to measure.

8.3 VARIOUS METHODS FOR ASSESSING ACCURACY

8.3.1 Holdout and Random Sampling

In hold out method, the given data set is randomly partitioned into two independent sets, named as training set and test set. Two-thirds of the data is allocated to the training set, and the remaining one-third id allocated to the test set. The training set is used to derive the model. The model's accuracy is then estimated with the test-set, as shown in the Fig. 8.3 given below. This type of estimation is pessimistic as only a portion of the initial data is used to derive the model.

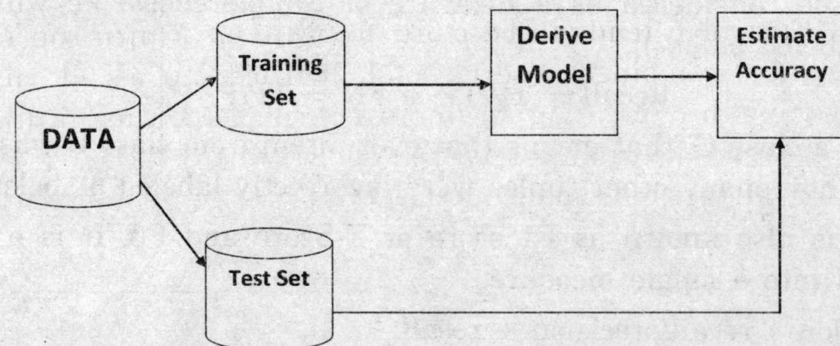

Fig. 8.3: Estimating Accuracy with Holdout Method

Random Sampling is a variation of the holdout method in which the holdout method is repeated n times. The overall accuracy estimate is taken as the average of the accuracies got from each iteration.

8.3.2 Cross-Validation

In a k-fold cross-validation, the initial data is randomly partitioned into k mutually exclusive subsets or folds, D1, D2......Dk, each of approximately equal size. Then training and testing is performed k times.

In ith iteration partition Di is reversed as the test set and the remaining partitions are collectively used to train the model.

In first iteration, subsets D2 .... Dk collectively serve as the training set to obtain a first model, which is tested on D1, the second iteration is trained on subsets D1, D3 .... Dk and tested on D2 and so on.

In this method, each sample is used for the same number of times for training and once for testing. The accuracy estimate is the overall number of correct classifications from k iterations, divided by the total number of tuples in the initial data.

8.3.3 Bootstrap Methods

This method samples the data uniformly with replacement. That is, each time a tuple is selected, it is equally likely to be selected again and re-added to the training set. There are various bootstrap methods, but the most commonly used is .632 bootstrap, in this method, Let a data set of d tuples is given, the data set is sampled d times, with replacement, resulting in a bootstrap sample or training set of d samples. It is possible that some of the original data tuples will occur more than once in the sample. The data tuples not included in training set are considered in the test set. Upon performing it many times, it is observed that 63.2% of the original data tuples will end up in the bootstrap sample and the remaining 36.8% will form the training set.

8.4 TECHNIQUES TO IMPROVE CLASSIFICATION ACCURACY

To improve the classification accuracy, we use ensemble methods. ***An ensemble for classification is a composite model, made up of a combination of classifiers.*** The individual classifier votes and a class label prediction is returned by the ensemble based on the votes collected. Ensemble tends to be more accurate as comparison to their component classifiers. An ensemble combines a series of k learned models or base classifiers M1, M2 .... Mk with the aim of creating an improved composite classification model. A given data set D is used to create k training sets, D1, D2.Dk where Di (1 < = i < = k – 1) is used to generate classifier Mi. An ensemble method tends to be more accurate than its base classifiers. The various ensemble methods are:

- Boosting.
- Bagging.

8.4.1 Boosting

Boosting was invented by two computer scientists at AT&T Labs (Freund and Schapire, 1997). Computer scientists tend to think of boosting as an "ensemble" method (a weighted average of predictions of individual classifiers), whereas statisticians tend to think of boosting as a sequential regression method. To understand why statisticians and computer scientists think about the essentially same algorithms in different ways, both approaches are discussed.

Adaboost, Adaptive Boosting: It is a popular boosting algorithm. It works only in the case where the response variable takes only one of two values: –1 and 1. (Whether the values are 0/1 or –1/1 is not important- the algorithm could be modified easily).

Assumptions of *AdaBoost:*

- Learning algorithm can handle weighted instances (usually handled by randomization schemes for selection of training data subsets).
- By weighting instances, the learning algorithm can concentrate on instances with high weights (called "hard" instances), i.e., incorrectly classified instances.

Main Features of the Algorithm:

- All instances are equally weighted.
- A learning algorithm is applied.
- The weight of incorrectly classified examples is increased ("hard" instances), correctly – classified examples is decreased ("easy" instances).
- The algorithm concentrates on incorrectly classified "hard" instances
- Some "hard" instances become "harder" some "softer".
- A series of diverse experts (classifiers) is generated based on the reweighed data.
- The observations that are repeatedly misclassified are given successively larger weights.
- The final "boosted" classifier consists of a majority-weighted vote of all previous classifiers.
- Boosting adds weak learners one at a time.
- A weight value is assigned to each training point.
- At each step, data points which are currently classified correctly are weighted down (i.e. the weight is smaller the more of the weak learners already trained classify the point correctly).

- The next weak learner is trained on the weighted data set: In the training step, the error contributions of misclassified points are multiplied by the weights of the points.
- Roughly speaking, each weak learner tries to get those points right which are currently not classified correctly.
- Weak learners can be trees (decision stumps are popular), Perceptrons, etc. In principle, any classifier that can be trained on a weighted training set will work.

General Procedure:

Part I: Classifier Generation

Step 0: Set the weight value, w = 1, and assign it to each object in the training data set.

For each of *t* iterations, perform:

Step 1: Apply a learning algorithm to the weighted training data set.

Step 2: Compute classification error e for the weighted training data set. If e = 0 or e > = .5, then terminate the classifier generation process and go to Step 4; otherwise multiple the weight w of each object by e/(1 – e) and normalize the weights of all objects.

Part II: Classification

Step 4: Assign weight q = 0 to each decision (class) to be predicted.

Step 5: For each of *t* (or less) classifiers, add –log e/(1 – e) to the weight of the decision predicted by the classifier and output the decision with the highest weight.

AdaBoost Algorithm: It creates an ensemble of classifier, each one gives a weighted vote.

Input
D, a set of d class labeled training tuples. k the number of rounds , where one classifier is generated per round. a classification learning Scheme.

Algorithm: Ada Boost
Initialize the weight of each tuple in D to 1/d For *m* = 1 to k (a) Sample D with replacement according to the tuple weights to obtain Di (b) Use training set Di to derive a model Mi. (c) Compute error(Mi), by using error(Mi) = Σ wj ∗ err(Xj), where j = 1 to d. (d) if error(Mi) > 0.5 then go back to step a and try again.endif. (e) for each tuple in Di that was correctly classified do (f) multiply the weight of the tuple by error (Mi) / (1- error(Mi)) (g) normalize the weight of each tuple. (h) end for.

To use the ensemble to classify tuple, X

1. Initialize weight of each class to o.
2. for i = 1 to k do
3. wi = log((1-error(Mi)/error(Mi) // weight of classifier's vote
4. c = Mi(X) //get class prediction for X from Mi
5. add wi to weight for class c
6. end for
7. return the class with the largest weight.

Algorithm 1: The AdaBoost algorithm for classification into two categories.

Friedman's Gradient Boosting Algorithm

The AdaBoost algorithm was inefficient on various grounds as the computational learning theory roots of the AdaBoost puzzled statisticians who have traditionally worked from likelihood-based approaches to classification and, more generally, to regression.

Then Friedman et al. (2000) were able to reinterpret this algorithm in a likelihood framework, enabling the authors to form a boosted logistic regression algorithm, a formulation more familiar to the statistical community. Once the connection to the likelihood existed, boosting could be extended to generalized linear models (Friedman 2001, Ridgeway, 1999). This meant that a boosting algorithm could be developed for all the error distributions in common practice: Gaussian, logistic, Poisson, Cox models, etc.

The interpretation of boosting in terms of regression for a continuous, normally distributed response variable is as follows:

The average y-value is used as a first guess for predicting all observations. This is analogous to fitting a linear regression model that consists of the intercept only. The residuals from the model are computed. A regression tree is fit to the residuals. For each terminal node, the average y-value of the residuals that the node contains is computed. The regression tree is used to predict the residuals.

(In the first step, this means that a regression tree is fit to the difference between the observation and the average y-value. The tree then predicts those differences.)

The boosting regression model - consisting of the sum of all previous regression trees - is updated to reflect the current regression tree. The residuals are updated to reflect the changes in the boosting regression model; a tree is fit to the new residuals, and so forth.

Algorithm : Friedman's Gradient Boosting Algorithm

1. Initialization: Set initial guess to y
2. For all regressions trees m = 1 to M:
   (a) Compute the residuals based on the current model $r_{mi} = y_i - f_{m-1}(x_i)$ where i indexes observations. Note that f_{m-1} refers to the sum of all previous regression trees.
   (b) Fit a regression tree (with a fixed number of nodes) to the residuals
   (c) For each terminal node of the tree, compute the average residual. The average value is the estimate for residuals that fall in the corresponding node.
   (d) Add the regression tree of the residuals to the current best fit $f_m = f_{m-1}$ + last regression tree of residuals.

Algorithm 2: Friedman's gradient boosting algorithm for a normally distributed Response

Each term of the regression model thus consists of a tree. Each tree fits the residuals of the prediction of all previous trees combined.

To generalize Algorithm 2 to a more general version with arbitrary distributions requires that "average y-value" be replaced with a function of y-values that is dictated by the specific distribution and that the residual (Step 2a) be a "deviance residual".

The basic boosting algorithm requires the specification of two parameters:

1. The number of splits (or the number of nodes) that are used for fitting each regression tree in step (2b). The number of nodes equals the number of splits plus one. Specifying one split (tree stumps) corresponds to an additive model with only main effects. Specifying two splits corresponds to a model with main effects and two-way interactions. Generally, specifying J splits corresponds to a model with up to J-way interactions. When J x-variables need to be considered jointly for a component of a regression model this is a J-way interaction. Hastie et al. (2001) suggest that $J = 2$ in general is not sufficient and that $4 \leq J \leq 8$ generally works well. They further suggest that the model is typically not sensitive to the exact choice of J within that range. In the Stata implementation J is specified as an option: *interaction*(J).
2. The second parameter is the number of iterations or the number of trees to be fit. If the number of iterations is too large the model will overfit; i.e., it will fit the training data well but not generalize to other observations from the same population. If the number of iterations is too small then the model is not fit as well either. A suitable value for *maxiter* can range from a few dozen to several thousand, depending on the value of a shrinkage parameter (explained below) and the data set. The easiest way to find a suitable number of iterations is to check how well the model fits on a test data set. In the Stata implementation the maximal number of iterations, *maxiter*, is specified and the number of iteration that maximizes the log likelihood on a test data set, *bestiter*, is automatically found. The size of the test data set is controlled by *trainfraction*. For example, if trainfraction = 0.5 then the last 50% of the data are used as test data.

8.4.2 Bagging

This method is used to increase the accuracy. Let a patient has certain symptoms, the patient consults a number of doctors and assign weights to the value or worth to the diagnosis of each doctor, based on accuracies of previous diagnoses made by them. The final diagnosis is then a combination of the weighted diagnoses. Now replace each doctor by a classifier, and it is the idea behind bagging.

Given a set of D of d tuples, the procedure of bagging works as:

1. For iteration i, a training set Di of d tuples is sampled with replacement from the original set of tuples, D. Bagging is also termed as bootstrap aggregation.
2. In this case, sampling with replacement is used where some of the original tuples of D may not be included in Di, whereas others may occur more than once.

3. A classifier model Mi is learned for each training set Di. to classify an unknown tuple, X each classifier Mi returns its class prediction which is counted as one vote. The bagged classifier M* counts the votes and assigns the class with the most votes to X.
4. Bagging can be applied to the prediction of continuous values by taking the average value of each prediction for a given test tuple.
5. The bagged classifier often has significantly greater accuracy than a single classifier derived from D, the original training data.
6. It is robust to the effects of noisy data and over fitting. The increased accuracy occurs as the composite model reduces the variance of the individual classifier.

Algorithm: This algorithm creates an ensemble of classification models for a learning scheme where each model gives an equally weighted prediction.

Input
D a set of d training tuples, k the number of models in the ensemble. A classification learning scheme (decision tree algorithm, naïve Bayesian)

Output
The ensemble- a composite model, M*.

Method:

(i) For i = 1 to k
(ii) Create bootstrap sample, Di by sampling D with replacement.
(iii) Use Di and the learning scheme to derive a model Mi
(iv) end for.

To use the ensemble to classify a tuple, X. Let each of the k models classify X and return the majority vote.

8.4.3 Boosting Vs Bagging

Boosting focuses on the misclassified tuples, it risks over fitting the resulting composite model to such data. So the resulting boosted model may be less accurate than a single model derived from the same data. Whereas, bagging is less susceptible to model over fitting. Both improve accuracy, but ***boosting tends to achieve greater accuracy.***

SUMMARY

- The ultimate aim of data mining is prediction; therefore, predictive data mining is the most common type of data mining and is the one that has the most application to businesses or life concerns.
- Predictive data mining has three stages: ***Data Preprocessing,*** which includes data preparation and data reduction, ***Data Mining,*** which involves the extraction of data from data warehouses using various data-mining techniques and finally, ***Data Post-Processing,*** which involves the interpretation of results and demonstrating important to estimate how accurately the classifier can predict the future trends.
- The various parameters used to measure the accuracy of a classifier are: **accuracy, error rate Sensitivity, specificity, precision, F, F1, F-score and Fβ.**
- Confusion Matrix is a powerful tool for analyzing how well the classifier can recognize tuples of different classes.
- A classifier will have good accuracy if most of the tuples have been represented along the diagonal of the matrix, and the result of the entries being zero or close to zero. i.e FP and FN are around zero, ideally.
- **Accuracy** is defined as percentage of test set tuples that are correctly classified by the classifier. i.e. Accuracy = TP + TN / P + N.
- **Error Rate is measured as,** Error rate = 1 - accuracy (M), where accuracy(M) is the accuracy of M.
- **Sensitivity** is defined as true positive rate or recognition rate, it is the proportion of positive tuples that are correctly identified. sensitivity = TP/P.
- **Specificity** is the proposition of negative tuples that are correctly identified. specificity = TN/N.
- **Precision calculates** what percentage of tuples labeled as positive are actually so. Precision = TP/TP + FP.
- **Recall calculates** what percentage of positive tuples is labeled as such. It is calculated as, Recall = TP/TP+FN = TP/P.
- F-measure is a way to combine precision and recall into a single measure.

  F = 2 * precision * recall/precision + recall.

  $F\beta = (1 + \beta^2) * \text{precision} * \text{recall} / \beta^2 * \text{precision} + \text{recall}$. *where β is a non-negative real number.*

  Other important parameters for measuring the accuracy of a classifier are, ***Speed, Robustness, Scalability and Interpretability.***
- Various Methods for Assessing Accuracy are: ***Holdout and Random Sampling, Cross Validation and Bootstrapping.***
- Ensemble methods can be used to increase the overall accuracy by learning and combining a series of individual classifier models. The most common methods in the category are, ***boosting and bagging.***

CHAPTER 9

CLUSTERING TECHNIQUES

9.1 MEANING OF CLUSTERING

Clustering is the process of grouping a set of data objects into various groups or clusters so that objects within a cluster have high similarity, but are very dissimilar to objects in other clusters. Dissimilarities and similarities are assessed based on the attribute values describing the objects and often involve distance measure. Clustering as a data mining tool has its roots in many application areas such as biology, security, business intelligence and web search.

In the process of clustering a set of data objects are partitioned into subsets. Each subset is a cluster, where the objects in a cluster are similar to each and are different from the objects in the other clusters. The process of creating clusters resulting from a cluster analysis is known as clustering.

> ***What is a Cluster?***
>
> *A collection of data objects that are:*
>
> - Similar (or related) to one another within the same group.
> - Dissimilar (or unrelated) to the objects in other groups.
>
> ***What is a Cluster Analysis?***
>
> Cluster Analysis (also termed as *clustering* or *data segmentation*)
>
> *Finding similarities between data according to the characteristics found in the data and grouping similar data objects into clusters*

Different clustering methods may generate different clustering on the same data set. The clustering is done by the clustering algorithm. It will help to discover the previously unknown groups within the data. Due to huge amount of data collected in data bases, cluster analysis has become a highly important topic in data mining research.

9.2 APPLICATIONS OF CLUSTERING

The technique of clustering can be used in following areas:

1. **Business Intelligence:** Clustering can be used to organize a large number of customers into groups, where customers within a group share similar characteristics. It will help in designing the business strategies according to the requirements of the particular cluster and hence the better customer relationship management can be achieved. Customized services as per the requirements of the cluster members can be provided, which will enhance the customer satisfaction and will reduce the efforts from the organization's point of view.
2. **Project Management:** To improve project management in a company having large number of projects, clustering can be applied to partition projects into categories based on which proper project management can be done effectively and efficiently. As it is obvious that the different projects have different requirement of resources, different conceptual framework and it is not possible to handle all projects by a common strategy, so it is required to group the projects with the similar characteristics into clusters and hence can be handled accordingly.
3. **Image Recognition:** In image recognition, clustering can be used to discover clusters or subclasses in handwritten character recognition systems. The images matching the given image can be found and can be grouped accordingly.
4. **Web Search:** While searching the data on the web by using a keyword may return a large number of web pages. Clustering can be used to organize the search results into groups and present the results in a concise and easily accessible way. Clustering can be used to cluster documents according to topics. Like if we are interested in searching data on Data Mining, which is a subject under the Category: Computer Science. If we search by providing the keyword Computer Science, then we will get a large number of results and we will get the data for all the subjects under the computer science category like, information technology, DBMS, Software Engineering and of Course Data Mining, and out of these large number of documents, it will be difficult to find the data related to data mining. But if the documents have been clustered according to subject, the user will get the data related to the subject Data Mining directly.
5. **Outlier Analysis:** Clustering can be used for outlier detection, where outliers are the values that are far away from any cluster. The user may be more interested in finding such cases rather than the common cases. It can be used to detect the credit card fraud and monitoring the criminal activities in e-commerce. Like tracing the very expensive and infrequent purchases may be of interest to detect the frauds. Like being a customer you make a number of transactions through your account and normally it ranges from 10000 to 50000, but if on some day the transaction for lakhs of rupees have been made then it will be considered as an outlier, and it should be reported to the user and the organization. A large number of students absent from the class on a particular day, is considered as an outlier and requires immediate action.

6. **Information Retrieval:** The huge size of ever growing databases makes it difficult for the users to retrieve the relevant documents as per the requirement. So documents pertaining to same area can be clustered and hence can be retrieved easily as per the requirement.
7. **Land Use:** Identification of areas of similar land use in an earth observation database will help to organize the lands of similar characteristics into clusters and can be used accordingly, whether for agriculture, industrial or residential purpose.
8. **Marketing:** Help marketers discover distinct groups in their customer bases, and then use this knowledge to develop targeted marketing programs. For an example: A call centre representative needs to sell a policy, that is meant for service class people, the call centre executive has been given a data of 5000 customers, some of which is related to service class people and the remaining is of the customers from business class, and the executive make 5000 calls and let us say, 3000 customers are from service class, who listen to the call and out of them 100 are interested, that means by making 5000 calls the result is 100 mature cases and the success rate is 100/5000 = 20 %. But instead of this if the customer data has been organized in to clusters, one belonging to the customers from service class and other belonging to business class, then we need to make the 3000 calls to the customers in first cluster only and out of which 100 matures and the success rate is 100/3000 = 33.3 %.
9. **City-Planning:** Identifying groups of houses according to their house type, value, and geographical location.

9.3 REQUIREMENTS TO USE CLUSTERING AS A DATA MINING TOOL

For using clustering as a data mining tool, the following requirements should be met:

1. ***Scalability:*** The size of data bases varies from having a few data objects to the data bases containing hundreds and thousands of data objects. Clustering if applied to a small sized database or to a subset of a given data set may lead to biased result. Therefore highly scalable clustering algorithms are needed.
2. ***Ability to handle Heterogonous Attributes:*** The databases in the present day scenarios consist of attributes of various types and the users need to cluster and hence analyze the data objects having attributes of various different types. Many cluster algorithms are designed to cluster numeric or interval based data items. Some applications may require clustering the data of different types like binary, nominal or ordinal or a mixture of these data types. The clustering algorithms should be able to handle data belonging to heterogeneous data types.
3. ***Ability to discover clusters with arbitrary shape:*** The studies of present day environment involve clustering of data into clusters, most of the times the clusters are spherical in shape. The clustering algorithms determine clusters based on euclidean distance measure. Algorithms based on such distance measure tend to find spherical clusters with similar size and density. But in real life scenarios the clusters can be of any shape, it is mandatory to develop algorithms that can detect clusters of arbitrary shape.

4. ***Ability to provide domain knowledge to determine input parameters:*** Most of the clustering algorithms require that the user should provide the information about the number and characteristics of the clusters and number and characteristics of parameters to be given in each cluster. And the result of clustering is dependent on these parameters and when these parameters change the clustering results change consequently. This requirement of the clustering algorithm is difficult to fulfil, users feel it difficult to provide this information as it requires the deep understanding of their data and the subsequent changes occurring in the data items. Moreover, it makes the quality of the clustering difficult to control.
5. ***Ability to handle noisy data:*** Most of the real world data sets contain missing values, unknown or erroneous data, noisy data or outliers. The errors most of the time occur due to wrong entry of data by the operator, inaccurate readings taken by the sensing mechanism, interferences from the surrounding objects during transmission of data. These inaccurate readings or information may prove to be fatal to be given as input to the clustering algorithms and hence will result in poor quality clusters and consequently the poor results will be obtained. So, it is the bare necessity that data to be given as input to the clustering algorithm should be free from error and it should be robust to any disturbance encountered by the data by any internal or external source.
6. ***Ability to handle incremental clustering:*** In the ever-changing dynamic environments where the updations are done in the data bases at the blink of the eye, the new data items may arrive at any time and it may require the changes in the existing clustering structure, which will add to overhead in re-designing the clustering structure from the scratch again. So the clustering algorithm should be able to incorporate incremental updates into existing structure, instead of recomputing the new cluster.
7. ***Ability to handle inputs in any order:*** As discussed earlier, the clusters will be created depending on the inputs received and many a times it is found that the clustering algorithms are sensitive to the order in which the input data is received and processed, as a result of which different clusters may be obtained depending the order in which the input is received for the same data sets. So the algorithms should be insensitive to the order in which input is received.
8. ***Ability to handle multi-dimensional data items:*** Most of the clustering algorithms are good at handling low-dimensional data like data sets involving only two or three dimensions. But the decision making required in the present day scenario requires that the data is to be analyzed on multiple dimensions so that results based on multiple factors can be obtained. Like in a student data base, user may require to analyze the data on the basis of marks in the qualifying exams, regular attendance, class participation and behavior of the students. So the need is to develop and incorporate algorithms which can handle high dimensionality data.
9. ***Constraint Based Clustering:*** The real world applications now a days are full of constraints, and the user is required to perform clustering under various kinds of constraints. Like in a student data base we need to find out the number of students

for a project. To decide this we may cluster the students keeping the constraints like the caliber of the student for the particular language, whether the student is a day scholar or a hostler, the punctuality and sincerity of the student. The objective is to find out the groups with good clustering behavior that satisfy the specified constraints.

10. ***Ability to Interpret the Clustering Results:*** The user wants the results of clustering algorithms should be easy to interpret, so the clustering algorithm should be designed in such a way that it should provide the results in lucid and easy to understand format.

> ***What is good clustering?***
>
> - A good clustering method will produce high quality clusters, the clusters will be of high quality if there is high intra-class similarity i.e high cohesiveness within the clusters and low inter-class similarity i.e distinctive between clusters.
> - The quality of a clustering method depends on the similarity measure used by the method, its implementation, and its ability to discover some or all of the hidden patterns.

9.4 CRITERIAS FOR ANALYZING VARIOUS METHODS OF CLUSTERING

1. ***Partitioning Criteria:*** Single level vs. hierarchical partitioning (often, multi-level hierarchical partitioning is desirable). In many cases, all the objects are partitioned so that no hierarchy exists among the clusters. In this case, all the clusters will be at the same level. Such a method will be helpful while partitioning students into groups so that each group has its own project guide. On the other hand, some methods may partition data objects hierarchically where cluster can be formed at different semantic levels. For example, Programming in C, C++, Java may exist as subtopics of Programming Languages.

2. ***Separation of Clusters:*** The data can be partitioned into following two types of clusters:

   Mutually Exclusive Clusters: In these clusters, each data object may belong to one cluster only, like one customer belongs to only one region, like students in a group is taken care of by one project guide only, a student can choose either of two specializations offered.

   Non-Exclusive Clusters: In this case, the data objects may belong to more than one cluster. For example, one document may belong to more than one class, like students if clustered according to their hobbies, we may find that the same student may have multiple hobbies and hence can be a member of more than one cluster.

3. ***Similarity Measure:*** It is important to measure the similarity between the clusters, the similarity measures play a fundamental role in the design of clustering methods. The following methods exist for the same:

   Distance-Based Methods: These methods determine the similarity between two objects by the distance between them; the examples of these methods are defined on

Euclidian Space, a road network, a vector space or any other space. These methods take advantage of optimization techniques.

Connectivity-based Methods: The connectivity based methods do not depend on the absolute distance between two objects, but define the similarity defined by connectivity based on density or contiguity.(e.g., density or contiguity). These methods may provide the clusters of arbitrary shape.

4. ***Clustering Space:*** While creating the clusters, it is important to find out the total clustering space to be taken into consideration. As the complete data space or a sub set of the data space may be considered for designing the clusters. Two broad categories can be:

   Full Space Consideration: In this category the whole data space or the database is considered for creating clusters, this method is suitable if the data has lesser number of dimensions.

   Sub Space Consideration: In this category the subspaces of the same data set is considered for creating clusters. It is considered when the user has high dimensional data, as in such cases there may be many irrelevant attributes which can make the similarity measurements unreliable, so clusters found in the full space may be meaningless and it is advisable to consider a subset of the same data set.

9.5 CLASSIFICATION OF VARIOUS CLUSTERING ALGORITHMS

There are a number of clustering algorithms; it is difficult to provide a fine differentiation between these, because these methods overlap. These techniques can be divided into following broad categories:

9.5.1 Partitioning Methods

It is the simplest method for cluster analysis. It organizes the objects of a set into several exclusive clusters. For a set of n objects, this method constructs k partitions of data, where each partition represents a cluster and k < = n, i.e it divides the data into k groups such that each group must contain atleast one object. Most of the partitioning methods perform exclusive cluster separation, where each object must belong to exactly one group. Most of the partitioning methods are distance based, given k, the number of partitions to construct, a partitioning method creates an initial partitioning. It then uses an iterative relocation technique that attempts to improve the partitioning by moving objects from one group to another. The good partitioning will emphasize on the fact that the objects in the same cluster are close to each other and objects in different clusters are far apart. The important parameter to start this method is the number of partitions required or done. The clusters are formed to optimize the objective partitioning criterion, such as dissimilarity function based on distance, so that the objects within a cluster are similar to one another and dissimilar to objects in the other clusters in terms of data set attributes. The most commonly used partitioning methods are:

- K-means.
- K-mediods.

k-Means: It is a centroid based technique. Let a data set D, contains n objects in Euclidean space. Partitioning methods distribute the objects in D into n clusters, c1, c2 .... cn, i.e Ci is subset of D and Ci ∩ Cj = ∅. For 1 < = i and j < = k. an objective function is used to assess the partitioning quality so that objects with in a cluster are similar to one other but dissimilar to objects in other clusters. It aims for high intracluster similarity and low intercluster similarity.

The centroid based partitioning technique uses the centroid of a cluster Ci, to represent that cluster. So the centroid of a cluster is its center point. It can be defined by the mean or mediods of the objects assigned to the cluster. The quality of cluster Ci can be measured by the within-cluster variation, which is sum of squared error between all objects in Ci and the entroid ci, defined as:

E = Σdist(p, ci)2, i = 1 to k, p belongs to Ci

Where E is the sum of the squared error for all objects in the data set,

p is the point in space representing a given object and

Ci(both p and ci are multidimensional).

Each object in each cluster, the distance from the object to its cluster center is squared and distance are summed. This objective function tries to make the resulting k clusters as compact and as separate as possible.

Algorithm: k-means

Input:

K: the number of clusters.

D: a data set containing n objects.

Output: A set of k clusters.

Procedure:

arbitrarily choose k objects from D as the initial cluster centers,

repeat

assign each object to the cluster to which the object is the most similar, based on the mean value of the objects in the cluster,

update the cluster means, that is, calculate the mean value of objects for each cluster,

until no change.

The k-means method is not guaranteed to cover the global optimum and often terminates at a local optimum and often terminates at a local optimum. The result may depend on the initial random selection of cluster centers. To obtain good results, it is coomon to run the k-means algorithm multiple times with different initial cluster centres.

The time complexity of the k-means algorithm is O(nkt),

where n is the total number of objects,

k is the number of clusters and

t is the number of iterations.

The k-means algorithm can be made more scalable by following means:

- Good size set of samples should be used in clustering.
- Use a filtering approach that uses a spatial hierarchical data index to save costs when computing means.
- Use the concept of micro-clustering, which first groups nearby objects into microclusters and then perform k-means clustering on the microclusters.

Limitation: The k-means algorithm is sensitive to outliers because such objects are far away from the majority of the data, when assigned to a cluster, they can distort the mean value of the cluster.

Algorithm: k-Mediods: In this method instead of taking mean value of the objects in a cluster as a reference point, we can pick actual objects to represent the clusters using one representative object per cluster. Each remaining object is assigned to the cluster of which the representative object is the most similar. The partitioning method is then perfomed based on the principle of minimizing the sum of the dissimilarities between each object p and its corresponding representative object. An absolute error criterion is used, defined as:

$$E = \Sigma dist(p, oi),\ i = 1 \text{ to } k,\ p \text{ belongs to } Ci.$$

Where E is the sum of the absolute error for all objects p in the data set,

oi is the representative object of Ci.

It is the base of k-medoids method, which groups n objects into k clusters by reducing the absolute error. This algorithm moves in an iterative and greedy method. The iterative process of replacing representative objects by other objects continues until the quality of resulting clustering cannot be improved by any replacement.

Algorithm: PAM, Partitioning Around Mediods
Input: k: the number of clusters. D: a data set containing n objects. **Output:** A set of k clusters.
Procedure: *arbitrarily choose k objects in D as the initial representative objects or seeds.* *repeat* *assign each remaining object to the cluster with the nearest representative object,* *randomly select a non-representative object, orandom,* *compute the total cost, S of swapping representative object, oj with orandom;* *If S < 0 then swap oj with orandom to form the new set of k representative objects.* *until no change.*

Which method is better?

The k-medoids method is more robust than k-means in the presence of noise and outliers as a medoid is less influenced by outliers or other extreme values than a mean. The complexity of each iteration in the k-medoids algorithm is O(k(n-k)2). For large values of n and k, such computations become costly as compared to the k-means method.

9.5.2 Hierarchical Methods

It creates a hierarchical decomposition of the given set of data objects. The data objects are organized into a hierarchy or tree of clusters. Representing data objects in the form of a hierarchy is useful for data summarization and visualization. The hierarchical methods can be categorized as:

Algorithmic Methods: These methods consider data objects as deterministic and compute clusters according to the deterministic distance between objects. It can be *agglomerative or divisive*, i.e based on how the hierarchical decomposition has been formed.

The *agglomerative approach* uses bottom up approach, as it starts with each object forming a separate group. It merges the groups close to one another, until all groups are merged into one. *The divisive approach* uses top-down approach, as it starts with all the objects in the same cluster, where in each successive iteration, a cluster is split into smaller clusters, until each object is in one cluster.

Hierarchical method suffers from the fact that once a step is done, i.e either merge or split is done, it is never be undone. Fig. 9.1(a) given below shows the application of AGNES (Agglomerative NESting), an agglomerative hierarchical clustering method and DIANA(Divisive ANAlysis), a divisive hierarchical clustering method.

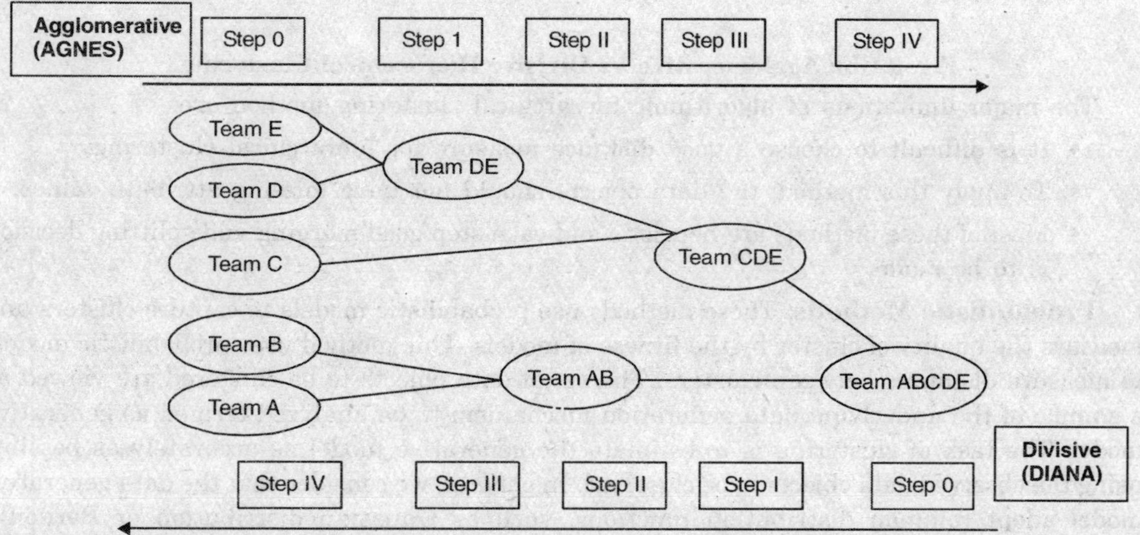

Fig. 9.1(a): Agglomerative and Divisive Hierarchical Clustering

Agglomerative Method places each object into a cluster of its own. The clusters are then merged step-by-step according to some specified condition.

DIANA, the divisive method proceeds with having all objects considered as one initial cluster. Then the main cluster is split according to some specified condition.

Fig. 9.1(b) is a tree structure known as dendrogram commonly used to represent the process of hierarchical clustering. The figure shows that when l = 0, all objects are present as a singleton cluster. At l = 1, objects team A and B are grouped together to form the first cluster and the process proceeds until all objects have been merged as a single cluster.

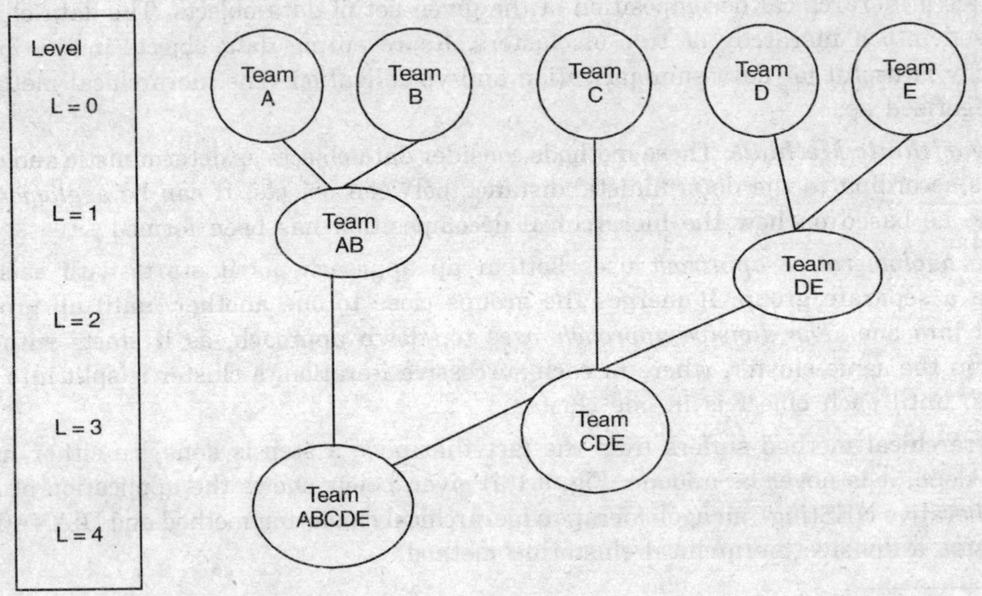

Fig. 9.1(b): Agglomerative Vs Divisive Hierarchical Clustering.

The major limitations of algorithmic hierarchical clustering method are:

- It is difficult to choose a good distance measure for hierarchical clustering.
- To apply this method, the data objects should not have missing attribute values.
- Most of these methods are heuristic and each step good merging and splitting decision is to be made.

Probabilistic Methods: These methods use probabilistic models to capture clusters and measure the quality of cluster by the fitness of models. This method uses probabilistic models to measure distances between clusters. The set of data objects to be clustered are viewed as a sample of the underlying data generation mechanism to be analyzed termed as generative model. The task of clustering is to estimate the generative model as accurately as possible using the observed data objects to be clustered. In general, we consider that the data generative model adopt common distribution functions, such as Gaussian distribution or Bernoulli Distribution, which are governed by parameters. The task of learning a generative model is then reduced to finding the parameter values for which the model best fits the observed data set.

Algorithm: A Probabilistic Hierarchical Clustering Algorithm
Input: D: a data set containing n objects. **Output:** A hierarchy of clusters.
Procedure: create cluster for each object Ci = {oi}, 1<= i <= n. for i = 1 to n find pair of cluster Ci and Cj such that Ci, Cj = arg max(log(P(Ci U Cj)/P(Ci). P(Cj))), i != j. if log (P(Ci U Cj)/P(Ci). P(Cj)) > 0 then merge Ci and Cj. else stop.

Limitation: The major limitation of this method are:

- It outputs only one hierarchy w.r.t chosen probabilistic model.
- It cannot handle the uncertainty of cluster hierarchies.

9.5.3 Density Based Method

Most of the partitioning methods cluster objects based on the distance between the objects. Such methods can find only spherical shaped clusters and encounter difficulty in discovering clusters of arbitrary shapes. So the methods based on the density have been developed. The general idea is to continue growing a given cluster as long as the density (number of objects or data points) in the neighborhood exceeds some threshold. Such methods can be used to filter out noise or outliers and discover clusters of arbitrary shape. Density based methods can divide a set of objects into multiple exclusive clusters or a hierarchy of clusters. These methods consider exclusive cluster only and do not consider fuzzy clusters. These methods can be extended from full space to subspace clustering.

Density-Based Approach: Most of the partitioning methods cluster objects based on the distance between the objects. Such methods can find only spherical shaped clusters and encounter difficulty in discovering clusters of arbitrary shapes. So the methods based on the density have been developed. The general idea is to continue growing a given cluster as long as the density (number of objects or data points) in the neighborhood exceeds some threshold. Such methods can be used to filter out noise or outliers and discover clusters of ***arbitrary shape.***

Density based methods can divide a set of objects into multiple exclusive clusters or a hierarchy of clusters. These methods consider exclusive cluster only and do not consider fuzzy clusters. These methods can be extended from full space to subspace clustering. These methods model clusters as dense regions in data space separated by sparse regions. This method can discover the clusters of non-spherical shape also.

Main Features:

1. It can find arbitrarily shaped clusters.
2. Clusters are dense regions of objects in space that are separated by low density regions.
3. Each point must have a minimum number of points within its neighborhood.
4. It may filter outliers.
5. It can handle noisy data also.
6. It need density parameters as termination condition

The various density based algorithms are:

1. **DBSCAN:** Ester, et al. (KDD'96)
2. **OPTICS:** Ankerst, et al (SIGMOD'99).
3. **DENCLUE:** Hinneburg & D. Keim (KDD'98)
4. **CLIQUE:** Agrawal, et al. (SIGMOD'98) (more grid-based)

Algorithm I: DBSCAN: Density Based Clustering Based on Connected Regions with High Density

This algorithm was developed by Ester. DBSCAN find core objects that are objects that have dense neighborhoods. It connects core objects and their neighborhoods to form dense regions as clusters. The density of an object o can be measured by the number of objects close to o.

How does DBSCAN quantify the neighborhood of objects?

A user specified parameter $\varepsilon > 0$ is used to specify the radius of a neighborhood, we consider for every object. Due to fixed neighborhood size parameterized by ε the density of neighborhood can be measured simply by the number of objects in the neighborhood. To determine whether a neighborhood is dense or not, DBSCAN uses another user-specified parameter MinPts, which specifies the density threshold of dense regions. An object is a core object if the ε neighborhood of object contains at least MinPts objects.

Given a set D of objects the user can identify all core objects w.r.t the given parameters e and MinPts. The clustering task is therefore reduced to using core objects and their neighborhoods to form dense regions, where dense regions are clusters. For a core object q and an object p, p is directly density reachable from q if p is within the ε-neighborhood of q.

An object p is directly density reachable from another object q iff q is a core object and p is the ε-neighborhood of q. using a directly density reachable relation, a core object can bring all objects from its ε-neighborhood into a dense region.

How does DBSCAN find Clusters?

In the start, all objects in a given data set D are marked as unvisited. This algorithm selects an unvisited object o, marks o as visited and checks whether the ε-neighborhood of o contains at least MinPts objects. If not, o is marked as a noise point, otherwise a new cluster C is created for o and all the objects in the ε-neighborhood of o are added to a candidate set, N. This algorithm iteratively adds to C those objects in N that do not belong to any other cluster. In this process, for an object o' in N that carries the label unvisited.

DBSCAN marks it as visited and checks its ε-neighborhood. If the ε-neighborhood of o' have atleast MinPts objects, those objects in the ε-neighborhood of o' are added to N. It continues adding objects to C until C can no longer be expanded, i.e N is empty. At this time cluster C is completed and it is the final output.

To find the next cluster, this algorithm randomly selects an unvisited object from the remaining objects and this clustering process continues until all objects are visited.

Algorithm: DBSCAN algorithm will find a set of density based clusters.

Inputs: A data set containing n objects, named as DB.

ε: the radius parameter and

MinPts: The neighborhood density threshold.

Procedure:

1. Mark all objects are unvisited.
2. do
3. randomly select an unvisited object o
4. mark o as visited.
5. if the ε-neighborhood of o has at least MinPts objects.
6. create a new cluster C and add o to C.
7. let N be the set of objects in the ε-neighborhood of o.
8. for each point o' in N.
9. if o' is unvisited, mark o' as unvisited.
10. if ε-neighborhood of o' has at least MinPts points.
11. add those points to N.
12. if o' is not yet a member of any cluster, add o' to C.
13. end for.
14. output C.
15. else mark o as noise.
16. until no object is unvisited.

The Complexity of DBSCAN algorithm is O(n log n), where n is the number of database objects.

Problems in DBSCAN Algorithm: This algorithm suffers from following problems:

- It can cluster objects given by the input parameters such as e (the maximum radius of a neighborhood) and MinPts(the minimum number of points required in the neighborhood of a core object), it gives the user the responsibility of selecting parameter values that will lead to the discovery of acceptable clusters. These parameter settings are difficult to determine, particularly if the data set contains high dimensional data sets.
- Most of the algorithms are sensitive to these parameter values, as the changes in these parameters will result in different clustering of the data.

- Most of the real world data sets are often skewed distributions and their intrinsic clustering structure may not be well defined by a single global parameter.
- This method is monotonic w.r.t the neighbourhood threshold, i.e for a fixed MinPts value and two neighbourhood thresholds, ε1 < ε2, a cluster C w.r.t ε1 and MinPts must be a subset of a cluster C' w.r.t ε2 and MinPts. That means if two objects are in a density-based cluster, they must also be in a cluster with a lower density requirement.

Algorithm II: OPTICS: To overcome the difficulty in using one set of global parameters in clustering analysis, another cluster analysis method called OPTICS was proposed. This method provides a cluster ordering i.e a linear list of all objects under analysis and represents the density based clustering structure of the data. Objects in a denser cluster are listed closer to each other in cluster ordering. This ordering is same as density based clustering obtained from a wide range of parameter settings. This algorithm does not require the user to provide a particular density threshold. The cluster ordering provided by this algorithm can be used to extract basic clustering information like the size of cluster, characteristics of a cluster, cluster centers and arbitrary shaped clusters.

In order to construct different clusterings at the same time, the objects are processed in a particular order. The object with high density w.r.t the lowest ε value is selected, it will ensure that the clusters with higher density i.e with lower ε will be finished first. According to this notion, the OPTICS need following parameters corresponding to each object:

1. ***Core-Distance:*** The core distance of an object O is the smallest value ε' s.t ε'-neighborhood of O has atleast MinPts objects. That is ε′ is the minimum distance threshold that makes O a core object. If O is not a core object w.r.t ε and MinPts, the core-distance of O is undefined.
2. **Reachability-Distance:** The reach ability distance of an object O from an object O' is the minimum radius value that makes O density reachable from O'. According to the definition of density reach ability, O' has to be a core object and O must be in neighborhood of O'. so we can say that the reach ability distance from O' to O is max{core-distance(q), dist(p,q)} and if O' is not a core object w.r.t ε and MinPts, the reachability distance to O from O' is undefined.

An object o may be directly reachable from multiple core objects. Therefore, o will have multiple reach ability distances w.r.t different core objects. The smallest reach ability distance of o is of particular interest as it gives the shortest path for which o is connected to a dense cluster.

This algorithm computes an ordering of all objects in a given database and for each object in the database, stores the core-distance and a suitable reach ability distance. This algorithm maintains a list called OrderSeeds to generate the output ordering. Objects in ordering seeds are sorted by the reach ability distance from their respective closest core objects, i.e by the smallest reach ability distance if each object.

OPTICS begins with an arbitrary object from the input database as the current object, O. it extracts the ε-neighborhood of O, determines the core-distance and sets the reachability distance to undefined. The current object O is then written to output.

If O is not a core object, this algorithm moves on to the next objects in the OrderSeeds list.

If O is a core object then for each object O', in the ε-neighborhood of O,it updates its reach ability distance from O and inserts O' into OrderSeeds if O' has not been processed. The iteration continues until the input is fully consumed and OrderSeeds is empty.

The structure of OPTICS algorithm is similar to DBSCAN and both the algorithms have same time complexity, i.e **complexity is O(n log n)** if a spatial index is used, otherwise complexity is $O(n^2)$, where n is the number of objects.

9.5.4 Grid-based Methods

These methods quantize the object space into a finite number of cells that form a grid structure. Then all operations are performed on this grid structure. The biggest advantage of this method is that it has fast processing time, which depends on number of cells in each dimension in quantized space. These methods can be integrated with other clustering methods like density based methods and hierarchical methods.

There are a large number of clustering algorithms, all of these have their individual characteristics and it is difficult to provide a crisp categorization of clustering methods as these categories may overlap so that a method may have features from several categories.

The clustering methods given earlier are ***data driven*** as they partition the set of objects and adapt to the distribution of the objects in the embedding space.

The grid based methods takes a ***space driven*** approach by partitioning the embedding space into cells independent of the distribution of the input objects.

It uses a ***multi-resolution grid data structure.***

It quantizes the object space into finite number of cells that form a grid structure.

All operation for clustering are performed on these grid structures.

The processing time is independent of number of data objects, but it is dependent on the number of cells in each dimension in the quantized space.

It is based on a multiple-level granularity structure.

The most common Grid Based methods are:

- STING
- WaveCluster and
- CLIQUE

STING: Statistical Information Grid

It is a grid-based multi-resolution technique in which the embedding spatial area of the input objects is divided into rectangular cells. The space can be divided in a hierarchical and recursive way.

Several levels of such rectangular cells correspond to different levels of resolution and form a hierarchical structure.

Each cell at a high level is partitioned to form a number of cells at the next lower level.

Statistical information regarding the attributes in each grid cell calculated are: mean, maximum and minimum values. These values are pre-computed and are stored as statistical parameters.

The statistical parameters of higher level cells can be computed from parameters of lower level cells.

Various statistical parameters calculated are:

- *Attribute- Independent Parameters:* Count
- *Attribute-Dependent Parameters:* mean, standard deviation, minimum, maximum.
- *Type of distribution:* It is followed by each attribute value in the cell, it be normal, uniform, exponential or none.

When the data is loaded into the database, the parameters count, max, min, standard deviation and mean of the bottom-level cells are calculated directly from the data. The value of distribution may be assigned by the user or can be obtained by hypothesis such as chi-square test. The type of distribution of a higher level cell can be computed with the help of corresponding lower level cells in association with the threshold filtering process. If the distribution of lower level cells disagrees with each other and fails the threshold test, then the distribution type of the high level cell is set to none.

Benefits of using Statistical Information for Query Processing

A layer in the hierarchical structure is to find out from which the query processing is started. This layer contains a small number of cells and for each cell in the current layer, computes the confidence interval reflecting the relevance of each cell to the given query. The irrelevant cells are removed and are not considered further. And for the processing of the next lower level only the relevant cells are considered. This process is repeated until the bottom layer is reached. If the data relevant to the query has been received, then the regions of relevant cells that satisfy the query are returned, else the data that fall in the relevant cells is retrieved and processed further until the requirements of the query are not met.

Advantages of STING Algorithm

The various advantages of STING algorithm are:

1. The grid-based computation is query independent as the statistical information stored in each cell shows the summary information of the data in the grid cell and this is independent of the query.
2. The grid structure facilitates parallel processing and incremental updating.
3. The time complexity of this algorithm is O(n), where n is the total number of objects. This algorithm traverses the database once to compute the statistical parameters of the cells. Moreover, once the hierarchical structure is created, the query processing time becomes O(g), where g is the total number of grid cells at the lowest level and it is much smaller than n.

9.6 EVALUATION OF QUALITY OF A CLUSTER

It is important to quantify the quality of the cluster generated through various clustering techniques. The various tasks of clustering evaluation are:

9.6.1 Assessing Clustering Tendency

It assess whether a nonrandom structure exists in the data or not. The analysis on the data set is meaningful only if there is a nonrandom structure in the data. If the clusters have been generated for a uniformly distributed point in a data space, then the clusters will be random and will be meaningless. To assess the randomness in the data, statistical tests for spatial randomness is used. The Hopkins statistic is a spatial statistics that tests the spatial randomness of a variable as distributed in a space. Given a data set D, which is considered as a sample of a random variable, o, we wish to find out how far away o is from being uniformly distributed in the data space. The Hopkins Statistics is calculated as:

1. Sample n points, p1 to pn uniformly from D. Where each point in D has the same probability of being included in this sample. For each point pi, find the nearest neighbor of pi in D and let xi be the distance between pi and its nearest neighbor in D., so xi = min{dis(pi, v)) where v belong to D.
2. Sample n points, q1 to qn uniformly from D, for each qi find the nearest neighbor of qi in D - {qi}, and let yi be the distance between qi and its nearest neighbor in D-{qi}, yi = min{dist(qi, v)}, v belong to D, v not equal to qi.
3. Calculate Hopkins statistic, H

   H = Σ yi / Σ xi + Σ yi (where i = 1 to n)

If D were uniformly distributed then Σyi and Σxi would be close to each other and H will be approximately close to 0.5.

If D were highly skewed then Σyi would be less than Σxi and H will be close to 0.

9.6.2 Determining the Number of Clusters in a Data Set

Finding the right number of clusters in a data set is important as the appropriate number of clusters control the proper granularity of cluster analysis. If the entire data set is considered as a single cluster, it will maximize the compression of data, but such a cluster analysis will have no value. On the other hand, if each object in a data set is considered as a cluster, but will make it difficult to handle the clusters. The right number of clusters depends on- ***shape of distribution, scale in the data set and the clustering resolution required by the user.*** A simple method is to set the number of clusters = n/2 for a data set of n points.

9.6.3 Measuring Clustering Quality

Measuring the quality of clustering is a daunting task, as it is a subjective matter. The method for measuring quality depend on the fact that whether the ground truth is available, ground truth is the ideal clustering that is built by human experts. Based on it the following two methods can be used:

Extrinsic Methods: These methods are used if the ground truth is available; these methods compare the clustering against the group truth and measure. In this method, the ground truth is compared with a clustering to assess the clustering.

Intrinsic Methods: These methods are used if ground truth is not available, and evaluate the goodness of a clustering by considering how well the clusters are separated and how compact the clusters are.

9.7 OUTLIER ANALYSIS

- **Outlier:** *A data object that* ***deviates significantly*** *from the normal objects as if it were* ***generated by a different mechanism.***
- **Outliers are interesting:** It violates the mechanism that generates the normal data. The data objects that are *not outliers* are considered as *normal* or *expected data* and the ***outliers*** are considered as ***abnormal data***.
- *Outlier detection is also known as anomaly detection*, It is the process of finding data objects with behavior that is very different from expectation.
- Outlier detection is important in many applications like fraud detection, medical care, public safety, security, industry damage detection, image processing and intrusion detection.

9.7.1 Applications of Outlier Analysis

- **Credit Card Fraud Detection:** The credit card companies try to protect the customers from credit card frauds and they pay attention to the usage pattern of the credit card and whenever the usage pattern is found to be different from the normal behavior then it notified and the appropriate action is taken accordingly. Most of the transactions done by a credit card are normal, but if it is stolen, then transaction pattern changes immediately, the location of purchase, the total amount of purchase and items purchased are different from the authentic user and hence it is considered as an outlier and the information about such a purchase and usage of card is given to the card owner and if the owner confirms the behavior as abnormal then the company takes the necessary action and the theft and thief are dealt accordingly. Let a credit card user usually makes a transactions in a range of 10000-30000 per month, and a transaction of 200000 in one go will be considered as outlier, and the details of the transaction is immediately informed to the user, so that user may check whether the transaction has been done by him or not.
- **Telecom Fraud Detection:** Telecommunication system is the best tool for the communication these days, and is used as a tool for authentic and unauthentic communication. A large number of phone calls made through a single number can be considered as outlier. Let a user makes international phone calls once a month and the duration varies from 5-10 min. and if the several calls have been on a single day and moreover the duration of calls varies from 40-45 min, it will be considered as an outlier and it may be possible that somebody else is using your connection, such a behavior is informed to the user. The telecom authority in association with investigation

department may black list some phone numbers, and if the user is getting phone calls from those numbers it will be considered as an outlier and the appropriate action will be taken.

- **Customer Segmentation:** The study of customer's transaction is of utmost importance to the organization. The abnormal or the unexpected behavior is considered as outlier and demands the required action and will work as a tool for designing future strategies. the unexpected sale on a particular day for a particular product is considered as an outlier, like demand of cold drinks increase drastically on a hot day, if a new product has been launched and its sale is more than expectation in all the regions except one region, which is the outlier, demanding introspection.
- Medical Analysis: The scans of any body part made by the physician, when investigated will highlight the areas which are problematic, will be the outlier.
- **Outlier Detection and Cluster analysis:** These are highly related topics; Clustering finds the majority patterns in a data set and organizes the data accordingly, whereas outlier detection tries to capture those exceptional cases that deviate from the majority pattern.

9.7.2 Types of Outliers

There are following three kinds of outliers:

1. **Global Outliers:** In a given data set, a data object is a global outlier if it deviates significantly from the rest of the data set. Global outliers are sometimes called point anomalies and are the simplest type of outlier. Most of the outlier detection methods are aimed at finding global outlier. If the user wishes to find out the global outlier, then the critical issue is to find the suitable measurement of deviation w.r.t the application. There are a variety of measurements which can be used in this category and depending on this the various outlier detection methods are partitioned into different categories. The most common example of global outliers is:
   - In intrusion detection system in a computer network, if the communication behavior of a system is quite different from the normal patterns, like a large number of packets are broadcasted from a particular system in a short span of time may be considered as a global outlier and the corresponding computer is considered as the victim of hacking.
2. **Contextual Outlier:** A data object is a contextual outlier if it deviates w.r.t a specific context of the object. These outliers are also known as *conditional outlier*, as these are conditional on the selected context. So in this case when the problem is defined or the query is being run, then the context has to be defined along with, so that the true analysis of data can be done. Like in a telephone company, there are phone connections given to the individuals and the organizations. A large number of phone calls done through an individual connection is an outlier but if it is done through the phone number of an organization, then it is not an outlier. A bad performance by a intelligent and sincere student, is considered as an outlier, but it is not an outlier for a notorious student. That means it depends on the context and may be some other

factors. In this case, the attributes of the data objects are divided into following groups:

- **Contextual Attributes:** The contextual attributes of a data object define the context of the object. As in the example given above, the contextual attributes are individual or the organization and sincere or notorious student.
- **Behavioral Attributes:** These attributes define the characteristics of the object and are used to evaluate whether the object is an outlier in the context to which it belongs.

The contextual outlier detection whether a data object is an outlier or not depends on the behavioral as well as contextual attributes. These outliers are the generalization of a local outlier where an object in a data set is a local outlier if its density significantly deviates from the local area in which it occurs. The biggest problem in finding contextual outlier is that how to formulate meaningful contexts in the contextual outlier. In some cases group-bys is used to find out the contexts, but this method may not be effective as many group-bys may have insufficient data.

3. **Collective Outliers:** *A subset of data objects collectively deviate significantly from the whole data set, even if the individual data objects may not be outliers.*

   Like in a college, if one or two students from each class are absent, it is not considered as an outlier, because it happens quite often. But if the whole class is absent or more than 50 percent of students from one or more classes are absent, then it may be considered as an outlier, here these deviations individually does not form an outlier, but collectively it is an outlier.

Detection of collective outliers is a tedious job because:

(i) It demands to study the behavior of not only the individual objects, but also that of groups of objects.

(ii) The users need to have the background knowledge on the relationship among data objects, such as a distance or similarity measure on objects.

(iii) A data set may have multiple types of outlier. One object may belong to more than one type of outlier.

9.7.3 Challenges in Outlier Detection

The outlier detection is used in many areas successfully, but there are following challenges being faced while performing these methods:

1. **Modeling Normal Objects and Outliers Properly:** The detection of an outlier depends on the modeling of normal objects and outlier. It is hard to enumerate all possible normal behaviors in an application. Building a comprehensive model for data normality is a challenging task. The border between normal and outlier objects is a daunting task. There exist some methods which define the object as normal or an outlier, while some other methods just enumerate the objects by measuring the degree of outlier-ness of the object. Moreover, the object can be an outiler for one and may not be for the others.

2. **Application-Specific Outlier Detection:** Choice of distance measure among objects and the model of relationship among objects vary from application to application. As in the real world scenarios, the different applications have different requirements. Like a small deviation in measurement of gold may be important enough to justify as an outlier, but the deviation while you are purchasing some vegetables a large deviation is needed to be considered as an outlier. The deviation in time (like in a fraction of time)when the traffic light signal shifts from red to green can be considered as an outlier, but if a train is delayed by that fraction of time, then it is not considered as an outlier. As outlier detection depends on the application under consideration, hence it is not possible to develop a universally applicable method. Instead of this, the outlier detection specific to a particular application must be developed.
3. **Handling Noise in Outlier Detection:** Low quality of data and the presence of noise create huge challenges to outlier detection. These can distort the data, make it difficult to distinguish between normal objects and the outliers. It may also hide outliers and may reduce the effectiveness of the outlier detection method.
4. **Understandability:** Along with finding the outliers it is also important to understand why these outliers have occurred and to justify the detections. The proper understanding and analysis of the outlier is very important and needs sensitive handling. Like, if the performance of a sincere student is not as expected and is considered as an outlier and the mentor takes the normal action decided to handle outlier will not work, the need is to identify the reasons for such an outlier and to handle the situation patiently and emphatically. Same way, it has been observed that a large number of calls have been received by a noble citizen from a black listed number, then it will be considered as an outlier, but it is not advisable to punish the citizen directly, but the need is to investigate and then to act. Handling the outlier without understanding may prove to be fatal.

9.7.4 Methods of Outlier Detection

There exist a number of outlier detection methods whichare used, but broadly these can be divided into following two categories:

9.7.4.1 Category I

Based on whether sample of data for analysis is given with domain expert provided labels that can be used to build an outlier detection model. The methods in the category are:

- Supervised Methods.
- Semi-Supervised Methods.
- Unsupervised Methods.

9.7.4.2 Category II

Based on the division of methods into groups according to their assumptions regarding normal objects vs outliers. The methods in this category are:

- Statistical Methods
- Proximity-based Methods.
- Clustering-based Methods.

Supervised Methods: Supervised methods model data normality and abnormality. Domain experts examine and label a sample of the underlying data. Outlier detection can then be modeled as a classification problem. The task is to learn a classifier that recognizes outliers. These samples examined by domain experts are used for training & testing. The methods for learning a classifier for outlier detection effectively model normal objects & report those not matching the model as outliers, or model outliers and treat those not matching the model as normal. The supervised methods of outlier detection must be careful in finding and interpreting the classification rates due to the fact that outliers are rare in comparison to other data samples.

Semi-supervised Outlier Detection: It may be regarded as applications of semi-supervised learning. In many cases, if some labeled normal objects are available whereas most of the data is unlabeled. The semi-supervised methods of outlier detection can be used to handle such situations. When some labeled normal objects are available the user can use them with the unlabeled objects that are quite close to it to train a model for normal objects. Then this model of normal objects can be used to detect outliers and in such cases the objects not fitting the model of normal objects are classified as outliers. If only some labeled outliers are available, a small number of labeled outliers many not cover the possible outliers well. To improve the quality of outlier detection, the user can get help from models for normal objects learned from unsupervised methods.

Unsupervised Methods: In some applications, objects labeled as normal or outlier are not available, in such cases unsupervised learning methods have to be used.

- These methods assume that normal objects are somewhat "clustered" into multiple groups, each having some distinct features.
- An outlier is expected to be far away from any groups of normal objects.
- The normal objects do not fall into one group sharing high similarity; rather they can form multiple groups, where each group has distinct features.

Drawbacks:

- It cannot detect collective outliers effectively.
- Normal objects may not share any strong pattern, but the collective outliers may share high similarity in a small area. These methods cannot detect such outliers effectively. In some applications, normal objects are diversely distributed, and many such objects do not follow strong patterns. Like in some intrusion or virus detection, normal activities are diverse and many do not fall into high quality clusters. In such cases, Un-supervised methods may have a high false positive rate but still miss many real outliers. As there is high similarity between intrusions and viruses (both attack the key resources in the target system). Modeling outliers using supervised methods may be far more effective.
- Many clustering methods can be adapted to work as unsupervised methods, the main idea in such methods is to find clusters first and then the objects not belonging to any cluster are detected as outliers. But in such methods it is difficult to differentiate between noise and outliers and it is costly to find clusters first and then to find the outliers.

Based on assumptions about normal data and outliers: In this category any of the following three methods can be used:

- Statistical Methods.
- Proximity-Based Methods.
- Clustering-Based Methods.

Statistical Methods:

- These methods are also known as model-based methods.
- These methods assume that the normal data follow some statistical model (a stochastic model) and the data not following the model is considered as an outlier.
- The normal objects in the data set are generated by a stochastic process and the normal objects are those that fall in the regions of high probability for the stochastic model and the objects in the regions of low probability are outliers.
- These methods generate a model fitting the given data set, and then identify those objects in the low probability regions of model as outliers.
- Effectiveness of statistical methods highly depends on whether the assumption of statistical model holds in the real data or not.
- There are rich alternatives to use various statistical models. e.g., parametric vs. non-parametric.

Parametric Methods assume that the normal data objects are generated by a parametric distribution with parameter α. The probability density function of parametric distribution f(x, α) gives the probability that object x is generated by the distribution. The smaller is the value, the more likely x is an outlier.

Non-parametric Methods, does not assume a priori statistical method, rather it tries to determine the model from the input data. Most of the non-parametric methods do not assume that the model is completely parameter free, rather these methods take the position that the number and nature of parameters are flexible and is not fixed in advance. Examples of these methods are histogram and kernel density estimation.

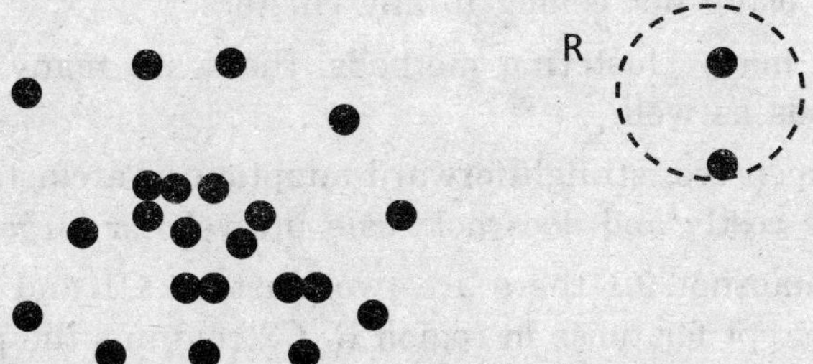

Snapshot 9.1: The objects in Region R are outliers

The data points which are not in region R fit a Gaussian distribution gD, where for a location x in the data space, gD(x) gives the probability density at x. then the Gaussian distribution gD can be used to model the normal data, i.e most of the data points in the data set.

For each object y in region R, estimate gD(y), the probability of y fits the Gaussian distribution

If gD(y) is very low, y is unlikely generated by the Gaussian model, thus an outlier

Proximity-Based Methods:

- An object is an outlier if the nearest neighbors of the object are far away in feature space i.e., the **proximity** of the object to its neighbors **deviates significantly** from the proximity of most of the other objects in the same data set.
- The effectiveness of proximity-based methods highly relies on the proximity measure.
- In some applications, proximity or distance measures cannot be obtained easily.
- These methods have difficulty in finding a group of outliers which stay close to each other.

Example: If we model the proximity of an object using its three nearest neighbors, then the objects in region R are substantially different from other objects in the data set. For the two objects in R, their second and third nearest neighbors are remote than those of any other objects.

Thus the objects in R are outliers.

Two major types of proximity-based outlier detection methods are:

- ***Distance-Based Method:*** These methods consider the neighborhood of an object which is defined by a given radius. And an object is then considered as an outlier if its neighborhood does not have enough other points.
- ***Density-Based Method:*** It calculates the density of an object and also of its neighbors. The object is considered as an outlier if its density is relatively much lower than the density of its neighbors.

Clustering Based Methods

These methods:

- Detect the outliers by examining the relationship between objects and clusters.
- Normal data belong to large and dense clusters, whereas outliers belong to small or sparse clusters, or do not belong to any clusters.
- Since there are many clustering methods, there are many clustering-based outlier detection methods as well.
- Clustering is expensive, straightforward adaption of a clustering method for outlier detection can be costly and does not scale up well for large data sets.

Example: In the snapshot 9.1 there are two clusters, C1 and C2, C1 contains all the points in the data set except for those in region R. C2 contains the points in R. C1 is bigger as comparison to C2. So a clustering based method asserts that the two objects in R are outliers.

There can be three cases for clustering based outlier detection:

(a) Check if the object belongs to any cluster? If not, it is considered as an outlier.

(b) Check is there a large distance between the object and the cluster to which it is closest? If yes it is considered as an outlier.

(c) Check if the object part of small or sparse cluster? If yes, then all the objects in that cluster are considered as outlier.

9.8 DATA VISUALIZATION

It is normally said that: *"A picture is worth a thousand words"*.

- Data visualization aims to communicate data clearly and effectively through graphical representation.
- Data Visualization techniques discover data relationships that are not observable by looking into the raw data.
- It is used in reporting, managing business operations and tracking progress of various tasks.

The various data visualization techniques are:

(A) Pixel Oriented Techniques.

(B) Geometric Projection Techniques.

(C) Icon-Based Techniques.

(D) Hierarchical and Graph Based Techniques.

9.8.1 Pixel Oriented Techniques:

- It is the simplest way to visualize the value of a dimension.
- This method uses a pixel to show the value of a dimension, the color of the pixel reflects the value of the dimension.
- For a data set with n dimensions, this technique creates n windows on the screen, one window for each dimension. And n dimension values of a record are mapped to n pixels at the corresponding positions in the windows and the color of the pixel represent the corresponding values.

Example: Let us consider the data stored in the customer information table, having the attributes: income, credit limit, volume of transactions and sex of the customer.

The customer data has been sorted in ascending order, order by income of the customer and use this data to lay out the customer data in visualization windows as shown below, the pixel colors are chosen so that smaller the value, the lighter is the shading. The Fig. 9.2 clearly show that:

- As income increase the credit limit also increases.
- Customers in the middle age group have more purchasing capacity.
- There is no correlation between income and sex.

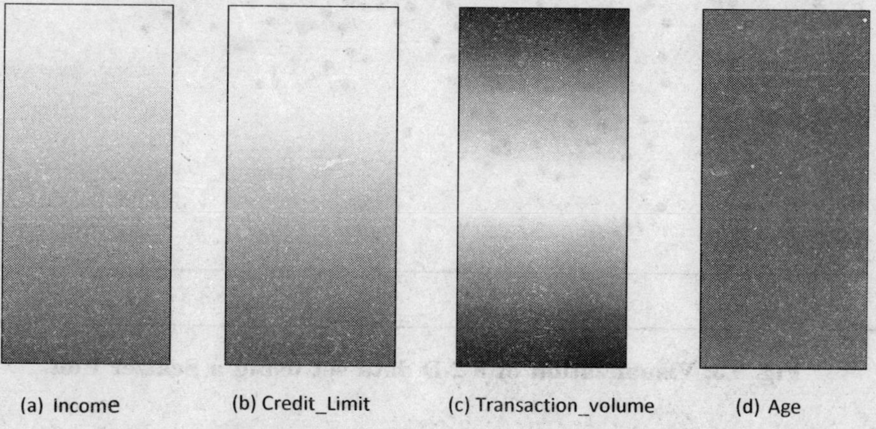

Fig. 9.2: Pixel Oriented Visualization of Four Attributes

Limitations:

- The biggest drawback of this technique is that this method is not suitable to handle data in a multidimensional space.
- Laying out the data records in a linear way does not work well for a wide window.
- The first pixel in a row is far away from the last pixel in the previous row, though they are next to each other in a global order.
- A pixel is next to the one above it in the window, although these two are next to each other in the global order.

9.8.2 Geometric Projection Visualization Techniques

- This technique helps the users in finding interesting projections in multidimensional data sets.
- It focuses on visualizing a high dimensional space on a 2-D display.
- The various techniques used are:

Scatter Plot: This method displays 2-D data points using Cartesian coordinates. The third dimension is added by using different colors or shapes to show different data points. Fig. 9.3 below show X and Y are two spatial attributes and the third dimension is shown by a different shape.

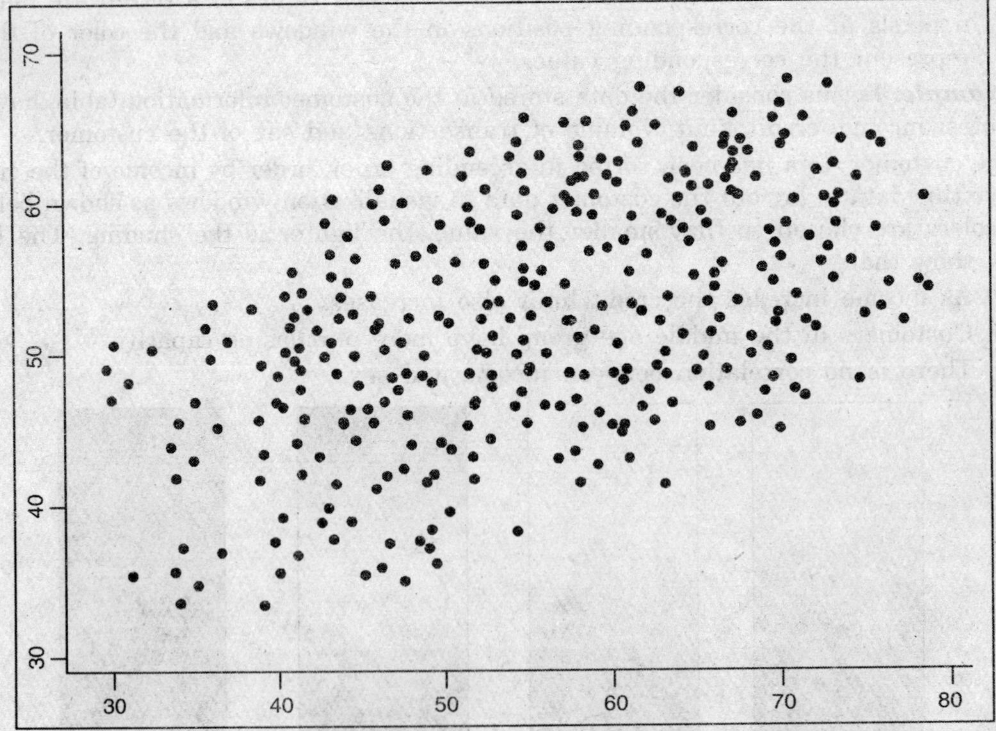

Fig. 9.3: Visualization of a 2-D data set using a Scatter Plot.

Limitations:

This method is not suitable for the data sets with four dimensions.

Scatter plot matrix technique is a useful extension to scatter plot, in which for an n-dimensional data set a scatter plot matrix is an n * n grid of 2-D scatter plots that provides visualization of each dimension with every other dimension.

Fig. 9.4 below show an example which visualizes the Iris data set. The data set consists of 450 samples from each of three spices of Iris flowers.

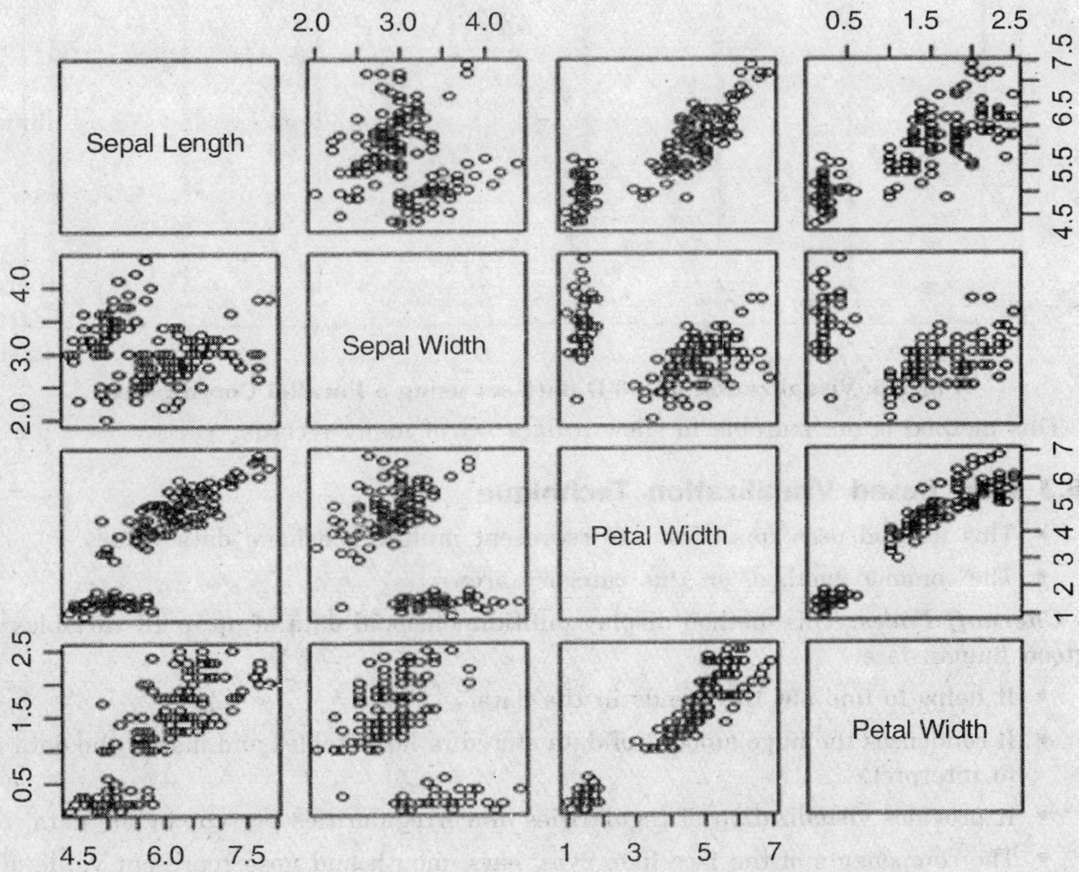

Fig. 9.4: Visualization of Iris data set using a Scatter-plot matrix.

This method becomes less effective as the dimensionality increases.

Parallel Coordinates Technique: This technique can handle high dimensional data. To visualize n-dimensional data points, this method draws n equally spaced axes, one for each dimension, parallel to one of the display axes. A data record is represented by a polygonal line that intersects each axis at the point corresponding to associated dimension value.

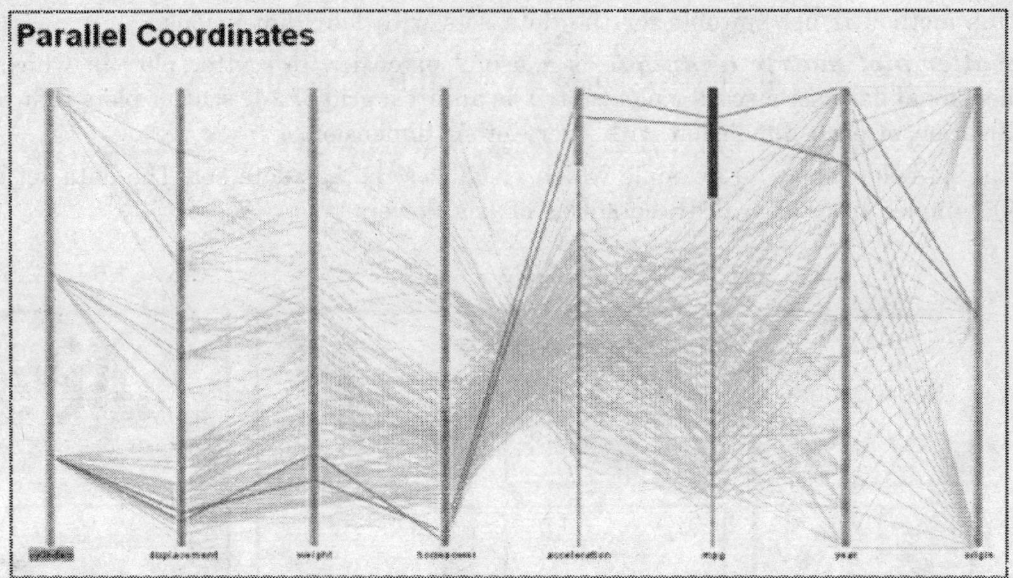

Fig. 9.5: Visualization of a 3-D data set using a Parallel Coordinates.

This method is not suitable to show a data set of many records.

9.8.3 Icon Based Visualization Technique

- This method uses small icons to represent multidimensional data values.
- The common methods in this category are:

Chernoff Faces: This method display multidimensional data of up to 18 variables as a cartoon human face.

- It helps to find out the trends in the data.
- It condenses the huge amount of data stored in large tables and makes the data easy to interpret.
- It provides visualization of regularities and irregularities present in the data.
- The components of the face like, eyes, ears, mouth and nose represent value of the dimension by their shape, size, placement and orientation. Dimensions can be mapped to the following facial characteristics: eye size, eye spacing, nose length, nose width, mouth curvature, mouth width, mouth openness, pupil size etc.
- This method makes use of the ability of the human mind to identify minute differences in facial characteristics.

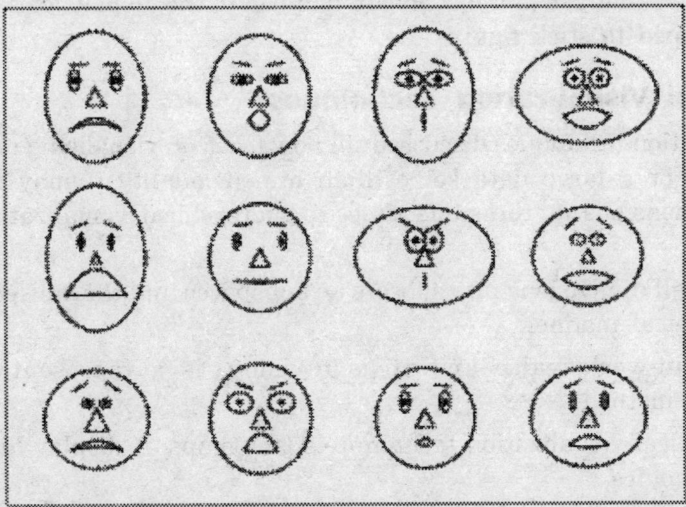

Fig. 9.6: Chernoff Faces, each face shows a n-dimensional data point(n<=18)

The main limitations of this method are:

- Inability to show specific data values.
- It cannot represent multiple relationships in the data.
- The facial features vary in perceived importance, which is the similarity of two faces can vary depending upon the order in which dimensions are assigned to facial characteristics.

Note: *Asymmetrical Chernoff faces have been proposed as an extension to the original technique, as it can allow 36 dimensions to be displayed.*

Stick Figure Visualization Technique: This technique maps multidimensional data to five-piece stick figures, where each figure has four limbs and a body. Two dimensions are mapped to the display axes and the remaining dimensions are mapped to the angle or length of the limbs.

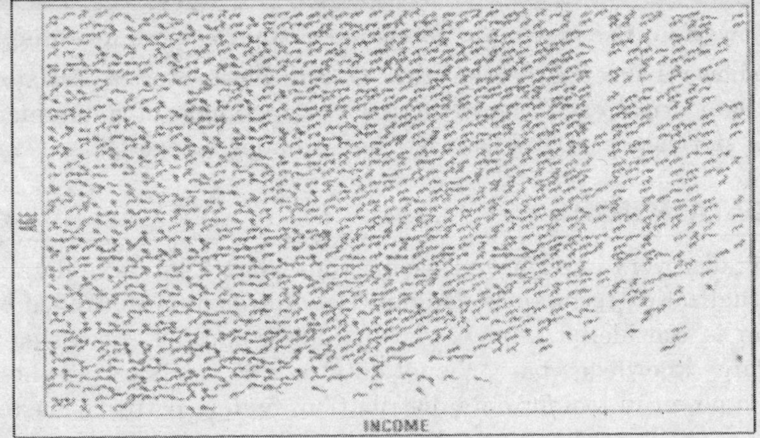

Fig. 9.7: Census Data represented using Stick Figures.

The Fig. 9.7 shows that age and income are mapped to the display axes and the remaining dimensions are mapped to stick figures.

9.8.4 Hierarchical Visualization Techniques

The various visualization techniques discussed till now focus on visualizing multiple dimensions at the same time. For a large data set of high dimensionality it may not be possible to visualize all the dimensions at the same time, so hierarchical visualization techniques are used.

- It partitions all dimensions into subsets i.e subspaces and the subspaces are visualized in a hierarchical manner.
- Worlds-within-worlds also known as n-vision, is a representative hierarchical visualization method.

Another hierarchical visualization technique is tree-maps, it display hierarchical data as a set of nested rectangles.

Fig. 9.8: Newsmap: Use tree-maps to visualize Google news headline stories.

The Fig. 9.8 shows a tree-map visualizing Google news Stories. All stories have been organized into 7 categories, each shown in a large rectangle of a unique color. In each category the news stories are further divided into smaller categories.

9.9 VISUAL DATA MINING

Visual data mining discovers implicit and useful knowledge from large data sets using data and knowledge visualization techniques. Human visual system is controlled by the eyes and brain, where brain is considered as a powerful, highly parallel processing and reasoning engine storing a large knowledge base. Visual data mining combines all these features and it has emerged as a powerful tool for data distribution, finding patterns clusters and outliers in the data.

Visual Data Mining can be viewed as an integration of two disciplines:

- Data Visualization
- Data Mining.

It is related to computer graphics, multimedia systems, human computer interaction, pattern recognition, multimedia systems, high performance computing and high performance computing.

Data Visualization and data mining can be integrated in following ways:

Data Visualization: Data in a data base or data warehouse can be viewed at different levels of abstractions or by combining attributes in many ways or dimensions. Data can be presented in various visual forms, such as boxplots, 3-D cubes, data distribution charts, link graphs. Visual display can help users in providing a clear impression and overview of data characteristics in a large data set.

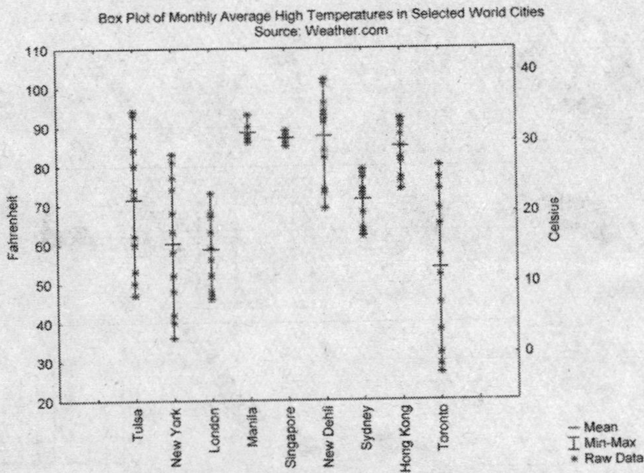

Fig. 9.9: Boxplots showing variables.

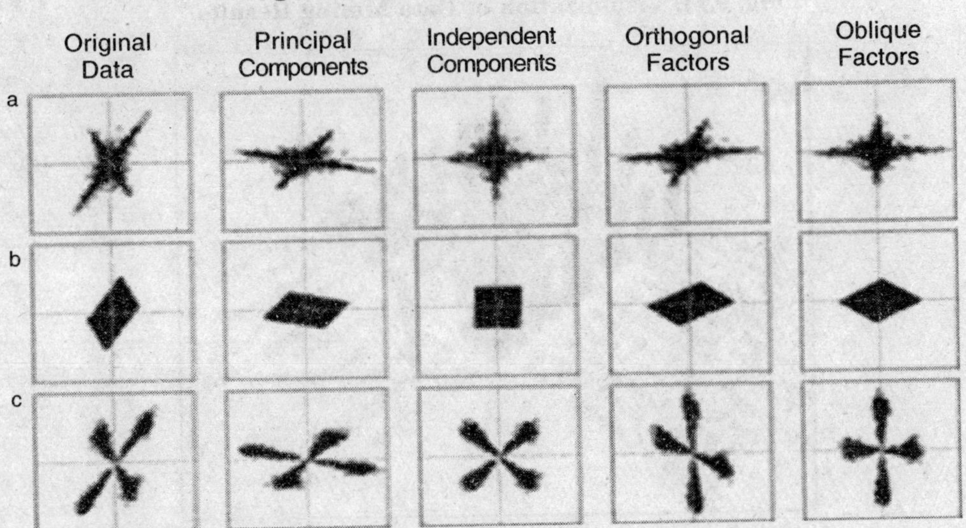

Fig. 9.10: Multidimensional Data Distribution Analysis in statsoft.

Mining result visualization: Visualization of data mining results is the presentation of the results obtained from data mining in visual forms. Such forms may include scatter plots and boxplots, decision trees, association rules, clusters, outliers and generalized rules. For Example Scatter Plots are shown in Fig. 9.11, from SAS Enterprise Miner, Fig. 9.12, from MineSet, sues a plane associated with a set of pillar to describe a set of association rules mined from a database. Fig. 9.13 also from MineSet presents a decision tree. Fig. 9.14 from IBM Intelligent Miner, presents a set of clusters and properties associated with them.

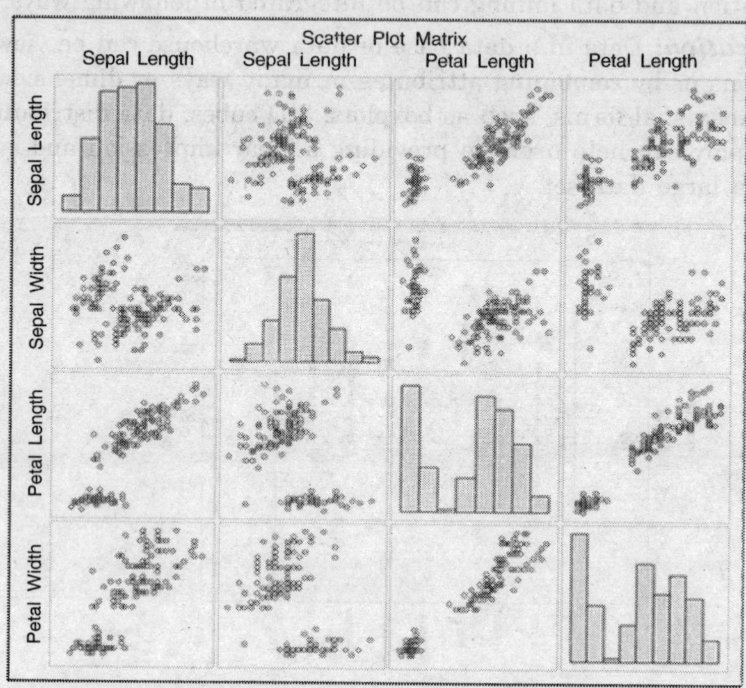

Fig. 9.11: Visualization of Data Mining Results

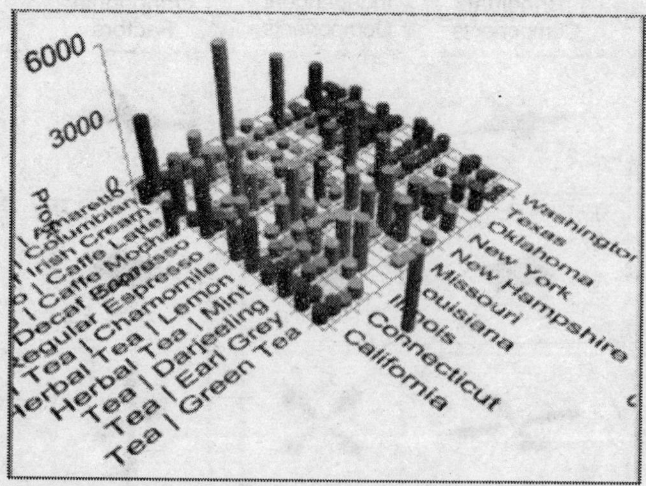

Fig. 9.12: Visualization of association rules in MineSet.

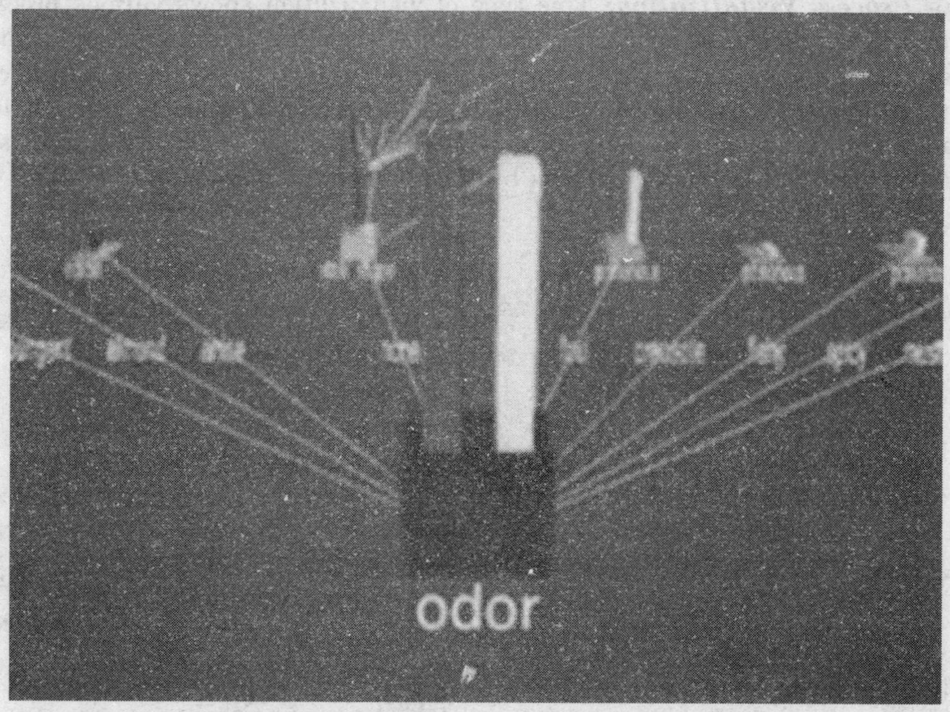

Fig. 9.13: Visualization of a decision tree in Mineset.

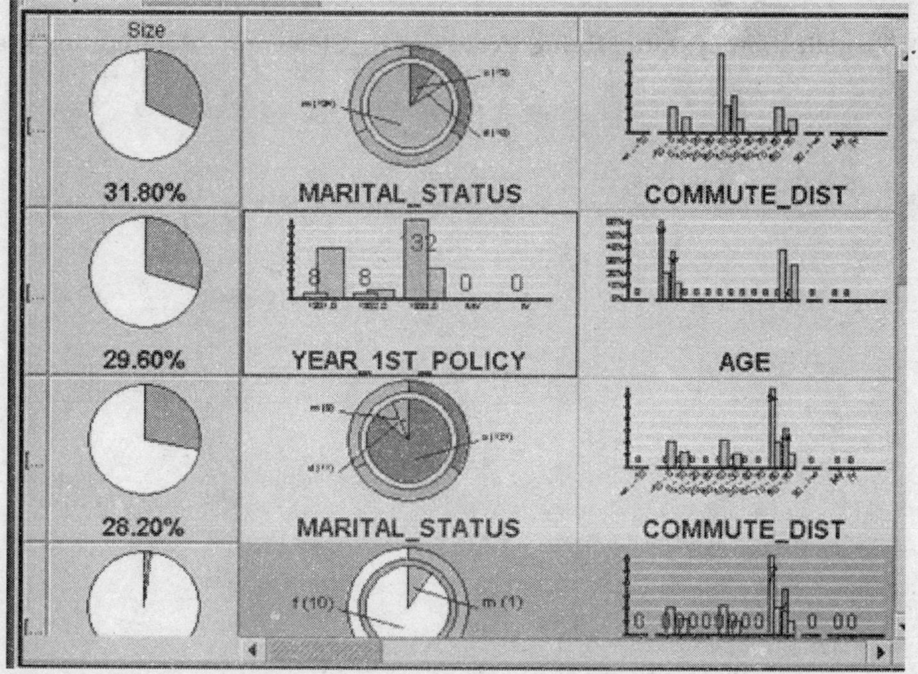

Fig. 9.14: Visualization of Cluster Grouping in IBM intelligent Miner.

Mining Process Visualization: This type of visualization shows various processes of data mining in visual forms so that users can see how the data is extracted and from which database or data warehouse they are extracted, as well as how the selected data is cleaned, Integrated, preprocessed and mined. It also show that which method is selected for data mining and where the results are stored and how they may be viewed. Fig. 9.15 shows a visual presentation of data mining process by the Clementine data mining system.

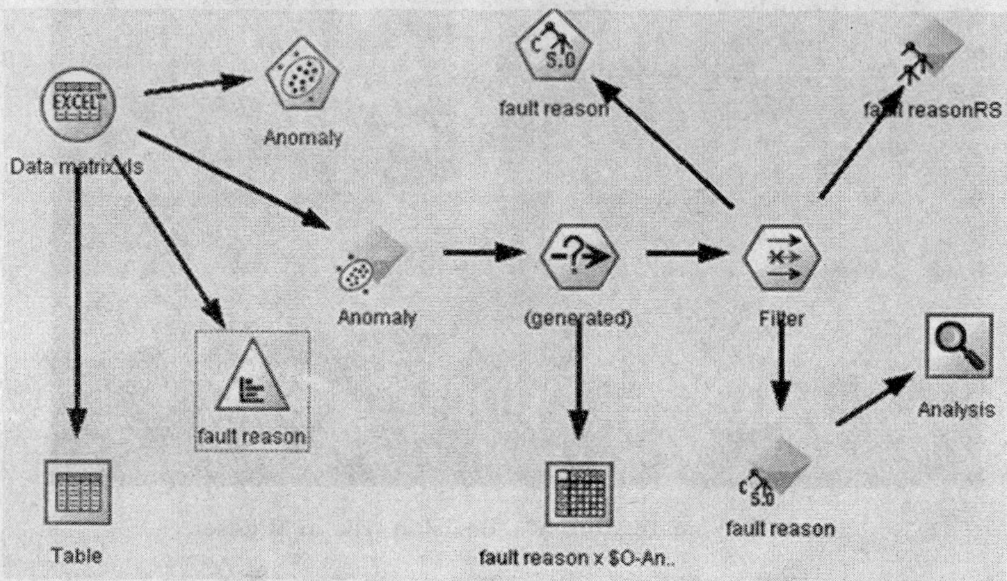

Fig. 9.15: Visualization of Data Mining Processes by Clementine data mining systems.

SUMMARY

- ***Clustering*** is the process of grouping a set of data objects into multiple groups or clusters so that objects within a cluster have high similarity, but are very dissimilar to objects in other clusters.
- A collection of data objects that are similar (or related) to one another within the same group and dissimilar (or unrelated) to the objects in other groups.
- Clustering Techniques can be applied in Business Intelligence, Project Management, Image Recognition, Web Search, Outlier Analysis, Information Retrieval, Marketing and Earth-quake studies.
- To use clustering as a Data Mining Tool, the clustering algorithm should be Scalable, able to handle heterogonous attributes, to discover clusters with arbitrary shape, to provide domain knowledge to determine input parameters, to handle noisy data ,to handle incremental clustering, to handle inputs in any order, ability to handle constraint based clustering and the power to interpret the clustering results.
- A cluster will be of high quality if there is high intra-class similarity i.e high cohesiveness within the clusters and low inter-class similarity i.e distinctive between clusters.
- Various clustering algorithms can be divide as hierarchical methods, partitioning methods and density based methods.
- Partitioning Methods divides the data into k groups such that each group must contain atleast one object. Most of the partitioning methods perform exclusive cluster separation, where each object must belong to exactly one group.
- Hierarchical Methods create a hierarchical decomposition of the given set of data objects. It can be agglomerative or divisive, i.e based on how the hierarchical decomposition has been formed.
- Hierarchical method suffers from the fact that once a step is done, i.e either merge or split is done, it is never be undone.
- Density Based Method clusters objects based on the concept of density. It grows clusters either according to the density of the neighborhood objects e.g in DBSCAN or according to a density function e.g. in DENCLUE. OPTICS is a density based method that generates an augmented ordering of the data's clustering structure.
- Grid-based Methods quantize the object space into a finite number of cells that form a grid structure. Then all operations are performed on this grid structure.
- Various density based algorithms are: DBSCAN, OPTICS, DENCLUE and CLIQUE.
- A data object that deviates significantly from the normal objects as if it were generated by a different mechanism.
- Applications of Outlier Analysis include, Credit Card Fraud Detection, Telecom Fraud Detection, Customer Segmentation:, Medical Analysis and Outlier Detection and Cluster analysis
- Various types of outliers are global outliers, contextual outlier and collective outlier.
- A data object is a global outlier if it deviates significantly from the rest of the data set. Global outliers are sometimes called point anomalies
- A data object is a contextual outlier if it deviates w.r.t a specific context of the object. These outliers are also known as conditional outlier, as these are conditional on the selected context. A bad performance by an intelligent and sincere student is considered as an outlier, but it is not an outlier for a notorious student.

- A subset of data objects collectively deviate significantly from the whole data set, even if the individual data objects may not be outliers
- Various challenges in Outlier Detection are inability to model normal objects and outliers properly, to handle application-specific outliers, handling noise in outlier detection and Understandability of the outlier results.
- Methods of Outlier Detection are Supervised Methods, Semi-Supervised Methods and Unsupervised Methods
- Outlier Methods based on assumptions about normal data and outliers are Statistical, Proximity-based, and Clustering-based methods.
- Data visualization aims to communicate data clearly and effectively through graphical representation. These techniques discover data relationships that are not observable by looking into the raw data. It is used in reporting, managing business operations and tracking progress of various tasks.
- Various data visualization techniques are, Pixel Oriented Techniques, Geometric Projection Techniques, Icon-Based Techniques, Hierarchical and Graph Based Techniques.

CHAPTER 10

APPLICATION AREAS OF DATA MINING

Data mining can play an important role in a decision-making system. It provides a methodology for problem solving, analysis, planning, diagnosis, detection, integration, prevention, learning and innovations. —**Hedelin & Allwood, 2002, Liao, 2003**

10.1 SELECTING AND USING RIGHT DM TECHNIQUE

One of the most difficult tasks in the knowledge discovery process is to choose the right data mining technique, as the commercial software tools provide more and more possibilities together and the decision requires more and more expertise to judge and choose the right technique suitable for the area under study. Indeed, there are a lot of data mining techniques available for an environmental scientist wishing to discover some model from the user's data. This diversity in the techniques can cause some troubles to the analysts who often have not a clear idea of what are the available methods, and which one of these techniques would be the most suitable method to be applied to solve a concrete domain problem.

In order to select the suitable method it is better to have an understanding of various methods of data mining and to classify them in order to choose the one which can be applied to the particular domain under consideration.

Apart from this, an intelligent data mining assistant is presented. It is oriented to provide model/algorithm selection support, suggesting the user the most suitable data mining techniques for a given problem.

The classical scheme of Knowledge Discovery from data provided by Fayyad in 1996 refers the following steps to complete the high level process of KDD, very often also called Data Mining (Spate et al. 2006):

- Developing and ***understanding the domain***, capturing relevant prior knowledge and the goals of the end-user is of paramount importance as the remaining process will be carried out keeping the problem domain under consideration.
- Creating the ***target data*** set by selecting a proper set of variables or data samples (including generation of proper queries to a central data warehouse if needed).
- ***Data cleaning and preprocessing:*** Quality of result strongly depends on the quality of input data, and therefore the preprocessing step is crucial. During this process, the

dirty data, noisy data and the irrelevant data is removed through various data flittering and preprocessing procedures.

- ***Data reduction and projection*:** Depending on the problem, it may be convenient to simplify the considered set of variables. The aim here is to keep a relevant set of variables describing the system adequately and efficiently.
- ***Choosing the data mining task*:** Many data mining techniques are available and each one of these has distinguish characteristics and the technique suitable to the problem domain is selected and is implemented with reference to the goal of the KDD process.
- ***Selecting the data mining algorithms*:** Once the task is decided and goals are codified, a concrete method (or set of methods) needs to be chosen for searching patterns in the data. Depending on the choice of techniques, parameter optimization may or may not be required.
- ***Data Mmining*:** The data mining algorithms are applied for searching the patterns in data. This will be significantly improved if previous steps were performed carefully.
- ***Interpreting mined patterns*:** This is crucial if the discovered patterns have to support effective improvement of expert's knowledge about the analyzed phenomenon or further decision-making.

  If results look inconsistent possible further iteration of previous steps may be required to refine the analysis.
- ***Consolidating discovered knowledge*:** Documenting and reporting results, or using them inside the target system so that the decision makers can get the maximum benefit from the results obtained.

This scheme is rarely followed fully by any computational system. Most of the commercial data mining systems provide collections of several preprocessing, data mining and support-interpretation tools, which have to be properly combined by the data miner itself to build a correct KDD process for every particular application.

10.2 CLASSIFICATION OF DATA MINING TECHNIQUES IN CONTEXT TO DECISION-MAKING

The classification given below is oriented to support the decisional problem of choosing the right one in real applications and it has been used as a reference for the construction of *intelligent data mining techniques recommenders (InDaMiTe-R).* The main criteria's taken into consideration while selecting a particular technique are:

- The main goals of the problem to be solved.
- The structure of the available data.

The various data mining techniques can be classified in many different ways depending on the purpose of classification. Here the classification provided is done to fulfil the requirement of the user to choose the technique best suited for the study. It will help in:

- Modeling the decision process itself.
- Helping non-expert data miners to improve their decisions.
- Building technical data miner recommenders that in the future can be included at a higher level in data mining systems.

The classification of various techniques has been shown in the form of a tree, having various levels of division:

These divisions have been done on the basis of following criterias:

Level I: Having no reference variable to be explained (response variable).

The left sub tree from root refers to *non-supervised* methods, without response variable, in which the main goal is to have a better *cognition* of the target phenomenon and description is enough as a result.

Whereas the right subtree refers to *supervised* models oriented to *re-cognition*, where a response variable is to be explained and prediction is pretended.

Level II: The division is based on the aim of describing relationships between objects (rows of data matrix), which are labeled as ***descriptive methods***, describing relationships between variables (columns of data matrix), labeled as ***associative methods***.

The various ***descriptive methods*** can be further subdivided as:

(*a*) *Conceptual Clustering*: It cluster the objects that are conceptually related to each other. This method
   - Provides grouping of homogeneous objects.
   - Requires hypothesis about the number of classes to be found.
   - Results of this type of clustering are directly understandable.
   - This method does not work with very big data sets.

(*b*) *Statistical Clustering*: This method:
   - Provides grouping of homogeneous objects.
   - It might not require the number of classes.
   - This method is very efficient with big data sets.
   - Sometimes it may be difficult to understand the meaning of grouping provided.

(*c*) *Clustering based on rules*:
   - It provides grouping of homogeneous objects and do not require number of classes as input.
   - It can introduce prior expert knowledge as semantic bias.
   - It guarantee interpretability of results and coherence with prior expert knowledge.

The various methods following the ***associative model*** can be classified as:

(*A*) *The first category in associative model is related to artificial intelligence and the various methods in this category are:*
   - *Association rules*: Provides patterns of associated values of variables and frequencies of appearance. Interpretable results.

- *Model-based reasoning*: Provides formal model of the causal relationships among the domain variables, by providing models for the dependencies among variables.
- *Qualitative reasoning*: Provides qualitative model of the causal relationships among the domain variables, by representing which variables increase or decrease values as a consequence of modifications in the values of other variables.

(*B*) *The second category is related to statistics and the various methods in this category are:*

- *Principal Component Analysis*: Provides graphical representation to see numerical variables which are associated or not. Extra work is required to be done to interpret the results.
- *Simple Correspondence Analysis*: Provides graphical representation to see modalities of two qualitative variables which behave associated or not. Extra work is required to be done to interpret the results.
- *Multiple Correspondences Analysis*: Provides graphical representation for associations among modalities of various qualitative variables. Extra work required for interpretation.

(*C*) *The methods in the third category use multi-disciplinary approach and use both the artificial intelligence and statistics, the method used in this category is:*

- *Bayesian Networks*: Provides graphical interpretation of causal relationships between variables together with conditional probabilities.

For methods related to prediction, the main distinction is regarding the nature of the response variable: where *discriminant methods* explain or predict qualitative variables, and the *predictive methods* refer to quantitative response variables.

The ***discriminant models*** can be further subdivided into:

(*A*) *Rule-based reasoning methods* group methods providing explicit knowledge model, which can be expressed by formal rules or not, to be applied for further prediction.

- **Rule-based Classifiers:** Provide a set of classification rules that can be used later to evaluate a new case and classify in a predefined set of classes.
- **Decision Trees:** Provide a graphical representation of a tree with conditions associated to nodes that permit to classify a new instance in a predefined set of classes. Problems with very big data sets. It works with qualitative variables.
- **Discriminant Analysis:** Provides an algebraic discriminant function and a cut-off as the rule to decide between two groups for a new instance. Only for numerical variables, two predefined classes and works only under linear separable classes.
- **Support Vector Machines (SVMs):** They can provide discriminant functions to distinguish between two predefined classes that can be non-lineary separable.
- Boxplot-based induction rules: Provide a set of probabilistic classification rules that can be used later on to classify a new instance in a predefined set of classes.
- **Regression-trees:** Provide decision trees for prediction of numerical values. Each leaf has a numerical value, which is the average of all the training set values that the leaf, or rule, applies to.

- **Model trees:** Provide regression trees combined with regression equations. The leaves of these trees contain regression equations rather than single predicted values. A model tree approximates continuous functions by several linear sub models.

(B) *Case-based reasoning methods* the predictive model is implicit in historical data;

- Instance-based learning: Uses historical data to classify a new instance of a problem in a predefined set of classes.

(C) *Bayesian Learning*: The third option is a mixture between prior explicit knowledge model and iterative refinements based on future data.

- Naïve Bayes Classifier: Provides an adaptive classifier that can improve initial knowledge-based predictions for the class of a new instance by refining the model on the basis of the evidences provided by the whole history of processed cases.

The predictive models can be classified as:

- **Connexionist Models:** It includes all artificial neural networks models. It permits to predict the value of one or more variables for a new instance on the basis of non-linear combination of the values of several input variables and intermediary layers.
- **Evolutionary Computation:** It provides the optimization of a certain objective function through the evolution of a population of individuals, which are subjected to several genetic operators. It includes techniques simulating the theory of evolution, like genetic algorithms and genetic programming.
- **Swarm Intelligence (SI):** It provides predictions of numerical variables by training the system under the metaphor of the collective behavior of decentralized, self-organized systems, natural or artificial. Local interactions between very simple agents lead to the emergence of intelligent global behavior. Natural examples of SI include ant colonies, bird flocking, animal herding, bacterial growth, and fish schooling.
- **Simple Linear Regression:** It predicts the value of a quantitative variable for a new instance as a linear equation of a single numerical variable. It requires normality, linearity and homocedasticity.
- **Multiple Linear Regressions:** It predicts the value of a quantitative variable for a new instance as a linear equation of several numerical variables. It requires normality, linearity, homocedasticity and independence
- **Analysis of Variance:** It predicts the value of a quantitative variable for a new instance as a linear combination of one or two qualitative variables. It requires conditional normality, linearity, homocedasticity and independence.
- **Generalized Linear Models:** It predicts the value of a quantitative variable for a new instance as a linear combination of several numerical and qualitative variables.
- **Time Series:** It predict the value of a quantitative variable for a future instance as a linear combination of past values of the same variable.

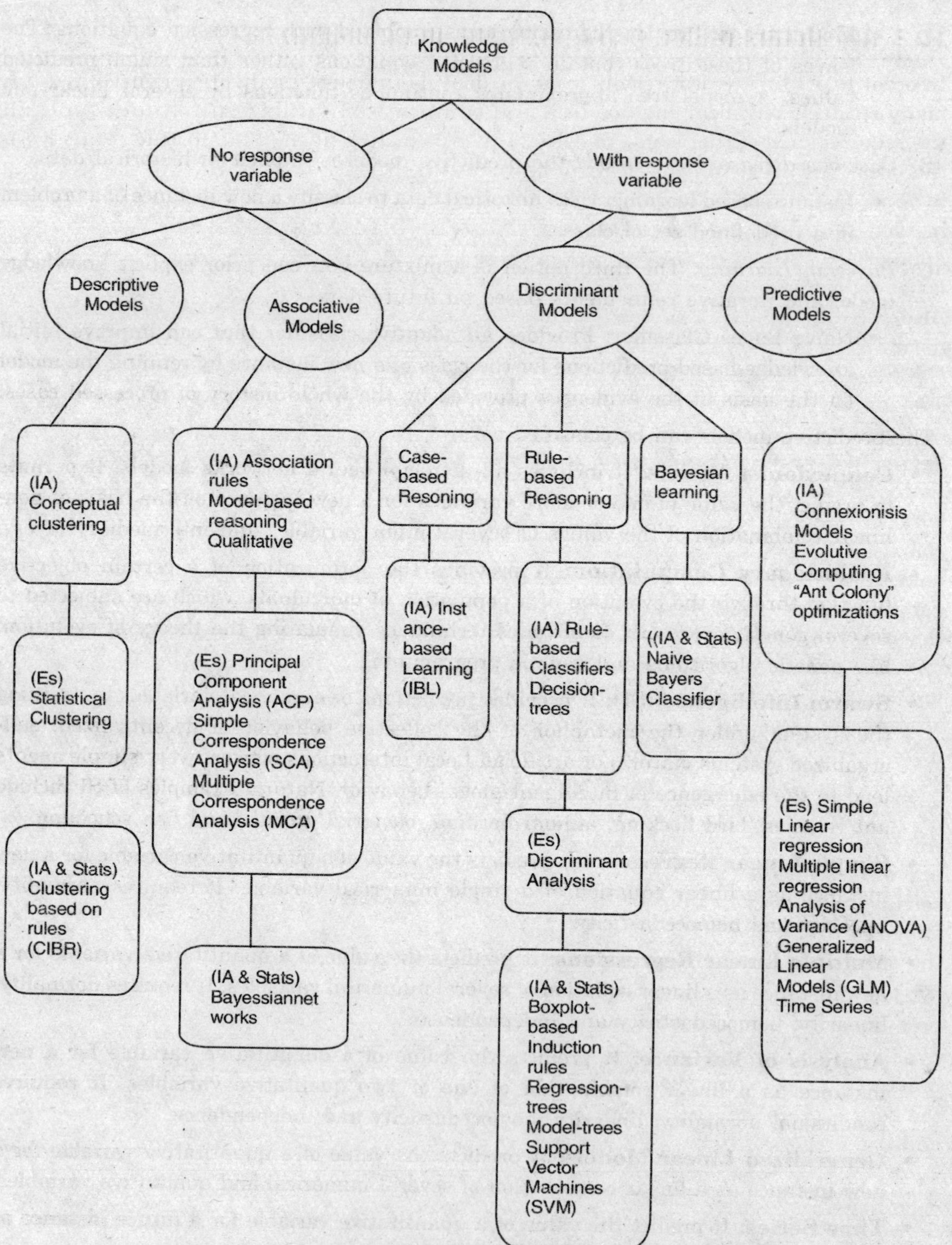

Fig. 10.1: Classification of Data Mining Techniques:

10.3 AN INTELLIGENT DATA MINING RECOMMENDER

In order to obtain the best results from the data mining process, the data miner has to tackle many strategic technical and non-technical decisions which will ultimately focus on fulfilling the requirements of the users. To select a particular technique it is important to understand the user's requirements and goals to be achieved, then the broader class of the technique is to be identified. The classification given in the previous selection in the Figure 10.1 will help in identifying the broader category in which the problem falls and hence the technique appropriate to the specific application can be selected and used. The classification given here is not exhaustive and the classification may be changed depending on the user's requirements. Also, the number of data mining techniques available grows incredibly fast every day and this means that the knowledge-based approach is constrained to continuous reviews and upgrades. On the other hand, the number of decisions made by an expert data miner to find the right subfamily of techniques (hierarchical clustering, or partitional or fuzzy), the right parameters of execution (once decided hierarchical clustering, choose the algorithm, the metric, the aggregation criterion, sometimes, weight on the metrics) in a particular case is so complex that it becomes difficult to mention them all explicitly in a conceptual map. That is the reason why we propose to move to a case-based reasoning approach, which is more flexible to changes in the future on the methodological framework and use implicitly the expertise of data miners by means of past experiences. In fact, a key characteristic that any intelligent data mining assistant should possess is the capacity to learn from past user's experiences, so the system can help the user to avoid the repetition of mistakes and motivates the knowledge reuse, and on the other hand, allow the user to adapt to new possibilities by including them in the system easily. Thus, a non-expert data miner could take advantage of the experiences of others users facing similar problems. And an expert can propose new solutions based on more recent trends.

System Overview

An intelligent DM assistant was developed, based on a pure Case-Based Reasoning (CBR) approach. This DM assistant is integrated within the GESCONDA tool. CBR is a problem solving methodology that tries to solve new problems by re-using specific past experiences stored in a case base, and its core proposition is that new problems can be solved by reusing the solutions to similar problems that have been solved in the past.

For this reason, a CBR approach naturally fits with the above mentioned challenge of promoting the knowledge reuse. Furthermore, this approach allows the construction of a dynamic system able to refine and adapt the suggestions over time, something that is of vital importance in a domain like the data mining processes, where it is extremely difficult to find the best solution due to the huge number of possible combinations of data mining techniques and training parameters.

As in most CBR approaches, the system relies on a unique case base in which past user's experiences are captured. Each case/experience is composed of:

- ***Case description***, a set of dataset characteristics describing the type of problem the data miner wants to solve (e.g. the number of attributes and records, the ratio of symbolic attributes and the relative probability of missing values);

- ***Case solution,*** a set of data mining techniques with its own configuration parameters and also associated with its corresponding evaluation measures such as the execution time and the error rate.

CBR is a cyclic and integrated problem solving process that supports learning from experience and can be described by four main phases.

Retrieve the most similar case(s) to the new case,

Reuse the solution(s) of the retrieved case(s) to solve the new case,

Revise the proposed solution,

Retain the new case into the existing case base.

For the particular problem domain of data mining processes our system conducts each one of these phases in the following manner:

1. **Retrieve:** The well-known K-nearest neighbour classification algorithm is employed in order to find the most similar cases. To do this, the system automatically extracts the metadata information of the dataset more relevant for the general type of task the data miner wants to solve (i.e. classification or regression task). The extracted dataset characteristics conform the case description.
2. **Reuse:** The solutions of the most similar cases are filtered and ranked according to how well they fit with the application restrictions provided by the user (if any), and how similar is the new case to the past case to which the solution belongs. The ordered list of data mining algorithms forms the preliminary case solution.
3. **Revise:** The user can execute the suggested algorithms or can modify/propose new configuration parameters and algorithms. During the user session each execution is automatically evaluated using a particular error rate measure according to the type of task the user is conducting. Furthermore, the user can explicitly evaluate the results of an execution and validating if the results are good or bad. Finally, the executed data mining algorithms constitute the final case solution.
4. **Retain:** The system will retain the new case if its solution contains at least the execution of one data mining algorithm whose evaluation results either have been validated by the user or its corresponding error rate is greater than a threshold.

10.4 APPLICATIONS OF DATA MINING

Data mining is an interdisciplinary field with wide and diverse applications. There exist nontrivial gaps between data mining principles and domain-specific applications. The organizations around the global are adopting and utilizing the new technologies to help them manage their businesses more efficiently and effectively, so that they can gain a competitive edge over others. The IT revolution is one of the biggest achievements of mankind. The use of information technology is very much prominent in all organizations irrespective of their size. Information and Communication Technologies (ICTs) are now widely accepted as key forces in shaping the economic landscape, transforming the way we live, learn, work and play(Danziger & Andersen, 2002). Today technology has allowed the production and storage of vast amounts of information. The size of data bases is growing at an alarming rate, but the problem is that the companies fail to reap the full benefits which can be gained from this great wealth of information. In such a situation, the techniques of data mining can be of immense help to the organization. The various commercial organizations are recognizing the need of generating relevant information out of the huge repositories of the data and they are trying to find out the ways and means for providing concise and crisp information as per the requirements of the organization and the users. In order to improve the quality of the decisions, the organizations need to critically analyze this information. In the business world for example, information obtained from market segmentation, customer profiling, trend forecasting, cross-selling can help decisions makers to learn more about their customers and to provide them more customized services. Technology provides the key to collating, classifying and manipulating this vast repository of information. Working in this direction, the business intelligence systems have played a vital and significant role in making the organizations capable of achieving their business objectives, which includes customer retention, profitability and increase in efficiency.

10.4.1 Data Mining in Banking and Retail Sector

The banking sector has witnessed a tremendous change in the way the banking operations are being carried out. Technology is as much part of the banking industry today as ship's engine is a part of the ship. Since 1990's the whole concept of banking has been shifted to centralized databases, online transactions, network connectivity and ATM's all over the world, which has made the banking system technically strong and more customer oriented. The banks have left their traditional functions and have been innovating, improving and coming out with new types of the services to cater the emerging needs of their customers. Massive branch expansion in the rural and underdeveloped areas, mobilization of savings and diversification of credit facilities to small scale industrial sector, agricultural and other preferred areas have resulted in the widening and deepening of the financial infrastructure. In the nutshell, the fundamental character of class banking has been transferred into mass banking. In spite of drastic changes in the ways in which business operations are being carried out by the banks, one factor that has remained unaltered is the need of the customers for the products and services provided by the banks and the objective of the banks i.e to provide customer-oriented services. Banks have to adjust to the changing needs of the societies, where people not only regard a bank account as a right rather than a privilege, but are also aware of the fact that their business is valuable to the bank, and if the bank does not look after them, they can take their business elsewhere.

Technology in banking is not just the automation of process, but it is much more than this. Where the age old ***product-strategy*** has be transformed to ***customer-focused*** strategy. The banks have realized that their biggest asset is the knowledge and not the financial resources. The organizations and individuals having right access to the right information at the right moment of time will be the one to rule the system.

The Indian banking sector is incorporating the concept of Management Information System, through which banks are generating various kinds of reports, which are analyzed for the decision making with in the organization. However these reports are available in the summarized form can be used for decision making purposes. But particularly for the banking sector, which is an information intensive industry, it is a cumbersome task. The banks at present generate reports from the periodic paper reports and the statements submitted by various constitute units. Such reports have a high degree of error, due to data being recorded and interpreted by various parties at various levels. Moreover the Total Branch Computerization (TBC) software packages being used at various branch levels are transaction oriented, as these were designed keeping day to day transactions in mind. Designing the new MIS or restructuring the existing ones would not be possible as such. The solution seems to be in incorporating the concept of *data warehousing and data mining*.

With the rapid development in the hardware and software industry, the terms like data warehouse and data mining are gaining importance, which basically equip the decision makers with the *what if* simulations. A step further, the present trend of mergers and acquitions has contributed a step further in highlighting the need of data warehouse and data mining techniques. The need is felt due to the fact that banking units use different operational systems in the different branches, but the top management still needs a consolidated view of the data for managing the future trends. Both the public and private sector banks are incorporating various types of techniques and tools to place themselves better in the market.

The data warehouses allow decision makers to have a prompt access to information for the purpose of reporting and analysis. Moving a step further, to extract, analyze, project and mine the data as per the requirements of the users and analysts, the data mining technology is helping the organization.

A data mining approach comprises of a variety of technological techniques and tools to explore, summarize, compare, analyze, forecast and estimate the data for various decisions to be taken by the organization.

The banking industry has been the leader in the use of data warehouses. Apart from the market driven reasons, compliance driven reasons are also behind the establishment of data ware houses and the use of data mining technology. Data collected in the banking and financial industry are often relatively complete, reliable and of high quality which facilitates systematic data analysis and data mining.

The retail industry collects a huge amount of data on sales, customer shopping history, goods transportation, consumption and service. The quantity of data collected continues to expand rapidly, especially due to the increasing availability, ease and popularity of business conducted on web. Today most of the major chain stores also have web sites where customers can purchase online. The application of data mining in retail can provide huge benefits to the decision maker. Retail data mining can help in identifying customer buying behavior, discover customer shopping trends and patterns, improve quality of service, better customer retention and satisfaction.

The application and usage of data mining in banking and retail sector are quite inter-related to each other.

According to Groth (1998), retailers are interested in creating data mining models to answer questions such as:

- How much are customers likely to spend over long periods of time?
- What is the frequency of customer purchasing behavior?

- What are the best types of advertisements to reach certain segments?
- What advertising mediums are most effective in reaching customers?
- What is the optimal timing to send mailers?

In the following sections, examples of how the retail industry has also been effectively utilizing data mining in the areas of (1) marketing, (2) risk management, (3) fraud detection, and (4) customer acquisition and retention.

Major Data Requirements of the Industry:

1. What is the profile, tastes, preferences and purchasing behavior of the customers?
2. What is the transaction behavior of the various customers?
3. Which products are often purchased together by the customers of which particular profile?
4. What services and benefits would the current customers likely desire?
5. Identifying the customers who are getting all types of services from the company.
6. Which set of customers are Loyal and which one are disloyal?
7. What set of transactions lead to a fraud?
8. Will the customer be able to repay the loans or not?
9. To predict the future trends and hence to design the future road map.

Major Goals the organization needs to achieve:

1. Cross selling the products.
2. Differentiating between Loyal and Disloyal Customers.
3. Target Marketing to focus on prospective customers.
4. Prevention of defaults, bad loans.
5. To increase customer retention.
6. To increase customer satisfaction.

The areas in which the data mining techniques can be implemented are:

1. Marketing: The data mining techniques can be used to know the customers well and to plan that how the banks can market their products in a better way. It is used to determine that how customers will react to adjustments in the interest rates, which customers will be likely to accept the new product offers, the risk profile of a customer segments for defaulting on loans etc. Data mining technique can be used to profile the likeminded customers in to one group and hence they can be dealt accordingly, the reaction of the customers for the existing and new products can be recorded, according to which the future strategies can be designed. They can also use the data mining techniques for cross selling. As we know that, the customers of a given geographic location and of a particular job profile demand a particular set of services, like in banking sector the customers from the service class always demand for the policy which ensures more security as they are not intending to take risks, likewise the same set of service class people in rural areas have the preferences for some particular brands which may differ from their counterparts in the urban areas. This information will help the organization in cross-selling their products, Instead of mass pitching a certain "hot" product, the bank's customer service representatives can be equipped with customer profiles enriched by data mining that help them to identify which products and services are more relevant to the callers. This technique will help the management in finding the solution of 80/20 principle of marketing, which says: Twenty per cent of the customers will provide 80 per cent of profits, then problem is to identify those 20 % and the techniques of clustering will help in achieving the same.

2. Risk Management: The customer and the banks while dealing with each other will always try to cover the risk factor. Data mining technique helps to distinguish borrowers who repay loans promptly from those who don't. It also helps to predict when the borrower is at default, whether providing loan to a particular customer will result in bad loans or not. Bank executives by using data mining techniques can also analyze the behavior and reliability of the customers. In commercial lending, risk assessment is usually an attempt to quantify the risk of loss to the lender while making a particular lending decision. It also helps to predict when the borrower is at fault, whether providing loan to a particular customer will result in bad loans or not. Such techniques come under the category of credit risk, where we wish to check the behavior of the prospective customers.

3. Customer Relationship Management: In the era of cut throat competition the customer is considered as the king and it is the customer only who is ruling the whole show. The huge data bases of various organizations are storing billions of data items about the customers. Data mining can be useful in all the three phases of a customer relationship cycle: *Customer Acquisition, Increasing Value of the Customer and Customer Retention.* Data mining technique can be used to create customer profile to group the likeminded people and hence they can be dealt accordingly. The information collected can be used for different purposes like making new marketing initiatives, market segmentation, risk analysis and revising company customer policies according to the need of the customers. The profiling can be done on the basis of demographic characteristics, life style and previous transactional behavior of a particular customer. Customer profiling is to characterize features of special customer groups. *Which customers in particular the organization will wish to keep? Which customers will drive most of the profits? Which customers might switch to the competitors and why? Which customers are dissatisfied with your services and products?* If the bank has the answers to these questions then they will be able to design customized services and offers, which will enhance customer satisfaction.

4. Cross Selling and Predicting the Future Trends: The techniques of data mining will be helpful in cross selling the products to existing customers. By profiling the customer data according to various factors like their demographic details, financial conditions, taste and preferences, the existing customers may be approached for the other products being offered by the banks. Data mining will help in predicting the future trends and organizations can offer the products accordingly, like if a customer has availed a home loan, then after some time he/she can be contacted again for buying furniture or refrigerator or TV etc. As these are the obvious requirements after the purchase of a home. By predicting customer needs in advance, businesses can then market their products in a better way. Customer satisfaction can also be improved through more effective marketing.

5. Attrition Analysis and Customer Retention: In the present day environment of cut throat competition, the customers are in a fix and are shifting from one bank to other. The studies show that customers switch from one bank to other, when they observe that the other bank is providing better rate of interests, better credit facilities or better customized services. The banks then need to classify the customers to identify that which set of customers might switch to the competitors and why? Which set of customers are dissatisfied with your services and products? The analysis will help the bank to identify such customers and hence the bank can plan strategies to prevent the attrition.

6. Fraud Detection: While dealing with banks, the customers and the banks have the chances of falling an easy prey to the frauds. So, both the parties wish to be secure while dealing with each other. The data mining techniques can help them to detect and hence prevent frauds. To detect such frauds it is important to integrate information from multiple, heterogeneous databases like transactional data bases of the bank and state's crime history database. Multiple data analysis tools can be used to detect unusual patterns like large amount of cash flow at a particular time by an individual or a group of customers. The tools like data visualization to display transaction activities using graph grouped by time or by customers, linkage and information network analysis tools to identify links among different customers and their activities, classification tools to group different cases, outlier analysis tools- to detect unusual fund transfers, sequential pattern analysis tools- to characterize unusual access sequences. It is important to:

- identify potentially fraudulent users and their usage pattern.
- attempts to gain fraudulent entry or unauthorized access to individual and organizational accounts.
- discover unusual patterns that may need special attention.

7. Multidimensional Analysis: when the organization wishes to analyze the customer's data, it is important to make decisions not only on a single factor, but multiple factors are required to be considered. Like the purchasing behavior of customer, not only depends on his tastes and preferences or his income, but is dependent on the market trends, pressure from peer groups also. It requires that the analysis should be done on multiple factors and hence multidimensional analysis is taken into consideration. The retail industry requires timely information regarding needs of the customers, product sales, trends and fashions as well as the quality, cost, profit and service of commodities. So it is important to provide powerful multidimensional analysis and visualization tools which includes the construction of data cubes according to the needs of data analysis.

8. Analysis of effectiveness of Sales Campaigns: The retail industry conducts sales campaigns using advertisements, coupons and various kinds of discounts and bonuses to promote products and attract customers. The analysis of the effectiveness of sales campaigns can help improve company profits. Multidimensional analysis can be used for this purpose by comparing the amount of sales and the number of transactions containing the sales items during the sales period vs those containing the same items before or after the sales campaign will help in designing the strategies.

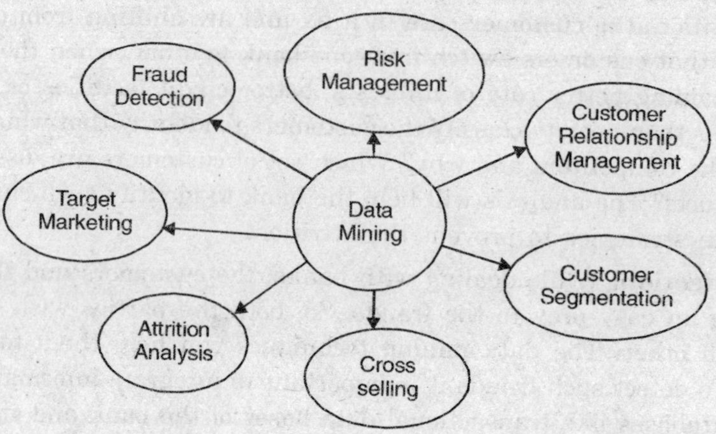

Fig. 10.2: Application Areas of Data Mining

The other benefits include:

1. The reaction of the customers for the existing and new products can also be known based on which banks will try to promote the product, improve on the quality of products and services and can gain competitive advantage over the other banks.
2. Bank analysts can also analyze the past trends to determine the present demand and forecast the customer behaviour of various products and services in order to grab more business opportunities and anticipate behavior patterns in the future.
3. Data mining techniques also help to distinguish between profitable and non-profitable customers.
4. Data mining techniques help to distinguish between the borrowers who repay loans promptly from those who do not.
5. It also helps to predict when the borrower is at default, whether providing loan to a particular customer will result in bad loans or not.
6. Bank executives by using data mining technique can also analyze the behavior and reliability of the customers while selling cards related products. It also helps to analyze whether the customer will make prompt or delay payment if the credit cards are sold to them.

There are numerous areas in which data mining can be used in the banking industry, which include customer segmentation and profitability, credit scoring and approval, predicting payment default, marketing, detecting fraudulent transactions, cash management and forecasting operations, optimizing stock portfolios, and ranking investments. In addition, banks may use data mining to identify their most profitable credit card customers or high-risk loan applicants. There is, therefore, a need to build an analytical capability to address the above-stated issues and data mining attempts to provide the answer.

Data Mining helps to increase sales by targeting the right customers and to make the right offers to customers. Banks, who have their ears to the ground regarding their customer's tastes and preferences, gather a lot of data...what data mining does is that it sifts through all the voluminous data and ekes out a pattern, which enables the bank to personalize its communication towards the customer as much as possible. With data mining, banks can get a better understanding what drives the customer relationship.

—Mudit Saxena (Vice-President (Retail Marketing) HDFC Bank)

Data Mining is really about understanding consumer behaviour.

Sriraman Jagannathan(Vice President(Internet and E-Commerce) Citibank)

10.4.2 Data Mining and Education

There are increasing research interests in using data mining in education. This new emerging field, called Educational Data Mining, concerns with developing methods that discover knowledge from data originating from educational environments. By using these techniques many kinds of knowledge can be discovered which can be used for prediction regarding enrolment of students in a particular course, alienation of traditional classroom teaching model, detection of unfair means used in online examination, detection of abnormal values in the result sheets of the students, prediction about student's performance and so on. Today, one of the biggest challenges that educational institutions face is the explosive growth of educational data and to use this data to improve the quality of managerial decisions. To face these challenges different systems are used such as Enterprise Resource Planning and data warehouse Systems. ***Enterprise Resource Planning (ERP)*** integrates internal and external management information of an entire organization like finance/accounting information, manufacturing, sales, service information and most important its customer relationship management. ERP systems automate all these activities to facilitate the flow of information between all business functions inside the boundaries of the organization and manage the connections to outside world. ERP systems operate in real time i.e. without relying on periodic updates, along with common database, which supports all applications. ERP plays a crucial role in decision making for businessmen to get quick decisions with fewer errors. OLTP (On-Line Transaction Processing) has been developed as complete ERP solution for academic institution. The primary objective of the OLTP is to facilitate students and faculty to get a robust and advanced atmosphere of learning. OLTP's academic IT Infrastructure helps us to manage thousands of students from a single integrated management control. It facilitates fast interaction between the students and teachers. These solutions use various modules like SMS integration, e-mail communication, biometric support, payment gateway integration, shared mail folders, e-mail group address and mobile mail access. These modules can be customized to the specific requirement of the institute. To keep a pace with the fast changing dynamic scenarios OLAP (On-Line analytic Processing) is required because it handles multi-dimensional queries.

Higher education institutions are interested in predicting the paths of students and alumni, thus identifying which students will join particular course programs.

A. Grouping the Students Sharing Similar Characteristics: It is required most of the times to group the students with similar characteristics into one group and to handle them by providing the customized services as per their requirements. Clustering technique of data mining can then be used to group the students. Clustering (as discussed earlier in Chapter 9), is the task of assigning a set of objects into groups called clusters) so that the objects in the same cluster are more similar (in some sense or another) to each other than to those in other clusters. Application of clustering in education can help institutes group individual student into class of similar behavior. Partition the students into clusters, so that students within a cluster (e.g. Average) are similar to each other while dissimilar to students in other clusters (e.g. Intelligent, Weak). The students clustered as toppers can be handled by providing more specialized trainings. These clusters/groups of students can be used by the instructor/developer to build a personalized learning system which can promote effective group learning. For Example: the students from a particular educational background want a training in particular course, so they can be clustered together and can be trained accordingly. It will help the trainer and trainee to focus on one particular core subject which will enhance the core competency of the student and teacher.

Table 10.1: Comparison of Data Mining Questions in Education and the Corporate World

Comparison of Data Mining Questions in Education and the Corporate World	
Questions in the Business World	***Counterpart Questions in Higher Education***
Who are my most profitable customers?	Who are the students taking most credit hours?
Who are the visitors visiting my website visitors?	Who are the ones likely to return for more classes?
Who are my loyal customers?	Who are the students loyal to the institution?
What are new products which can be launched in the recent future?	What type of courses can we offer to attract more students?
How to retain the existing customers? What services we can provide to retain them?	How to retain the existing students?

B. To provide associated courses to students: Association and correlation is usually to find frequently used data items in the large data sets. It is the technique of finding patterns where one event is connected to another event. Students acquiring a professional degree should have a good communication and analytical skills in order to get a good placement, so by using the techniques of data mining the management may find out such associations and can provide the course structure which will help the student in the long run. Like student studying in MCA Course can be given training in personality development, interview training and other associated courses, so that his/her employability can be increased. Students developing a project in ASP.NET need to have a good knowledge of some graphical tool, so if they are offered training in Corel Draw/Photoshop, it will add the course value and the course will sell like hot cakes.

C. To pinpoint and handle the exceptional cases: Students having exceptionally good or bad record needs special attention and it will be possible only if such cases have been identified. Due to large size of student base, extracting such knowledge is quite difficult. The data mining technique known as Outlier analysis can be used for this purpose, where an

Outlier can be defined as *"An outlying observation, or outlier, is one that appears to deviate markedly from other members of the sample in which it occurs"*. Outlier detection has been used to detect and remove anomalous observations from data. Like the students record showing any unusual behavior may be termed as outlier. A hostler coming late in the evening, a student getting less attendance in all subjects for more than a normal period, can be considered as an outlier and the corresponding message can be send to the concerned authority and the preventive and corrective actions can be taken accordingly, well in time.

D. Predicting Student Performance: In this case, we estimate the unknown value of a variable that describes the student. In education, the values normally predicted are student's performance, their knowledge, score, or marks. Regression analysis is used to find relation between a dependent variable and one or more independent variables. Prediction of a student's performance is the most popular applications of data mining in education. Different techniques and models are applied like neural networks, Bayesian networks, rule based systems, regression, and correlation analysis to analyze educational data. This analysis helps us to predict student's performance i.e. to predict about his success in a course and to predict about his final grade based on features extracted from logged data. Different types of rule-based systems have been applied to predict student's performance (mark prediction) in an e-learning environment (using fuzzy-association rules). Several regression techniques are used to predict student's marks like linear regression for predicting student's academic performance, stepwise linear regression for predicting time to be spent on a learning page, multiple linear regressions for identifying variables that could predict success in colleges courses and for predicting exam results in distance education courses.

E. Target Marketing: Marketing the course is the new is area of education sector added recently. Targeting the right student with the right course at the right time is very important. Students classified and clustered depending upon their various characteristics like gender, age, and educational qualification, family income, hobbies and future plans, can be offered customized courses. The girl students not willing to work out of home can be trained in cooking, interior designing, fashion technology and the other business which can be operated while sitting at home only. The students having the wish to pursue their career in IT sector can be offered courses for specialization like CCNA, MCSE, and OCP etc, along with their regular MCA or B.Tech courses. These techniques have been used successfully in service sectors like banks, where the customer call representative is not calling all 100 prospective customers for the same policy, rather depending upon the characteristics of the customers, a particular policy is offered only to those 20 pc customers who seem interested in a particular policy and let 10 out of them are ready, which will increase the success rate manifold.

F. Forecasting: Regression technique can be adapted for predication. Regression analysis can be used to model the relationship between one or more independent variables and dependent variables. In data mining independent variables are attributes already known and response variables are what we want to predict. Student purchasing a book on Programming in C, can be contacted after six months for a book on Programming in C++, student doing a course in MCA, can be offered a training course in a particular language and hence the educational institutes can plan and design their curriculum in better and customer centric way.

G. Customer Relationship Management: CRM can be defined as the process of predicting customer behavior and selecting actions to influence that behavior for the benefit of the company.

Major Goals the organization needs to achieve are:

1. Cross selling the courses.
2. Target Marketing to focus on prospective customers.
3. To increase customer retention.
5. Expanding the Customer Base by acquiring new and profitable customers
6. Lengthening the relationship with your top customers
7. Increasing Customer Delight through customized services:

10.4.3 Data Mining for Intrusion Detection and Prevention

The security of our computer systems and data is of paramount importance, the growth of internet and increasing availability of techniques for intrusion and attacking network have prompted intrusion detection and prevention to become an important part of networked system. *An intrusion can be defined as any set of actions that threaten the integrity, confidentiality or availability of a network resource. Intrusion detection systems monitor network traffic and try to trace malicious activities. As the size of networks and the data movement being handled by these systems is increasing day by day finding the intrusions is very challenging task.* Data mining methods can help an intrusion detection and prevention system to enhance its performance in following ways:

-Data mining algorithms can be used for both *signature based and anomaly based detection*. In case of signature based methods, detection mechanism utilizes signatures which are the attack patterns preconfigured and predetermined by domain experts. A signature based intrusion prevention system monitors the network traffic for matches of these signatures. If the match is found, the intrusion detection system will report the anamoly and the prevention system will take additional appropriate actions. In these systems, training data is labeled as either normal or intrusion. A classifier can be derived to detect known intrusions. In case of anomaly based detection methods, model is built regarding the normal network behavior and these are then used to detect new patterns that significantly deviate from the profiles. Such deviations may represent actual intrusion. The benefit of this method is that novel intrusion not detected so far can be detected. These methods use clustering, outlier analysis and classification algorithms and statistical approaches.

- Association, Correlation and pattern analysis help in selecting and building discriminative classifiers which can be applied to find relationships between systems attributes describing the network data.
- As the attacks are dynamic in nature, it is crucial to perform intrusion detection in the data stream environment. An event may be normal if considered individually, but may be malicious if viewed as a part of a sequence of events. Therefore, it is necessary to study what sequences of events are frequently encountered together and to find sequential patterns and identify outliers.

- Intrusions can be initiated from several different locations and may be targeted to many different destinations. So distributed data mining methods can be used to analyze network data from several network locations to detect distributed attacks.
- Visualization tools should be available for viewing any anomalous pattern detected. Such tools may include features for viewing associations, discriminative patterns, clusters and outliers. Intrusion detection systems should also have a graphical user interface that allows security analysts to pose queries regarding network data or intrusion detection results.

10.4.4 Data Mining in Telecommunication

The telecommunication industry handles a huge amount of data and is providing telephone services which include cellular phones, smart phones, internet access, email, text messages, images, computer and web data transmissions and other data traffic. The telecommunication is being integrated with computer network, internet and various other means of communication and computing. It has given birth to the demand for data mining to help understand business dynamics, identify telecommunication patterns, make better use of resources and improve service quality.

Data mining tasks in telecommunication share many similarities with those discussed in retail sector. Common tasks include:

- Fraudulent pattern analysis and the identification of unusual patterns.
- Identify potentially fraudulent users and their typical usage patterns.
- Detect attempts to gain fraudulent entry to customer accounts.
- Discover unusual patterns which may need special attention.
- Multidimensional association and sequential pattern analysis.
- Find usage patterns for a set of communication services by customer group, by month, etc.
- Promote the sales of specific services.
- Improve the availability of particular services in a region.
- Customer Retention.
- Use of visualization tools in telecommunication data analysis.

Although each industry has its own characteristics data sets and applications demands, they share common principles and methodologies.

10.4.5 Data Mining in Science and Engineering

In the earlier times, the scientific data analysis tasks tended to handle relatively small and homogeneous data sets. Such data were typically analyzed using the model - *formulate hypothesis, build model and evaluate results*. But today, scientific data can be collected at much higher speeds and at much lower costs, due to which huge volumes of high dimensional data, stream data and heterogeneous data, containing rich spatial and temporal information is collected and transferred. Therefore, scientific applications are shifting from the hypothesize and test to the new model - *collect and store data, mine for new hypotheses, confirm with data or experimentation process.*

Vast amounts of data have been collected from scientific domains including-

- Geo Sciences.
- Astronomy.
- Meterology
- Geology and biological sciences.

Data mining in science often collect massive amounts of data and require data preprocessing, data warehousing and scalable mining of complex data types of data.

In Social Sciences: massive amounts of human communication data pour into our daily life such communication exist in many forms like news, blogs, articles, web pages, online discussions, product reviews, messages, advertisements and communication both on the web and in various kinds of social networks. The feedback of users regarding products, speeches and articles can be analyzed to deduce general opinions and sentiments on the views of those in society. It can help to predict trends, improve work and help in decision making.

***In Computer Science*:** Data mining can be used to help monitor system status, improve system performance, isolate software bugs, detect software plagiarism, analyze computer system faults, detect network intrusions and recognize system malfunctioning. Data mining for software and system engineering can operate on static or dynamic data depending on whether the system dumps traces beforehand for post-analysis or it must react in real time to handle online data.

Application of Data Mining in Designing Recommender System: Recommender system helps the customers by providing product recommendations that are likely to be of interest to the users. Recommender system use a broad range of techniques like information retrieval, statistics, machine learning and data mining to find similarities among items and customers preferences. Recommender System can use any of the following approaches:

- ***Content Based Approach*** recommends items that are similar to the items the user preferred or enquired in past. It is based on product features and textual item description. The textual information can be collected from web sites, articles and news messages.
- ***Collaborative Approach***- It considers user's social environment. It recommends items based on the opinions of other customers who have similar tastes or preferences as the user.
- ***Hybrid Approach***- This approach combines the features of both the content based and collaborative methods.

These systems have the advantage of providing the personalized information for customers of e-commerce, promoting one-to-one marketing. It can benefit both the customer and the company, by having accurate models of the customers needs and preferences and hence companies gain a better understanding of customer's need. It helps in cross selling of related products, up-selling, product affinities, one-to-one promotions and customer retention.

10.4.6 Data Mining Pharmaceutical Sector

Pharmaceutical sector can get benefit from healthcare CRM and data mining, too.

- By tracking which physicians prescribe which drugs and for what purposes, pharmaceutical companies can decide whom to target, show what is the least expensive or most effective treatment plan for an ailment, help identify physicians whose practices are suited to specific clinical trials (for example, physicians who treat a large number of a specific group of patients), and map the course of an epidemic to support pharmaceutical salespersons, physicians, and patients.
- Pharmaceutical companies can also apply data mining to huge masses of genomic data to predict how a patient's genetic makeup determines his or her response to a drug therapy.

10.4.7 Data Mining in Sports

Sports are ideal for application of data mining tools and techniques. In the sports, the vast amounts of statistics are collected for each player, team, game, and season.

- Data mining can be used by sports organizations in the form of statistical analysis, pattern discovery, as well as outcome prediction. Patterns in the data are often helpful in the forecast of future events.
- Data mining can be used for scouting, prediction of performance, selection of players, coaching and training and for the strategy planning.
- The data mining techniques are used to determine the best or the most optimal squad to represent a team in a team sport in a season, tour or game.

The 'Cy Young Award' has been presented annually to the best pitcher in the major league of baseball. The award is based largely on statistics compiled over the course of the baseball season. A Bayesian classifier is developed to predict Cy Young Award winners in American major league baseball.

10.4.8 Data Mining in Health Care

The huge amounts of data generated by healthcare transactions are too complex and voluminous to be processed and analyzed by traditional methods. Data mining provides the methodology and technology to transform these amounts of data into useful information for decision making. Data can be a great asset to healthcare organizations, but it has to be transformed into information. Yet another factor motivating the use of data mining applications in healthcare is the realization that data mining can generate information that is very useful to all parties involved in the healthcare industry. For example, data mining applications can help healthcare insurers detect fraud and abuse, and healthcare providers can gain assistance in making decisions, Data mining applications also can help healthcare providers, such as hospitals, clinics and physicians, and patients, for example, by identifying effective treatments and best practices. The management of pharma industry starts to recognize the relevance of the definition of drugs and products in relation to management information. The delivery of healthcare has always been information intensive, and there are signs that the industry is recognizing the increasing importance of information processing in the new managed care environment. There is a growing need to do more with the data of an organization than to use them for administration only. A lot of information is hidden in the legacy systems. Most of the times this cannot be done directly from the legacy systems, because these are not build to answer questions that are unpredictable.

There is vast potential for data mining applications in healthcare. Generally, these can be grouped as the evaluation of treatment effectiveness; management of healthcare, customer relationship management and detection of fraud and abuse.

Treatment effectiveness: Data mining applications can be developed to evaluate the effectiveness of medical treatments. By comparing and contrasting causes, symptoms, and courses of treatments, data mining can deliver an analysis of which courses of action will prove effective. For example, the outcomes of patient groups treated with different drug regiments for the same disease or condition can be compared to determine which treatments work best and are most cost-effective.

Healthcare Management: To aid healthcare management, data mining applications can be developed to better identify and track chronic disease states and high-risk patients, design appropriate interventions, and reduce the number of hospital admissions and claims.

The Lightweight Epidemiological Advanced Detection Emergency Response System (LEADERS) is one such effort. In the past, LEADERS can be used for hospital infection control or as an automated early-warning system in the event of epidemics.

Customer Relationship Management: While customer relationship management is a core approach in managing interactions between commercial organizations—typically banks and retailers—and their customers, it is no less important in a healthcare context. Customer interactions may occur through call centers, physicians' offices, billing departments, inpatient settings, and ambulatory care settings. As in the case of commercial organizations, data mining applications can be developed in the healthcare industry to determine the preferences, usage patterns, and current and future needs of individuals to improve their level of satisfaction. These applications can also be used to predict other products that a healthcare customer is likely to purchase, whether a patient is likely to comply with prescribed treatment or whether preventive care is likely to produce a significant reduction in future utilization.

Fraud and abuse: Data mining applications that attempt to detect fraud and abuse often establish norms and then identify unusual or abnormal patterns of claims by physicians, laboratories, clinics, or others. Among other things, these applications can highlight inappropriate prescriptions or referrals and fraudulent insurance and medical claims.

Data Mining tools helps greatly to study DNA analysis and to find various patterns and functions. Data Mining helps the researches of Biomedical and DNA data analysis in the following ways:

- The DNA data is generally heterogeneous, highly distributed and uncontrolled in nature but this data is highly used in various areas of research in medical science. For the research purpose data must be systematic. Data Cleansing and integration approaches of data mining helps to systemize the data and store this data in the data base or data warehouse for further use in research.

- One of the main tasks related to DNA data analysis is to compare various sequences of the data and search for the similarities among this DNA data. Comparison mainly involves the gene sequence of healthy and diseased tissues to find the difference between these two types. This can be done by retrieving the gene sequence of both healthy and disease tissue classes and then finds the frequently occurring patterns of both classes. This analysis helps to find the similarities and dissimilarities in genetic sequence.
- In Biomedical research, it is studied that most of the diseases are triggered by combination of genes. Association analysis method is used to determine the co occurrence of the group of genes and also the user can study the interaction and relationships between the genes.
- There are different combinations of genes contributes to diseases but these different genes becomes activate at different level of stages. Path analysis is used to link the different genes to different stages of disease development.
- Visualization tools also play an important role in biomedical data mining. The visualization tools helps to present complex genes structure in graphs, trees and chains. The visual representation helps in better understanding of complex genes structures, for knowledge discovery and data exploration.

The neural networks with back-propagation and association rule mining used for tumor classification in mammograms. The data mining effectively used in the diagnosis of lung abnormality that may be cancerous or benign.

The data mining algorithms significantly reduce patient's risks and diagnosis costs. Using the prediction algorithms the observed prediction accuracy was 100% for 91.3% cases. The use of data mining in health care is the widely used application of data mining. The medical data is complex and difficult to analyze. A REMIND (Reliable Extraction and Meaningful Inference from Non-structured Data) system integrates the structured and unstructured clinical data in patient records to automatically create high quality structured clinical data. The high quality of structuring allows existing patient records to be mined to support guidelines compliance and to improve patient care.

SUMMARY

- Choosing the right data mining technique is a difficult task.
- *Intelligent data mining techniques recommenders* (*InDaMiTe-R*) is a system that can be used as a tool for selecting the right data mining technique.
- The main criteria's taken into consideration while selecting a particular technique are that, the main goals of the problem to be solved and the structure of the available data should be clear.
- Intelligent DM assistant was developed, based on a pure Case-Based Reasoning (CBR) approach. This DM assistant is integrated within the GESCONDA tool.
- Case-Based Reasoning is a cyclic and integrated problem solving process that supports learning from experience and can be described by four main phases.
- *Retrieve the most similar case(s) to the new case.*
- *Reuse the solution(s) of the retrieved case(s) to solve the new case.*
- *Revise the proposed solution.*
- *Retain the new case into the existing case base.*
- Data mining techniques can be applied in banking, telecommunication, health care, pharmaceutical, education and intrusion detection and prevention.

CHAPTER 11

INTRODUCTION TO BUSINESS INTELLIGENCE

11.1 INTRODUCTION

Business Intelligence refers to a set of methods and techniques that are used by organizations for tactical and strategic decision making. It leverages technologies that focus on counts, statistics and business objectives to improve business performance. Business intelligence equips enterprises to gain business advantage from data. *It is all about getting right information, to right decision makers at the right time in right format* Once an organization is powered with BI it can anticipate enhanced turnaround time on data collection, come up with fresh ideas for novel business initiatives, foresee accurate picture of customer needs and demands, and perform more targeted marketing campaigns. Decisions purely based on the gut feeling cannot assure success; but with BI's fact-based decision-making framework, confident decisions can be made for assured business success. Further, BI makes an organization agile thereby giving it a competitive edge in today's evolving market condition. Business intelligence is a concept or approach and is much more than a technology.

It leads to fact based decision making and provides a single version of truth.

In simple words,

Business Intelligence provides:

- *Fact Based Decision Making*
- *Single Version of Truth.*
- *360° perspective of business.*
- *Virtual Team Members on Same Page.*
- *Visibility to enterprise performance.*

The whole concept of BI starts with collection of raw data and ultimately by passing through various phases it is used for business use, the path followed is:

Raw Data -> Meaningful Information -> Knowledge Repository -> Beneficial Insights -> Impactful Decisions -> Business Benefits.

11.2 MEANING AND DEFINITIONS OF BUSINESS INTELLIGENCE

In a 1958 article, IBM researcher Hans Peter Luhn used the term business intelligence. He defined intelligence as: ***"the ability to apprehend the interrelationships of presented facts in such a way as to guide action towards a desired goal."***

BI refers to a set of tools and techniques that enable a company to transform its business data into timely and accurate information for the decisional process, to be made available to the right persons in the most suitable form."

Business Intelligence (BI) is the new technology for understanding the past & predicting the future. It is a collection of a broad category of technologies that allows for:

- gathering, storing, accessing & analyzing data to help business users to make better decisions.
- analyzing business performance through data-driven insight and
- a broad category of applications, which include the activities of: decision support systems, query and reporting, online analytical processing (OLAP), statistical analysis, forecasting, and data mining.

Business Intelligence (BI) is a set of theories, methodologies, processes, architectures, and technologies that transform raw data into meaningful and useful information for business purposes. BI can handle large amounts of information to help identify and develop new opportunities. Making use of new opportunities and implementing an effective strategy can provide a competitive market advantage and long-term stability.

Business intelligence (BI) is "about how to capture, access, understand, analyze and turn one of the most valuable assets of an enterprise - raw data - into actionable information in order to improve business performance"

It pairs data gathering, data storage, and knowledge management with analytic tools to provide decision-makers with competitive information that often act as differentiators in today's fierce business environment (Negash, 2004).

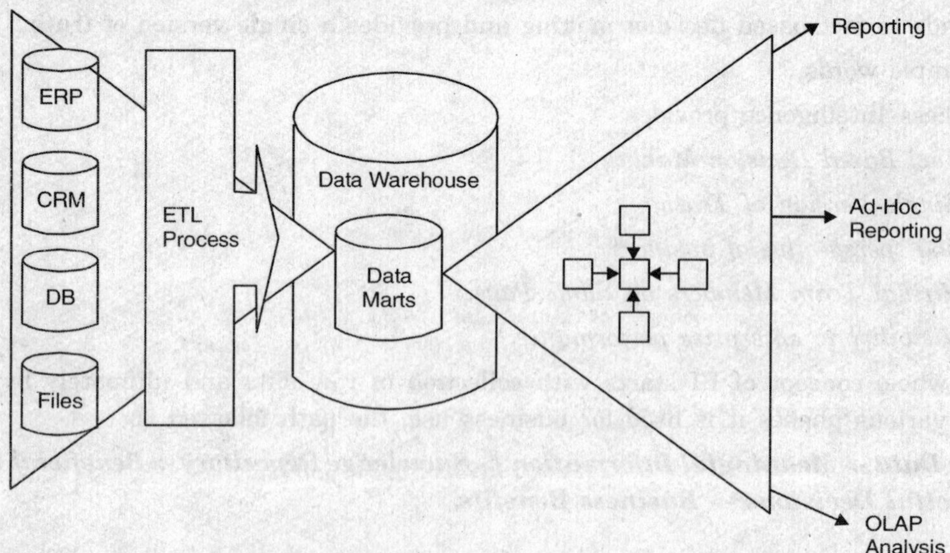

Fig. 11:1. Basic Business Intelligence Framework

BI technologies provide historical, current and predictive views of business operations. Common functions of business intelligence technologies are reporting, online analytical processing, analytics, data mining, process mining, complex event processing, business performance management, benchmarking, text mining, predictive analytics and prescriptive analytics.

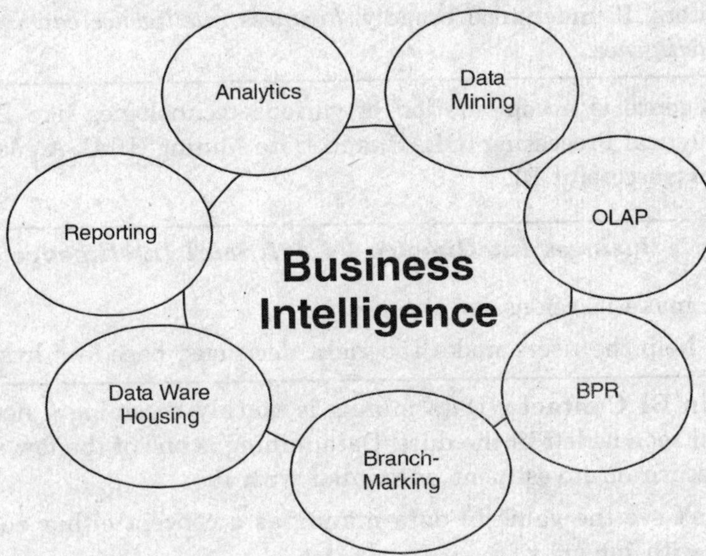

Fig. 11.2: Various Disciplines Integrated in Business Intelligence

Business intelligence (BI) is a broad category of application programs and technologies for gathering, storing, analyzing, and providing access to data from various data sources, thus providing enterprise users with reliable and timely information and analysis for improved decision making. To put it simply, BI is an umbrella term that refers to an assortment of software applications for analyzing an organization's raw data for intelligent decision making for business success. BI as a discipline includes a number of related activities, including decision support, data mining, online analytical processing (OLAP), querying and reporting, statistical analysis and forecasting.

In 1989, Howard Dresner (later a Gartner Group analyst) proposed ***"business intelligence"*** as an umbrella term to describe ***"concepts and methods to improve business decision making by using fact-based support systems."***

According to Forrester Research, ***"Business Intelligence is a set of methodologies, processes, architectures, and technologies that transform raw data into meaningful and useful information used to enable more effective strategic, tactical, and operational insights and decision-making."***

As per this definition, business intelligence also includes technologies such as data integration, data quality, data warehousing, master data management, text and content analytics, and many others that the market sometimes lumps into the information management segment.

Business Intelligence Vs Competitive Intelligence

Though the term business intelligence is sometimes used as a synonym for competitive intelligence (because they both support decision making), but there exist stubble difference between these two, ***business intelligence*** uses technologies, processes, and applications to analyze mostly internal, structured data and business processes, while ***competitive intelligence*** gathers, analyzes and disseminates information with a topical focus on company competitors. If understood broadly, *business intelligence can include the subset of competitive intelligence.*

Business Intelligence is a combination of various technologies like Data Warehousing (DW), On-Line Analytical Processing (OLAP) and Data Mining (DM). A good data warehouse is a prerequisite for successful BI.

Business Intelligence Vs Artificial Intelligence

- AI systems make decisions for the users.
- BI systems help the users make the right decisions, based on available data.

Data Mining in BI Contacts: Data mining is quickly becoming a necessity, and those who do not do it will soon be left in the dust. Data mining is one of the few software activities with measurable return on investment associated with it."

"People who can't see the value in data mining as a concept either don't have the data or don't have data with integrity."

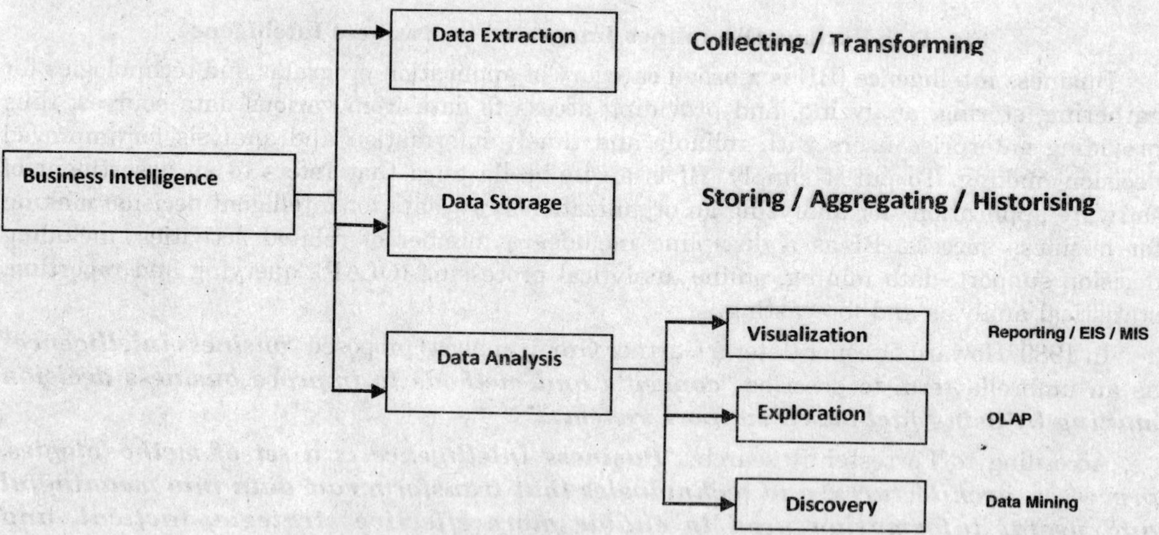

Fig. 11.3 Data Mining in BI Context

An Example: Fig. 11.4 given below provides a live example of business intelligence.

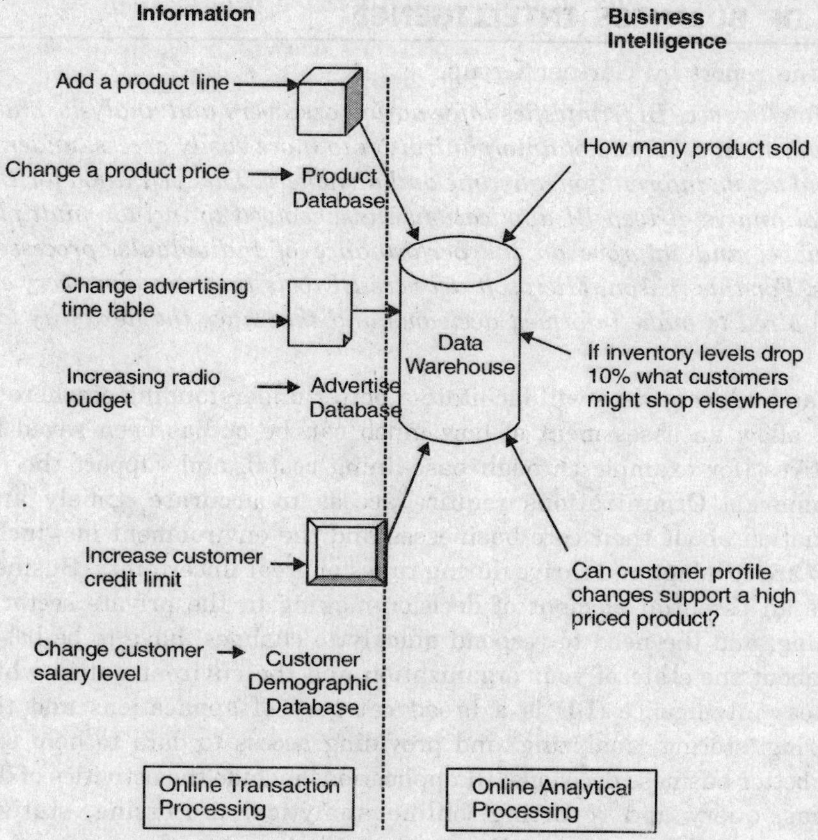

Fig. 11.4: An example of Business Intelligence System

Fig. 11.5 given below the Business Intelligence vision as provided by SAS.

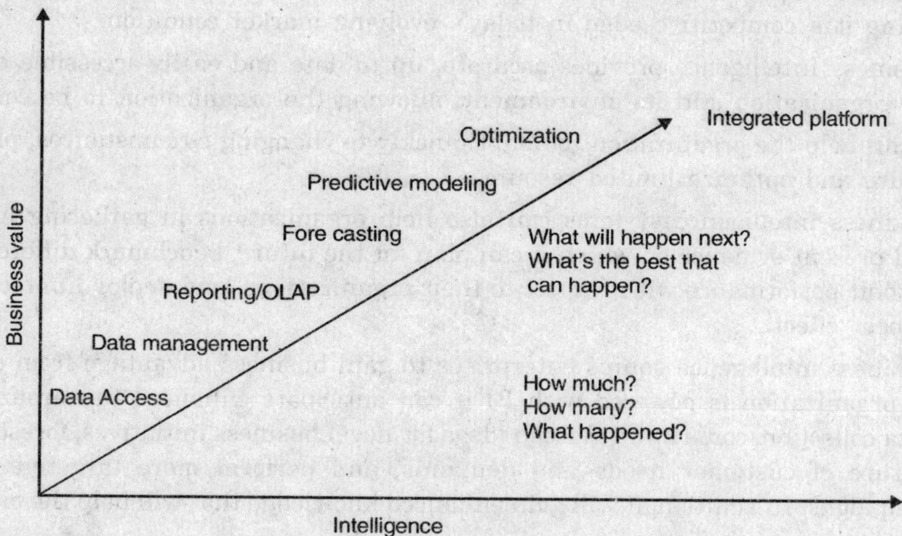

Fig. 11.5: SAS Vision of Business Intelligence

11.3 NEED OF BUSINESS INTELLIGENCE

According to the report by Gartner Group,

Business Intelligence (BI) simplifies information discovery and analysis, making it possible for decision-makers at all levels of an organization to more easily access, understand, analyze, collaborate, and act on information, anytime and anywhere. This definition for BI demonstrates that traditional analyst-driven BI applications have evolved to include multiple initiatives to measure, manage, and improve on the performance of individuals, processes, teams, and business units. For this reason, Microsoft delivers BI tools that can give every employee access to the data required to make informed decisions and that have the flexibility to work the way they do.

- Good and relevant data will facilitate a better understanding of where savings can be made, allow an assessment of how much can be or has been saved from efficiency initiatives (for example through base-lining costs), and support the development of benchmarks. Organizations require access to accurate, timely and meaningful information about their core businesses and the environment in which they operate, if they are to adapt and thrive during times of great uncertainty. Business Intelligence (BI) is an essential element of decision-making in the private sector. Strategy and planning, and the need to respond quickly to changes, have to be based on accurate data about the state of your organization and the environment in which it operates. Business intelligence (BI) is a broad category of applications and technologies for gathering, storing, analyzing, and providing access to data to help enterprise users make better business decisions. BI applications include the activities of decision support systems, query and reporting, online analytical processing, statistical analysis, forecasting, and data mining. Decisions purely based on the gut feeling cannot assure success; but in BI's fact-based decision-making framework, confident decisions can be made for assured business success. Further, BI makes an organization agile thereby giving it a competitive edge in today's evolving market condition.
- Business Intelligence provides accurate, up to date and easily-accessible data about the organization and its environment, allowing the organization to be competitive.
- It can help the organization to adapt quickly to changing circumstances, plan for the future and optimize limited resources.
- Business intelligence systems can also help organizations in gathering information and present evidence on which it can plan for the future, benchmark different aspects of their performance with respect to their organizations, and deploy limited resources to best effect.
- Business intelligence equips enterprises to gain business advantage from data. Once an organization is powered with BI it can anticipate enhanced turnaround time on data collection, come up with fresh ideas for novel business initiatives, foresee accurate picture of customer needs and demands, and perform more targeted marketing campaigns. In addition, it will gain enhanced knowledge that will help the organization to:

   - *advance its brand into the top slot in terms of market share,*
   - *cut down its client churn,*
   - *reduce its overheads and*
   - *Diminish delays in supply chain.*

- It creates a hierarchy of performance metrics and benchmarking informs business leaders about progress towards business goals.
- It provides the facility of analytics, which is a program that builds quantitative processes for a business to arrive at optimal decisions and to perform business knowledge discovery. It involves, data mining, process mining, statistical analysis, predictive analysis, predictive modeling and prescriptive analytics.
- It provides the facility of enterprise reporting, which is a program that builds infrastructure for strategic reporting to serve the strategic management of a business, not operational reporting. It frequently involves data visualization, executive information system and OLAP.
- It facilitates knowledge management, that is a program to make the company data driven through strategies and practices to identify, create, represent, distribute, and enable adoption of insights and experiences that are true business knowledge. Knowledge management leads to learning management and regulatory compliance.
- Business intelligence also can provide a pro-active approach, such as ALARM function to alert immediately to end-user. There are many types of alerts, for example if some business value exceeds the threshold value the color of that amount in the report will turn RED and the business analyst is alerted. Sometimes an alert mail will be sent to the user as well. This end to end process requires data governance, which should be handled by the expert.

BI can catalyze a business's success in terms of:

Revenues

- Distinguish the products and services that drive revenues.
- Rank customers and locations based on profitability.

Customer Relationship Management

- Categorize low-value customers and work toward improving their value.
- Find customer relationship issues early and take timely action to resolve them.
- Finding Loyal and Disloyal Customers.
- Providing Customized Services to the customers.

Sales and Marketing

- Aim at high-value customers to minimize marketing risk.
- Rank the success of product promotions based on product and market segment.
- Find what is in the sales pipeline

11.4 BUSINESS INTELLIGENCE COMPONENT FRAMEWORK (ARCHITECTURE)

It is a framework for organizing the data, information management and technology components that are used to build business intelligence systems for reporting and data analytics. The underlying BI architecture plays an important role in business intelligence projects because it affects development and implementation decisions.

The data components of a BI architecture include the data sources that corporate executives and other end users need to access and analyze to meet their business requirements. Important criteria in the source selection process include autenticated source of data, providion of data concurrence, data quality and the level of detail in the data. Both structured and unstructured data may be required as part of a BI architecture, as well as information from both internal and external sources.

Information management architectural components are used to transform raw transaction data into a consistent and coherent set of information that is suitable for BI uses. For example, this part of a BI architecture typically includes data integration, data cleansing and the creation of data dimensions and business rules that conform to the architectural guidelines. It may also define structures for data warehousing or for a data federation approach that aggregates information in virtual databases instead of physical data warehouses or data marts.

The technology components are used to present information to business users and enable them to analyze the data. This includes the BI software suite or BI tools to be used within an organization as well as the supporting IT infrastructure - i.e., hardware, database software and networking devices. There are various types of BI applications that can be built into an architecture reporting, ad hoc query, data mining and data visualization tools, online analytical processing software, business intelligence dashboards and performance scorecards.

Through literature review, it is found that there are several existing BI architectures (e.g., Baars & Kemper, 2008; Balaceanu, 2007; Shariat & Hightower, 2007; Turban et al., 2008; Watson, 2009).

These architectures are different in their structures such as layers, components, processes, and relationships to guide BI implementation efforts. However, there are some common components among these BI architectures (e.g., source systems, data storage, and reporting tools). Here the five layered architecture given by In Lih Ong, Pei Hwa Siew and Siew Fan Wong has been explained. Fig. 11.6 shows the five layered architecture of BI.

There is a centralized metadata repository that is connected with various components such as the ETL layer, the data warehouse layer, and the end user layer. Such consideration overcomes limitations of unidirectional data flow in many existing BI architectures. A multi-directional flow can enhance query performance and improve accuracy because data error at one layer can be returned to the previous layer for clarification if error occurs. For instance, if an error in data is found in the ETL layer, that particular piece of data can be sent back to the data source layer (i.e., internal sources) for modification.

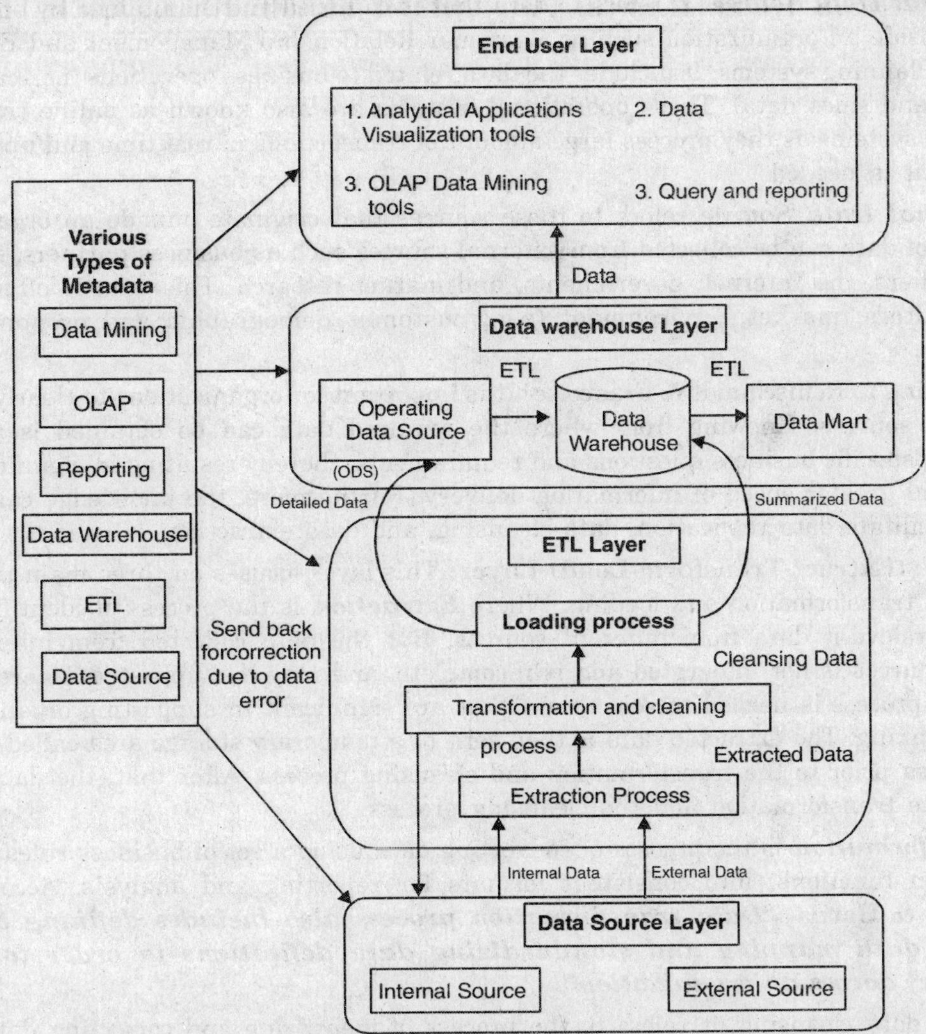

Fig. 11.6: Five Layered architecture for Business Intelligence

The Five layered architecture has been developed taking into consideration the value and quality of data as well as information flow in the system. The five layers are:

1. Data Source
2. ETL (Extract-Transform-Load)
3. Data Warehouse
4. End User and
5. Metadata

Data Source Layer: The applications today require various types of data like structured, unstructured and semi-structured data to make effective and timely decision. This data can be acquired from two types of sources:

Internal Data Source, It refers to data that is captured and maintained by operational systems inside an organization such as Customer Relationship Management and Enterprise Resource Planning systems. It includes the data related to business operations (i.e., customers, products, and sales data). These operational systems are also known as online transaction processing systems as they process large amount of transactions in real time and update data whenever it is needed.

External Data Source refers to those sources that originate outside an organization. This type of data can be collected from external sources such as business partners, syndicate data suppliers, the Internet, governments, and market research. This data is often related to competitors, market, environment (e.g., customer demographic and economic), and technology.

According to Reinschmidt & Francoise- It is important for organizations to clearly identify their data sources. Knowing from where the required data can be obtained is useful in addressing specific business questions and requirements, thereby resulting in significant time savings and greater speed of information delivery. Furthermore, the knowledge can also be used to facilitate data replication, data cleansing, and data extraction

2. ETL (Extract-Transform-Load) Layer: This layer focuses on three main processes: extraction, transformation and loading. Where ***Extraction*** is the process of identifying and collecting relevant data from different sources. But the data collected from internal and external sources is not integrated and is incomplete, and may be duplicated. Therefore, the extraction process is needed to select data that are significant in supporting organizational decision making. The extracted data is then sent to a temporary storage area called the data staging area prior to the transformation and cleansing process. After that, the data will go through the transformation and the cleansing process.

Transformation is the process of converting data using a set of business rules (such as aggregation functions) into consistent formats for reporting and analysis. According to Davenport & Harris- ***"Data transformation process also includes defining business logic for data mapping and standardizing data definitions in order to ensure consistency across an organization".***

As for data cleansing, it refers to the process of identifying and correcting data errors based on pre-specified rules. If there is an error found in the extracted data, then it is sent back to the data source for correction. Once data have been transformed and cleansed, they are stored in the staging area. This can prevent the need of transforming data again if the loading processes fail or terminate.

Loading is the last phase of the ETL process. The data in staging area are loaded into target repository.

(ETL process has been explained in detail in chapter 4).

3. Data Warehouse Layer: There are three components in the data warehouse layer-operational data store, data warehouse, and data marts. Data flows from operational data store to data warehouse and subsequently to data mart.

Operational Data Store

An operational data store (ODS) is used to integrate all data from the ETL layer and load them into data warehouses. ODS is a database that stores subject-oriented, detailed, and current data from multiple sources to support tactical decision making. It provides an integrated view of near real-time data such as transactions and prices. In addition, the data stored in ODS is volatile, which means it can be over-written or updated with new data that blow into ODS. ODS does not store any historical data. Generally, ODS is designed to support operational processing and reporting needs of a specific application by providing an integrated view of data across many different business applications. It is normally used by middle management level for daily management and short-term decision making.

Data Warehouse

Data warehouse is one of the most important components in BI architecture. Inmon (2005) defines data warehouse as "a subject-oriented, integrated, time-variant, and non-volatile collection of data in support of management's decision making process". In summary, data warehouse is a central storage that collects and stores data from internal and external sources for strategic decision making, queries, and analysis.

In addition, it also stores large amount of historical data for the purpose of long term analysis. Data is stored in data warehouse longer (5 to 10 years) than in ODS (60 to 90 days). Data in a data warehouse is updated regularly, for instance weekly or sometimes daily. Data warehouses are designed to support OLAP (Online Analytical Processing) applications by storing and maintaining data in multi-dimensional structures for query, reporting, and analysis.

Data Mart

While the data in a data warehouse is mainly used to support various needs across the whole organization, it is not equipped to support the needs and requirements of specific departments.

A data mart is a subset of the data warehouse that is used to support analytical needs of a particular business function or department. Like data warehouses, it contains historical data that can help users to access and analyze different data trends. It can only keep data for 60 to 90 days. Therefore, the amount of data stored in a data mart is much lesser than the data stored in a data warehouse. There can be many data marts inside an organization.

(Data Mart has been explained in detail in chapter 4).

4. Metadata Layer: Metadata refers to data about data. It describes where data is being used and stored, the source of data, what changes have been made to the data, and how one piece of data relates to other information (Giovinazzo, 2003). Metadata repository is used to store technical and business information about data as well as business rules and data definitions. Good management and use of metadata can reduce development time, simplify on-going maintenance, and provide users with information about data source. It is essential to ensure that metadata in repositories are maintained and updated regularly.

Metadata repository is also used to document the information about data contained in the data warehouse layer. It includes description of data structure (schema, dimensions, and hierarchies) and definitions of conformed dimensions and conformed facts. This metadata guide the process of extracting, transforming, and loading data into target repository. OLAP metadata provides descriptions about structure of cubes, dimensions, hierarchies, levels, and the type of drill paths being taken.

5. End User Layer: The end user layer consists of tools that display information in different formats to different users. The various components in this layer are:

Query and Reporting Tools

Query and reporting tools are very useful tools which allow end users to access and query data quickly, and to produce reports for decision making and management purposes. There are many different types of reports including standard reports, adhoc reports, budgeting and planning reports, and metadata reports.

BI portal is a popular end user tool to deliver information. It is a single, secure interface that integrates data and information from various sources so that users can have a one-stop access to different types of information.

OLAP (Online Analytical Processing)

One or more OLAP servers can manage data in the data warehouse layer for reporting, analysis, modelling, and planning to optimize business. OLAP server is a "data manipulation engine that is designed to support multidimensional data structures". OLAP server can provide multi-dimensional and summarized views of aggregated data.

OLAP is a user-friendly graphical tool that allows users to quickly view and analyze business data from different perspectives. Besides that, OLAP also allows users to easily compare different types of data and complex computations. In order to reduce query time, data in OLAP server are organized in the form of data cubes instead of tables as in relational data model. Data cubes are dimensional models stored in multi-dimensional OLAP structures. They contain fact and dimensional tables to store and manage multi-dimensional data so that users can analyze data easily and in a faster manner. Four basic OLAP operations used in analyzing multidimensional data are: **Roll-up or drill-up, Slice and dice and Pivot.**

Data Mining: It is the process can be achieved with the integration of data warehouses and OLAP servers by performing further data analysis in OLAP cubes. Since the amount of data in an organization is growing rapidly, it is necessary to have data mining to make decisions faster. Basically, data mining is a process that automatically identifies useful information such as unusual patterns, trends, and relationships that are hidden within large amount of data. This can be achieved by applying statistical techniques such as classification, time-series analysis or clustering.

Data Visualisation Tools

Data visualisation tools such as dashboard and scorecards can be provided to managers and executives who need an overall view of their business performance.

Dashboard is a useful tool that allows users to visualize data using charts, coloured metrics or tables. Users can also view more detailed information about key performance indicators across their organizations. As a result of which, managers can closely and more effectively monitor their business performance and progress toward defined goals.

Analytical Applications

According to Hobbs, "Analytical applications provide functionalities such as modeling, forecasting, sales analysis, and what-if scenarios. These applications can be used to support both internal and external business processes. Applications that are equipped with analytical capabilities allow users to gain insights into improving the performance of business operations. By employing analytical applications, decision makers can also identify and understand what factors drive their business value, and thus able to leverage opportunities faster than their competitors.

For a BI system to work smoothly, all five layers described above have to be linked together in a systematic manner. Data originating from internal and external sources have to be extracted, transformed, and loaded into the data warehouse layer.

When the data passes through the ETL layer, it can flow to both directions, either to ODS (and then to data warehouse) or to data warehouse directly. Since data warehouse is developed for the usage of the entire organization, data from the warehouse is sent to data marts to fulfill specific operational needs. At end user layer, data in the ODS, data warehouse, and data marts can be accessed by using a variety of tools such as query and reporting tools, data visualisation tools, and analytical applications.

11.5 BUSINESS APPLICATION OF BUSINESS INTELLIGENCE

Scope of BI should include making the best use of information for strategic, tactical, and operational needs of the users at the various levels in the organization. The main purpose of building BI strategy is to help business with long-term planning, help middle management with tactical reporting, and help operations with day-to-day decision making to run the business efficiently. BI is all about providing people with the information they need to do their jobs more effectively. A wide range of BI services need to be provided to meet a wide range of requirements. Scope of BI Strategy should be determined by the business drivers and business goals. The business intelligence framework should always account for the changing business requirements to keep the BI strategy aligned with business goals and objectives. BI strategy should include a broad set of processes, technologies, and stakeholders for collecting, integrating, accessing, and analyzing information for the purpose of helping enterprise make better business decisions. BI solutions should enable users to be able to quickly adapt to new business requirements and evolving sources of information. Overall, BI vision should be planned in advance of any iteration being implemented. It is vital to establish a BI vision to ensure that implementation of specific components fits in the overall BI strategy. BI strategy should state and document the needs as identified by the stakeholders, highlighting how BI fits into the broader enterprise vision. BI strategy should take into consideration appropriate framework, methodology, processes, governance, systems, and technology to deliver value that aligns with the business objectives and priorities. As discussed earlier,

"Business Intelligence is the process of gathering high-quality and meaningful information about the subject matter being researched that will help the individual(s) analyzing the information, draws conclusions or make assumptions."

Business Intelligence refers to the use of technology to collect and effectively use information to improve business effectiveness. An ideal BI system gives an organization's employees, partners, and supplier's easy access to the information they need to effectively do their jobs, and the ability to analyze and easily share this information with others.

"Information workers at all levels of the organization need to be able to interact with the data: to drill down, drill up, slice and dice business information to quickly find the relevant facts on their own, without administrative intervention."

Business intelligence is the emerging class of IT applications that use information assets to aid in better decision-making. A variety of tools and techniques such as data mining, predictive analytics and data visualisation are employed to provide valuable insights into past, current and future business metrics.

BI applications serve a critical function in achieving operational efficiency, integrated planning and coordination and monitoring.

The objective of BI is to drive more intelligent processes and decisions - with business intelligence software.

Business Intelligence (BI) applications are decision support tools that enable real-time, interactive access to data and analysis of mission-critical corporate information. BI applications bridge the gaps between information silos in an organization. Their sophisticated analytical capabilities have access to such corporate information resources as data warehouses, transaction processing applications, and enterprise applications like ERP. This enables users to access and leverage vast amounts of data for analysis, giving users valuable insight into potential opportunities and areas for business process refinement.

It is vital for enterprises to be well-informed and take quick, fact-based decisions in the dynamic marketplace. Business intelligence offers a ripe set of solutions that plug into existing IT infrastructure and bring out valuable insights.

BI applications can be classified as follows:

- Personalized Dashboards for Process Monitoring and Highlighting Exceptions.
- Decision Support with Drill-Down and "What-If" Analysis.
- Data-Mining to Understand and Discover Patterns and Behaviors.
- Automated Agents to Drive Rule-Based Business Strategy via Integrated Processes.
- Support for ODI across all sources.
- Data model and release integration across Fusion and Applications Unlimited.
- User Experience Redesign (partial).
- Cost of Ownership Improvements: Data Lineage, ETL Data Validation, Golden Gate.

11.6 BENEFITS OF BUSINESS INTELLIGENCE

Single version of the truth: It provides consistent information in real time across the enterprise, thereby eliminating debates on the validity of data. It also visualises information through meaningful dashboards to allow for coordinated decision-making.

Metric trees: Business performance metrics are related to KPIs and are computed at various levels within the enterprise. Metrics are linked to each other to create a metric tree, which connects the low-level performance metrics with high-level outcome measures.

The golden triangle (budget, time and quality): One can foresee impact of changes in specifications and business case. This helps to manage the trade-off between budget, time and quality.

Business modelling: It captures business dynamics in robust and transparent models. These are useful for sensitivity analysis, simulation and scenario-based decision-making.

Looking backward, moving forward: It does not rely only on historic data to look into the future, but integrates external and internal data for better forecasting and predictive analytical capabilities.

Other Benefits Include

- Greater ability to access and analyze data without IT involvement
- Faster and more collaborative decision making
- Improved performance metric tracking
- More accountability, with visibility into key performance indicators by line of business
- Faster response times, when exceptions and events occur

11.7 DO'S AND DON'T FOR DESIGNING A BI STRATEGY

Steps to ensure success of the BI strategy: To ensure the success of this mission critical business intelligence system, following factors should be kept in mind:

- Create a business case and outline the expected benefits.
- Enumerate the expectations of the various users and try to create a balance between them.
- Avoid tunnel vision and have an enterprise-wide perspective.
- Pen down the priorities and establish criteria for success.
- Keep in mind that information is an asset.
- Adopt best practices and standards and adhere to them.
- Develop and execute change management procedures.
- Develop the BI strategy that should align with the overall IT strategy and enterprise goals.
- Think big and start small with baby steps.
- Establish governance body to control the overall process.
- Use iterative implementation approach with parallel tracks
- Work with frameworks and adopt proven and tested methodologies.
- Assess BI readiness of the organization and identify related gaps and bottlenecks.
- Document and analyze the constraints and assumptions.

Potential pitfalls to avoid when designing the BI strategy:

- Don't fall into the trap of starting with a narrow tunnel vision. Rather, BI strategy needs to be holistic and prepared in the context of the wider BI definition.

- Don't plan to use big-bang implementation approach. It has been proven that iterative implementation works better for BI initiatives.
- Remember that scope of BI is not limited to just selection and implementation of technology. Often mistake is made by BI architects to associate the BI initiatives to specific technology components, such as implementing parallel processing database technology or building OLAP cubes or dimensional modeling.
- BI iterations should not be done in the haphazard manner. BI strategy document is the necessary roadmap that you should follow as you begin designing BI environment.
- Don't just focus on data integration and state-of-art BI tools. BI strategy should be comprehensive and it should incorporate much more than a data warehouse or BI tools. During warehouse-centric planning, don't lose sight of the broad vision to ensure the design of a successful enterprise-wide informational asset.
- Don't adopt inflexible approach. BI strategy should be treated as a living artifact. It should be constantly tuned and adjusted to reflect the needs of your business.

11.8 VARIOUS TYPES OF OLAP ARCHITECTURES

1. Relational OLAP (ROLAP).
2. Multidimensional OLAP (MOLAP) and
3. Hybrid OLAP (HOLAP) refers to technologies that combine MOLAP and ROLAP.

ROLAP: It is defined as Relational On-Line Analytical Processing. This methodology relies on manipulating the data stored in the relational database to give the appearance of traditional OLAP's slicing and dicing functionality. In essence, each action of slicing and dicing is equivalent to adding a "WHERE" clause in the SQL statement.

Data is stored in a relational database (R = "relational") using multidimensional criteria. These systems have virtually no limitations regarding data volume and users have direct access to "raw" data.

ROLAP stores all data, including aggregations, in the source relational database. This type of storage is good for enterprises that need larger data warehousing. ROLAP uses an SQL reporting tool to query data directly from the data warehouse.

Two well-known ROLAP solutions are SAP BI and Cognos. The main features of ROLAP architecture are:

- Relational OLAP
- Data is stored in relational tables.
- Star (or snowflake) schemas used for modeling
- SQL used for querying

Advantages

- It can handle large amounts of data. The data size limitation of ROLAP technology is the limitation on data size of the underlying relational database. In other words,

ROLAP itself places no limitation on data amount.

- It can leverage functionalities inherent in the relational database. Often, relational database already comes with a host of functionalities.
- Most of the companies are already following relational models and implementation of this technology on the basis of this already implemented technology can provide better results.
- It is scalable to handle a large amount of facts.
- It has flexible structure which is easy to change.
- It has incorporated some of the new performance enhancing techniques adapted from MOLAP.
- It provides the facility of indices, materialized views and special treatment of star schemas.
- ROLAP's advantages include better scalability, enabling it to handle huge amounts of data, and the ability to efficiently manage both numeric and textual data.
- It provides the facility of reliability, security and ease of loading of the data warehouse based on Relational DBMS (RDBMS) technology.
- It provides the facility to "drill down" to the leaf details or the lowest level of a hierarchy structure.

Disadvantages

- It suffers from the problem of slow performance. It is because of the reason that each ROLAP report is essentially a SQL query (or multiple SQL queries) in the relational database, the query time can be long if the underlying data size is large.
- ROLAP architectures suffers from the limited functionalities of SQL.ROLAP technology mainly relies on generating SQL statements to query the relational database, and SQL statements do not fit all needs of the users, like it is difficult to perform complex calculations using SQL. So, ROLAP technologies are therefore traditionally limited by what SQL can do.
- ROLAP architecture consumes a large amount of storage space, which is normally 3-4 times the requirement of MOLAP architecture.
- However, ROLAP applications display a slower performance as compared to other style of OLAP tools since, oftentimes, calculations are performed inside the server. Another demerit of a ROLAP tool is that as it is dependent on use of SQL for data manipulation, it may not be ideal for performance of some calculations that are not easily translatable into an SQL query.

MOLAP: It is defined as Multidimensional Online Analytical Processes and it should not be confused with Mobile On-Line Analytical Processes.

MOLAP is the more traditional OLAP type. It is widely regarded as the classic form of OLAP. Data storage usually takes place in a multidimensional database (M = "multidimensional") but in a condensed form. Multi-dimensional OLAP (MOLAP) makes use of specially tailored data structures like arrays and associated dimension lists or bitmaps. Data is stored in special multidimensional data structures known as multidimensional cube. The storage is not in the relational database, but in proprietary formats.

The various features of MOLAP are:

- In MOLAP architecture, both the source data and the aggregation calculations are stored in a multidimensional format. This type is the fastest option for data retrieval, but it also requires the most storage space.
- Data are pre-summarized and are stored in an optimized format in a multidimensional cube, instead of in a relational database.

Advantages

- MOLAP systems are more optimized for fast query performance and retrieval of summarized data. These systems are optimal for slicing and dicing operations.
- Data are structured into proprietary formats in accordance with a client's reporting requirements with the calculations pre-generated on the cubes.
- These systems are fast as presenting the data requires less overall processing than in ROLAP.
- It requires less storage space, as foreign keys are not stored.
- This is probably by far, the best OLAP tool to use in making analysis reports since this enables users to easily reorganize or rotate the cube structure to view different aspects of data. This is done by way of slicing and dicing.
- MOLAP analytic tool are also capable of performing complex calculations. Since calculations are predefined upon cube creation, this result in the faster return of computed data.
- MOLAP systems also provide users the ability to quickly write back data into a data set.
- Moreover, in comparison to ROLAP, MOLAP is considerably less heavy on hardware due to compression techniques.

Examples of MOLAP are: Oracle Essbase (previously Hyperion Essbase), Cognos TM1 (previously Applix TM1).

Disadvantages

- Limited in the amount of data it can handle: Because all calculations are performed when the cube is built, it is not possible to include a large amount of data in the cube itself. This is not to say that the data in the cube cannot be derived from a large amount of data. Indeed, this is possible. But in this case, only summary-level information will be included in the cube itself.
- Requires additional investment: Cube technology is often proprietary and does not exist in the organization. Therefore, to adopt MOLAP technology additional investments in human and capital resources are needed.
- MOLAP tool is less scalable than a ROLAP tool as the former is capable of handling only a limited amount of data.
- The MOLAP approach also introduces data redundancy. There are also certain MOLAP

products that encounter difficulty in updating models with dimensions with very high cardinality.

- MOLAP is less flexible, e.g., cube must be re-computed when design changes.

HOLAP: Hybrid systems (H = "hybrid") combine MOLAP and ROLAP and, therefore provide the benefits of both systems - in a common architecture. HOLAP technologies attempt to combine the advantages of MOLAP and ROLAP. This tool tried to bridge the technology gap of both products by enabling access or use to both multidimensional database (MDDB) and Relational Database Management System (RDBMS) data stores. For summary-type information, HOLAP leverages cube technology. When detail information is needed, HOLAP can "drill through" from the cube into the underlying relational data.

Advantages

- HOLAP systems store larger amounts of data in relational tables, and aggregations are stored in the pre-calculated cubes, offering better scalability, quick data processing and flexibility in accessing data sources. The relational model is used to store replicated and low-level aggregates, while the multi-dimensional model is responsible for high-level aggregates.
- HOLAP also has the capacity to "drill through" from the cube down to the relational tables for delineated data.
- HOLAP uses cube technology, which provides the benefit of fast performance.
- HOLAP provide the facility of better scalability.
- It provides the flexibility in accessing of data sources.

Disadvantages

- HOLAP has complexity and has all the limitations which ROLAP and MOLAP has.

Apart from these basic architectures, some newly invented architectures providing the facility for specialized scenarios are:

RTOLAP - Real Time On-Line Analytical Processes: RTOLAP systems store data in-memory, enabling real time analysis of data as required. Real time OLAP systems do not store pre-calculated values, avoiding "data explosion" as less data is stored. Data updates are immediate, queries are preformed on-demand, and results are immediately available as well.

WOLAP - Web-based On-Line Analytical Processes: WOLAP is an OLAP application accessible through a web browser. This type of application offers lower investment and enhanced accessibility, as there are lower deployment costs and all a user needs is an internet connection and web browser, but it is limited in its performance. The ActivePivot solution provides web-access by allowing users to access their OLAP data using a three-tiered architecture that consists of the user, ActivePivot software, and a database server. Unlike traditional client/server OLAP applications, WOLAP is considered to have a three-tiered architecture which consists of three components: a client, a middleware and a database server.

DOLAP - Desktop On-Line Analytical Processes: It is also known as LOLAP - Local On-Line Analytical Processes. DOLAP is based on the idea that a user can download a section of the data from the database or source and work with that dataset locally or on their desktop. This type of application is easy to deploy and has lower costs, but it is very limited in its performance. With ActivePivot, Excel sheets can be saved to the user's desktop, for local access to OLAP data.

MOLAP - Mobile On-Line Analytical Processes: It is also known as ROLAP - Remote On-Line Analytical Processes. Mobile OLAP refers to functionalities of OLAP solutions that are accessible through a wireless or mobile device, enabling the user to access OLAP data and functionalities remotely via the user's mobile device. ActivePivot provides mobile OLAP accesses through its ActivePivot Live solution, which allows accessing data and certain capabilities through your smartphone, iPad, or any other mobile device.

SOLAP - Spatial On-Line Analytical Processes: It was created based on the idea to integrate GIS and OLAP capabilities in one system to handle both spatial and non-spatial data. With the aim of integrating the capabilities of both Geographic Information Systems (GIS) and OLAP into a single user interface, "SOLAP" or Spatial OLAP emerged. SOLAP is created to facilitate management of both spatial and non-spatial data, as data could come not only in an alphanumeric form, but also in images and vectors. This technology provides easy and quick exploration of data that resides on a spatial database.

SUMMARY

- BI refers to a set of tools and techniques that enable a company to transform its business data into timely and accurate information for the decisional process, to be made available to the right persons in the most suitable form.
- Business intelligence (BI) is "about how to capture, access, understand, analyze and turn one of the most valuable assets of an enterprise - raw data - into actionable information in order to improve business performance"
- BI as a discipline includes a number of related activities, including decision support, data mining, online analytical processing (OLAP), querying and reporting, statistical analysis and forecasting.
- ***Business Intelligence*** uses technologies, processes, and applications to analyze mostly internal, structured data and business processes, while ***competitive intelligence*** gathers, analyzes and disseminates information with a topical focus on company competitors. If understood broadly, *business intelligence can include the subset of competitive intelligence.*
- Business Intelligence is a combination of various technologies like Data Warehousing (DW), On-LineAnalytical Processing (OLAP) and Data Mining (DM).
- A good data warehouse is a prerequisite for successful BI.
- AI systems make decisions for the users, whereas, BI systems help the users make the right decisions, based on available data.
- Data mining is quickly becoming a necessity, and those who do not do it will soon be left in the dust. Data mining is one of the few software activities with measurable return on investment associated with it."
- Business Intelligence provides accurate, up to date and easily-accessible data about the organization and its environment, allowing the organization to be competitive, help the organization to adapt quickly to changing circumstances, plan for the future and optimize limited resources.
- BI will provide enhanced knowledge that will help the organization to: *advance its brand into the top slot in terms of market share, cut down its client churn and reduce its overheads and diminish delays in supply chain.*
- The Five layered architecture of BI comprises of following layers: Data Source Layer, ETL (Extract-Transform-Load) Layer, Data Warehouse Layer, End User Layer and Metadata layer.
- Various BI applications include, Personalized Dashboards for Process Monitoring and Highlighting Exceptions, Decision Support with Drill-Down and "What-If" Analysis, *Data-Mining to Understand and Discover Patterns and Behaviors etc.*
- *Various types of OLAP Architectures are Relational OLAP (ROLAP), Multidimensional OLAP (MOLAP) and Hybrid OLAP (HOLAP).*
- In ROLAP, data is stored in a relational database (R = "relational") using multidimensional criteria. It stores all data, including aggregations, in the source relational database.
- MOLAP refers to Multidimensional Online Analytical Processes. Multi-dimensional OLAP (MOLAP) makes use of specially tailored data structures like arrays and associated dimension lists or bitmaps. Data stored in special multidimensional data structures. In MOLAP, data is stored in a multidimensional cube.
- Hybrid systems (H = "hybrid") combine MOLAP and ROLAP. It uses cube technology, which provides the benefit of fast performance, facility of better scalability and flexibility in accessing of data sources.

CHAPTER 12

CONCEPTS OF DATA MANAGEMENT AND ENTERPRISE REPORTING

12.1 INTRODUCTION TO DATA INTEGRATION

Almost all organizations run different but coexisting information systems. In the present era of cut throat competition, bringing all these heterogeneous systems under one umbrella and hence performing data integration is a difficult task (although it is not impossible). But in order to dynamically meet business and customer needs the data integration of existing information systems is becoming more and more indispensable. Although it needs huge investment both in concern to hardware and software, it is being considered as necessary for survival. Integration of multiple information systems aims at combining selected systems so that they form a unified view of data and give users the illusion of interacting with one single information system. Users are provided with a homogeneous logical view of data that is physically distributed over heterogeneous data sources. The reason for integration is two fold:

- Given a set of existing information systems, through which an integrated view can be created to facilitate information access and reuse through a single information access point.
- Given a certain information, data from different complementing information systems is combined to gain a more comprehensive basis to satisfy the need.

In the enterprise context, the integration problem is commonly referred to as enterprise integration (EI). Enterprise integration denotes the capability to integrate information and functionalities from a variety of information systems in an enterprise. This encompasses enterprise information integration (EII) that concerns integration on the data and information level and enterprise application integration (EAI) that considers integration on the level of application logic.

For this, all data has to be represented using the same unified global data model and unified semantics. This task includes detection and resolution of schema and data conflicts regarding structure and semantics. In general, information systems are not designed for integration. Thus, whenever integrated access to different source systems is desired, the sources and their data that do not fit together have to be coalesced by additional adaptation and reconciliation functionality. Integrated data will be consistent and logically compatible in different systems or databases, and can use across time and users

Definition of Data Integration: According to Heimbigner and McLeod, 1985; Litwin, et al., 1990- "Data Integration is the process of the standardization of data definitions and data structures by using a common conceptual schema across a collection of data sources."

According to Goodhue et al. Data Integration is "the use of common field definitions and codes across different parts of an organization".

According to Goodhue, et al. (1992), data integration will increase along one or both of two dimensions: (1) the number of fields with common definitions and codes, or (2) the number of systems or databases adhering to these standards.

Data Integration involves combining data residing in different sources and providing users with a unified view of these data. This process becomes significant in a variety of situations, which include both commercial (when two similar companies need to merge their databases) and scientific (combining research results from different bioinformatics repositories, for example) domains.

> ***Definition:*** Data integration systems are formally defined as a triple <G, S, M> where
>
> G is the global (or mediated) schema,
>
> S is the heterogeneous set of source schemas, and
>
> M is the mapping that maps queries between the source and the global schemas.
>
> Both G and S are expressed in languages over alphabets composed of symbols for each of their respective relations. The mapping M consists of assertions between queries over G and queries over S. When users pose queries over the data integration system, they pose queries over and the mapping then asserts connections between the elements in the global schema and the source schemas.

A database over a schema is defined as a set of sets, one for each relation (in a relational database). The database corresponding to the source schema S would comprise of sets of tuples for each of the heterogeneous data sources and is called the *source database.* Note that this single source database may actually represent a collection of disconnected databases. The database corresponding to the virtual mediated schema G is called the *global database.* The global database must satisfy the mapping M with respect to the source database. The legality of this mapping depends on the nature of the correspondence between G and S. Two popular ways to model this correspondence exist: *Global as View* or GAV and *Local as View* or LAV.

12.1.1 Factors Affecting the Process of Data Integration

While the goal is always to provide a homogeneous, unified view on data from different sources, the particular integration task may depend on:

- the architectural view of an information system.
- the content and functionality of the component systems,
- the kind of information that is managed by component systems (alphanumeric data, multimedia data; structured, semi-structured, unstructured data),
- requirements concerning autonomy of component systems,
- Intended use of the integrated information system (read-only or write access),

- Performance requirements, and
- The available resources (time, money, human resources, know-how, etc.)

Major Issues while performing Data Integration are: These include differences in:

- Hardware and Operating Systems.
- Data Management Software.
- Data Models, Schemas, and Data User Interfaces.
- Business rules and Integrity Constraints.
- Identification of an optimal subset of the available data sources for integration.
- Estimation of the levels of noise and distortions due to sensory, processing, and environmental conditions when the data is collected.
- The spatial resolution, the spectral resolution, and the accuracy of the data.
- The formats of the data, the archive systems, and the data storage and retrieval.
- The computational efficiency of the integrated data sets to achieve the goals of the users.

12.1.2 Need of Data Integration

- Most enterprises contain multiple systems that were never designed to work together. The business units that fund these information systems are primarily concerned with functional requirements rather than technical architectures. Because information systems vary greatly in terms of technical architecture, enterprises often have a mix of systems, and these systems have incompatible architectures.
- When multiple systems are integrated, we usually want to be as noninvasive as possible. Any change to an existing production system is a risk, so it is wise to try to fulfill the needs of other systems and users while minimizing disturbance to the existing systems.
- The user usually wants to isolate applications' internal data structures. Isolation means that changes to one application's internal structures or business logic do not affect other applications. Without isolated data structures, a small change inside an application could cause a ripple effect and require changes in many dependent applications.
- Reading data from a system usually requires little or no business logic or validation. In these cases, it can be more efficient to access raw data that a business layer has not modified.
- Many preexisting applications couple business and presentation logic so that the business logic is not accessible externally. In other cases, the business logic may be implemented in a specific programming language without support for remote access. Both scenarios limit the potential to connect to an application's business logic layer.
- When making updates to another application's data, the user should generally take advantage of the application's business logic that performs validations and data integrity checks. The user can use *Functional Integration* to integrate systems at the logical business layer.

- Direct access to an application's data store may violate security policies that are frequently implemented in an application's business logic layer.
- The availability of commercial tools can influence the integration strategy between applications. Commercial tools usually carry a lower risk and expense when compared to a custom solution.

12.1.3 Design Issues in Data Integration

While implementing *Data Integration*, the user should consider the following design tradeoffs:

- **Latency tolerance:** Some forms of data integration imply a delay between updates to the data that is used by multiple applications. For example, in the data replication pattern, the data is extracted from the source system, and it is transported over a network. The data might then be modified, and then it is inserted in a target database. This delay means that one system may have access to data that is more up to date than another system. This latency in propagating data can play an important role in integration.
- **Push versus pull:** When accessing a data source's database, a system can either pull the data from the database or let the database itself push the data when a change occurs. Pull approaches are generally less intrusive, while push approaches minimize latency.
- **Granularity:** Getting a larger chunk of information at one time is generally more efficient than propagating each small change by itself. This requires an understanding of the cohesion between multiple data entities. If one entity changes, are other entities also likely to be affected? And if the other entities are getting affected, then up to what extent it happens and how this is being handled.
- **Master/subordinate relationships:** If updates are made only to one application's data, propagating these changes is relatively simple. However, if multiple applications are allowed to update the information, synchronization issues are taken into account.
- **Synchronization logic versus latency:** For geographically dispersed applications, sharing a single database may cause excessive network latency. To overcome this problem, the user can use distributed databases that contain copies of the same data. However, distributed databases add the additional complexity of synchronization and replication logic.

12.1.4 Benefits of Data Integration

There are some obvious advantages in integrating information from multiple data sources. Such integration alleviates the burden of duplicating data gathering efforts, and enables the extraction of information that would be impossible otherwise.

Subrahmanian, et al. (1996) gives the following examples of benefits of data integration:

- "... law enforcement agencies such as Interpol benefit from the ability to access databases of various national police forces, to assist their effort in fighting international terrorism, drug trafficking, and other criminal activities.

In the age of information, the basic benefits of information sharing are:

- **Assessing Current Conditions and Performance**
  - Analyze historical and spatial conditions more conveniently.
  - Quickly identify assets that need immediate attention.
  - Standardize condition rating procedures and establish more uniform criteria for evaluation.
  - Store condition/investment analysis data and results more conveniently.
  - Support collective decision making across various skills sets within an agency.
- **Determining and Evaluating Future System Needs**
  - Facilitate integrated decision making.
  - Support investment trade-off analysis (across asset categories and modes).
  - Allow for more thorough and detailed assessment of investment requirements and help minimize the risk of flawed funding projections.
  - Effectively determine future funding needs.
  - Support the development of comprehensive improvement programs that cover multiple assets.
  - Enhance communication and improve the overall alignment of investment programs.
- **Evaluating and Selecting Strategies for Current and Future Needs**
  - Develop more effective management strategies by combining data about previous activities or decisions with existing condition data.
  - Reduce the risk of choosing inappropriate or ineffective action.
  - Prevent the inadvertent development of multiple strategies for a single asset.
  - Evaluate the economic viability of various alternatives.
  - Readily store and retrieve results of analyses.
  - Support fact-based strategies.
- **Evaluating the Effectiveness of each Strategy**
  - Improve performance through immediate feedback.
  - Calculate performance measures and indicators with a higher level of confidence.
  - Promote more consistent performance measures agency-wide.
  - Calculate and evaluate multiple performance measures for many assets in less time.
  - Conduct different types of analysis with data more flexibly.
  - Quickly compare assets, resources, personnel and activities.
- **Availability/Accessibility:** Asset data that is easily retrieved, viewed, queried, and analyzed by anyone within an organization encourages the integration of such data into every area of an organization that can benefit from it, spurring both innovation and better decision-making.

- **Timeliness:** Well-organized data can be quickly updated; one input will often apply the data across a variety of linked systems, and the information can be transmitted to various participating components easily at the same time.
- **Accuracy and Integrity:** Errors are greatly reduced because the integration environment drives a higher quality of input and can include automatic or convenient error checking and verification. Moreover, as the same information is provided to all the components, they all receive the same consistent information, which ensure that integrity of data is maintained.
- **Consistency and Clarity:** Integration ensures clear and unique definition of various types of data, avoiding confusion or conflict in the meaning of terms and usage. All users through out the organization get a consistent view of data and hence ensures the clarity in concepts and operations.
- **Completeness:** All available information, including both historical and recent data, is accessible in an integrated database, with any missing records or fields identified and flagged via the integration process.
- **Reduced Duplication:** Identical data is eliminated reducing the need for multiple updates and ensuring everyone is working from the exact same information.
- **Faster Processing and Turnaround Time:** Less time is spent on consolidating and transmitting data to various users in the organization. The integrated data environment saves time by eliminating consolidation and transmittal to disparate users and allows many users to conduct separate analyses concurrently.
- **Lower Data Acquisition and Storage Cost:** Data is collected or processed only once, and the information is consolidated and stored at locations supporting optimal convenience and ease of maintenance.
- **Informed and Defensible Decisions:** Highly organized, comprehensive databases allow users to drill down through successive levels of detail for an asset, supplying more information to support decisions and supporting different types of analysis using various data combinations.
- **Enhanced Program Development:** Comprehensive and coordinated system information advances program development by providing timely data for high-priority actions, promoting efficient distribution of funding among competing programs, and improving consistency in programs from year to year and across departments, among other benefits.
- **Greater Accountability:** Data integration allows rapid and more accurate reporting of costs and accomplishments, including full attribution of results to relevant agency units and functions.
- **Optimized Asset Inventory:** Acquire and upload data from a single source just once.
  - Update and process inventory records in a single transaction.

- Determine more easily how much data exists and how much need to be collected.
- Reduce data handling and processing time with built-in data checking and verification.

- **Ensuring Nonintrusive Approach:** Most databases support transactional multiuser access, ensuring that one user's transaction does not affect another user's transaction. This is accomplished by using the Isolation property of the Atomicity, Consistency, Isolation, and Durability (ACID) properties set. In addition, many applications permit you to produce and consume files for the purpose of data exchange. This makes Data Integration a natural choice for packaged applications that are difficult to modify.
- **High bandwidth:** Direct database connections are designed to handle large volumes of data. Likewise, reading files is a very efficient operation. By performing integration, high bandwidth will be available to access multiple entities at the same time, which will ensure the faster execution of queries.
- **Metadata:** Metadata is data that describes data. If the solution that we use for data integration connects to a commercial database, metadata is usually available through the same access mechanisms that are used to access application data. The metadata describes the names of data elements, their type, and the relationships between entities. Access to this information can greatly simplify the transformation from one application's data format to another.
- **Good tool support:** Most business applications need access to databases. As a result, many development and debugging tools are available to aid in connecting to a remote database. Almost every integration vendor provides a database adapter component that simplifies the conversion of data into messages. Also, Extract, Transform, and Load (ETL) tools allow the manipulation of larger sets of data and simplify the replication from one schema to another. If straight data replication is required, many database vendors integrate replication tools as part of their software platform.

12.1.5 Common Data Integration Approaches

The various approaches for data integration can be used:

Approach I: Architectural Perspective: This classification distinguishes integration approaches according to the level of abstraction where integration is performed. Information systems can be described using a layered architecture, as shown in Fig. 12.1: On the topmost layer, users access data and services through various interfaces that run on top of different applications. Applications may use middleware - transaction processing (TP) monitors, message oriented middleware (MOM), SQL-middleware, etc. - to access data via a data access layer. The data itself is managed by a data storage system. Usually, database management systems (DBMS) are used to combine the data access and storage layer.

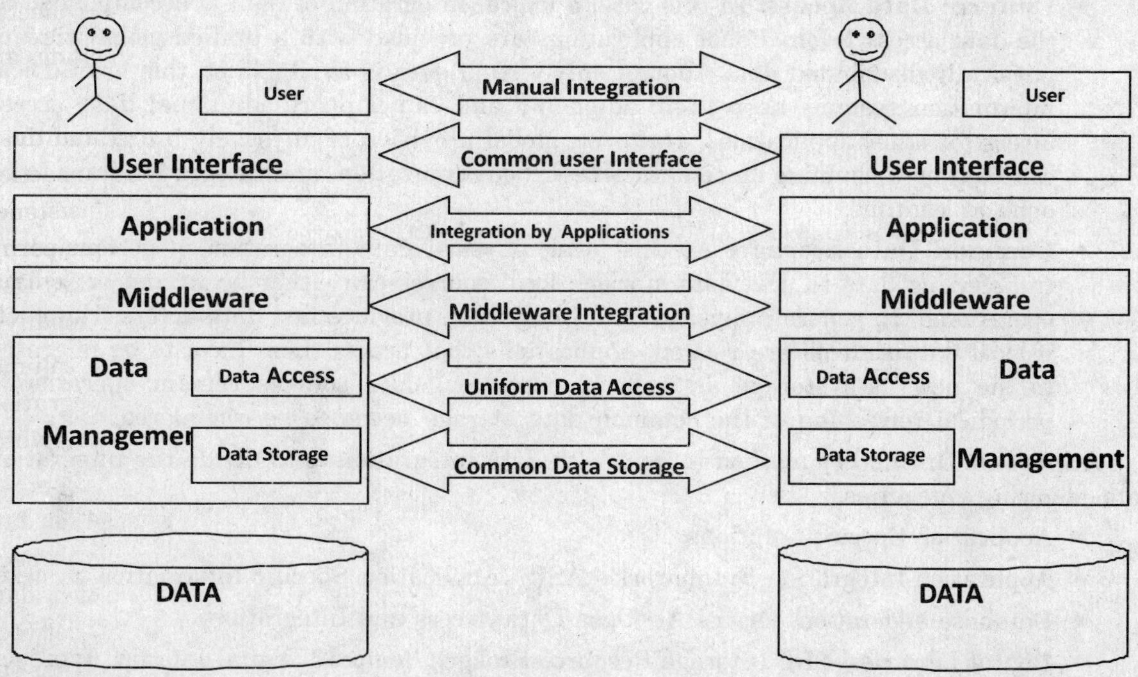

Fig. 12.1

In general, the integration problem can be addressed on each of the presented system layers. For this, the following principal approaches are available:

- **Manual Integration:** The users directly interact with all relevant information systems and manually integrate selected data. That is, users have to deal with different user interfaces and query languages. Additionally, users need to have detailed knowledge about the location, logical data representation, and data semantics.
- **Common User Interface:** The user is supplied with a common user interface (e.g., a web browser) that provides a uniform look and feel. Data from relevant information systems is still separately presented so that homogenization and integration of data yet has to be done by the users (for instance, as in search engines).
- **Integration by Applications:** This approach uses integration applications that access various data sources and return integrated results to the user. This solution is practical for a small number of component systems. However, applications become increasingly fast as the number of system interfaces and data formats to homogenize and integrate grows.
- **Integration by Middleware:** Middleware provides reusable functionality that is generally used to solve dedicated aspects of the integration problem, e.g., as done by SQL-middleware. While applications are relieved from implementing common integration functionality, integration efforts are still needed in applications. Moreover, different middleware tools usually have to be combined to build integrated systems.

- **Uniform Data Access:** In this case, a logical integration of data is accomplished at the data access level. Global applications are provided with a unified global view of physically distributed data, though only virtual data is available on this level. Local information systems keep their autonomy and can support additional data access layers for other applications. However, global provision of physically integrated data can be time-consuming since data access, homogenization, and integration have to be done at runtime.
- **Common Data Storage:** At this level, physical data integration is performed by transferring data to new data storage; local sources can either be retired or remain operational. In general, physical data integration provides fast data access. However, if local data sources are retired, applications that access them have to be migrated to the new data storage as well. In case local data sources remain operational, periodical refreshing of the common data storage needs to be considered.

Approach II: Another method to deal with data integration is to divide the integration into following categories:

- Application Specific Solutions
- Application-Integration Framework - ASIS (Application Specific Information System)
- Database Federation- Ogsa-DAI (Ogsa-Data Access and Integration)
- Digital Libraries- SRB (Storage Resource Broker), Sompel's Digital Library Approach

I: Application Specific Solutions: It is the most common means of data integration, the main features of this approach are:

- It requires time and expertise to develop and manage this approach. Hence, is expensive -in terms of time and skills.
- To develop and use the application specific solution requires deep system knowledge.
- Application Specific Solutions provide customized services and hence provide better results for special-purpose applications.
- These solutions are inflexible and fragile as changes to the underlying sources may easily break the application.
- These solutions are hard to extend as a new data source requires new code to be written.

II: Application-Integration Framework: It is also known as component-based framework. In this approach various applications can be integrated into one common application. The main features of this approach are:

- It is based on common data model (such as CML and GML) with adaptors, if the source changes the adaptor may have to change, but application may never see it.
- It is easy to add a new source, in which a new adaptor may either be written or can be purchased or obtained from any other offline or online source.
- It does not require the detailed system knowledge.

Examples: ASIS - OGC GIS Application Integration Framework

Features of ASIS: It enables inter-service communication through well-defined service interfaces, message formats and capabilities. The main features of this approach are:

- This data model uses Application Specific Language (ASL), which is a community-accepted application specific language.
- In this case, data and metadata have common predefined schemas.
- The various services provided are: Filter Services, Web Services, Information/data services enabling distributed access, querying and transformation through their predictable input/output interfaces.
- Chainable structure that help in updating the metadata manually or dynamically.
- In this approach, data can be integrated into the system after transforming to Application Specific Language.
- This approach handles heterogeneity at the end-filters with adaptors.
- The various common service interfaces used are: getCapabilities, getData, getFeatureInfo.
- The various requests to Filter's interfaces are: getCapabilitiesReq, getDataReq, getFeatureInfoReq.
- It offers data integration through Filters' capability metadata and Metadata is stored in local Filter's file system as a flat file.

III: Database Federation: The main features of this approach are:

- It has middleware consisting of database management system.
- It provides uniform access to number of heterogeneous data sources.
- It provides query language used to combine, contrast, analyze and manipulate the data.
- In this approach data integration is done through database integration.
- It combines data from multiple sources in to a single SQL statement.

Examples: Ogsa-DAI (Open Grid Service Architecture - Data Access and Integration)

Features of Ogsa-DAI: The main features are:

- It provides common Java API for accessing and integrating data resources -such as relational and XML databases, and files- in Grid environment.
- It is specifically designed for OGSA architecture.
- It provides data pipelining (similar to Filter chaining) via an XML document called "perform" document. The main components perform document includes,
  - The list of activities and their XML schemas and implementation classes.
  - The list of role mappers and details
  - The information about data resources, their origin, processing and final storage.
- It allows developers to easily add or extend functionality within Ogsa-DAI, ***"activity"*** document.
- In this approach, data is stored in XML or relational databases, files.
- It does not have a common data model; rather data is provided through GDS (Grid Data Services).

- It uses Ogsa-DQP (Distributed Query Processor) to coordinate to access to multiple data services.
- It incorporates the metadata storage model, where metadata is kept in Catalog Service (MCS), which in turn enables attribute-based querying.
- It performs data integration through XML based activity file which mix activities (in SQL queries) and metadata.
- It does not have common schema for metadata like capability, rather defines metadata for the datasets.
- It defines Metadata for the datasets, but schema is designed in XML, rather data is stored in database tables as attributes.
- It defines metadata for the Database system to enable querying and defining activities.

Difference between ASIS vs. Ogsa-DAI		
1.	Ogsa-DAI does not define metadata and data in XML schema. Metadata is mixed with database schema.	ASIS has predefined data and metadata models.
2.	Ogsa-DAI's data integration is coded in XML structure perform and activity documents.	ASIS's data integration is on demand and based on capability federation.
3.	Ogsa-DAI has central (MCS), meta data approach.	ASIS has distributed metadata approach.
4.	Ogsa-DAI uses GridFTP	ASIS uses NaradaBrokering for the performance issues in data transfers

IV: Digital Libraries: In this approach the main focus is on publishing and discovering of the digital objects, like, file, URL, SQL command string and any string of bits.

- It collects data from multiple different data sources.
- It is little bit different from the other data integration approaches, as it provides data curation services like publishing and removing data from the data sources.

Ex***amples: SRB (Storage Resource Broker) and Sompel's Digital Library Approach***

Features of SRB: (Storage Resource Broker): The main features of this approach are:

- It is a federated client server system, where each server manages a set of resources.
- It provides a base for implementation architecture for Data grids and Digital Libraries.
- It has storage resources which include digital libraries, MSS, UniTree and file systems.
- It consists of *three components:*

- MCAT services,
- SRB servers to access storage repositories and
- SRB clients.

- It works as a mediator to access distributed heterogeneous resources.
- It uses MCAT (Metadata Catalog Service) to facilitate brokering and attribute based querying.
- SRB server spawns SRB agent to authenticate the user/application by comparing it with information stored in MCAT. This server performs the following jobs:
  - Find the location in MCAT.
  - Check user request against permissions stored in MCAT.
  - SRB agent contacts user with the result of his request.
  - SRB agent communicates with the user through a port specific to this client session.
  - SRB server chaining scenario (integrated SRBs):
  - SRB agent contacts remote SRB agent via remote SRB server.
  - SRB agent returns the pointer to the data item to the first SRB agent which passes it on to the user.
  - The SRB client interact with the data item directly. The federated SRB scheme -SRB server acts as a client to another.

ASIS vs. SRB		
S.No	**ASIS**	**SRB**
1.	ASIS define metadata in XML structure.	SRB does not define metadata in XML Structure.
2.	ASIS uses ASL.	SRB uses any type of data.
3.	ASIS uses XML structured capability metadata.	SRB keeps the metadata in Catalogue Services (MCAT)
4.	ASIS has distributed metadata handling approach.	It has distributed metadata handling approach.
5.	The data integration is based on metadata federation.	The data integration is based on SRB server federation.
6.	It uses filters for accessing the various data sources.	It uses SRB server and agents for accessing data sources.

- The second

Sompel's DL: The main features are:

- Instead of Filters and ASL in ASIS, Sompel defines "repositories" and "digital objects", respectively, where, repository is a networked system that provides services pertaining to a collection of Digital Objects.
- Repositories are active nodes. Repositories enable the use and re-use of materials in many contexts.
- These repositories have common service interfaces, like - "Obtain", "Harvest" and "Put".
- It has two classes of participants- Data providers (DP) and Service providers (SP)
- Service Provider collects metadata from Data Providers.
- Data Providers offer some type of search mechanism for their own repositories.
    - Different storage types used are: book repositories, teaching object repositories, dataset repositories etc.
- Chaining for integrating data is handled differently,
    - Application/User doesn't need to use workflow engine or script to create or run the chain. (As in ASIS), here chain (also termed as "value chain") is hidden in the surrogates.
    - Surrogates are updated through the common interfaces ("put" "obtain" and "harvest") of the resources.
    - Chain is defined in the "Entity" element in the surrogate document with the "Lineage" sub element.

ASIS vs. Sompel's Approach		
	ASIS	**Sompel's Approach**
1.	It uses the concept of filters and ASL.	It uses the concept of "repositories" and "digital objects".
2.	The service interfaces used are : "getData" and "getCapabilities".	The service interfaces used are: "Obtain" and "Harvest".
3.	It supports distributed metadata approach for data integration. It supports direct communication between filters by using "GetCapabilities" interface.	It supports distributed metadata approach for data integration. It supports direct communication between repositories and services by using "Harvest" interface.
4.	It uses its own schema for representation of the resources.	It uses Dublin Core for representation of the resources.
5.	It uses ASL for the representation of the data.	It does not have common data model.

12.1.6 Applications of Data Integration

The common applications of data integration are:

- ***Mediated query systems:*** It represent a uniform data access solution by providing a single point for read-only querying access to various data sources. A mediator contains a global query processor which is employed to send subqueries to local data sources; and in turn the local query results are then combined.
- ***Portals:*** It is another form of uniform data access, which provides personalized doorways to the internet or intranet where each user is provided with information according to his information needs. Usually, web mining is applied to determine user-profiles by click-stream analysis; thereby, information the user might be interested in can be retrieved and presented.
- ***Data warehouses:*** It uses a common data storage approach to integration. Data from several operational sources (on-line transaction processing systems, OLTP) are extracted, transformed, and loaded (ETL) into a data warehouse. Then, analysis, such as online analytical processing (OLAP), can be performed on cubes of integrated and aggregated data.
- ***Operational data stores:*** It also uses common data storage approach. Here, a "warehouse with fresh data" is built by immediately propagating updates in local data sources to the data store. Thus, up-to-date integrated data is available for decision support. Unlike in data warehouses, data is neither cleansed nor aggregated nor are data histories supported.
- ***Federated database systems (FDBMS):*** It achieve a uniform data access solution by logically integrating data from underlying local DBMS. Federated database systems are full-fledged DBMS; that is, they implement their own data model, support global queries, global transactions, and global access control.
- ***Workflow management systems (WFMS):*** It implements business processes where each single step is executed by a different application or user. Generally, WFMS support modeling, execution, and maintenance of processes that are comprised of interactions between applications and human users. WFMS represent an integration-by-application approach.
- ***Integration by web services:*** It performs integration through software components (i.e., web services) that support machine-to-machine interaction over a network by XML-based messages that are conveyed by internet protocols. Depending on their offered integration functionality, web services either represent a uniform data access approach or a common data access interface for later manual or application-based integration.
- ***Model Management:*** It introduces high-level operations between models (such as database schemas, UML models, and software configurations) and model mappings; such operations include matching, merging, selection, and composition. Using a schema algebra that encompasses all these operations, it is intended to reduce the amount of hand-crafted code required for transformations of models and mappings as needed for schema integration. Model management falls into the category of manual integration.

- ***Peer-to-peer (P2P) integration:*** It is a decentralized approach to integration between distributed, autonomous peers where data can be mutually shared and integrated through mappings between local schemas of peers. P2P integration constitutes, depending on the provided integration functionality, either a uniform data access approach or a data access interface for subsequent manual or application-based integration.
- ***Grid data integration:*** It provides the basis for hypotheses testing and pattern detection in large amounts of data in grid environments, i.e., interconnected computing resources being used for high-throughput computing. Here, often unpredictable and highly dynamic amounts of data have to be dealt with to provide an integrated view over large (scientific) data sets.Grid data integration represents an integration by middleware approach.
- ***Personal data integration systems:*** These are a special form of manual integration. Here, tailored integrated views are defined (e.g., by a declarative integration language), either by users themselves or by dedicated integration engineers. Each integrated view precisely matches the information needs of a user by encompassing all relevant entities with real-world semantics as intended by the particular user; thereby, the integrated view reflects the user's personal way to perceive his application domain of interest.
- ***Collaborative integration:*** It is another special form of manual integration, which is based on the idea to have users to contribute to a data integration system for using it. Here, initial partial schema mappings are presented to users who answer questions concerning the mappings; these answers are then taken to refine the mappings and to expand the system capabilities.

12.1.7 Problems with Data Integration

Although the concept of data integration offers a bundle of benefits and is applied in various areas, but it also suffers from following problems:

- **Unpublished schemas:** Most packaged applications consider the database schema to be unpublished. This means that the software vendor reserves the right to make changes to the schema at will. A solution based on *Data Integration* is likely to be affected by these changes, making the integration solution unreliable. Also, many software vendors do not document their database schemas for packaged applications, which can make working with a large physical schema difficult.
- **Bypassed business logic:** Because data integration accesses the application data store directly, it bypasses most of the business logic and validation rules incorporated into the application logic. This means that direct updates to an application's database can corrupt the application's integrity and cause the application to malfunction. Even though databases enforce simple constraints such as uniqueness or foreign key relationships, it is usually very inefficient to implement all application-related rules and constraints inside the database. Therefore, the database may consider updates as valid even though they violate business rules that are encoded in the application logic. In this case *Functional Integration is used* instead of *Data Integration* if it is required that the target application should enforce complex business rules.

- **No encapsulation:** Accessing an application's data directly provides the advantage of immediate access to raw data. However, the disadvantage is that there is little or no encapsulation of the application's functionality. The data that is extracted is represented in the format of an application-internal physical database schema. This data very likely has to be transformed before other applications can use it. These transformations can become very complex because they often have to reconcile structural or semantic differences between applications. In extreme scenarios, the data store may contain information in a format that cannot be used by other systems. For example, the data store might contain byte streams representing serialized business objects that cannot be used by other systems.
- **Different storage paradigms:** Most data stores use a representation that is different from the underlying programming model of the application layer. For example, both relational databases and flat-file formats usually represent entities and their relationships in a very different way from an object-oriented application. The difference in representation requires a translation between the two paradigms.
- **Semantic Dissonance:** Semantic dissonance is a common problem in integration. Even though the user can easily resolve syntactic differences between systems, resolving semantic differences can be much more difficult. For example, although it is easy to convert a number into a string to resolve a syntactic difference, it is more difficult to resolve semantic differences between two systems that have slightly different meanings for the Time, Customer, and Region entities. Even though two databases might contain a Customer entity, the semantic context of both entities might be dramatically different.
- **Coarse-grained security:** Because *Data Integration* bypasses the application logic, it also bypasses any security rules that are enforced by the application logic. Many databases manage access privileges at the table level. At the table level, a user either has access to the Customer table or the user does not have access. Most applications enforce security at an object level. At the object level, a specific user has access only to those customer records that are associated with the user.
- **Privacy policies may not be enforced:** Many corporate databases are subject to privacy policies that are based on corporate or legal guidelines. Directly accessing these data stores may be in violation of these policies because it is difficult to control the ways the retrieved data may be used.
- **Data may be encrypted:** Data inside the database may be encrypted so that it is not accessible for data integration unless the integration solution obtains the key to decrypt the data. Providing the key to the data integration solution could present a security risk unless the key is properly protected.

12.2 INTRODUCTION TO DATA QUALITY

Data quality has serious consequences, of far-reaching significance, for the efficiency and effectiveness of organizations and businesses. Data is collected, stored, elaborated, retrieved, and exchanged in *information systems* used in organizations to provide services to business processes. Different criteria can be adopted for classifying the different types of information systems, and their corresponding architectures; they are usually related to the overall organizational model adopted by the organization or the set of the organizations that make use of the information system.

Data quality management incorporates a "virtuous cycle" in which continuous analysis, observation, and improvement lead to overall improvement in the quality of organizational information across the board. The results of each iteration can improve the value of an organization's data asset and the ways that data asset supports the achievement of business objectives. This cycle turns on the execution of five fundamental data quality management practices, which are ultimately implemented using a combination of core data services. Those practices are:

- data quality assessment.
- data quality measurement.
- integrating data quality into the application infrastructure.
- operational data quality improvement.
- data quality incident management.

Data quality management practices can improve the value of an organization's data asset and the ways it supports the achievement of business objectives.

The virtuous cycle of data quality: Data quality management incorporates a "virtuous cycle" in which continuous analysis, observation, and improvement lead to overall improvement in the quality of organizational information. The objective of this cycle is to perform transition from being an organization in which the data stewards react to acute data failures into an organization that proactively controls and limits the introduction of data flaws into the environment. In turn, this virtuous cycle incorporates five fundamental data quality management practices, which are ultimately implemented using a combination of core data services. Those practices are:

1. ***Identify & Assess the degree to which poor data quality impedes business objectives:*** Data quality assessment, as a way for the practitioner to understand the scope of how poor data quality affects the ways that the business processes are intended to run, and to develop a business case for data quality management;
2. ***Define business-related data quality rules, perform measurements, and set performance targets:*** Data quality measurement, in which the data quality analysts synthesize the results assessment and concentrate on the data elements that are deemed critical based on the selected business users' needs. This leads to the definition of performance metrics that feed management reporting via data quality scorecards;
3. ***Design quality improvement processes that remediate process flaws:*** Integrating data quality into the application infrastructure, by way of integrating data requirements analysis across the organization and by engineering data quality into the system development life cycle.
4. ***Move data quality improvements and process into production:*** operational data quality improvement, where data stewardship procedures are used to manage identified

data quality rules, conformance to acceptability thresholds, supported by organisational objected are emforced to the live data.

5. ***Inspect, monitor and perform data quality incident management:*** It allows the data quality analysts to review the degree to which the data does or does not meet the levels of acceptability, report, log, and track issues, and document the processes for remediation and improvement.

Research areas related to data quality: Data quality is fairly a new research area. several other areas in computer science and other sciences have in the past treated related and overlapping problems; at the same time, such areas have developed in the last decades (in the case of statistics, in the last centuries) paradigms, models, and methodologies that have proved to be of major importance in grounding the data quality research area. we now discuss such research areas.

1. ***Statistics*** includes a set of methods that are used to collect, analyze, present, and interpret data. statistics has developed in the last two centuries a wide spectrum of methods and models that allow one to express predictions and formulate decisions in all contexts where uncertain and imprecise information is available for the domain of interest. Statistics and statistical methodology are the basis of data analysis and is concerned with two basic types of problems: (i) summarizing, describing, and exploring data, (ii) using sampled data to infer the nature of the process that produced the data. As low quality data are an inaccurate representation of the reality, a variety of statistical methods have been developed for measuring and improving the quality of data.
2. ***Knowledge Representation:*** *It is important to understand that* how knowledge about an application domain can be represented, and what kinds of reasoning can be done with that knowledge (this is called *knowledge reasoning*). Knowledge about an application domain may be represented procedurally in form of program code, or implicitly as patterns of activation in a neural network. alternatively, the area of knowledge representation assumes an explicit and declarative representation, in terms of a *knowledge base*, consisting of logical formulas or rules expressed in a representation language. Providing a rich representation of the application domain, and being able to reason about it, is becoming an important leverage in many techniques for improving data quality.
3. ***Data Mining:*** It is an analytic process designed to explore usually large sets of data in search of consistent patterns and/or systematic relationships between attributes/ variables. *Exploratory data mining* is defined as the preliminary process of discovering structure in a set of data using statistical summaries, visualization, and other means. In this context, achieving good data quality is an intrinsic objective of any data mining activity, since otherwise the process of discovering patterns, relationships and structures is seriously deteriorated. from another perspective, data mining techniques may be used in a wide spectrum of activities for improving the quality of data;
4. ***Management Information Systems:*** *These systems* are defined as systems that provide the information necessary to manage an organization effectively. As data and

knowledge are becoming relevant resources both in operational and decision business processes, and poor quality data result in poor quality processes, it is becoming increasingly important to supply management information systems with functionalities and services that allow one to control and improve the quality of the data resource.

5. ***Data Integration*** It has the goal of building and presenting a unified view of data owned by heterogeneous data sources in distributed, cooperative, and peer-to-peer information systems. Data integration is one of basic activities whose purpose is improving data quality. Data integration is related to providing query results on the basis of a quality characterization of data at sources, and identifying and solving conflicts on values referring to the same real-world objects.

12.3 DATA PROFILING

The collection of data and hence its use for the benefit of the organization is the need of hour. Many organizations around the globe find that their data is as confusing and disorienting as the whimsical world of Wonderland. Many business and IT managers face the same problem when sifting through corporate data. Often, organizations cannot make the best decision because they can't get access to the right data. Most of the time, a decision is made based on data that is faulty or untrustworthy. The normal methods of data collection has various problems *like data inconsistencies, anomalies in data, missing data, duplicated data, data that does not meet business rules, orphaned data and many more problems.* Before using the data, the user/organization needs to consider the following points:

- ***Can the user trust the quality of the data which is being used?***
- ***Will the existing data support the needed functionality?***
- ***Is the data being used is complete enough to populate the needed data repository?***
- ***Does the data for this initiative conform to the expected business rules and structure rules?***
- ***Can the user access the needed data sources for the concerned initiative?***

If the above issues have not been taken in to consideration, it may result in faulty development and the project cost increases and subsequently there are chances of project failures. Gartner Group estimates that through 2005, *"more than 50 percent of business intelligence and customer relationship management deployments will suffer limited acceptance, if not outright failure, due to lack of attention to data quality issues."*

Data profiling is a fundamental, yet often overlooked, step that should begin every data-driven initiative. Every ERP implementation, CRM deployment, data warehouse development and every application rewrite should start with data profiling. The research shows that most of the ERP and data warehouse implementation projects fail or go over-budget. The basic reason of these project failures is misunderstanding about the quality, meaning or completeness of the data. So this problem needs to be identified and fixed in the beginning itself. And by identifying data quality issues at the front-end of a data driven project, the user can drastically reduce the risk of project failure.

Data profiling provides a proactive approach to understanding your data.

Data profiling, also known as data discovery or data auditing, is specifically about discovering the data available in your organization and to understand the characteristics of that data.

Data profiling is a critical diagnostic phase that arms the user with information about the quality of the data. This information is essential in helping the user in determining not only what data is available in your organization, but how valid and usable that data is.

Data Profiling is the process of examining the data available in an existing data source, database or a file and collecting statistics and information about that data.

Data profiling is an analysis of the candidate data sources for a data warehouse to clarify the structure, content, relationships and derivation rules of the data. Profiling helps not only to understand anomalies and to assess data quality, but also to discover, register, and assess enterprise metadata. So, the purpose of data profiling is both to validate metadata when it is available and to discover metadata when it is not.

With proper data profiling methodologies, the organization can also gain valuable insight into their business processes and refine these procedures over time. For instance, a data analyst conducts a profiling routine on a CRM database and finds that over 50% of the product information is inaccurate, incorrect or outside of the standard parameters. The data analyst consults the other departments and investigates that how product data is entered into the system and find ways to refine and enhance this process.

12.3.1 Need of Data Profiling

To investigate whether the existing data can easily be used for other purposes or not.

- To improve the ability to search the data by tagging it with keywords, descriptions, or assigning it to a category.
- To define metrics on data quality, to check whether the data conforms to particular standards or patterns or not.
- To assess the risk involved in integrating data for new applications.
- To assess whether metadata accurately describes the actual values in the source database or not.
- To understand data challenges early in any data intensive project, so that late project surprises are avoided. Finding data problems late in the project can lead to delays and cost overruns.
- To have an enterprise view of all data, for master data management.

12.3.2 When and How to do Data Profiling?

Data Profiling utilizes different kinds of descriptive statistics such as minimum, maximum, mean, mode, percentile, standard deviation, frequency, count, sum and variation. Additional metadata information obtained during data profiling is data type, length, discrete values, and uniqueness, occurrence of null values, typical string patterns, and abstract type recognition.

The metadata can then be used to discover problems such as illegal values, misspelling, missing values, varying value representation, and duplicates. Different analyses are performed for different structural levels e.g. single columns could be profiled individually to get an understanding of frequency distribution of different values, type, and use of each column. Embedded value dependencies can be exposed in cross-columns analysis. Finally, overlapping value sets possibly representing foreign key relationships between entities can be explored in an inter-table analysis. Normally purpose-built tools are used for data profiling to ease the process. The computation complexity increases when going from single column, to single table, to cross-table structural profiling. Therefore, performance is an evaluation criterion for profiling tools.

When to Conduct Data Profiling?

According to Kimball, data profiling is performed several times and with varying intensity throughout the data warehouse developing process. A light profiling assessment should be undertaken as soon as candidate source systems have been identified right after the acquisition of the business requirements for the DW/BI. The purpose is to clarify at an early stage if the right data is available at the right detail level and that anomalies can be handled subsequently. More detailed profiling is done prior to the dimensional modeling process in order to see what it will require to convert data into the dimensional model, and extends into the ETL system design process to establish what data to extract and which filters to apply.

12.3.3 Various Techniques of Data Profiling

To help the user to "begin at the beginning," data profiling encompasses many techniques and processes that can be grouped into three major categories:

- Structure Discovery
- Data Discovery
- Relationship Discovery

- **Structure Discovery:** *It deals to check:*

Whether the organizational data match the corresponding metadata?

Does the patterns of the data match expected patterns?

Does the data adhere to appropriate uniqueness and null value rules?

Does it follow the various constraints enforced on the data?

Structure discovery techniques help in understanding data patterns and metadata, it performs this by examining complete columns or tables of data, structure analysis helps the user to determine whether or not the data in that column or table is consistent and meets the expectations that the user have for the data. There are many techniques that can validate the adherence of data to expected formats. Any one of these techniques provides insight about the validity of the data.

Common Structure Analysis Techniques:

(a) ***Validation with metadata:*** Most data has some associated metadata or description of the characteristics of the data. It may be in the form of a COBOL copy book, a relational database repository, a data model or a text file. The metadata will contain information that indicates data type, field length, whether the data should be unique and if a field can be missing or null. This metadata is supposed to describe the data that is present in the table or column. Data profiling tools scan the data to infer this same type of information. Often, the data and the metadata do not agree, causing far-reaching implications for the data management efforts. For example, consider a 10 million row field with a field length of 255 characters. If the longest data element in the data is of 210 characters, the field length is longer than required, and you are wasting memory space on the disk. Missing values in a field can cause joins to fail and reports to yield erroneous results. Metadata analysis helps determine if the data matches the expectations of the developer when the data files were created. Has the data migrated from its initial intention over time? Has the purpose, meaning and content of the data been intentionally altered since it was first created? By answering these questions, user can make decisions about how to use the data.

(b) ***Pattern Matching:*** Pattern matching is used to determine if the data values in a field are in the expected format. This technique can quickly validate that the data in a field is consistent across the data source-and that information is consistent with user's expectations. For example, pattern matching would analyze if a phone number field contains all phone numbers. Or if a registration number field contains all registration numbers of the students. Pattern matching will also tell if a field is all numeric, if a field has consistent lengths and other format-specific information about the data.

As an example, consider a pattern report for phone numbers. There are many valid phone number formats, but all valid formats consist of three sets of numbers for country code, city code and then the phone number. Valid patterns might include: 91- 01628- 222111

Like registration number of students has the fileds: nameofcollege(year of joining the course)registration number, like dbim(2011)1234.

The majority of the data in these field contain valid data. There are, however, some data entries that do not match a valid data pattern. A data profiling tool will let you drill through a report like this to view the underlying data or generate a report containing the drill-down subset of data to help you correct those records.

- **Basic Statistics:** The user can learn a lot about the data just by reviewing some basic statistics about the data. This is true for all types of data, especially numeric data. Reviewing statistics such as minimum/maximum values, mean, median, mode and standard deviation can give the user an insight into the validity of the data. Basic statistics give a snapshot of an entire data field. Checking basic statistics of new data prior to entering it into the system can alert the user to inconsistent information and help prevent adding problematic data to a data source. Table below shows the statistical data about the marks obtained by a student, the marks range from 0 to 100. A student database with incorrect value of marks obtained can lead to many problems, from poor analysis of results to incorrect promotion of the students. Let's take a look at some basic statistics from a marks obtained column in the student database.

Field: Marks Obtained Data Type: integer	
Metric Name	Metric value
Data Type	integer
Primary Key Candidate	no
Minimum Value	**-90**
Maximum Value	100
Null Count	**4**
Mean	**11789.17**

This report uncovers many potential problems with the attribute marks obtained. The minimum value of marks is a negative value. There are four missing values (Null Count). The mean is unexpectedly large numbers. All of these indicate potential problems for this data file.

Metadata analysis, pattern analysis and basic statistics are a few of the techniques that profiling tools use to discover potential structure problems in a data file. There are a variety of reasons that these problems appear in files. Many problems are caused by incorrectly entering data into a field (which is most likely the source of the negative value in the student data). Some problems occur because a correct value was unknown and a default or fabricated value is used. Other structure problems are the result of legacy data sources that are still in use or have been migrated to a new application.

2. Data Discovery: Are the data values complete, accurate and unambiguous? This technique focuses to check the business rule validation and data completeness. Structure discovery provides a broad sweep across the organization data and often points to problem areas that need further investigation. Whereas, data discovery digs deeper and helps to determine which data values are inaccurate, incomplete or ambiguous. Data discovery techniques use matching technology to uncover non-standard data, frequency counts and outlier detection to find data elements that don't make sense, and performs data verification according to specific business rules that may be unique to the organization.

The various techniques under Data Discovery are:

- **Standardization:** Data in an organization often comes from a variety of sources: different departments, different data entry clerks and different partners. This is often the root of an organization's data quality issues. The data collected from various heterogeneous sources lacks in uniformity.

For example:

- "IBM", "Int. Business Machines", "I.B.M", "ibm" and "Intl Bus Machines" all represent the same company.

- Does the value "GM" in a database represent "General Motors" or "General Mills" or "General Manager"?"

Each of these values have the same meaning, but they are represented differently. The analytical and operational problems of this non-standard data can be very costly, as the user cannot get a true picture of the customers, businesses or items.

In addition, consider a marketing campaign that personalizes its communication based on a household profile. If there are a number of profiles for customers at the same address, the addresses are represented inconsistently. Variations in addresses can have a nightmare effect on highly-targeted campaigns, causing improper personalization or the creation of too many generic communication pieces. These inefficiencies lead to waste of time and money both on material production and creative efforts of the group, while alienating customers by ineffectively marketing to their preferences.

- **Frequency Counts:** When there are hundreds or even thousands of records that need to be profiled, it may be possible for a business analyst to scan the file and look for values that don't look right. But, as the data grows, this becomes an immense task and it require a lot of effort and money. Many organizations spend hundreds of thousands of dollars to pay for manual validation of data. This is not only expensive and time-consuming, but manual data profiling is inaccurate and prone to human error. Frequency counts and outlier detection are the techniques that can limit the amount of these faults. These techniques highlight the data values that need further investigation.

Consider the following frequency distribution of a field containing state and province information.

Field: STATE **Data Type: Varchar** **Length: 20 Characters**	
Value	**Count**
Punjab	78
New Delhi	89
Haryana	77
PUN	67
ND	66
Maharashtra	66
PB	67
Jammu and Kashmir	34
J&K	56

Fig. : Frequency distribution on state data.

The frequency distribution shows a number of state entries. But, the report also shows data that needs to be corrected. Incorrect state spellings, invalid state abbreviations and multiple representations of states can all cause problems. Punjab is represented as "Punjab" "PUN," and "PB". These Non-standard representations will have an adverse impact on the time and effort when the user tries to do state-level analysis. The invalid state entries may prevent from contacting certain individuals; the missing state values make communication even more problematic.

- **Outlier Detection:** It also helps in pinpointing problematic data. Whereas frequency count looks at how values are related according to data occurrences, outlier detection examines the few data values that are remarkably different from other values. Outliers show the highest and lowest values for a set of data. This technique is useful for both numeric and character data.

Consider the following outlier report (showing the 10 minimum and 10 maximum values for the field). In Figure , the field is weight of player in sport data base, measured in kg, A business analyst would understand that the valid weights are between 45 and 90 kg.

Field: Weight of Player **Data type: float(decimal)** **Defined Length: 4 Characters**		
Name Of Player	**Weight**	
Vansh	75	
Ajay	64	
Amar	50000	
Amit	0	

Fig. Outlier report on product weight.

There are many outliers on both the low end and the high end. On the high end, the values were probably entered in grams instead of kilograms. On the low end, the impossible values have been entered. Outlier detection allows you to quickly and easily determine if there are gross inconsistencies in certain data elements. Data profiling tools can let you drill through to the actual records and determine the best mechanism for correction.

3. Relationship Discovery: This aspect of profiling discovers what data is in use and links data in disparate applications based on their relationships to each other or to a new application being developed. Different pieces of relevant data that are spread across many separate data stores make it difficult to develop a complete understanding of the data. Organizations today maintain an enormous amount of data, such as customer data, supplier data, product data, operational and business intelligence data, financial and compliance data and so on. In addition, organizations get data from partners, purchase data from list providers and acquire industry-specific data from other sources. Relationship discovery helps you understand how data sources interact with other data sources Companies typically don't fully understand all of their data-and cannot effectively manage their data-until they understand all of these sources and the relationships of data across different applications. The main areas of concern in relationship discovery are:

- Does the data adhere to specified required key relationships across columns and tables?
- Are there inferred relationships across columns, tables or databases?
- Is there redundant data?

Consider some of these problems that can occur when data sources are not properly aligned:

- A product ID exists in your invoice register, but no corresponding product is available in the product database. According to systems, the user has sold a product that does not exist.
- A customer ID exists on a sales order, but no corresponding customer is in the customer database. In effect, we have sold something to a customer with no possibility of delivering the product or billing the customer.
- Your customer database has multiple customer records with the same ID.

Relationship discovery provides you with information about the ways that data records relate. These records can be multiple records in the same data file, records across data files or records across databases. With relationship discovery, you can profile your data to answer the following questions:

- Are there potential key relationships across tables?
- If there is a primary/foreign key relationship, is it enforced?
- If there is an explicit or inferred key relationship, is there any orphaned data (data that does not have a primary key associated with it)?
- Are there duplicate records?

Relationship discovery starts with metadata to determine relationships, using any metadata available about key relationships. The documented metadata relationships need to be verified. Relationship discovery should also determine, in the absence of metadata, what fields (and therefore, what records) have relationships.

Once potential relationships are determined, further investigation is needed. Does the relationship provide a primary/foreign key? If so, is the primary key unique? If not, which records prevent it from being unique? With the key relationships, are there any outstanding records that do not adhere to the relationship?

12.3.4 Benefits and Applications of Data Profiling

The benefits of data profiling is to:

- Improve data quality
- Shorten the implementation cycle of major projects, and
- Improve understanding of data for the users.

- Discovering business knowledge embedded in data.
- Improve data accuracy in corporate databases
- Fix business rule violations.
- Standardize and normalize data sources.
- Consolidate data across data sources.
- Remove duplicate data and choose the best surviving information.

12.4 INTRODUCTION TO ENTERPRISE REPORTING

Reporting from the subordinates to the head is a very important part of any organization. The decision making is one of the most important job in any organization. In the present era of cut throat competition making right decisions at the right time is of paramount importance. One wrong decision can prove to be fatal to the survival of the organizations. The importance of making right decision increases as we move up the organizational hierarchy i.e from operational level to tactical level and then to the top level of management. To make the right decisions, enterprises need the systems which can provide fast, efficient and crisp reports, based on which the efficient decisions can be taken. Hence the topic of enterprise reporting is gaining importance. Enterprise reporting provides the basis for making decisions at all levels in an organization.

The main features of enterprise reporting are:

- Enterprise Reporting provides business intelligence to the enterprise.
- It provides single version of truth to the people at any level of organization, it means it provides the same fact value irrespective of the way the data is stored, transformed and extracted.
- It helps in providing right information to the right person in the right format.
- It provides the detailed information to the decision-makers of the enterprise.
- It provides the flexibility of providing customized information as per the user's requirements.
- It provides information in the format as required by the users.
- People at all level of the organization rely on the enterprise reporting system, so the enterprise reporting system should be strong and powerful.
- It should provide the data in easy to understandable format.
- The users of the enterprise report can use the OLAP tools to analyze the data contained in the enterprise report.
- The enterprise report can take the form of graphs, text, tables etc.

12.4.1 Features of a Good Report

- It should be efficient and well formatted.
- The matter of the report should be analytical and directive.
- In the report the actual facts must be depicted clearly.

- The matter in the report should be relevant enough to get the desired result.
- Information collected in the report must be relevant and focused to derive desired results.
- The graphical presentation of may be include to make the data more understandable.
- The Report should follow the exact predefined goals and objectives.
- The report should contain the executive summary of the work.
- The report should also contain the reasons to prepare the report.
- The report should clearly define the methodology used to create the report.
- The report should also define the possibility of errors if any.
- The report should also clearly define questionnaires used in analysis.
- The report should also define the prediction regarding the goal.
- The report should be flexible.

12.4.2 Types of Enterprise Report

The common types of enterprise report are:

12.4.2.1 Dashboards

The term dashboard originates from the automobile dashboard. A dashboard provides the overall view of the entire enterprise. It helps the organization to see the information differently and to analyze it. A good dashboard should give the answers to What, Where, and How like questions. Dashboards are used to show summaries, key trends, comparisons, and exceptions.

In a management information system, a **dashboard** is defined as *"An easy to read, often single page, real-time user interface, showing a graphical presentation of the current status (snapshot) and historical trends of an organization's key performance indicators to enable instantaneous and informed decisions to be made at a glance."*

Dashboard can be a strategic dashboard or an analytic dashboard:

1. Strategic Dashboard: It provides the support to managers at executive level(top level of management). This type of dashboard mainly focuses on high level measures of performance, and forecasts. It provides information for long term planning. It provides static snapshots of data that is not constantly changing from one moment to the next.
2. Analytic Dashboards: It contains more context, comparisons, and history, along with subtler performance evaluators. Analytical dashboards typically support interactions with the data, such as drilling down into the underlying details.

The dash board can be created by using either of the following:

- Bar Charts
- Maps
- Trend Lines
- Speeddos
- Correlation.

Steps to Create a Dashboard

Step 1: Collect of the data for Enterprise Dashboard, the data collected may be quantitative or non quantitative.

Step 2: Set the timeframe for which the dashboard is designed, it depends on the requirements of the decision maker, i.e for which time period analysis is to be done. The timeframe can be a year, quarter, month or day.

Step 3: Set comparative measure: The next important point to be considered is the basis on which the comparative analysis is to be done. The analysis can be done on the basis of a single dimension or it can be on the basis of multiple dimensions. Moreover, the basis of analysis can be same whenever the analysis is done or it can different for different scenarios.

Step 4: Set the evaluation mechanisms: It is to design that what should be the basis of evaluation and how the results are to be presented. Mostly, visualization is the best way to depict the results.

Types of Corporate Dashboards

1. Enterprise Performance Dashboards: It provides a holistic view of the organization's health. It gives an overall view of the entire enterprise, rather than specific business functions. Typical players in an Enterprise Performance Dashboard include: Financial Statement of the Enterprise, Sales revenue, Key Performance Indicators for the organization as a whole, Information regarding Supply Chain, Information regarding Compliance or regulatory data and balanced scorecard information

2. Customer Support Dashboards: This dashboard is particularly designed to cater the needs of an individual customer. The organizations provide such a dashboard to its customers as a value-add service. They provide the customer with their personal account information as pertaining to the business relationship, such as: online trading, utility Services and entertainment.

3. Divisional Dashboards: As the name specifies, this dashboard is used to cater the needs of a particular division or department. It is used to provide at-a-glance actionable information to division heads, operational managers and department managers. Each division has its own set of KPIs which can be visually displayed on the enterprise dashboard. Number of divisional dashboards depends on the number of divisions available in the enterprise, most common divisional dashboards are: purchasing dashboards, manufacturing dashboards, quality control dashboards, marketing dashboards, sales dashboards, finance dashboards and Human Resources Dashboards .

4. Advantages of Dashboard: Dashboards are the life line of any organization. It provides the snapshot the organization's position as a whole, with respect to a particular department from the perspective of a particular dimension. It is hence required for better analysis, better tracking and proactive alerting. The other benefits include:

1. It helps in placing all important information at one place.
2. It is helpful in decision making process.
3. It helps in problem detection.

4. It helps in performance analysis.
5. It helps in identifying the trends and corrective actions to improve the performance of the organization

12.4.2.2 Balanced Scorecard

The **balanced scorecard** (**BSC**) is a performance measurement tool used as semi-standard structured report.

Robert S. Kaplan and David Norton introduced the Balanced Scorecard in a 1992.The various design methods and automation tools may be used for creating balanced scorecards. The balaced scorecard is used by the managers of an organization to monitor the activities of employees.

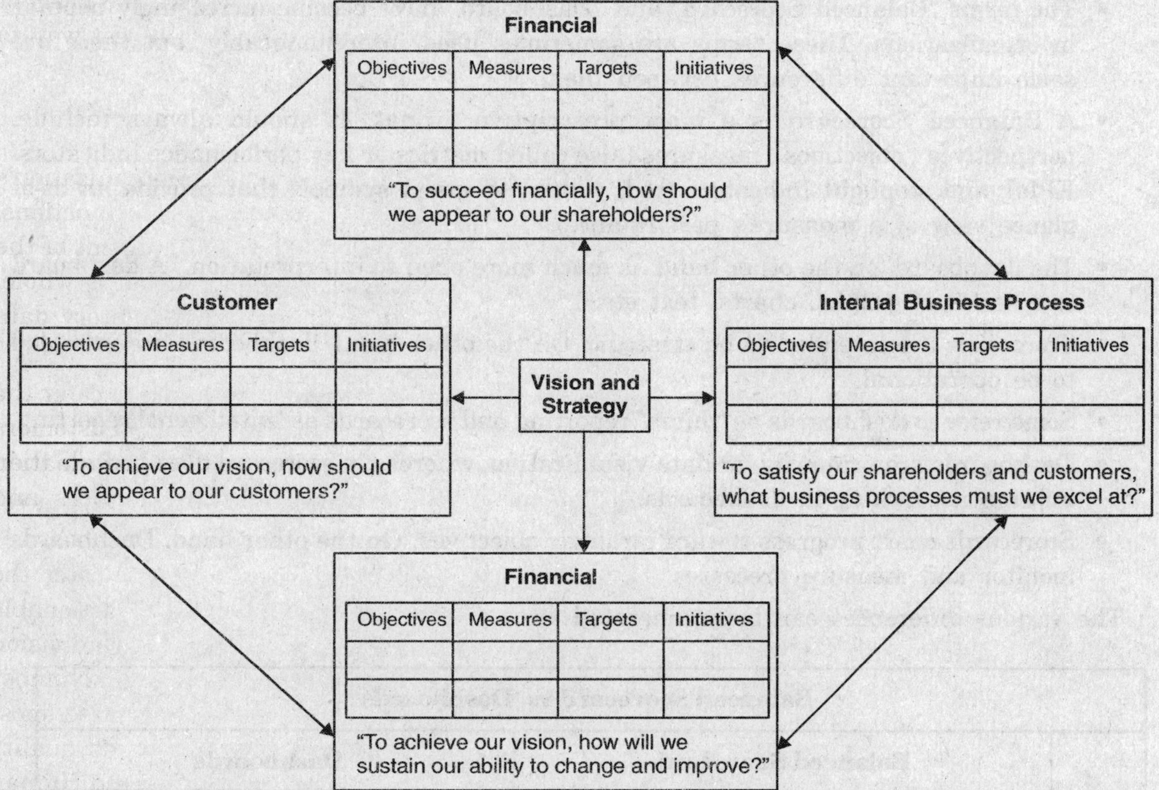

Shows the original structure for the Balanced Scorecard (BSC) as proposed by Robert S. Kaplan and David Norton . The BSC retains financial metrics as the ultimate outcome measures for company success, but supplements these with metrics from three additional perspectives – customer, internal process, and learning and growth – that we proposed as the drivers for creating long-term shareholder value.

To elaborate the Balanced Score Card (Kaplan & Norton's) proposes four contexts:

- **Financial Context:** It pertains to the financial goals of the organization. It addresses the questions like: View of stakeholder about the company, companies financial statement and which financial goals are desired from the shareholder's perspective.

- **Customer Context:** It pertains to how customers views the organization and tries to answer whether the company will be able to fulfil the customer's expectations or not.
- **Process Context:** It pertains to the operational objectives and processes for achieving financial and customer satisfaction goals. It tries to focus on the processes which should be considered on the priority basis to fulfil the customer's expectations and overall business objectives.
- **Growth and Learning Context:** It deals and focuses on the employee training, culture of the organization, leadership, CSR etc.

12.4.3 Difference between Balanced Scorecard and Enterprise Dashboard

- The terms "Balanced Scorecard" and "Dashboard" have become increasingly popular in organizations. These terms are sometimes used interchangeably, but there are some important differences between them.
- A Balanced Scorecard is a more prescriptive format. It should always include: perspectives , objectives , measures (also called metrics or key performance indicators/ KPIs), and stoplight indicators (red, yellow, or green symbols that provide an at-a-glance view of a measure's performance).
- The dashboard, on the other hand, is much more open to interpretation. A dashboard is a series of graphs, charts, text etc.
- Scorecards are intended to be strategic. On the other hand, dashboards are intended to be operational.
- Some refer to dashboards as "dumb" reporting and scorecards as "intelligent" reporting.
- Dashboards are primarily for data visualization, whereas, a scorecard does provide the information lacking in dashboards.
- Scorecards chart progress toward strategic objectives. On the other hand, Dashboards monitor and measure processes.

The various differences can be enumerated as:

Balanced Scorecard vs. Dashboards		
	Balanced Scorecard	**Dashboards**
1.	It is used in business to measure the Performance.	It is used to monitor the operations.
2.	It is used by Senior Executives.	It is used by Operation Managers.
3.	It is used at the Corporate/Unit level.	It is used at Corporate/Department level.
4.	It provides Summarized data.	It provides detailed data.

SUMMARY

- Data Integration is the process of the standardization of data definitions and data structures by using a common conceptual schema across a collection of data sources."
- ***Major Issues while performing Data Integration are***: Hardware and Operating Systems, Data Management Software, Data Models, Schemas, and Data User Interfaces and Business rules and Integrity Constraints.
- Data quality management incorporates a "virtuous cycle" in which continuous analysis, observation, and improvement lead to overall improvement in the quality of organizational information across the board.
- Data quality management practices can improve the value of an organization's data asset and the ways it supports the achievement of business objectives.
- ***Data profiling provides a proactive approach to understanding your data.***
- *Data profiling, also known as data discovery or data auditing, is specifically about discovering the data available in your organization and to understand the characteristics of that data.*
- *Data profiling is a critical diagnostic phase that arms the user with information about the quality of the data. This information is essential in helping the user in determining not only what data is available in your organization, but how valid and usable that data is.*
- *Data Profiling is needed to* improve the ability to search the data by tagging it with keywords, descriptions, or assigning it to a category, to define metrics on data quality, to check whether the data conforms to particular standards or patterns or not and to assess the risk involved in integrating data for new applications.
- **Various Techniques of Data Profiling are** Structure Discovery, Data Discovery and Relationship Discovery.
- **Benefits of Data Profiling are improvement in** data quality, Shorten the implementation cycle of major projects, better understanding of data for the users and discovering business knowledge embedded in data.
  - Enterprise Reporting provides business intelligence to the enterprise. It provides single version of truth to the people at any level of organization, it means it provides the same fact value irrespective of the way the data is stored, transformed and extracted.
- The most common types of enterprise reports are dashboards and balanced scorecards.
  - Various types of Corporate Dashboards are: Enterprise Performance Dashboards, Customer Support Dashboards and Divisional Dashboards.
  - The balanced scorecard (BSC) is a performance measurement tool used as semi-standard structured report.
- Robert S. Kaplan and David Norton introduced the Balanced Scorecard in a 1992.

  The balanced scorecard is used by the managers of an organization to monitor the activities of employees.

APPENDIX I

DATA MINING SOFTWARES

There is a wide range of data mining softwares available in the market. The major companies involved in the development of data mining softwares are: IBM, Oracle and Microsoft. These products vary in their features and cost, so while choosing the software, the user should spend some time, so that the appropriate software can be chosen as per the requirements of the organization. The various data mining softwares available in the market are:

Name of the Package	Description
KnowledgeSTUDIO	Designed by Angoss Software, it is a complete data mining package that includes the facilities for classification, cluster analysis and prediction. It provides a visual, easy to use interface.
KnowledgeSEEKER	Designed by Angoss software, it is designed to support decision tree classification.
SPSS Clementine	This software from SPSS is a well known and comprehensive package that provides association rules, classification, cluster analysis, factor analysis, forecasting, prediction and sequence discovery. It provides GUI approach to data mining.
Intelligent Miner	This is a comprehensive data mining package from IBM. It uses DB2 but can access data from other databases also. Its functionality includes association rules, classification, cluster analysis, prediction, sequential patterns and time series. It also includes facility for text mining including mining of email and web pages.
SAS Enterprise Miner	This software is designed by SAS. It is a comprehensive integrated data mining package. It provides user friendly icon based GUI front end using the process model called SEMMA(Sample, Explore, Modify, Model, Access). It is available as distributed client server system that is well suited for data mining in large organizations.
Weka 3	This package was designed by Witten and Frank; it is a collection of machine learning algorithms for solving data mining problems. It is written in Java that runs on almost any platform.

CART and MARS	This software was designed by Salford systems and includes CART decision trees, MARS predictive modeling, automated regression, TreeNet classification and regression, modeling, clustering and anomaly detection.
Ghost Miner	It was developed in Poland. It is a complete data mining suite including data preprocessing, feature selection-nearest neighbours, neural nets, decision tree, SVM, PCA, clustering and visualization.
Oracle Data Miner	Oracle Data Miner is a graphical user interface for oracle data mining. Oracle 10g has data mining facilities embedded in it. Users of oracle have access to techniques for association rules, classification and prediction.
Darwin	It is also a product from Oracle. It also provides GUI environment for cluster analysis, prediction, classification and association rules.
MiningMart	This package was developed at University of Dortmund in Germany. This software focuses on data cleaning and provides graphical tools for data preprocessing. It provides the facility of mining on relational data bases and supports development, documentation, re-use and exchange of complete knowledge discovery processes.
DBMiner	This software was designed by Han and Kamber, who are the authors of the book, Data Mining: Concepts and techniques. It provides facilities for association rules, classification and cluster analysis. It interfaces with SQL Server and is able to use some of the facilities of SQL Server.
MineSet	It was developed by SGI, but now it is owned and further developed by Purple insight. It specializes in visualization and provides a variety of visualization tools including the scatter visualizer, the tree visualizer, the statistics visualize and the map visualize.
Data Miner Software Kit	It is a collection of data mining tools, offered in combination with the book Predictive Data Mining: A practical Guide by Weiss and Indurkhya.

APPENDIX II

DATA MINING AND INDUSTRY

RBI'S INITIATIVE ON DATA MINING

Source: Report of the Committee on Technology Upgradation in the Banking Sector, Chairman, Dr A.Vasudevan, www.rbi.org.in.

The committee opines that use of information technology is wide spread in all banks and recommends the use of data warehouse and data mining. It is not necessary to wait for all bank branches to be computerised for setting up of data warehouse. Neither is it necessary for all branches to have the same TBC software package. Data warehouse can be established even across multiple computer platforms as long as the transaction details are made available to the data warehouses in standardised formats. Therefore, banks should standardise the data formats and start supplying the data on a continuous basis from the branches which have already been computerised. It is expected that the computerised branches themselves would provide the critical data for a data warehouse to go live. The Committee recommends that all banks should put in place their data warehouse strategy by January 1, 2001. The banks with a large number of computerised branches may start their pilot projects by warehousing certain categories of data (if not all the transactions) by April 1, 2001. Some illustrative application areas are, Investment Analysis, Credit Analysis, Customer Base Analysis and Defaulters Analysis.

SBI Launches Hard Drive on Software

Source: Business Standard, February 7, 2010, Abhijit Lele & Shivani Shinde

As per this article, SBI has placed all 13,000 branches on core banking platform. The customers walking into a State Bank of India branch could soon be greeted by name as soon as they reach the counters. That's because scanners at the doorstep will detect an RFID chip embedded in their debit cards and flash an alert on the bank's computers. Having spent close to Rs 2,300 crore over the last five years on information technology, the bank is planning to spend another Rs 900 crore over the next three years. The report explains that SBI has 170 to 180 million accounts and the average daily transaction done on IT system is about 25 million. SBI Deputy Managing Director (IT) Krishna Kumar disclosed that SBI has signed an eight-year contract with IBM for data mining and warehousing. According to Mr. Krishan Kumar, ***"This will allow us to get qualitative information about customers. That in turn will help our employees to make informed decisions. This is still at a preliminary***

stage. The real benefit of this will take a few more years but in the next few months we will start extracting monthly information reports. We are investing about Rs 80 - 90 crore for this system,"

Banks Take to Data Mining in a Big Way

Source: Indian Express Newspapers, *Leena Baliga(2000)*

The article highlights that Citibank, HDFC Bank and ICICI Bank have taken the lead in using data mining along with leading mobile telephony service providers. The intention is to profile each other's customers so well that the companies can cross-sell products and services. Not just cross-sell, but data is mined in such a way that the companies can customize their offerings. The objective is to increase the existing customer base and enhance loyalty.

According to HDFC Bank's Vice-President (retail marketing), Mudit Saxena: "Data mining helps to increase sales by targeting the right customers and to make the right offers to customers. Banks, who have their ears to the ground regarding their customer's tastes and preferences, gather a lot of data...what data mining does is that it sifts through all the voluminous data and ekes out a pattern, which enables the bank to personalize its communication towards the customer as much as possible.

With data mining, banks can get a better understanding of the facts which are responsible for better customer relationship. Citibank is now doing the same in association with Hutchison Max in Mumbai and Airtel in Delhi. HDFC Bank with all of its mobile service providers - Hutchison Max, BPL Mobile, Tata Cellular, RPG, Airtel, Aircell, Cellphone and Command. ICICI Bank has followed suit with Hutchison Max, Airtel and Command in Calcutta. Based on the information captured, one can find the consumer's transacting behavior and can make necessary conclusions. Data mining is about collecting information about consumers through various sources - one of the sources being mobile operators and then can design tailor-made products for specific consumers".

Data Mining Used in US Department of Agriculture

Source: Assessing Loan Risks: A Data Mining Case Study, Rob Gerritsen IT Pro November x December 1999

Basic data mining techniques and models also proved useful in a project for the US Department of Agriculture. The USDA's Rural Housing Service administers a loan program that lends or guarantees mortgage loans to people living in rural areas. To administer these nearly 600,000 loans, the department maintains extensive information about each one in its data warehouse. As with most lending programs, some USDA loans perform better than others. The USDA chose data mining to help it better understand these loans ,improve the management of its lending program, and reduce the incidence of problem loans. The department wants data mining to find patterns that distinguish borrowers who repay promptly from those who don't. The hope is that such patterns could predict when a borrower is heading for trouble. Primarily, it's the USDA's role as lender of last resort that drives the difference between how it and commercial lenders use data mining. Basic data mining techniques helped the official of rural housing service to understand and classify the loyal and disloyal customers. Using data mining techniques, they planned to sift through this information and extract the patterns and characteristics common in the defaulters. Data mining increases understanding of the given problem by identifying the important factors for specific outcomes. In the near future, the department plans to expand the limited number of attributes available for data mining. In particular, it plans to include payment histories in the warehouse, and we hope that this data will help further improve the model's accuracy. Eventually, the USDA will use these models to identify loans for added attention and support, with the goal of reducing late payments and defaults.

Data Mining in Malaysian Banking Environment

Source: Investigating the Status of Data Mining in Practice, Teh Ying Wah,Zaitun Abu Bakar(2003) InSITE - "Where Parallels Intersect" June ***2003***

Investigated the status of data mining in practice, and highlighted the need of. It has been reported that e-business revenues will increase from $61 billion in 2001 to $148 billion in 2005 (James, 2001). The need of data warehouse performance tuning process is felt by the people at the various levels in the organization. The reasons for not implementing data mining to improve processing time of queries are lack of required expertise, high software cost, and high training cost.

Data Mining applied at Chase Manhattan Bank in New York

Source: Data Mining: A Competitive Tool in the Banking and Retail Industries- Madan Lal Bhasin (2006)- The Chartered Accountant October 2006

The writer explains when the bank began to lose customers to competitors, it began using data mining to analyse customer accounts and make changes in its account requirements, thereby allowing the bank to retain its profitable customers.

Data Mining applied at Bank of America's West Coast Customer Service Call Centre

Source: Data Mining: A Competitive Tool in the Banking and Retail Industries- Madan Lal Bhasin (2006) - The Chartered Accountant October 2006

Bank of America's West Coast customer service call centre has its representatives ready with customer profiles gathered from data mining to pitch new products and services that are the most relevant to each individual caller. Enterprises can also use data mining to minimize purchasing costs; identify the most effective promotions; and address numerous other organizational needs, including fraud detection, failure analysis, predictive maintenance, risk management and demand forecasting.

Shenandoah Life Insurance Company United States

The company was facing the difficulty in policy approval process; it was being handled on papers and hence was cumbersome. Another problem was routing of these paper copies to various departments, there was delays in approval. The use of data mining empowered management with current information on pending policies, which reduced the time required to issue certain policies by 20 percent and improved underwriting and employee performance review processes.

Soft Map Company Ltd., Tokyo

The major challenge the customers were having was the difficulty in making hardware and software purchasing decisions, which was hindering online sales. Using the data mining techniques and tools, page views increased 67 percent per month after the recommendation engine went live and profits tripled in 2001, as sales increased 18 percent versus the same period in the previous year.

Data Mining at Dexia Bank

Source: Geert Van den Berge, Data Miner, Dexia Bank, www.sas.com

Dexia Bank is part of the Dexia Group, which operates in Belgium, Luxembourg, France, Germany, Austria, Spain, the United Kingdom, Portugal, Switzerland, Sweden, Italy and the United States. Dexia Group's three main activities cover three areas: the funding of public utilities and financial services to the public sector and major corporate customers, general commercial banking services, and private banking and administrative and financial wealth management. In a recent data mining project, Dexia Bank set out to determine what products its customers are likely to purchase. Bank uses data mining to create a model for cross-selling and up selling.

ICICI Bank would undertake Data Mining

Source: Posted: Friday, Jun 14, 2002 at 0000 hrs IST

ICICI Bank to focus on cross-selling retail products. Targeting a rapid expansion of its retail portfolio, ICICI Bank is opting for extensive data-mining, packaging the products with additional incentives and double its distribution network for cross-selling of various loan products in 2002-03. The bank official, Ms Kochhar.Branches opined that ***"The bank sees good opportunity in cross-selling home, auto and personal loans and credit cards and we plan to double our distribution network for retail products in the current fiscal from the present 120-150 locations," said would be geared up to offer all products"***

Data Mining used at FBTO Dutch Insurance Company

The company was facing the challenges, to reduce direct mail costs, to increase efficiency of marketing campaigns and increase cross-selling to existing customers, using inbound channels such as the company's sell center and the internet a one year test of the solution's effectiveness. The use of data mining provided the marketing team with the ability to predict the effectiveness of its campaigns, help them in enhancing the efficiency of marketing campaign creation, optimization, and execution. The mail cost was decreased 35 percent and the conversion rate was enhanced by 40 percent.

Data Mining at ECtel Ltd., Israel

This telecom company was facing challenges in identifying the fraudulent activity in telecommunication services. The company used data mining and has significantly reduced telecommunications fraud for more than 150 telecommunication companies worldwide and moreover, saved money by enabling real-time fraud detection.

Provident Financials Home credit Division, United Kingdom

The biggest challenge the company was going through was that they were unable to detect and prevent fraud. The application of data mining helped in reduction of frequency and magnitude of agent and customer fraud, which helped in saving the money through early fraud detection and hence investigator's time and increased prosecution rate.

India to set up Data Mining Unit to Fight Fraud

Source: By Jamie Yap December 31, 2012, www.zdnet.com

India's Corporate Affairs Ministry is setting up a new intelligence unit to carry out data mining that will help detection and investigation of fraud. In a Press Trust of India (PTI) report, Indian Corporate Affairs Minister Sachin Pilot said "***The number of financial fraud cases in the country is increasing and by mining data from all possible sources, company wrong doings can be detected at the earliest possible stage. The unit is currently at a nascent stage and will comprise technical people with experience and expertise to mine data***".

Pilot said. ***"The idea is to have a set of people to do the data mining, collection and checking of records that is available on various platforms, and then link them with the inputs from investigating agencies."***

The information needed to detect possible corporate fraud at an early stage is generally available on various platforms, and what is actually needed is "the sense to mine it", the minister pointed out. "For any financial fraud, you need to have companies registered, institutions, bank accounts, statements, filing and reporting... Investigating agencies have to find the links and they need to talk to each other," Pilot noted. "Unless agencies talk to each other, you cannot have a smart, proactive machinery to stop things before they go wrong." In addition, the new division will seek help from various agencies to detect possible frauds as well as provide information to others in their investgations, he added.

Data Mining applied at Fleet Bank in Boston

Source: Data Mining: A Competitive Tool in the Banking and Retail Industries- Madan Lal Bhasin (2006)- The Chartered Accountant October 2006

Data mining is also being used by Fleet Bank, Boston, to identify the best candidates for mutual fund offerings. The bank mines customer demographics and account data along different product lines to determine which customers may be likely to invest in a mutual fund, and this information is used to target those customers.

MULTIPLE CHOICE QUESTIONS ANSWERS

1. Data dictionary is

A. Large collection of data mostly stored in a computer system

B. The removal of noise errors and incorrect input from a database

C. The systematic description of the syntactic structure of a specific database. It describesthe structure of the attributes the tables and foreign key relations hips.

D. None of these

Ans: C

2. Data warehouse is

A. The actual discovery phase of a knowledge discovery process

B. The stage of selecting the right data for a KDD process

C. A subject-oriented, integrated, time-variant and non-volatile collection of data in supportof management

D. None of these

Ans: C

3. Data cleaning is

A. Large collection of data mostly stored in a computer system

B. The removal of noise errors and incorrect input from a database

C. The systematic description of the syntactic structure of a specific database. It describesthe structure of the attributes the tables and foreign key relationships.

D. None of these

Ans: B

4. Decision support systems (DSS) is

A. A family of relational database management systems marketed by IBM

B. Interactive systems that enable decision makers to use databases and models on a computer in order to solve ill-structured problems

C. It consists of nodes and branches starting from a single root node. Each node represents a test, or decision

D. None of these

Ans: B

5. Adaptive system management is

A. It uses machine-learning techniques. Here program can learn from past experience and adapt themselves to new situations

B. Computational procedure that takes some value as input and produces some value as output.

C. Science of making machines performs tasks that would require intelligence when performed by humans

D. None of these

Ans: A

6. Data warehouse data is static in nature,

A. True B. False

Ans: A.

7. Algorithm is

A. It uses machine-learning techniques. Here program can learn from past experience and adapt themselves to new situations

B. Computational procedure that takes some value as input and produces some value as output

C. Science of making machines performs tasks that would require intelligence when performed by humans

D. None of these

Ans: B

8. Data warehouse can be employed for the following applications:

A. Information Processing: B. Analytical Processing:

C. Data Mining: D. All of Above:

Ans: D

9. Background knowledge referred to

A. Additional acquaintance used by a learning algorithm to facilitate the learning process

B. A neural network that makes use of a hidden layer

C. It is a form of automatic learning.

D. None of these

Ans: A

10. Case-based learning is

A. A class of learning algorithm that tries to find an optimum classification of a set of examples using the probabilistic theory.

B. Any mechanism employed by a learning system to constrain the search space of a hypothesis

C. An approach to the design of learning algorithms that is inspired by the fact that when people encounter new situations, they often explain them by reference to familiar experiences, adapting the explanations to fit the new situation.

D. None of these

Ans: C

11. Classification is

A. A subdivision of a set of examples into a number of classes

B. A measure of the accuracy, of the classification of a concept that is given by a certain theory

C. The task of assigning a classification to a set of examples

D. None of these

Ans: A

12. Binary attribute are

A. This takes only two values. In general, these values will be 0 and 1 and they can be coded as one bit

B. The natural environment of a certain species

C. Systems that can be used without knowledge of internal operations

D. None of these

Ans: A

13. Classification accuracy is

A. A subdivision of a set of examples into a number of classes

B. Measure of the accuracy, of the classification of a concept that is given by a certain theory

C. The task of assigning a classification to a set of examples

D. None of these

Ans: B

14. Which of the following method can be used for Assessing Accuracy ?

A. Holdout and Random Sampling

B. Cross validation

C. Booting

D. Bagging

Ans: Both A and B

15. Cluster is

A. Group of similar objects that differ significantly from other objects

B. Operations on a database to transform or simplify data in order to prepare it for a machine-learning algorithm

C. Symbolic representation of facts or ideas from which information can potentially be extracted

D. None of these

Ans: A

16. Black boxes are

A. This takes only two values. In general, these values will be 0 and 1 and they can be coded as one bit.

B. The natural environment of a certain species

C. Systems that can be used without knowledge of internal operations

D. None of these

Ans: C

17. A definition of a concept is——if it recognizes all the instances of that concept

A. Complete
B. Consistent
C. Constant
D. None of these

Ans: A

18. Data mining is

A. The actual discovery phase of a knowledge discovery process
B. The stage of selecting the right data for a KDD process
C. A subject-oriented integrated time variant non-volatile collection of data in support of management
D. None of these

Ans: A

19. A definition or a concept is .... if it classifies any examples as coming within the concept

A. Complete
B. Consistent
C. Constant
D. None of these

Ans: B

20. Data selection is

A. The actual discovery phase of a knowledge discovery process
B. The stage of selecting the right data for a KDD process
C. A subject-oriented integrated time variant non-volatile collection of data in support of management
D. None of these

Ans: B

21. Classification task referred to

A. A subdivision of a set of examples into a number of classes
B. A measure of the accuracy, of the classification of a concept that is given by a certain theory
C. The task of assigning a classification to a set of examples
D. None of these

Ans: C

22. Which of the following is a schema for multidimensional data models:

A. Star Schema
B. Snowflake Schema
C. Fact Constellation
D. All of Above.

Ans: D

23. Which of the following multi-dimensional data stores data in normalized tables.

A. Star Schema
B. Snowflake Schema
C. Fact Constellation
D. All of Above.

Ans: B

24. Discovery is

A. It is hidden within a database and can only be recovered if one is given certain clues(an example IS encrypted information).

B. The process of executing implicit previously unknown and potentially useful information from data

C. An extremely complex molecule that occurs in human chromosomes and that carriesgenetic information in the form of genes.

D. None of these

Ans: B

25. Which of the following OLAP operation is performed by climbing up a concept hierarchy

A. Roll-Up
B. Dice
C. Drill Down
D. None of These.

Ans: A

26. Hidden knowledge referred to

A. A set of databases from different vendors, possibly using different database paradigms

B. An approach to a problem that is not guaranteed to work but performs well in most cases

C. Information that is hidden in a database and that cannot be recovered by a simple SQL query.

D. None of these

Ans: C

27. Enrichment is

A. A stage of the KDD process in which new data is added to the existing selection

B. The process of finding a solution for a problem simply by enumerating all possible solutions according to some pre-defined order and then testing them

C. The distance between two points as calculated using the Pythagoras theorem.

D. None of these

Ans: A

28. Heterogeneous databases referred to

A. A set of databases from different b vendors, possibly using different database paradigms

B. An approach to a problem that is not guaranteed to work but performs well in most cases.

C. Information that is hidden in a database and that cannot be recovered by a simple SQL query.

D. None of these

Ans: A

29. A selection of some specified data based on two or more dimensions of the given cube isdone in which of following OLAP operation?

A. Slice B. Dice C. Both Slice or Dice

D. Pivot

Ans: B

30. Which of the following OLAP operation is also termed as rotate operation?

A. Dice B. Roll Up C. Pivot D. Slice

Ans. C

31. A data base may be designed by

A. Top-down approach B. Bottom-up approach

C. Either A or B D. None of these

Ans: C

32. Which of the following skill(s) is/are required to built a data warehouse?

A. rogram Management Skills B. Business Skills

C. Technical Skills D. All of the above

Ans: D

33. Incremental learning referred to

A. Machine-learning involving different techniques

B. The learning algorithmic analyzes the examples on a systematic basis and makes incremental adjustments to the theory that is learned

C. Learning by generalizing from examples

D. None of these

Ans: B

34. Knowledge engineering is

A. The process of finding the right formal representation of a certain body of knowledge inorder to represent it in a knowledge-based system

B. It automatically maps an external signal space into a system's internal representationalspace. They are useful in the performance of classification tasks.

C. A process where an individual learns how to carry out a certain task when making atransition from a situation in which the task cannot be carried out to a situation in whichthe same task under the same circumstances can be carried out.

D. None of these

Ans: A

35. Which of the following is data access and analysis tool?

A. Query and reporting tools

B. application development tools,

C. online analytical processing tools

D. data mining tools

E. All of above.

Ans: E

36. Inductive learning is

A. Machine-learning involving different techniques

B. The learning algorithmic analyzes the examples on a systematic basis and makes incremental adjustments to the theory that is learned

C. Learning by generalizing from examples

D. None of these

Ans: C

37. The data warehouse architecture must support which of the following *view:*

A. The Top-Down View

B. The Data Source View

C. The Data Warehouse View

D. Business Query View

E. All of the above

Ans: E

38. KDD (Knowledge Discovery in Databases) is referred to

A. Non-trivial extraction of implicit previously unknown and potentially useful information from data

B. Set of columns in a database table that can be used to identify each record within this table uniquely.

C. collection of interesting and useful patterns in a database

D. none of these

Ans: A

39. Which of the following is an essential property for a Data Warehouse?

A. Separation

B. Scalability

C. Extensibility

D. Flexibility

E. All of above

Ans: E

40. In which of the following component in data warehouse architecture, *cleaning, preprocessing and filtering* of data is done.

A. Analysis
B. Warehouse
C. Staging Area
D. Data Sources

Ans: C

41. *Apex Cuboids* is also termed as:

A. 0-D cuboid
B. 1-D cuboid
C. 2-D Cuboid
D. 3-D Cuboid

Ans: A

42: Knowledge is referred to

A. Non-trivial extraction of implicit previously unknown and potentially useful information from data

B. Set of columns in a database table that can be used to identify each record within this table uniquely

C. collection of interesting and useful patterns in a database

D. none of these

Ans: C

43. For a cube with n dimensions, there are a total of:

A. 2*n cuboids.
B. 2^n cuboids
C. n/2 cuboids
D. n^2 cuboids

Ans: B

44. The selection of the subset of cuboids to materialize should take into account:

A. The workload of the queries.

B. The frequency of occurrence of queries.

C. The cost of execution of queries and accessing the data

D. The cost for incremental updates.

E. All of above.

Ans: E

45. Which of the following types of data can be used in a data warehouse

A. Data Streams
B. Ordered/Sequence Data
C. Graph or Networked Data
D. Spatial and Multimedia Data
E. All of above

Ans: E

46. Data Mining Systems can be classified as:

A. According to the type of data source mined.

B. According to the data model

C. According to the kind of knowledge discovered

D. According to mining techniques used:

E. all of above

Ans: E

47. Support (A => B) is equal to

A. P(A U B)

B. P(A + B)\

C. P(A\B)

D. P(B\A)

Ans: A

48. Multi-dimensional knowledge is

A. A class of learning algorithms those try to derive a Prolog program from examples

B. A table with n independent attributes can be seen as an n-dimensional space

C. A prediction made using an extremely simple method, such as always predicting the same output.

D. None of these

Ans: B

49. Prediction is

A. The result of the application of a theory or a rule in a specific case

B. One of several possible enters within a database table that is chosen by the designer asthe primary means of accessing the data in the table.

C. Discipline in statistics that studies ways to find the most interesting projections of multi-dimensional spaces.

D. None of these

Ans: A

50. Query tools are

A. A reference to the speed of an algorithm, which is quadratically dependent on the size of the data

B. Attributes of a database table that can take only numerical values.

C. Tools designed to query a database.

D. None of these

Ans: C

51. Operational database is

A. A measure of the desired maximal complexity of data mining algorithms

B. A database containing volatile data used for the daily operation of an organization

C. Relational database management system

D. None of these

Ans: B

52. Noise is

A. A component of a network

B. In the context of KDD and data mining, this refers to random errors in a database table.

C. One of the defining aspects of a data warehouse

D. None of these

Ans: B

53. confidence (A => B) =

A. P(A U B)

B. P(B \ A)

C. P(A \B)

D. None of these

Ans: B

54. Which of the following method can be used to improve efficiency of Apriori's Algorithm?

A. Hash-based Itemset Counting

B. Transaction Reduction

C. Partitioning

D. All of above

Ans: D

55. Patterns is

A. General class of approaches to a problem.

B. Performing several computations simultaneously.

C. Structures in a database those are statistically relevant

D. Simple forerunner of modern neural networks, without hidden layers

Ans: C

56. Unsupervised algorithms

A. It do not need the control of the human operator during their execution

B. An arrow in a multi-dimensional space. It is a quantity usually characterized by an ordered set of scalars.

C. The validation of a theory on the basis of a finite number of examples

D. None of these

Ans: A

57. Which of the following criterias can be used for the evaluation of various ClassificationTechniques?

A. Predictive Accuracy.

B. Speed and Robustness.

C. Scalability

D. Interpretability

E. All of above

Ans: E

58. The most common attribute selection measures are:

A. Information gain.

B. Gain ratio.

C. Gini Index.

D. All of above

Ans: D

59. Which of the following techniques can be used to improve classification accuracy?

A. Boosting
B. Bagging
C. Cross Validation
D. Bootstrap

Ans: Both A and B.

66. Visualization techniques are

A. A class of graphic techniques used to visualize the contents of a database

B. The division of a certain space into various areas based on guide points

C. A branch that connects one node to another

D. None of these

Ans: A

61. Data scrubbing is which of the following?

A. A process to reject data from the data warehouse and to create the necessary indexes

B. A process to load the data in the data warehouse and to create the necessary indexes

C. A process to upgrade the quality of data after it is moved into a data warehouse

D. A process to upgrade the quality of data before it is moved into a data warehouse

Ans: D

62. The active data warehouse architecture includes which of the following?

A. At least one data mart

B. Data that can extracted from numerous internal and external sources

C. Near real-time updates

D. All of the above.

Ans: D

63. A goal of data mining includes which of the following?

A. To explain some observed event or condition

B. To confirm that data exists

C. To analyze data for expected relationships

D. To create a new data warehouse

Ans: A

64. An operational system is which of the following?

A. A system that is used to run the business in real time and is based on historical data.

B. A system that is used to run the business in real time and is based on current data.

C. A system that is used to support decision making and is based on current data.

D. A system that is used to support decision making and is based on historical data.

Ans: B

65. A data warehouse is which of the following?

A. Can be updated by end users.

B. Contains numerous naming conventions and formats.

C. Organized around important subject areas.

D. Contains only current data.

Ans: C

66. A snowflake schema is which of the following types of tables?

A. Fact

B. Dimension

C. Helper

D. All of the above

Ans: D

67. The generic two-level data warehouse architecture includes which of the following?

A. At least one data mart

B. Data that can extracted from numerous internal and external sources

C. Near real-time updates

D. All of the above.

Ans: B

68. Fact tables are which of the following?

A. Completely denormalized

B. Partially denormalized.

C. Completely normalized

D. Partially normalized

Ans: C

69. Data transformation includes which of the following?

A. A process to change data from a detailed level to a summary level

B. A process to change data from a summary level to a detailed level

C. Joining data from one source into various sources of data

D. Separating data from one source into various sources of data

Ans: A

70. Reconciled data is which of the following?

A. Data stored in the various operational systems throughout the organization.

B. Current data intended to be the single source for all decision support systems.

C. Data stored in one operational system in the organization.

D. Data that has been selected and formatted for end-user support applications.

Ans: B

71. The load and index is which of the following?

A. A process to reject data from the data warehouse and to create the necessary indexes

B. A process to load the data in the data warehouse and to create the necessary indexes

C. A process to upgrade the quality of data after it is moved into a data warehouse

D. A process to upgrade the quality of data before it is moved into a data warehouse

Ans: B

72. The extract process is which of the following?

A. Capturing all of the data contained in various operational systems

B. Capturing a subset of the data contained in various operational systems

C. Capturing all of the data contained in various decision support systems

D. Capturing a subset of the data contained in various decision support systems

Ans: B

73. A star schema has what type of relationship between a dimension and fact table?

A. Many-to-many

B. One-to-one

C. One-to-many

D. All of the above.

Ans: C

74. Transient data is which of the following?

A. Data in which changes to existing records cause the previous version of the records to be eliminated

B. Data in which changes to existing records do not cause the previous version of the records to be eliminated

C. Data that are never altered or deleted once they have been added

D. Data that are never deleted once they have been added

Ans: A

75. A multifield transformation does which of the following?

A. Converts data from one field into multiple fields

B. Converts data from multiple fields into one field

C. Converts data from multiple fields into multiple fields

D. All of the above

Ans: D

76. A data object is a ———————— outlier if it deviates w.r.t a specific context of the object.

A. Global outlier

B. Contextual

C. Collective

D. None of these

Ans: B

77: A multifield transformation does which of the following?

A. Converts data from one field into multiple fields

B. Converts data from multiple fields into one field

C. Converts data from multiple fields into multiple fields

D. All of the above

Ans: D

78. What is ETL Stand for?

A. Execute transmit and load

B. Extract transform and load

C. Excute Transform and load

D. All the above

Ans: B

79. Successful data warehousing requires that a formal program in total quality management (TQM) be implemented.

A. True

B. False

Ans: A

80. Joining is the process of partitioning data according to predefined criteria.

A. True

B. False

Ans: B

81. The role of the ETL process is to identify erroneous data and to fix them.

A. True

B. False

Ans: B

82. Star schema is suited to online transaction processing, and therefore is generally used in operational systems, operational data stores, or an EDW.

A. True

B. False

Ans: B

BIBLIOGRAPHY

Data Mining Concepts & Techniques, Jiawei Han & Micheline Kamber, Second Edition, Morgan Kaufmann Publishers.

Konstantinos Tsiptsis,Antonios Chorianopoulos- Data Mining Techniques in CRM: Inside Customer Segmentation

Berry, M., J., A., & Linoff, G., S., (2000). *Mastering data mining*. New York: Wiley.

Edelstein, H., A. (1999). *Introduction to data mining and knowledge discovery (3rd ed)*. Potomac, MD: Two Crows Corp.

Fayyad, U. M., Piatetsky-Shapiro, G., Smyth, P., & Uthurusamy, R. (1996). *Advances in knowledge discovery & data mining*. Cambridge, MA: MIT Press.

Han, J., Kamber, M. (2000). *Data mining: Concepts and Techniques*. New York: Morgan-Kaufman.

Hastie, T., Tibshirani, R., & Friedman, J. H. (2001). *The elements of statistical learning : Data mining, inference, and prediction*. New York: Springer.

Pregibon, D. (1997). *Data Mining*. Statistical Computing and Graphics, 7, 8.

Weiss, S. M., & Indurkhya, N. (1997). *Predictive data mining: A practical guide*. New York: Morgan-Kaufman.

Effective Data Governance in Banking - Failure is Not an Option- IBM Global Business Services, White Paper.

J Hanes, M. Kamber, "Data Mining Concepts and Techniques", Morgan Kaufmann Publishers, 2002.

Joseph Guerra, Vice President & Chief Architect David Andrews, President-Why You Need a Data Warehouse

K. H. Chye and C. K. L. Gerry [2002]"Data Mining and Customer Relationship Marketing in the Banking Industry". Singapore Management Review, vol. 24, no. 2, pp. 1–27.

D. Muraleedharan- PHI Learning Private Limited [2009] - Modern Banking: Theory and Practice.

C.S.R. Prabhu (2008) - Data Warehousing-Concepts, Techniques, Products and Applications- PHI Learning Private Limited.

G. K. Gupta (2009)- Introduction to Data Mining with case Studies- PHI Learning Private Limited.

Glenn J. Myatt, "Making Sense of Data", Wiley 2007.

Boris Kovalerchuk, Evgenii Vityaev Data Mining and Knowledge Discovery Handbook: A Complete Guide for Practitioners and Researchers.

Larose, D. T., "Discovering Knowledge in Data: An Introduction to Data Mining". ISBN 0-471-66657-2, John Wiley & Sons, Inc, 2005.

In Lih Ong, Pei Hwa Siew and Siew Fan Wong,Selangor, Malaysia- pagesA Five-Layered Business Intelligence Architecture,IBIMA Publishing Communications of the IBIMA http://www.ibimapublishing.com /journals/CIBIMA /cibima.html Vol. 2011 (2011), Article ID 695619, 11.

Prashant Pant Deloitte Consulting LLP-Business intelligence (BI) How to build successful BI strategy

Christian S. Jensen Torben Bach Pedersen Christian Thomsen -Introduction to Data Warehousing and Business Intelligence

Castellanos, M., Dayal, U., Simitsis, A., & Wilkinson, k. (2009). Data integration flows for Business Intelligence. Proceedings of the 12th International Conference on Extending Database Technology: Advances in Database Technology, 1-11.

Negash, S. (2004). Business intelligence. Communications of the Association for Information Systems, 177-195.

Olszak, C., & Ziemba, E. (2006). Business intelligence systems in the holistic infrastructure. Interdisciplinary Journal of Information, Knowledge and Management, 47-58.

Vercellis, C. (2009). Business Intelligence: Data Mining and Optimization for Decision Making. John Wiley & Sons.

Data Mining, Data Warehousing and OLAP, Sharma, Gajendra, Second Edition

Principles of Data Mining, Hand,David

RN Prasad and Seema Acharya- Fundamentals of Business Analytics" [2011] Wiley India Pvt. Ltd. All rights reserved.